D1204079

Oxford University Press, Ely House, London W.1

GLASGOW NEW YORK TORONTO MELBOURNE WELLINGTON
CAPE TOWN SALISBURY IBADAN NAIROBI LUSAKA ADDIS ABABA
BOMBAY CALCUTTA MADRAS KARACHI LAHORE DACCA
KUALA LUMPUR HONG KONG TOKYO

1. Eleanor Marx

THE LIFE OF ELEANOR MARX
1855-1898

A Socialist Tragedy

BY

CHUSHICHI TSUZUKI

CLARENDON PRESS · OXFORD
1967

92
M3921t

© *Oxford University Press* 1967

Printed in Great Britain by
The Camelot Press Ltd., London and Southampton

To the memory of
Junko

MAY 7 '68

HUNT LIBRARY
CARNEGIE-MELLON UNIVERSITY

PREFACE

This book is an attempt to evaluate the life of Eleanor Marx, the daughter of Karl Marx. It is her misfortune that she has been remembered mainly as the daughter of her distinguished father, with a paternal halo that obscured her remarkable career. Moreover, the materials necessary for a balanced study of her life are widely and almost hopelessly scattered, from London to Tokyo, from Moscow perhaps even to Peking!

This study would have been impossible without generous help from many people. I wish to express my special gratitude to M. Emile Bottigelli for the great favour of allowing me extensive use of the family letters of Eleanor Marx in his possession. Dr. Muriel Radford very kindly allowed me to quote correspondence between her parents-in-law and my subject. The International Institute of Social History in Amsterdam gave me permission to consult the Marx-Engels *Nachlass* and other archives relating to Eleanor Marx. I am also indebted to the British Museum, Institute of Marxism-Leninism (Berlin), and Ohara Institute of Hosei University in Tokyo for other manuscript sources.

I am very grateful to Mr. Henry Pelling for his constant advice on the subject, and especially for his generous help in improving my English style. Professor Isaiah Berlin, Mr. James Joll, Mr. Siegfried Bünger, Mr. Chimen Abramsky, and Mr. Bert Andreas assisted me with their expert knowledge on various aspects of international Socialism. I am under special obligations to Mr. Richard Storry, Mr. Geoffrey Bownas, Mr. H. P. Harstick, Mr. Heinrich Gemkow, Mr. Ernst K. Herlitzka, M. Marcel Lederman, and Mr. Chuhei Sugiyama. I am grateful to the Staff of the Clarendon Press and their advisers for their help. I am also indebted to the staff of the following libraries for their co-operation: the

viii PREFACE

British Museum, Bodleian Library, British Library of Political and Economic Science, Nuffield College Library, St. Antony's College Library, Library of Congress, New York Public Library, Library of New York State School of Industrial and Labor Relations, State Historical Society of Wisconsin, Illinois State Historical Library, Österreichische Staatsbibliothek, Bibliothèque Nationale, and Institute of Marxism-Leninism (Moscow). I wish to make grateful acknowledgement of financial assistance given by St. Antony's College and Hitotsubashi University while I was engaged in research for the present work.

CHUSHICHI TSUZUKI

Hino, Tokyo.

CONTENTS

LIST OF PLATES

LIST OF ABBREVIATIONS

BLPES   British Library of Political and Economic
                Science

B.M.Add.MSS.   British Museum Additional Manuscripts

IISH   International Institute of Social History,
                Amsterdam

IML (Berlin)   Institut für Marxismus-Leninismus beim
                ZK der SED

I ✤ DAUGHTER OF REVOLUTION

History would be of a mystical nature if 'accidents' played no part in it. It is by 'accidents including the "accident" of the character of the people who first head the movement' that the general course of development is either accelerated or delayed. This was the view expressed by Karl Marx at the time of the Paris Commune.[1] The First International, which he himself headed, soon disintegrated amidst bitter internal dissensions and hostility from outside. With the spread of industrialization, however, Socialism recovered, and in the last two decades of the nineteenth century the working-class movement groped its way to a position of power and influence in major European countries. Among the 'accidents' which conditioned its history stands out an incident which involved Eleanor Marx, the daughter of Karl Marx. It attracted wide attention mainly because of its unusual, pathetic nature and human interest, though its impact on the movement was also considerable.

Among the three daughters of Karl Marx, Eleanor alone grew into a fighter dedicated to a cause, a brave, ingenious, never tiring champion of Socialism. She harangued, organized, and led the unskilled workers in the East End of London. She skilfully handled negotiations and consultations which contributed much to securing success for the Marxist

[1] Karl Marx to L. Kugelmann, 17 April 1871, Marx and Engels, *Selected Correspondence* (Moscow, n.d.), 320.

International when it was revived. Already in her childhood her father used to say in jest that she should have been a man. Yet she was very feminine in her nature, tender and and affectionate, and was loved by her friends and esteemed by her opponents. It is true that her informal union with her husband Edward Aveling shocked the respectable. Yet acts of defiance of the conventional standard of morality presented the main theme of the new drama of which she was a dedicated protagonist. Together with her husband she sought to conquer the new theatre of naturalism. Together with him she hoped to direct a succession of Socialist organizations in England to the acceptance of Marxist theories and tactics. But the character of the man, who was believed by many to be an arch-knave, disappointed all her hopes. Most of the English Socialists and trade union leaders avoided the 'Mecca of Socialism', the London home of Friedrich Engels, because he patronized Aveling.[1] Moreover, it turned out in the end that Aveling was mainly responsible for the violent death of his wife, an incident which greatly alarmed the Socialist world.

It was a tragedy of Socialism, and the record of Eleanor's tragic life and death has been compared to that of Ferdinand Lassalle.[2] Yet the full extent of her trouble has been wrapped in mystery. Indeed, her life constituted one long struggle: she went through a series of conflicts which involved her father and later her husband and which generally took the shape of a struggle between her sense of duty and her desire for freedom. While she was seeking a solution of this conflict, she worked hard for the nascent Socialist movement, which had its own prejudices. When she was in trouble, however, she could tell herself as she once wrote to her sister: 'From childhood we have known what it is to devote oneself to the "prolétaire".'[3] After all, she was the daughter

---

[1] Gustav Mayer, *Friedrich Engels* (Haag, 1934), ii. 471.

[2] William Collison, *The Apostle of Free Labour* (1913), 81.

[3] Eleanor Marx Aveling to Laura Lafargue, 12 April 1885, Marx Family Archives in the care of M. Émile Bottigelli, hereafter referred to as Bottigelli Collection.

of the proletarian revolution. With this father and with her childhood we shall now begin, in order to appreciate the character of our subject as well as the depth of its tragedy.

*   *   *

It was the summer of 1849. Hopes for a democratic Germany and for the emancipation of the working class had been shattered by the forces of reaction that had swept major European capitals. The author of the *Communist Manifesto*, who had sought to direct the course of the revolution from his editorial offices on the bank of the Rhine, was now crossing the Channel, a fugitive but still a fighter, expecting to see the ashes of the revolution glowing red once more. There was, however, no sign of revolution to be detected in England, where he came to stay. Chartism, for which he had great admiration, never recovered from the ignominious blow it had received in 1848. The discovery of gold in California seemed to give a new lease of life to capitalism, whose death-knell he had hoped to hear ringing all around. In fact, a period of prosperity and contentment had begun, and in the atmosphere of solid bourgeois security all revolutionary sentiments of foreign exiles and surviving Chartists were either tolerated or ignored by the triumphant middle class in Britain.

Marx, together with his comrade-in-arms Engels, who had also arrived in London after a belated *putsch* in Baden, in which he had taken part, had now to examine the whole situation, and came to the conclusion that a revolution could succeed only when the bourgeois form of production was at variance with the modern forces of production, and that consequently they would have to wait patiently for a crisis in capitalist production. Now Marx and Engels, with only half a dozen followers, set themselves against the whole community of revolutionary exiles who somehow believed that a revolution could be made by crying 'war to the knife' and 'vive la guerre'. As a result the Communist League, for which they had written the historic document, split and was soon to dissolve itself. In a mood of self-pity Marx wrote to Engels, who had just gone to Manchester in order to take up 'filthy business' in a cotton mill in which his father had a partnership: 'The open, authentic isolation in which we two, you and I, now find ourselves, pleases me very much. It entirely corresponds to our position and our principles.'[1] To this Engels replied: 'What will happen to all the gibble-gabble which the whole *émigré* gang can make at your cost, if you answer them with a work on economics?'[2] In such total isolation, there was in fact no alternative left for Marx but to concentrate himself on the work of scholarship, which he now undertook at the British Museum.

* * *

Marx and his family had settled in Chelsea shortly after their arrival in England in the early autumn of 1849, and had to undergo all kinds of hardship as denizens in a strange land. Even their bitter political disappointment was dwarfed by the harassing effects of the poverty and squalor in which they were obliged to live in London, and the misery of a *petit-bourgeois* existence was felt all the more acutely as it was accompanied by lingering illness and hovering shadows of death that came to stay, as it seemed, with his growing family. Even with the long rabbinical tradition of his ancestors Marx often failed to maintain his stoicism, and recurring misfor-tunes almost wrecked the tender nerves of his wife, Jenny, who came from an aristocratic family of Westphalia and whose ancestral tree on her grandmother's side could be traced to a Duke of Argyll.

When Jenny joined her husband in London, she was accompanied by three little children, all bearing marks of her uprooted life. Jenny, the eldest daughter, was born in Paris in 1844: her young parents, who had married only a

[1] Marx to Engels, 11 Feb. 1851, Marx-Engels, *Werke*, Bd. 27 (Berlin, 1963), 184–5.
[2] Engels to Marx, 13 Feb. 1851, ibid. 191.

year before, had come to the French capital in order to resume radical journalism, which had been suppressed in Germany. In the sharp and creative mind of Marx, theories of Communism were then being formulated, but for him and his family there was no resting place for some time to come. As a result of Prussian intervention he had to move again, this time to Brussels, where two children were born, Laura in 1846 and Edgar in 1847. During the European Revolution of 1848–9 Frau Marx with her children followed her husband to Paris, Cologne, back to Paris, and then finally to London. At Frankfurt she had been forced to exchange some of her family silver at a pawn-shop, and a few pieces that still remained bearing the arms of the Argylls Marx himself, to his great embarrassment indeed, later brought to a London pawnshop. There was yet another member of his household, Helena Demuth or 'Lenchen', a housemaid of 26 years of age at the time. When she was a small girl she had come to serve the Westphalen family, and she had grown up with Karl and Jenny, who were playmates at the small town of Trier in the Rhineland. Shortly before the birth of Laura, Karoline von Westphalen, Jenny's mother, sent to Brussels 'the faithful, dear Lenchen' 'as the best she could send'.[1]

Now in London the fourth child was born, Heinrich Guido, on Guy Fawkes Day in 1849, and was nicknamed 'Little Fawkes' or 'Foxchen'. It was from about this time that the monetary troubles of the family became acute. Marx's new journalistic venture was delayed and, even when it materialized, came to nothing in pecuniary terms. In spite of its cheerful name, the new-born child 'drank in so much sorrow and secret worries with the milk', as the unhappy mother wrote, 'that he was continually fretting, and in violent pain day and night'.[2] In the spring of the following year the family

[1] Eleanor Marx quoted in Wilhelm Liebknecht, *Karl Marx* (Chicago, 1901), 163.
[2] Mrs. Marx to Joseph Weydemeyer, 20 May 1850, Marx-Engels, op. cit. 608.

was evicted from its Chelsea home; bailiffs came and seized everything that could be taken, including the baby's cradle and the girls' toys. The family stayed for a week at a German hotel in Leicester Square. 'But we did not stay there long', wrote Frau Marx in her memoirs:

> One morning our worthy host refused to serve us our breakfast and we were forced to look for other lodgings. The small help I got from my mother often saved us from the bitterest privations. We found two rooms in the house of a Jewish lace dealer and spent a miserable summer there with the four children.[1]

The two rooms were in 28 Dean Street, Soho, the squalid and noisy quarter inhabited mostly by poor foreigners, and in this dilapidated flat Marx and his family were to spend the following six years, the worst period of their life. Here 'Foxchen' suddenly died of pneumonia at the age of one year. Frau Marx was in a terrible state, 'in a really dangerous excitement and exhaustion', wrote Marx, and the thought that the poor child had been 'a victim of the bourgeois misery' aggravated her despair.[2] In March 1851 a fifth child, Franziska, was born. Frau Marx was 'very strained'. Lenchen, too, gave birth to a child, but the father's name was not stated. This was a boy, born on 23 June 1851 at 28 Dean Street, and was registered on 1 August under the name of Henry Frederick Demuth. There seems to have been utter confusion in Marx's household at this time, and even Engels began to worry about his friend of whom he had heard nothing for a fortnight. To an anxious inquiry from Manchester, Marx replied on 31 July: 'For about 14 days I have not been able to write, for I was hunted like a dog all the time when I was not in the library.'[3] Little is known as to what happened to the Demuth child until he reappeared on the fringe of the Marx family in the 1880's. It is most likely that at a very early stage he was taken as a foster-child to a

[1] Mrs. Marx in *Reminiscences of Marx and Engels* (Moscow, n.d.), 226.
[2] Marx to Engels, 23 Nov. 1850, Marx-Engels, op. cit. 144.
[3] Ibid. 291

working-class family somewhere in London. In his letter to Engels mentioned above Marx added: 'My wife troubles me. . . . Upon her falls the main burden and *au fond* she is right. Industry ought to be more productive than marriage. In spite of everything you remember that I am by nature very little patient . . . so that from time to time I lose my temper.'[1] A few days later Marx wrote to Weydemeyer, a member of the Communist League in Germany, who was then on his way to emigrate to America:

You can imagine that my situation is very gloomy. It will be the end of my wife if it goes on much longer. The never-ending worries of the petty, paltry, bourgeois struggle wear her out. To add to it there are all the infamies of my opponents, who never dared attack me positively but avenge themselves for their impotence by spreading the most unspeakable infamies about me and making me socially suspect.[2]

Again it is not clear what he meant by the 'unspeakable infamies about me', though it is not unlikely that rumour spread by his opponents made him the father of Frederick Demuth.

There seemed no end to the grief and humiliation that fell mercilessly upon the unfortunate family. Around Easter 1852 Franziska died, but there were no means at hand to bury the little corpse. 'She had no cradle when she came into the world', wrote her mother, 'and for a long time was refused a last resting place.'[3] 'My wife is sick, Jennychen is sick, Lenchen has a sort of nervous fever', wrote Marx a few months later: 'I cannot and could not call the doctor, because I have no money for the medicine. For the last eight or ten days I have fed my family on bread and potatoes, and it is still doubtful whether I can procure even these to-day.'[4]

[1] Ibid. 293.
[2] Marx to Joseph Weydemeyer, 2 August 1851, Marx-Engels, op. cit. 565. For an English translation of this letter, see Marx-Engels, *Letters to Americans* (New York, 1953), 24.
[3] *Reminiscences of Marx and Engels*, 228.
[4] Marx to Engels, 8 Sept. 1852, Marx-Engels, *Werke*, Bd. 28, 128.

The family continued to live in dingy surroundings and in a state of great confusion—an impasse from which there seemed little hope of breaking away. A Prussian spy who visited Marx's flat in 1853 wrote in his report:

He occupies two rooms. The room looking out on the street is the parlour, and the bedroom is at the back. There is not one clean or decent piece of furniture in either room, but everything is broken, tattered and torn, with thick dust over everything and the greatest untidiness everywhere. In the middle of the parlour there is a large old-fashioned table, covered with oilcloth. On it there lie manuscripts, books and newspapers, besides the children's toys, bits and pieces from his wife's sewing basket, and cups with broken rims, dirty spoons, knives, forks, lamps, an ink-pot, tumblers, some Dutch clay-pipes, tobacco ash—all in a pile on the same table.[1]

Even a spy must have felt compassion for the pitiful state of their living, which was indeed threatened from all sides, and in the following year there was even an outbreak of cholera in this quarter of the city.

*　　　　*　　　　*

By this time, however, Marx had begun writing regular articles on European affairs for the *New York Tribune*, a radical newspaper with a very large circulation. Although at first and sometimes even later he had to rely on Engels in sending dispatches, his strained circumstances were now considerably eased, and for a while his children grew up in better conditions. Christmas 1853 was the first cheerful feast the Marx family celebrated in London. But gloom soon returned and shrouded the entire household. His favourite child Edgar, now six years old, began to show symptoms of the family disease—tuberculosis. It was as if it were to replace this hopelessly weakening son that a sixth child was born on 16 January 1855. On the following day Marx wrote to Engels: 'I could not of course write to the *Tribune* yesterday

[1] Boris Nicolaievsky and Otto Maenchen-Helfen, *Karl Marx* (London, 1936), 241–2.

and could not either to-day and for some time in the future, for yesterday between 6 and 7 o'clock in the morning my wife was delivered of a bona fide traveller—unfortunately of the "sex" par excellence.'[1] She was named Jenny Julia Eleanor, and the last of these names, by which she was to be known, was taken from one of her Scottish ancestors.

A 'Weltbürgerin' was born, proudly reported her father to Lassalle, with whom he was still on friendly terms.[2] Yet she was the only child of Jenny's who was born in London and survived, and was the only member of the family who was a British subject. Small Eleanor was 'a merry little thing, as round as a ball and like cream and roses', said Wilhelm Liebknecht, who since his arrival in London in 1850 had visited the Marx family almost every day.[3] But the child was immature and weak at birth, and was often in a critical state. In March her condition grew worse and disturbed the whole family, as her brother was also seriously ill. In April Edgar died in the arms of his father. Marx, who felt keenly the loss of his male heir, now almost broke down and, as he confessed in a letter to Engels, knew for the first time 'what a real misfortune is'.[4] As for Eleanor, there was 'a grand consultation' with the family physician, Dr. Allan, and upon his advice the child was fed solely on milk until five and mainly on the same diet until ten. This diet appears to have saved her life.[5] After Edgar's death, all the family's affection for him was transferred to the baby sister. 'The elder girls fostered and fondled her with almost motherly care', wrote her mother: 'It is true that there can hardly be a more lovable child, so pretty, simple and good-humoured.'[6]

Eleanor did not remain long in the Soho flat and had

[1] Marx to Engels, 17 Jan. 1855, *Werke*, 28, 423.

[2] Marx to Ferdinand Lassalle, 23 Jan. 1855, ibid. 612.

[3] *Reminiscences of Marx and Engels*, 115; Liebknecht, op. cit. 134.

[4] Marx to Engels, 12 April 1855, *Werke*, 28, 444.

[5] Liebknecht, op. cit. 134–5.

[6] Mrs. Marx to Luise Weydemeyer, 11 March 1861, *Reminiscences of Marx and Engels*, 245.

practically no memory of the worst privation and humiliation her family experienced in their lives. Indeed, their existence was so desperate at the time that the death of kinsfolk was not always unwelcome and could even be 'a very happy event', as Marx put it, when it entailed an inheritance on the impoverished family.[1] Heinrich Georg von Westphalen, Frau Marx's uncle, died in 1855, and one of her Scottish relatives passed away shortly afterwards, both making bequests to Jenny. With these windfalls from the misfortunes of their relations, the family resolved to move from the scene of so many sorrows; they paid all their debts and redeemed silver, linen, and clothes from the pawn-shop. Then in the summer of 1856 Frau Marx with her three daughters went to Trier in order to be at the bedside of her own mother, who died in July. From this source also Frau Marx received a legacy. Upon her return in September, the family rented a house at 9 Grafton Terrace, Maitland Park, Haverstock Hill, on the southern slope of Hampstead Hill—'a palace for us in comparison with the places we had lived in before', wrote Frau Marx.[2]

* * *

Marx's family, however, had not been relieved from the nagging worries of daily life. The economic crisis of 1857, while falsifying his prophecy of a revolution, reduced his regular income from New York. Marx was much troubled by the high cost of education for the two elder daughters, Jenny and Laura, as they grew up. Eleanor, the smallest, became his real pet, and her chatter dispelled many of his worries.

'The baby is a remarkably witty fellow, and insists that she has got two brains', wrote Marx.[3] She was even allowed to scribble on the edge of his letters. The indulgent father carried her on his shoulder round the small garden at Grafton

---

[1] Marx to Engels, 8 March 1855, *Werke*, 28, 438.
[2] *Reminiscences of Marx and Engels*, 229–30.
[3] Marx to Engels, 23 April 1857, *Werke*, 29, 130.

Terrace, putting convolvulus flowers in her brown curls, and acted as 'a splendid horse' as she later put it.[1] 'The most striking thing about her', wrote her mother:

is her love for talking and telling stories. This she got from the Grimm Brothers, with whom she does not part night or day. We all read her those tales till we are weary, but woe betide us if we leave out a single syllable about the Noisy Goblin, King Brossel-bart or Snow-White. It is through these tales that the child has learned German, besides English which she breathes here with the air.[2]

In fact, the household language had become English by the time that Eleanor was learning to talk, and as a result even in her later life she wrote German only when she was obliged to do so, though she spoke it well.[3]

Little Eleanor was 'restless, curious, wanting to know everything, and constantly widening the horizon of her mind', wrote Liebknecht, who often accompanied her and her sisters on strolls about Primrose Hill and Hampstead Heath.[4] Liebknecht, too, had to tell her many a story for hours, and Marx himself was a wonderful story-teller. He spun a series of narratives on the curious life of 'Hans Röckle' which went on for months and enchanted the small child. Hans kept a toyshop where all kinds of wonderful products were displayed: wooden men and women, giants and dwarfs, kings and queens, workmen and masters. He was a Hoff-mann-like magician, but was always 'hard up', like Marx himself, and 'could never meet his obligations either to the devil or the butcher'. The toys, which he was obliged to sell to the devil, went through marvellous adventures, some grim and some comic, but they always ended up by returning to his shop.[5] 'Hans Röckle' had its moral: in this charming

[1] *Reminiscences*, 250, originally in Eleanor Marx, 'Karl Marx: Lose Blätter', *Österreichische Arbeiter-Kalender*, 1895.
[2] *Reminiscences*, 245.
[3] Liebknecht, op. cit. 155.
[4] Liebknecht in *Social-Democrat*, Sept. 1898.
[5] Eleanor Marx in *Reminiscences of Marx and Engels*, 251–2.

story Marx made fun of himself and of bourgeois life in general in which one's own personal dignity, it was implied, tended to be submerged under the devilish process of the circulation of commodities.

Marx also read to Eleanor, as he had done to her sisters, the whole of Homer, the whole *Nibelungenlied*, *Gudrun*, *Don Quixote*, and the *Arabian Nights*. But Shakespeare was the Bible of the house, inherited as it were from Ludwig von Westphalen, Eleanor's grandfather, who could recite whole plays both in English and in German. When she was three or four years old she knew whole passages. 'My favourite scenes', wrote Eleanor, 'were the soliloquy of Richard IIIrd ("I can smile and smile and be a villain", which I *know* I loved because I had to have a knife in my hand to say it!) and the scene between Hamlet and his mother!' Frau Marx occasionally did the Queen, and the lines 'Mother, you have my father much offended' were an attraction, as Eleanor used to look at her father 'very pointedly' when she spoke the words.[1] On her sixth birthday she was presented by her father with her first novel, Frederick Marryat's *Peter Simple*. The little girl, fired by this epic of heroic action at sea, declared that she would become a 'Post Captain', whatever it might be, and consulted Marx quite seriously as to whether it was possible for her to dress up like a boy and run away to join a man-of-war. While the idea was developing in her mind, to the amusement of her father, she fell under the spell of Sir Walter Scott and was shocked to learn that she herself partly belonged to the detested clan of Campbell.[2]

For Eleanor, her father was a friend and companion. 'I am getting on very well with my chess. I nearly always win and when I do Papa is *so* cross', she wrote in one of her earliest letters.[3] A precocious child, she even discussed religion with

[1] Eleanor Marx Aveling to Karl Kautsky, 1 Jan. 1898, IISH.

[2] *Reminiscences of Marx and Engels*, 252.

[3] Eleanor Marx to Lion Philips, 25 June 1864, IISH, published in W. Blumenberg, 'Ein unbekanntes Kapitel aus Marx' Leben', *International Review of Social History*, i (1956) Part i, 103–4.

Marx. When she was five or six years old the family paid a visit to a Roman Catholic Church to hear the music, and Eleanor suddenly felt the call of religion. She told her father, who as she later recalled 'quietly made everything clear and straight, so that from that hour . . . no doubt could ever cross my mind again.'[1]

*　　　*　　　*

Meanwhile, illness ruthlessly pursued the family even in its healthier surroundings at Haverstock Hill. In the autumn of 1860 Frau Marx, who had been working hard at copying out the theoretical and polemical works of her husband, suddenly felt ill, and the ailment was diagnosed as smallpox. The children were hurriedly taken to the Liebknechts, who were then living in nearby Kentish Town, and stayed with them till after Christmas. Marx himself often fell ill with his chronic liver disease, which took an acute turn about this time. Eleanor, too, had bad whooping cough for some months. She took advantage of her illness and insisted upon open house being kept for all the children of the neighbourhood. 'The whole family became my bond slaves,' she wrote later, 'and I have heard that as usual in slavery, there was general demoralisation.'[2] At the age of six she had jaundice. 'I remember well,' she continued, 'that seeing myself quite yellow I declared I had become a Chinaman and insisted on my curls being made into a little pig-tail.'[3] She did not stop bothering her father until he promised to send a letter which she pretended to be written in Chinese characters.[4] She was absorbed in everything Chinese. She would send for a cotton ball from Manchester for her birthday, as 'that little humbug loves all Chinese formalities',

---

[1] *Reminiscences*, 252–3.
[2] Eleanor Marx Aveling to Karl Kautsky, 19 June 1897, IISH.
[3] Ibid.
[4] Marx to Lion Philips, 20 Feb. 1864, *International Review of Social History*, i (1956), 95.

HUNT LIBRARY
CARNEGIE-MELLON UNIVERSITY

amusingly commented her father.[1] She was indeed a 'wild hoyden' difficult to tame. When she was fit and healthy, she would refuse to take an ordinary lunch, as Lenchen recalled later, hastily drink a glass of milk, and with a piece of bread in her hand run into the street to join her playmates.[2]

The real 'demoralization' of the family, however, was not due to the behaviour of Eleanor. As the American Civil War approached, the *New York Tribune*, which had helped to 'keep Marx's head above water', reduced by half the number of articles which it required from its chief European correspondent. This change took place early in 1861, and Marx's association with the paper came to an end one year later. The blow was felt all the more acutely as all other sources of income had dried up. Marx now turned to his relatives for help and in the spring of 1861 paid a flying visit to Holland, where he was able to secure a considerable amount of money from his uncle, Lion Philips, a banker at Zaltbommel, who acted as the administrator of Marx's own mother Henrietta's estate. He also obtained assistance from Lassalle, whom he visited in Berlin at the time. Lassalle, as friendly as ever, presented him with fashionable mantillas for his wife and his two elder daughters. Frau Marx was delighted with the gift and informed her benefactor: '... Even I look quite dignified in mine, and when I proudly walked up and down the room in it, little Eleanor called out after me: "Just like a peacock!"'[3] In spite of all this, however, the familiar round of poverty continued, and Marx confided to Engels his sad intention to let himself be declared bankrupt, to entrust his elder daughters to a family as governesses, to dismiss Lenchen, and to move to a cheap lodging house with his wife and Eleanor.[4] Marx also received

---

[1] Marx to Engels, 11 Jan. 1868, Marx-Engels, *Briefwechsel* (Berlin, 1950), iv. 15.

[2] Eduard Bernstein in *Neue Zeit* (xiv–ii, Nr. 30), 119.

[3] Quoted in E. H. Carr, *Karl Marx* (1934), 169.

[4] Marx to Engels, 24 Jan. 1863, Marx-Engels, *Briefwechsel*, iii. 144.

2. Karl Marx with his three daughters and Friedrich Engels

occasional contributions from Engels, though it was only in 1864 that the latter became a full partner in the management of his firm at Manchester and could spare much for his friend.

Yet the education of the children, especially that of the two elder daughters, was not neglected. They took lessons in French and Italian, also in drawing and singing. Laura set herself to piano exercises, and Frau Marx hired an old piano. Indeed, maintaining the appearances of a bourgeois family became a serious problem as the children grew up. In the middle of the winter of 1863–4 Marx visited Germany in order to obtain a legacy—about £580—from his mother, who died in November at Trier. The following Easter the family moved to a larger house at 1 Modena Villas, Maitland Park, Hampstead, where each daughter was given a separate room for the first time. A further substantial income was expected, as Wilhelm Wolff, an old member of the Communist League who died in Manchester in that year, left £825 for Marx in his will. Thus for a while the family was saved from harassing money difficulties. Marx was now more or less able to devote his energy to the direction of the International Working Men's Association, which was founded in the same year, and to the completion of his life work, *Das Kapital*, the first volume of which was to appear in three years' time with a dedication to his benefactor Wilhelm Wolff.

*   *   *

At home Marx was a genial father and retained his old nickname 'Moor' or 'Mohr', given for his dark complexion. Each member of the family had one or more such names. Frau Marx was called 'Möhme'; Jenny, the eldest daughter, was 'Qui-qui', 'Di', and 'the Empress of China'; Laura was called 'Hottentot' and 'Kakadu'. Eleanor, too, had a series of nicknames: 'Quo-quo', 'Dwarf Alberich', 'Successor to the Empress of China', 'Ellee', 'Secretary', and 'Tussy'. The last name, by which she was to be known even outside the family, seems to have been derived from 'pussy', for she was very fond of kittens.[1] The faithful Lenchen, whom Marx used to call 'his Demuth, Wehmuth, Hochmuth', had 'the dictatorship' in the house, while Frau Marx had 'the supremacy', and 'Marx submitted like a lamb to this dictatorship', recalled 'Library', *alias* Liebknecht, who had left for Germany in 1862 after twelve years' exile and intimate association with the Marx family.[2]

In 1865 a young Frenchman, Paul Lafargue, visited Marx. He was a mulatto, born in Cuba, and was now a medical student in Paris and a Positivist and Proudhonian. He came to London to present to the General Council of the International a report on the French working-class movement. At Marx's house he found Eleanor 'a charming child with a sunny disposition' and her elder sisters, Jenny and Laura, respectively the image of their father and mother.[3] Lafargue, on his return to France, was expelled from his university and decided to continue his studies in London. He joined the General Council, paid frequent visits to Marx, and was soon engaged to Laura, to the pleasant surprise of Frau Marx, who admired his fortune as well as his good character. Now Tussy became his favourite, and he built a swing in the garden for her to use. 'Paul has given me a delicious swing, on which as Mama says I would willingly forget school and everything else', wrote Eleanor to Alice, the daughter of Liebknecht, with whom she now started correspondence.[4]

She told Alice, her old playmate, that she was collecting stamps of all nations 'like every body is doing now', and complained that her time had been so much taken up with school. She did not appear to be keen on school, and it is

[1] Jean Longuet in *Nouvelle Revue Socialiste*, no. 25 (1928).

[2] Eleanor Marx to Wilhelm Liebknecht, 12 March 1896, Liebknecht, *Briefwechsel mit Marx und Engels* (The Hague, 1963), 445; Liebknecht, *Marx*, 123.

[3] Paul Lafargue in *Reminiscences*, 82.

[4] Eleanor Marx to Alice Liebknecht, 14 Oct. 1866, IISH.

said that it took nearly a year to induce her to go.[1] In April 1868 Marx asked Engels to send '£5 for school and £1 5s. for gymnastic school for Tussy' and was proud of the 'great things she achieved' in gymnastics.[2] Her school education, however, was overshadowed by the more attractive form of education that she was receiving from her father.

Indeed, Tussy seemed more absorbed in her own world of imagination. She opened a 'Museum of Curiosity' in her room, probably a 'Shakespeare museum' mentioned in one of her mother's letters, for which she sold tickets at various prices as 'sole proprietor and manager'.[3] Her 'Confession', which was a popular party game at the time, was an indication of her happy family life and her own serious nature, and it was naturally adorned with childish pleasantries:

Your favourite virtue   Truth
Your favourite virtue in man   Courage
Your favourite virtue in woman   (no answer)
Your chief characteristic   Curiosity
Your idea of happiness   Champagne
Your idea of misery   The Toothache
The vice you excuse most   Playing the truant
The vice you detest most   Eve's Examiner
Your aversion   Cold mutton
Your favourite occupation   Gymnastics
Your favourite poet   Shakespeare
Your favourite prose writer   Captain Marryat
Your favourite hero   Garibaldi
Your favourite heroine   Lady Jane Grey
Your favourite flower   All flowers
Your favourite colour   White
Your favourite names   Percy, Henry, Charles, Edward
Your favourite maxim and motto   'Go ahead'.[4]

[1] Eleanor Marx to Alice Liebknecht, n.d., IISH; Bernstein in *Neue Zeit* (xvi–ii, Nr, 30), 119.

[2] Marx to Engels, 8 Jan. and 18 April 1868, Marx-Engels, *Briefwechsel*, iv. 8, 48.

[3] Manuscript handbill, Feb. 1866, IISH; Nicolaievsky, op. cit. 244.

[4] Eleanor Marx, 'Confession', 20 March 1865, photocopy supplied by the Institute of Marxism-Leninism (Moscow).

Her choice of hero and heroine is interesting. Her own father 'Moor' hardly qualified as a hero, and she thought of the romantic figure of Garibaldi, whose sensational visit to England at the time made a great impression on her, as on many other English people. Her heroine was the niece of Henry VIII, Lady Jane Grey, who became Queen of England for nine days, but who died on the scaffold. Indeed, tragedy lived in Eleanor's mind, constantly reinforced by her reading of Shakespeare and later by fateful turns in her own life.

Tussy was very much attached to her father. In April 1867 Marx, after having submitted his manuscript of *Das Kapital* to a Hamburg publisher, was staying with Ludwig Kugelmann, a surgeon and his close friend at Hanover. Eleanor sent him a charming letter: 'I have not as I used to do looked in the beds for you, but I constantly sing "Oh! Would I were a bird that I might fly to thee & breathe a loving word to one so dear to me".' Then she added the latest news of herself and the family:

Paul has been keeping me in books, he got me Cooper's Deer-slayer, Homeward Bound, The Eppingham. . . . Good Friday I ate 16 hot cross buns, Laura & Jenny ate 8. . . . Tommy, Blacky & Whisky [her pets] send their compliments. Paul & Laura have had three riding lessons. Laura looks very nice in her riding habit, & Paul looks a little shaky.[1]

Already in July 1865, less than a year after his removal to Modena Villas, Marx had begun to complain about money troubles again, but this time his impecuniosity was largely due to his attempt to keep up a higher and more respectable standard of living than before. 'I live at any rate too dear for my conditions', he wrote to Engels:

. . . But it is the only means with which the children . . . can enter into connections and relations which can secure them a future. I believe, you yourself will be of the opinion that even from the

[1] Eleanor Marx to Karl Marx, 26 April 1867, Bottigelli Collection.

Your favourite virtue   Truth
  —   .   .   in man   Courage
  —   .   .   in woman
Your chief characteristic   Curiosity
Your idea of happiness   Champagne
  —   .   .   of misery   The Toothache
The vice you excuse most   Playing the truant
  .   .   .   you detest most   Eve's Examiner
Your aversion   Cold meat &c
Favourite occupation   Gymnastics
  —   .   .   Poet   .   Shakespeare
  Prose writer   Captain Marryat
  Hero   .   Garibaldi
  Heroine   Lady Jane Grey
  Flower   All flowers
  Colour   White
  Names   Percy, Henry, Charles, Edward
Your favourite maxim   "Go a head"
  & motto

Eleanor Marx
March 20th/65.

3. Eleanor Marx's 'Confession'

mere commercial point of view a pure proletarian arrangement would be unsuitable here, though it would be all right if my wife and I were alone or the daughters were young.[1]

Indeed, Marx allowed his wife to open her 'meagre purse' in order to buy bonnets and cloaks for the two elder daughters, who had been chosen as bridesmaids for a society wedding, 'a great distinction' as Frau Marx called it.[2] When the first volume of *Das Kapital* came out, he hoped for immediate success. 'This is necessary,' he wrote to Kugelmann, 'if I am to find a publisher in England and *without that* my miserable material position will remain so difficult and disturbing, that I shall find neither the time nor the peace for rapid completion [of the second volume].' 'My circumstances are harassing,' he wrote again, '. . . yet certain appearances must be maintained for the children's sake.' He had spent so much money on blue books and 'Yankee reports' that he had almost nothing left for his engaged daughter.[3] In spite of all the worries of her parents, however, Laura was duly married to Lafargue in April 1868, and in October they left for Paris.

*   *   *

Meanwhile Tussy, like her sisters before her, had inevitably been initiated into politics, but it was a natural and gradual process of unconsciously adopting one or other of the views held by the father she loved. Towards the end of 1862 when Lassalle visited London, Marx definitely parted company with his old friend, of whose ambitious role as the workers' dictator he disapproved and whose views of Socialist action by the state of Prussia he thought nonsense. In the summer of 1864, when the news reached Marx that Lassalle had been fatally wounded in a duel, he wrote to

[1] Marx to Engels, 31 July 1865, Marx-Engels, *Briefwechsel*, iii. 333.
[2] Mrs. Marx to Mrs. Liebknecht, n.d. (Oct. 1866?), Liebknecht, *Briefwechsel*, 82.
[3] Marx to Kugelmann, 11 Oct. 1867, 6 and 17 March 1868, Marx, *Letters to Dr. Kugelmann*, 51, 64, 65.

his wife, who was then convalescing at Brighton: 'Tussy's latest. As it comes out . . . that Lassalle had the duel for the sake of a lady whom he wanted to marry, Laura suggested that he would declare to every lady "he can love her only for 6 weeks". So, said Tussy, "he is *warranted* for 6 weeks".'[1] It is probably too much to expect more than this innocent remark from a child of nine years of age, but it shows that she was allowed to poke her nose into the personal affairs of her father's friends and foes. Indeed, she was even allowed to play with the wider problems of international politics.

At the time of the Polish insurrection of 1863, Eleanor wrote in a letter to her great uncle, Lion Philips: 'I hear from Papa that you are a great politician, so we are sure to agree. How do you think Poland is getting on? I always hold up a finger for the Poles those brave little fellows.'[2] The Prussian war against Denmark over Schleswig and Holstein in 1864 elicited further remarks from her: she 'begs me to tell you', wrote her father in a letter to his uncle, 'that "she don't care for such stuff", and that "she considers one of the parties to the quarrel as bad as the other, and perhaps worse".'[3] On the more popular issue of the Civil War in America she again addressed herself directly to the old man at Zaltbommel: 'What do you think of affairs in America? I think the Federals are safe. . . . Were you not delighted about the Alabama? Of course you know all about it; at all events a politician like you ought to.'[4] It was with such characteristically childish arrogance that she felt at the time that 'Abraham Lincoln badly needed my advice as to the war', and wrote long letters addressed to the President, all of which her father pretended to post but of course did not.[5]

---

[1] Marx to Mrs. Marx, 2 Sept. 1864, Istituto Giangiacomo Feltrinelli, *Annali*, i (1958), 159.

[2] Eleanor Marx to Lion Philips, n.d. (Dec. 1863?), IISH., published in *International Review of Social History*, i (1956), 94–95.

[3] Marx to Lion Philips, n.d. (March 1864?), ibid. 97.

[4] Eleanor Marx to Lion Philips, 25 June 1864, ibid. 103–4.

[5] Eleanor Marx in *Reminiscences*, 253.

After the Civil War came the Irish Insurrection of 1867, in which Irish-American officers took the lead. It was a dismal failure, but Colonel T. J. Kelly, formerly of the U. S. Army, now leader of the Irish Republican or Fenian Brotherhood, resuscitated the movement with headquarters in Manchester. He was soon arrested, and a successful rescue operation organized by his followers cost the life of a policeman. Three of the accused involved in the operation were hanged, and the whole incident shook the two nations profoundly. Tussy's political sympathy was now definitely with the Irish, 'the convicted nation' as she put it.[1] Neither her father nor Engels, however, approved of the Fenian tactics of conspiracy and violence, though Marx proceeded diplomatically in his work for the Irish in the International.[2] Yet Eleanor became a 'fanatical partisan' of the cause of the Fenians. So did her sister Jenny, and Marx perhaps cheerfully supported his children's wild but innocent demonstrations of sympathy for the Irish.

*   *   *

Eleanor's interest in the Fenians had been developed mainly through her personal contact with Engels and his home in Manchester. An Irish factory girl, Mary Burns, who had introduced Engels to proletarian circles in Manchester in the forties, later became his wife by free union. After Mary's death in 1863 her sister Lizzie Burns took her place. Now Lizzie was passionately interested in the fate of the revolutionary Fenians, and Engels's little household on the outskirts of Manchester—though certainly not his official residence in the centre of town where he received his business friends—became a safe refuge for the Irish extremists.

From her early childhood Tussy placed unbounded trust

---

[1] Marx to Engels, 14 Dec. 1868, Marx-Engels, *Briefwechsel*, iv. 168.

[2] Henry Collins and Chimen Abramsky, *Karl Marx and the British Labour Movement* (1965), 133.

in her father's greatest friend. She would write to him for 'a few bottles of hock and claret' for her mother's birthday. 'Alberich, der Grimme Zwerg', i.e. Tussy, would rail at Engels—'You bad boy, why haven't you answered my letters?—I suppose you and the hedgehog [Engels's pet] have been on the spree again.' Now, in June 1868 Marx and Tussy paid a short visit to Manchester, and upon her return she solemnly declared: 'Formerly I clung to a man, now I cling to a nation.'[1] Tussy was then regularly reading the *Irishman*, an organ of the Irish nationalist movement, and she sent the latest Fenian news to 'Mrs. Burns', who was almost illiterate: 'The Fenians have been having a congress, at which they sat for *19* hours without interruption! I should think they were tired after that.' In the paper she also found new words for the national anthem, such as 'God save our flag of green, Soon may it bright be seen', which, she said, 'you as a Fenian sister will appreciate'.[2]

Her interest in Ireland was to some extent interrupted, first by Christmas, which was always a big occasion for the Marx family, and second by a visit to France. In a letter to her sister Laura, who had gone to Paris with her husband, she complained of 'shameful treatment', as 'we had neither goose nor turkey for our Christmas dinner, but a hare!!', though the 'sham' was amply compensated by a good dinner they had at the Lormiers, a French family living in London who were on very friendly terms with Marx. She also informed her sister that members of the Lormier family would come to her house shortly, when 'Louis, Ludovic and I are going to act a little play. I think Beauty and the Beast. Louis to be the Beast, Ludovic the Beauty, I to be the Prince.' Her interest in acting, which was indeed a family craze, was already taking shape. It was characteristic of her to send, as

[1] Eleanor Marx to Engels, 13 Feb. 1865, IISH; Eleanor Marx to Engels, 3 Jan. 1868, Marx to Engels, 26 June 1868, Marx-Engels, *Briefwechsel*, iv. 5, 79.

[2] Eleanor Marx to Lizzie Burns, 14 Oct. 1868, IISH.

she wrote in this letter, 'a little satin collar, with a green ribbon in it, and pinned with a harp' to Lizzie Burns, and 'a very pretty steel cross in a green ribbon' to Mary Ellen, Lizzie's niece, for a Christmas present.[1] In the spring of 1869 Eleanor spent two months in Paris staying with the Lafargues. She saw a play by Sardou and visited a fair, but spent most of the time nursing a newly born child of Laura's which, like the other Lafargue children, did not live for long.[2] Her father sent her the *Irishman* from home and also gave her news of her animals—'*Dicky* treats me like Luther treated the devil'.[3]

In May Tussy returned from Paris with her mother, who had gone there to fetch her, and a few days later she went to Manchester with her father. Lizzie Burns showed her around the working-class quarters in the town, and the Irish question again absorbed her attention. 'Yesterday', she wrote to her sister Jenny:

Mrs. Burns and I went to see the Market, and Mrs. Burns showed me the stall where Kelly sold pots, and the house where he lived. It was really very amusing, and Mrs. B. has been telling me a great many amusing thing about 'Kelly and Daisy [Deasy]', whom Mrs. B. knew quite well, having been to their house, and seen them 3 or 4 times a week.[4]

'After the restraint at Paris', added Marx to this letter, 'she feels here quite at her ease like a newfledged bird.' Early in June Engels's whole company including Tussy and her father paid a three-day visit to a farm near Bolton Abbey, in Yorkshire. There were also two intimate friends of Engels, Samuel Moore, a barrister and manufacturer, and Karl Schorlemmer or 'Jollymeier', a German who taught

---

[1] Eleanor Marx to Laura Lafargue, 29 Dec. 1868, IISH.

[2] Eleanor Marx to Mrs. Marx, 31 March 1869, Bottigelli Collection.

[3] Marx to Eleanor Marx, 26 April 1869; (French Version) *Nouvelle Revue Socialiste*, no. 25 (1928), (German version) *Familie Marx in Briefen*, 148.

[4] Eleanor and Karl Marx to Jenny Marx, 2 June 1869, Bottigelli Collection.

chemistry at Owens College, Manchester. Marx returned to London shortly afterwards, and Eleanor was left in the care of Engels and his wife. One hot summer day all the female members of the household were lying on the floor 'the whole day drinking beer, claret, etc. . . . with no stays, no boots, and one petticoat and a cotton dress on'. Engels would return in the evening 'as drunk as jelly'. Eleanor did not like Lizzie calling her 'Miss Marx'—so she made a rule that if anyone did not call her Tussy he or she was to stand on a chair and say Tussy six times. 'One evening they had all called me "Miss Marx". So I made Auntie [Lizzie] and Moore and Jollymeier and Sarah [housekeeper] all stand in a row and say Tussy 24 times.' 'The Prince and Princess of Wales go through Manchester tomorrow', she informed Jenny: 'We're going to see them. What fun if a lot of children sing "The Prince of Wales in Belle Vue jail for robbing a man of a pint of ale". It's a song that's sung very much here so perhaps they will. Belle Vue is the large jail here.'[1]

But Tussy did not idle away her days in Manchester. She visited theatres and gave piano lessons to Mary Ellen. Under Engels's tutelage she went through Goethe from *Götz von Berlichingen* and *Egmont* to *Hermann und Dorothea*, and read some of the sagas such as the Icelandic *Edda* and Danish *Kjämpeviser*, and even Persian books of kings by Firdausi and Serbian folksongs in German translation.[2] In September Engels, accompanied by Lizzie and Tussy, made a short trip to Dublin, Killarney, and Cork. Upon their return he reported to Marx that the two ladies became 'yet more Hibernian' than before.[3] In the autumn Tussy returned to London, but she 'did not rest', wrote her sister Jenny, 'until she had persuaded Mohr, Mama and me to go with her' to attend a great demonstration held in Hyde Park on 24

---

[1] Eleanor Marx to Jenny Marx, 20 July 1869, Bottigelli Collection.
[2] Engels to Marx, 22 June, 6 July, 25 July, 30 July 1869, Marx-Engels, *Briefwechsel*, iv. 234, 244, 255, 258.
[3] Ibid, 27 Sept. 1869, 273.

October to demand an amnesty for the Fenian prisoners. 'We are all of us downright Fenians', wrote Jenny. When they received the news of the election to Parliament of an imprisoned Fenian, Jeremiah O'Donovan Rossa, 'we all danced with joy—Tussy went quite wild'.[1]

Meanwhile, Engels had come to terms with his partner on the withdrawal of his capital and compensation for his goodwill in the firm. Tussy was still in Manchester when he 'reached the end of his forced labour'. 'I shall never forget', she later recalled, 'the triumph with which he exclaimed: "For the last time!" as he put on his boots in the morning to go to the office for the last time.'[2] From July 1869 Engels became 'a free man', and in the autumn of the following year he and Lizzie moved to London. Marx was now assured of financial support—an annual allowance of £350—to enable him to work in peace, and his family was relieved of its constant economic worries.

Indeed, as a result of the 'false appearance' which Marx had often been obliged to assume for the sake of his daughters, Tussy had spent her childhood without being aware of these worries. Her health was carefully attended to by her parents, who had had so many sad experiences of the sick bed. Her education at home was of an excellent kind; she grew up in an atmosphere in which she befriended her 'Moor' and her 'bad boy'. In political matters she already showed an interest, indeed a passionate interest, in the cause of the oppressed nations, though she was still too young to be initiated into Socialism. She was now a girl of 15, and her years of adolescence, with increasing consciousness of political and human interests, were to a large extent to be affected by the dramatic events in Europe in the seventies.

[1] Jenny Marx to Kugelmann, 30 Oct., 27 Dec. 1869, Bert Andréas, 'Briefe und Dokumente der Familie Marx aus den Jahren 1862–73', *Archiv für Sozialgeschichte*, ii (1962), 200, 205.

[2] Eleanor Marx in *Reminiscences*, 185–6.

II ❧ LOVE AND POLITICS

In July 1870 when war broke out between France and Prussia, Marx wished victory for the Germans, because, as he wrote at the time, 'the definite defeat of Bonaparte is likely to provoke Revolution in France, while the definite defeat of the Germans would only protract the present state of things for 20 years'.[1] Engels began to write a series of war notes in the *Pall Mall Gazette* in which he accurately predicted, a week in advance, the capitulation of MacMahon's army at Sedan, and his reputation for excellent military knowledge led Jenny to give him a lasting nickname 'General'.[2] When the *Pall Mall* sent Marx a cheque for Engels's first article, Tussy, 'the ferocious girl' as Marx called her, and Jenny, who must have done something to help him or Engels, were excited and declared that 'they should seize upon these first spoils of war as due to them for brokerage'.[3] Meanwhile, 'a war of defence', as Marx at first saw it, for the Germans 'degenerated' into an aggressive war against the French. The Empire fell and an armistice was negotiated. Many of the agitated and almost starving citizens of beleaguered Paris felt themselves betrayed. They deeply distrusted the new Republican Government, led as it was by Thiers, one of the liquidators of the 1848 Revolution, with

[1] Marx to Paul and Laura Lafargue, 20 July 1870, photocopy at IML (Berlin).

[2] Liebknecht claims that this nickname derived from Engels's equally excellent articles on the revolutionary war in Hungary published in the *Neue Rheinische Zeitung*. Liebknecht in *Reminiscences*, 138–9.

[3] Marx to Engels, 3 August 1870, Marx-Engels, *Briefwechsel*, iv. 425.

the support of a strong monarchist-clerical majority in the
new National Assembly. The Commune was proclaimed in
March 1871, and Marx, in spite of his great caution before
the event, was now overwhelmed by the courage of the
heroic Parisians. 'The struggle of the working class against
the capitalist class and its state has entered upon a new
phase with the struggle in Paris. Whatever the immediate
results may be, a new point of departure of world-historic
importance has been gained', he wrote to Kugelmann in
April.[1] He was then preparing the historic address on the
Commune for the General Council of the International.

On 22 April a passport was issued for 'Miss Eleanor Marx
(British Subject) accompanied by her sister, going to
Bordeaux'. There the emissary of the Commune Paul
Lafargue had been trying to organize provincial support for
Paris. The two sisters arrived in Bordeaux in May to help
Laura and her children. In that month Paris, under the
merciless attack of the Versailles army, finally capitulated
and was turned into a scene of terror. In order to escape arrest
the Lafargues and the Marx sisters moved to Luchon in the
Pyrenees. Early in August, Paul had to retreat farther across
the border to a small Spanish town, Bosost. The French and
Spanish peasants of the Pyrenees, according to Jenny, formed
'a league, offensive and defensive, against their respective
governments'[2] and helped the agent of the International
and the daughters of Karl Marx. Their spying upon the
official spies, however, was not quite effective. Jenny and
Eleanor entered the Spanish territory, accompanying Laura,
who was to join her husband at Bosost, but on their way
back they were arrested on the frontier. Eleanor now
protested that the police had no right to touch a British
citizen, but they were conducted by twenty-four gendarmes
back to Luchon, where a search was made of their room and

[1] Marx to Kugelmann, 17 April 1871, *Letters to Kugelmann*, 124.
[2] Jenny Marx in *Woodhull & Claflin's Weekly*, 21 Oct. 1871, in Liebknecht, *Briefwechsel*, 483.

their interrogation began. The police 'looked in the mat-
tresses for bombs, and thought that the lamps in which we
had warmed the milk for the poor little baby who died, was
full of "petrole"', wrote Tussy some months later.[1] Jenny
managed to dispose of a letter from Gustave Flourens, her
old friend and a leader of the Commune who had been killed
by the Versailles army, a letter which, if discovered, would
have become 'a sure passport for the two girls to go to New
Caledonia'.[2] After an anxious night spent at the 'gen-
darmerie', they were released, and finally allowed to proceed
to Spain.

*   *   *

They returned home in time to find their father busy
preparing a conference of the International to be held in
London in September. They were present at the conference
itself, an irregularity that shocked even a sympathetic
delegate from Spain.[3] They also attended the sessions of a
subcommittee appointed by the conference to deal with the
Bakuninist opposition, which met at their own house. Indeed,
as Liebknecht said, Tussy was growing into 'the International
Working Men's Association personified'.[4] In fact, the London
conference was a turning-point in the history of the International, for Marx now envisaged the need for transforming
the organization into a number of separate national political
parties having their central direction in the General Council.
At the same time his attempt to do this precipitated the
final struggle with Bakunin, who now became the champion
of local autonomy against what he regarded as authoritarian
dictatorship.

For the first time since the 1848 Revolution Marx took an

---

[1] Eleanor Marx to Liebknecht, 29 Dec. 1871, Liebknecht, *Briefwechsel*,
414.

[2] Engels in *Sozialdemokrat*, 18 Jan. 1883, quoted ibid. 404.

[3] Miklos Molnar, *Le Déclin de la Première Internationale* (Geneva, 1963),
112.

[4] *Social-Democrat*, Sept. 1898.

open and active part in the leadership of a revolutionary political movement. As the rulers of Europe sought in panic to identify the International with the hated Commune, he became 'the best calumniated and the most menaced man of London'. 'That really does one good after a tedious twenty years' idyll in my den', wrote Marx to Kugelmann.[1] Eleanor, too, in her mother's words, became 'eine Politikerin von top to bottom'.[2] The whole Marx family went to The Hague when the last congress of the International was held in that town in September 1872. The congress passed a resolution, which had been adopted at the London conference, urging the proletariat to constitute 'its own distinct political party, opposed to all the old parties formed by the possessing classes', a resolution that was to become a guiding principle for the development of international Socialism in the following decades. Bakunin was expelled, and it was decided that the seat of the General Council was to be transferred from London to New York. After the congress Marx and Engels invited the delegates to a dinner at Scheveningen where they were introduced to Marx's daughters. A public meeting was also held at Amsterdam, at which Marx made one of his most celebrated speeches. He now declared that allowance should be made for the distinct institutions, manners, and traditions of the various countries in considering the means to achieve political power. Although force would be the lever for a revolution in most of the Continental countries, he said 'We do not deny that there exist countries like America, England, and, if I knew your institutions better, I would add Holland, where the workers may be able to attain their ends by peaceful means'.[3]

These events must have made a great impression on Eleanor, who later wrote on the Hague congress: '*Of course*

[1] Marx to Kugelmann, 18 June 1871, *Letters to Kugelmann*, 126.
[2] Mrs. Marx to Liebknecht, 26 May 1872, Liebknecht, *Briefwechsel*, 170.
[3] Quoted in Nicolaievsky, *Marx*, 364.

the 2nd volume of *Capital* was not the *reason* for the removal of the Council to New York. . . . Gott sei dank jetzt kommt man wieder zur Arbeit—as I've heard him [Marx] say again and again . . . but the reasons for the removal were quite others.' In England, the only country where the General Council could function, its position had become 'difficult' owing to quarrels among the French refugees, and it was rendered 'impossible' by the attitude of the English section. Prominent trade union leaders withdrew one after another from the International protesting against its endorsement of the Commune, and there was a marked hostility between the British Council created at the London conference and the General Council. 'Many opposed Mohr but he was firm for the New York change. He knew what it meant, but he said the *real* work of the International *is done*; we must not outlive ourselves and fall ignobly to pieces; the end must be voluntary and decent.' She added that she 'knew all that went on' at the time.[1]

Indeed, she had by this time often acted as 'secretary' for Moor, and wrote in a letter to Nicolai Danielson, the Russian translator of *Capital*:

Papa thinks you would do well to retard Russian edition in no way, but to continue as quickly as possible. —I am in great hopes that when once a French edition of 'Das Kapital' has appeared, an English one will soon follow—The English ape everything the French do, only when a thing comes from Paris does it meet with success here.[2]

The Russian translation came out in 1872 and a French one in 1872–5, but for an English edition she had to wait fifteen years.

*   *   *

Meanwhile, many of the Communard refugees who had fled to London had found warm hospitality at Marx's house.

[1] Eleanor Marx Aveling to Kautsky, 3 Dec. 1896, IISH.
[2] Eleanor Marx to Nicolai Danielson, 23 Jan. 1872, photocopy at IML (Berlin).

Most of them, when they arrived, were without means, and Eleanor even wished 'they'd taken some of the millions they're accused of having stolen'.[1] Her sympathy with their suffering was a reflection of her admiration for their valiant deeds. She, like her sister Jenny, had once been attracted to Flourens, the knight errant of revolution and 'a most extraordinary mixture of a savant and an homme d'action', as Jenny called him.[2] Then Eleanor was a child, but now she was a girl of 17 years of age. In May 1872 the Communards in London held a festive evening at Marx's house, and among those present there were Charles Longuet and Lissagaray, who were then winning the hearts of Jenny and Tussy respectively. Longuet, a Proudhonian Socialist and a medical student like Lafargue, had actively participated in the International in the sixties and had been editor of an official journal of the Commune. He became engaged to Jenny in May, though Frau Marx was rather disapproving. She regretted that her daughter's choice had not fallen 'for a change' on an Englishman or a German rather than on a Frenchman and was sorry for Jenny's prospects as a 'political wife'—a role whose sorrows and anxieties she knew too well.[3] Tussy, however, was quite satisfied with her sister's decision and looked 'as if she should not mind to follow suit', as Engels informed her married sister Laura.[4]

Hippolyte Prosper Olivier Lissagaray, to whom Tussy became increasingly attached, was a French Basque, about twice her age—he was 34 at the time. A journalist under the Empire, he had made attempts to rally a democratic opposition, first at Toulouse, then in Paris. During the

---

[1] Eleanor Marx to Liebknecht, 29 Dec. 1871, Liebknecht, *Briefwechsel*, 415.

[2] Jenny Marx to Kugelmann, 8 May 1870, *Archiv für Sozialgeschichte*, ii (1962), 216.

[3] Mrs. Marx to Liebknecht, 26 May 1872, Liebknecht, *Briefwechsel*, 169.

[4] Engels to Laura Lafargue, 11 March 1872, Engels-Lafargue, *Correspondance*, i. 27.

Franco-Prussian war he was appointed a commissar of defence in the south-west and soon found himself working for the cause of the Commune as a national guard and again as a journalist. In the heroic week in May his newspaper *Tribune du Peuple* advocated a fight to a finish with the accent, as it was said, of 1793. In London he naturally came under Marx's influence, but as a born individualist he repudiated all orthodoxy.[1] As a result Tussy's choice did not augur well.

In September 1872, shortly after the Hague congress, a friend called Maggie sent her a letter in which she mentioned a man whom Eleanor regarded with affection—apparently Lissagaray himself. 'What you tell me of his visit puzzles entirely my brain', she wrote: 'I cannot imagine what he is "up-to", whether it is a change of nature or restraint, perhaps some promise which may eventually turn out for your good.' Maggie promised to do her best to find out his real feeling about Eleanor: 'Try & pump my dear—all is fair in love & war—I do hope you are no longer miserable.'[2] Indeed, Tussy had reason to feel miserable, for Lissagaray was not always a welcome guest at her house. The Lafargues, who had recently settled in London, treated him unkindly. 'Last night Lissa came again', wrote Tussy to Jenny, now Mme Longuet:

. . . and again Laura and Lafargue shook hands with everybody . . . and not with him! Altogether they behave most oddly. Either Lissagaray is the perfect gentleman Paul's letter and his own behaviour proclaim him to be, and then he should be treated as such, or else he is no gentleman, and then he ought not to be received by us—one or the other—but this really unladylike behaviour on Laura's part is very disagreeable. I only wonder Lissagaray comes at all—He told me, too, that he would come one day this, or early next week to read me some extracts from the second edition of his book which is shortly to appear.[3]

---

[1] A note on Lissagaray by Amédée Dunois in Lissagaray, *Histoire de la Commune de 1871* (Paris, 1947), *passim*.

[2] Maggie to Eleanor Marx, 18 Sept. 1872, Bottigelli Collection.

[3] Eleanor Marx to Jenny Marx, 7 Nov. 1872, ibid.

In the previous year Lissagaray had published a short volume entitled *Huit journées de mai derrière les barricades,* which was to be enlarged into the classic work on the Commune. From him Tussy also learned many things that went on among the community of foreign refugees in London. Among them, Leo Frankel, a Communard and Hungarian Socialist, and Nicolai Outine, Russian *émigré* and a bitter opponent of Bakunin, sought to befriend her.

Her father, however, did not approve of her relationship with Lissagaray, and it can easily be assumed that Frau Marx was not at all happy about the possible union of her daughter and a French journalist in exile with no adequate resources. Marx seems to have tried to persuade Tussy to be cautious in her relations with him. 'Today I have written to Tussy,' he said in a letter to Engels, 'and am sure that Herr Lissagaray will be obliged for the moment to put a good face on a bad business.'[1] Eleanor reproached Moor that he was unjust towards her lover. But Marx was set in his attitude as he wrote in another letter to Engels:

I want nothing from him except that he would give proofs instead of phrases, that he would be better than his reputation, and that one could have certain right to rely on him. You will see from the answer [from Tussy] how the man continues to act. The damned thing is that I have to proceed with much consideration and foresight for the child's sake.[2]

It is difficult to know what was the actual reputation of Lissagaray at that time, but Paul Lafargue, who had worked hard for the International after the fall of the Commune, formed a low opinion of the Communard refugees in general. Even many years later he could utter harsh, though not unjustified, words about them:

The manifesto of the civil war drawn up by Marx for the General Council invested the Commune with a socialist character that it had certainly not possessed during its ephemeral existence. The

[1] Marx to Engels, 23 May 1873, Marx-Engels, *Briefwechsel,* iv. 473.
[2] Ibid., 31 May 1873, ibid. 480.

Communist refugees thereafter took themselves quite seriously as representing a socialism of which they did not know a single letter.[1]

It was only to be expected that the Basque individualist was on especially bad terms with Lafargue, who was soon to lead 'orthodox' Marxism in France.

*   *   *

Eleanor had been anxious to gain independence by taking a job, and as early as February 1870 she was asking Engels for a reference for such a purpose. In May 1873 she at last secured a teaching position at a boarding school for ladies conducted by a certain Miss Hall at Brighton. From there she wrote to her Moor:

I shall let the Misses Hall know that I shall come in on Monday evening. I hope too that I shall get some lessons for the morning. I have enlisted in my service two clergymen. . . . My conscience pricks me now and then for having anything to do with these people. I have also been to the Agency of which old Ruge wrote to me. You see I'm 'going in' for it with a vengeance.[2]

Ruge was probably Arnold Ruge, who had edited the *Deutsch-Französische Jahrbücher* with Marx in the forties and was now living in England, possibly at Brighton.[3] One of her pupils at the school was a girl of inferior intellect but with 'an immense interest in the Commune, the International, etc.'. 'Is it not odd that I should always hit on such girls?' she wrote to her mother.[4] But she was not always happy at Brighton. She could not swallow Moor's objections to Lissagaray, felt miserable, and often became ill. Frau Marx was anxious about her health and persuaded Miss

[1] Paul Lafargue, 'Socialism in France from 1876 to 1896', *Fortnightly Review*, Sept. 1897.

[2] Eleanor Marx to Karl Marx, 3 May 1873, photocopy in Bottigelli Collection.

[3] *Page's Brighton Directory* for 1873 listed Dr. and Mrs. Arnold Ruge, German language teachers.

[4] Eleanor Marx to Mrs. Marx, 31 May 1873, photocopy at IISH.

Hall to allow her to leave the school. Towards the end of the year Eleanor and her father, who was again suffering from his liver complaint, spent some time at Harrogate.

Change of air, rest, and 'the waters', however, failed to cure her nervous trouble, which was rooted in the conflict in her mind between love and filial duty. It was probably some months after her return from Harrogate that she wrote a pathetic letter imploring her father to show her some leniency and understanding:

I want to know, dear Mohr, when I may see L[issagaray] again. It is so *very* hard *never* to see him. I have been doing my best to be patient, but it is so difficult, and I dont feel as if I could be much longer.—I do not expect you to say that he can come here —I should not even wish it, but could I not, now and then go for a little walk with him? You let me go out with Outine, with Frankel, why not with him?—No one moreover will be astonished to see us together, as every body knows we are engaged. . . .

When I was so very ill at Brighton (during a week I fainted 2 or 3 times a day) L[issagaray] came [to] see me, each time left me stronger and happier, and more able to bear the rather heavy load laid on my shoulders. It is *so* long since I saw him, and I am beginning to feel so very miserable notwithstanding all my efforts to be merry and cheerful. I cannot much longer.—Believe me, dear Mohr, if I could see him now and then it could do me more good than all Mrs. Anderson [her doctor]'s prescriptions put together—I know that by experience.[1]

Marx yielded to her desire, if not at once, possibly at a later date when her health was fairly restored. He was indeed very concerned about her 'severe illness'. 'Eleanor is now up again', he wrote to Kugelmann:

much sooner than her doctor (Madame Dr. Anderson-Garret [*sic* for Garrett-Anderson]) had hoped. She is able to travel, though of course still delicate. Madame Anderson thinks the Karlsbad waters will help considerably to restore her health, just as Dr. Gumpert [Marx's own doctor] ordered rather than recommended me to go there. It is difficult for me to leave Jenny

[1] Eleanor Marx to Karl Marx, n.d., photocopy in Bottigelli Collection.

[Frau Marx] now. . . . I am in this respect less stoical than in others and family afflictions always hit me hard. The more one lives, as I do, almost cut off from the outside world, the more one is caught in the emotional life of one's own circle.[1]

Thus it was not for Tussy alone that the family ties caused emotional upset; but her father was able to look upon his own agitated feelings as well as his daughter's with cool reasoning and reflections. 'Tussy is much better', he wrote shortly afterwards to Engels: 'Her appetite grows in geometrical proportion, but that is the peculiarity of this women's disease where the hysterical element plays into it.'[2] A few days later father and daughter set off for the celebrated spa in Bohemia.

*   *   *

Karlsbad, now called Karlovy Vary, had acquired international fame as a health resort since the middle of the century. The town is situated on the bank of the Eger in the pine-forested foothills of the Erzgebirge. Here Kugelmann with his wife and daughter arrived on 16 August to make the necessary arrangements for a sojourn with Marx and his daughter. Three days later there was an entry in the official list of visitors at Karlsbad: 'Herr Charles Marx, Privatier, with daughter Eleanor from London—residence: "Germania"—Schlossberg, arrival 19 August.' The 'Germania' was not a fashionable hotel, but it had a terrace-garden behind it, beyond which was the deep forest at the foot of Berg Hirschensprung. In this garden Marx and Eleanor often sat together, reading books and writing letters.[3] It was on advice from Kugelmann that he registered himself as 'Charles Marx, Privatier' and sought to avoid suspicion, though he had to pay twice as much bath-tax as 'Dr. Karl Marx' would to the Austrian exchequer.

[1] Marx to Kugelmann, 4 August 1874, *Letters to Kugelmann*, 138.
[2] Marx to Engels, 14 August 1874, Marx-Engels, *Briefwechsel*, iv. 501.
[3] Egon Erwin Kisch, *Karl Marx in Karlsbad* (Berlin, 1953), 9–12.

In spite of its admirable scenery, with which both father and daughter were enchanted, Karlsbad had one disadvantage, and that was the company, especially Kugelmann himself, 'an impossible man' as Eleanor called him. 'The Kugelmanns have been a great drawback to Papa in his cure', she wrote to her sister Jenny:

> . . . he [Kugelmann] & Papa could not help quarrelling. . . . I am very intimate with Mrs. Kugelmann & indeed it is impossible not to like & to pity her when one sees the life she leads. It's a hard thing when a woman has no money of her own & her husband tells her every minute that she is ungrateful for all his 'Wohltaten' to her & the child. . . . The grand scene began because Mrs. K. did n't lift up her dress in a dusty day! . . . In all this of course Papa has had much bother but we shall take no notice of him now.[1]

In fact the whole episode, itself rather a trivial matter, put an end to the close friendship between the master and his Hanoverian disciple.

'Still I think Papa is better, & the waters are sure to have a good effect', wrote Eleanor in the same letter: 'We are very exact indeed in all our "duties". Fancy Papa being ready dressed & at the "brunnen" by six o'clock, frequently still earlier! We take long walks, & altogether get on very well here.' She observed the peculiarities of various acquaintances they made at the resort, among whom was a certain Count Plater, a Pole—'Good fellow enough in his way. A regular old aristo & catholic, but good Pole & Russian-hater. He was described in the local paper here [the Viennese paper *Sprude*] as "chef" of the Nihilists (you may suppose how horrified the old fellow was) & was announced as being here with the "chef" of the International.' Moor and Tussy avoided Hanover on their return journey; instead they visited Prague and called on the Liebknechts at Leipzig. The old 'Library' had just come out of prison after having served two years' sentence for his opposition to the war with France

---

[1] Eleanor Marx to Jenny Longuet, 5 Sept. 1874, Bottigelli Collection.

and all its consequences. The travellers also made a detour to Bingen near Mainz where Marx had spent his honeymoon with Tussy's mother.

*   *   *

By this time Marx seems to have removed some of the restrictions he had imposed on Tussy's association with her fiancé. Already at Leipzig she had told Liebknecht about her relationship with Lissagaray and his work. Shortly after her return to London she sent a letter to Leipzig in which was enclosed a message from Lissagaray announcing the publication of his weekly review of politics written from the revolutionary point of view and inviting Liebknecht's collaboration. 'The French press as you know, is so thoroughly abject', wrote Eleanor in her letter:

. . . That a socialistic movement is going on in Germany is a fact which the French people are quite ignorant of! It is necessary then for France that some publication should take place in which the Socialistic movement in all countries will be spoken of. . . . I think, therefore, and heartily hope that Lissagaray's 'revue' will be of some use.[1]

The first number of the 'revue', *Rouge et Noir*, came out at Brussels on 24 October 1874. It was a collection of Lissagaray's personal comments on current French politics and had very little to do with international Socialism, though the author expressed certain Socialist sentiments, an indication of the degree to which he had come under Marx's influence. 'Everywhere the governments arm themselves one against the other and within each country against the workers', he wrote: 'everywhere burst suddenly into view the presages of these political and social struggles of which the war of 1870 and the Commune are nothing but forerunners.' Commenting on the reconstruction of the Vendôme column, he says that what was important was 'a protest against military

[1] Eleanor Marx to Liebknecht, 13 Oct. 1874, Liebknecht, *Briefwechsel*, 416.

glory, a warning given to the world that the war of classes
was henceforth going to replace that of peoples'.[1] The 'revue'
was full not only of bitter remarks about Thiers, who had just
left office, but also of caricatures of Louis Blanc and Victor
Hugo, radical spokesman in the Assembly. As a result the
Brussels publisher refused to print the second number, which,
after considerable delay, came out in London on 20 November. In this appeared a vigorous appeal for relief made on
behalf of a London committee which had been formed to
collect subscriptions for those Communards who had been
deported to New Caledonia, but there was again no reference
to any Socialist movement, and in fact there were as yet few
signs even in Germany of Socialist recovery from the repres-
sion which had taken place after the fall of the Commune.
Liebknecht seems to have proposed to Tussy that she should
prepare a German edition of the 'revue', but she declined on
the ground that her German was not good enough for such
an undertaking. However, for Lissagaray's benefit she
translated into French Liebknecht's Reichstag speech on the
imprisoned Social Democrats, but it was too late, for the
third number of the review which came out on 27 November
turned out to be its last. Again the utmost he could write on
Socialism were such Proudhonian lines as 'Qu'est ce-que
la bourgeoisie?—Tout. Que doit-elle être?—Rien'.[2]

Apparently Tussy had by now recovered from her mental
depression and somewhat regained her health. She was
allowed to continue her association with the man of her
choice. When Marx visited Karlsbad again in the summer
of 1875, she was permitted to stay behind. Through Lissagaray she now took a keen interest in the controversy over
the amnesty question, the outcome of which would decide
the future of her fiancé and possibly of herself. The Conservative National Assembly had been replaced by a Republican
Chamber of Deputies during the winter of 1875–6, and this
encouraged those who were working for an amnesty. A bill

[1] *Rouge et Noir*, 24 Oct. 1874, 6, 15.   [2] Ibid., 27 Nov. 1874, 128.

for a complete amnesty was introduced, and this caused intensified argument for and against reconciliation with the former rebels. 'I suppose that at this moment one is very much occupied with the amnesty in Paris', wrote Eleanor to Karl Hirsch, the German Socialist who under the Bismarckian persecutions had fled to the French capital: 'At any rate the newspapers start talking about it. At last we shall know shortly who will be able to return to France. For I think the assembly will be forced to give fairly numerous pardons.'[1] Tussy's sanguine expectation, however, was soon disappointed, for the bill was killed both in the Chamber and in the Senate shortly afterwards.

After the failure of his journalistic venture Lissagaray devoted himself solely to the completion of his monumental work, *l'Histoire de la Commune de 1871*, which came out at Brussels in the autumn of 1876. By writing a full and objective history of the event and by doing justice to the work of the Communards, it has been said that the author contributed more than anybody else towards hastening the day of reparation for the defeated. Eleanor gave as much assistance as she could in the preparation of his work. Early in the summer, for instance, she was writing to Hirsch, asking for information as to certain details about the last days of the Commune. Shortly after the publication of the book she informed Hirsch of an intended visit of Kistemaeker, Lissagaray's publisher, who was making arrangements for the book to be introduced into Paris, and asked him to take every precaution so as not to put the police on their guard.

Meanwhile, in the summer of the same year, Tussy accom-

---

[1] Eleanor Marx to Karl Hirsch, 12 May 1876, Ohara Institute (Tokyo), published in Society for the Study of Labour History, *Bulletin*, No. 8 (Spring 1964). Hirsch had been placed under police surveillance in Paris: letters from Marx were opened and there was one from Eleanor in which she commented on the French elections in the previous year. Résumés of letters from Karl and Eleanor Marx to Karl Hirsch, Préfecture de Police Secretariat General Archives, photocopy at IML (Berlin).

panied her father on his third journey to Karlsbad, because, as she wrote later, 'he had missed me too much the preceding year'.[1] There she met two professors from Breslau, 'two nice fellows', and they were so nice that she could not conceal her affection for the author of the *History of the Commune*. One of them, Professor Heinrich Graetz, an eminent Jewish historian to whom she sent a copy of the book when it came out, later wrote a letter to Marx in which he added a few lines addressed to Eleanor:

Finally please allow me to write to you, dear Fräulein. You were probably already an incognito fiancée at Carlsbad? Then your happy disposition. In fact one must congratulate you on such a fiancé. The book by Herr Lissagaray is well written and has style and conviction. . . . Will you give your betrothed greetings from an admirer.[2]

Even Marx was induced to assist his daughter in translating Lissagaray's book into English, a labour of love which she undertook at the express wish of the author. In fact, her manuscript was thoroughly revised and corrected by Marx, though its publication was delayed until several years after his death.

*   *   *

Yet Marx never withdrew his fundamental objections to Lissagaray. Writing of French politics to Engels, he said:

In France is shown what I have for a long time, though in vain, expounded to Lissagaray (he now seems too rosy again), that the real industrial and commercial bourgeoisie is republican . . . and

---

[1] Eleanor Marx in Marx-Engels, *Reminiscences of Marx and Engels*, 126. 'How proverbially stupid one gets at Carlsbad', she wrote to her mother at the time: '. . . Carlsbad is still very full. There are as many Jews as ever, & more anxious than ever to get as much water as possible. Still an American has outdone them. He came to Carlsbad but being unable to stay more than two days took 42 glasses a day! It's a marvel he didn't die of it.' Eleanor Marx to Mrs. Marx, 19 August 1876, Bottigelli Collection.

[2] Heinrich Graetz to Karl Marx, 1 Feb. 1877, *Yivo Studies in History*, ii (Wilno, 1937), 662.

that the 'hommes de combat' represent only the 'beaux restes' of professional politicians of old parties, but no class. The workers (in Paris) have given the watchword that c'est cette fois l'affaire de Messieurs les bourgeois. Hence they keep themselves in reserve.[1]

The letter was written at a time when the Republic was threatened by a determined attempt made by the Right, who sought to rid France of the Republican majority in the Chamber. Yet its failure, itself a reflection of the growing strength of the *bourgeoisie* under the Third Republic, paved the way for the final struggle for an amnesty in which working-class and Socialist elements played an increasingly important role. A partial amnesty bill was adopted in March 1879, from which, however, Collectivists were excluded. Now the issue at stake was full amnesty against partial amnesty, or Socialism against the Republic. In London a Committee of the Excluded was set up of which both Lissagaray and Charles Longuet were prominent members.

In the meantime, Jules Guesde, a journalist and eloquent agitator who had been in exile in Switzerland and Italy, where he was associated with Anarchists, returned to France in 1876 and devoted himself to the self-appointed task of propagating Marxism in his country. He came into contact with Hirsch and through him with German Socialists, and founded *L'Égalité*, the earliest Marxist organ in France, the first series of which appeared from November 1877 to July 1878. He was a leading figure at the Socialist Workers' Congress held at Marseilles in October 1879, which inaugurated le Parti ouvrier français. Eleanor had been asked by Hirsch, on behalf of the *Égalité* group, to collaborate in their paper, but she had to decline the offer on account of her other engagements. The new *L'Égalité*, which was resuscitated in January 1880, took the lead in the struggle for a full amnesty and declared that the ballot box should be used 'to liberate, to amnesty the nine million French wage

---

[1] Marx to Engels, 31 May 1877, Marx-Engels, *Briefwechsel*, iv. 544.

slaves locked up in the penal colonies of capitalism'.[1] After certain compromises, a virtually full amnesty was granted in July 1880. In the same month Lissagaray returned to Paris, but he kept away as much as he could from the internecine struggles of the French Socialists. Longuet, too, on his return worked for Clemenceau on his radical organ, *La Justice*. Longuet was soon joined by his wife, Jenny, but the Basque individualist was left alone.

*   *   *

Shortly after her return from her first visit to Karlsbad, Eleanor wrote to Frau Liebknecht: 'Since I have been in Germany, and have seen how much the police do to help our Cause, I cannot but regret that the Prussian regime is not possible in England. It would do more than all the Trade Unions and Working men's Societies put together to bring life into the movement here.'[2] In Germany repressive measures adopted in the early years of the Reich had drawn together both the Lassalleans and the Marxists. As a result of the initiative taken by Liebknecht on behalf of the latter, a unity congress was held at Gotha in 1875 at which a new organization, Sozialistische Arbeiterpartei Deutschlands, later to be known as Sozialdemokratische Partei Deutschlands or S.P.D., was formed. A few weeks before the congress, Marx sent Liebknecht and his colleagues a criticism of the draft programme in which he stated his objections to what he regarded as its too great concessions to the Lassalleans. He repudiated such Lassallean concepts as the 'iron law of wages' and State-aided co-operative associations which were included in the draft. His letter, however, was virtually suppressed, though it helped to clarify certain clauses in the programme. It was apparently with great interest that Eleanor watched the progress of the German party as well

[1] *L'Égalité*, 23 June 1880, quoted in Jean T. Joughin, *The Paris Commune in French Politics*, ii (Baltimore, 1955), 470.

[2] Eleanor Marx to Natalie Liebknecht, 23 Oct. 1874, Liebknecht, *Briefwechsel*, 418.

as her father's reaction to it, but it was not before the dramatic turn of its fortune in 1878 that she became in any way involved in its struggles.

In May and June in that year there were two attempts on the life of Kaiser Wilhelm I. The White Terror began, and Bismarck proceeded with an Anti-Socialist bill. Shortly after the second attempt, Eleanor, not knowing anything about the would-be assassin Dr. Karl Nobiling—who was in fact a desperate man of no political connexion—wrote to Hirsch:

What do you think of Nobiling? Do you know something about this man?—The English press is indignant—perhaps more so than the German. One can see how delighted they would be to make Socialists in all the countries responsible for everything in order to start prosecutions again. They are delighted that Germany will have a bit of reaction and of terrorism—if only one could taste a little of it here! I fear for my friends, Liebknecht and others, for that is going to be a nasty affair for them. A little persecution does good, but not a reaction which suppresses newspapers, meetings—finally all the means of propaganda.[1]

In October the bill passed the Reichstag and Eleanor's fears became realities. Hirsch, who had been expelled from Paris on the passing of the law, founded *Die Laterne* at Brussels, and his paper, together with *Die Freiheit* (started in London by Johann Most, the former Socialist member of the Reichstag who was now a deportee from Berlin), became unofficial organs in exile of the proscribed party. In March 1879 Hirsch was expelled from Belgium and proceeded to London, where he continued his work. In the autumn of the following year, when a state of siege was proclaimed in the Hamburg area, Eleanor appealed to thirty-eight London and provincial newspapers, though very few of them took any notice. 'Englishmen' she wrote, 'have sympathised with Bulgarians and Turks, with Russians and Greeks, will they not give some measure of justice at least if not of sympathy to the

---

[1] Eleanor Marx to Karl Hirsch, 8 June 1878, Ohara Institute, Society for the Study of Labour History, loc. cit.

Social Democrats of Germany?'[1] With Hirsch she also made an attempt to organize a committee to collect funds for the victimized families in Hamburg.

The German leaders, however, refused to recognize the two journals in foreign countries as organs of their party, and they set themselves against the two editors, Most for his 'amateur revolutionism' and Hirsch for his 'vindictiveness and quarrelsomeness'. They thus acted in defiance of Marx and Engels, for the two London masters placed confidence at least in Hirsch. Liebknecht and even more August Bebel, a journeyman carpenter whom Liebknecht had converted to Socialism and who was now an eloquent member in the Reichstag, gave their support to a Zurich group of German Socialists. This group included among others an idealistic but wealthy Socialist called Karl Höchberg, whom Hirsch came to distrust, and Höchberg's literary adviser, a former bank clerk, Eduard Bernstein. In September 1879 *Der Sozial-demokrat* was founded in Zurich with Höchberg's financial assistance and was adopted as official organ of the party in the following summer. Hirsch, who had wound up his own paper shortly before, was elected to its editorship—a deliberate move by the party leaders to conciliate Marx and Engels—but in December 1880 Bebel, accompanied by Bernstein, paid a visit to London to explain to his masters the merits of Bernstein and certainly the defects of Hirsch, whom Bebel regarded as 'a man who knows no discipline'. The 'journey to Canossa', as his visit was called among the German leaders, had its effect: Hirsch, who refused to move to Zurich, was dismissed, and instead Bernstein became editor and conducted the paper throughout the remaining long years of the Anti-Socialist law.[2] Meanwhile, Hirsch— 'the unamoured Hirsch' according to Jenny Longuet—

[1] Eleanor Marx to Liebknecht [Nov. 1880], Liebknecht, *Briefwechsel*, 425.

[2] Franz Mehring, *Karl Marx*, Engl. tr. (1951 ed.), 519–22; Mehring, *Geschichte der deutschen Sozial-demokratie* (Stuttgart, 1906), iv. 16off.; Bebel, *Aus meinem Leben* (Berlin, 1946), iii, 137f., 139–41.

earnestly sought Eleanor's hand.[1] His aspirations, however, remained unfulfilled, and he soon disappeared from the official circles of the Marxist movement.

There was a prominent recruit to the inner circle of orthodoxy who was soon to become an intimate friend of Eleanor. This was Karl Kautsky, an Austrian Socialist born in Prague. He had joined the German party, and, like Bernstein, worked for Höchberg as a literary counsellor at Zurich. He spent a few months in London in 1881 and came into contact with Marx and Engels. From the beginning of 1883 he edited the *Neue Zeit*, a new Socialist journal which he founded at Stuttgart and in which Eleanor too was to collaborate.

*   *   *

There were several Russian visitors at Marx's house, which was now at 41 Maitland Park Road, Hampstead, where the family had moved in 1875. Lev Hartmann, most prominent among them, was a member of the executive committee of the Narodnaya Volya. With his 'wife' Sofya Perovskaya and others, he had made an attempt to blow up the royal train in 1879, and after its failure escaped to France. In spite of a strong Russian demand for his extradition he was allowed to proceed to London, where he came to know Marx and Engels. He introduced N. Morozov, another leading member of the Narodnaya Volya, to Marx. Morozov was one of those who had gone 'to the people' in the famous Populist propaganda movement of the summer of 1874, and had also taken part in Hartmann's attempt referred to above. He visited Marx in December 1880 and saw his youngest daughter. 'Eleanor kept running in and taking part in the conversation, sitting a little aside on the couch', he later recalled: '. . . The conversation was mainly on Narodnaya Volya matters, in which Marx showed a great interest. He said that he, like all other Europeans, imagined our struggle

[1] Jenny Longuet to Eleanor Marx, 23 March 1882, photocopy, IISH.

with the autocracy as something fabulous, like a fantastic novel.'[1] Morozov on his return to Russia in February 1881 was arrested, and in March Czar Alexander II was assassinated by his organization, with Sofya Perovskaya as the actual leader of the operation.

Eleanor had been fascinated by the heroic struggles of the Russian revolutionaries. She prepared articles on Russia for a London paper,[2] and took a strong interest in the arrest of Johann Most. Most, now an Anarchist, had sought to justify the Russian act of tyrannicide in his London *Freiheit*, and this led to his imprisonment, which attracted wide attention. Eleanor was indignant—not for his sake but because she thought 'the government are doing Most a great service' by treating him as if he had been a really dangerous man.[3] Most, when he came out of prison, emigrated to America, where he became a leading figure in the transatlantic Anarchist movement.

Meanwhile, Hartmann stayed behind and seems to have thoroughly enjoyed his sojourn in London. He was among those who gathered around Mary Ellen or 'Pumps'—who had taken Lizzie's place when the latter died in 1878—at Engels's famous Sunday evenings. Eleanor amusingly observed affairs among them, while Marx indignantly exclaimed—'From Perovskaya to Pumps—truly that is too much'.[4] Hartmann soon emigrated to America, and this put an end to his political career.

In February 1878 Marx in a letter to Liebknecht made a

*   *   *

[1] Morozov in *Izvestia*, 7 Nov. 1935, reproduced in *Reminiscences*, 303.

[2] 'I am rather busy just now with my articles on Russia for the *St. James's Gazette*', she wrote in a letter to Liebknecht (November 1880, Liebknecht, *Briefwechsel*, 425), but it is very difficult to identify her contributions to that paper, which published a number of anonymous articles on the subject at this time.

[3] Eleanor Marx to Jenny Longuet, 7 April 1881, Bottigelli Collection.

[4] Karl Marx to Jenny Longuet, 6 June 1881, *Nouvelle Revue Socialiste*, no. 26. See also *Familie Marx in Briefen*, 148.

remark which later became famous through an amplification by Engels: 'Little by little through the period of corruption since 1848 the English working-class had more and more thoroughly been demoralised and had finally gone so far as to constitute merely the tail of the great Liberal party of Capitalists, i.e. their *servants*.'[1] Prominent English members of the International had gone over or returned to the fold of Liberalism. The trade unions of skilled workers, after they had secured legal status by the Act of 1871, lost interest in an international organization. 'There is a still-stand [*sic*] so far as political movement is concerned', wrote Eleanor in a letter to Frau Liebknecht:

A kind of internal movement (strikes etc) never entirely ceased in England, but John Bull has been accustomed for so long a while to behave himself that he goes the way he should go to an alarming extent. . . . It passes all understanding how the thousands of men and women starving in the East End of London—and starving by the side of the greatest wealth and luxury do not break into some wild struggle.[2]

The only event of some interest for Eleanor at the time was the foundation of a London Medical School for Women, the promoters of which included Mrs. Anderson, her own doctor. 'It is of course chiefly an advantage for "bourgeoises"', she told Frau Liebknecht, 'but it is always something and it is time that women too may be able to work, and have other occupations than dress.'[3] She now took a keen interest in education, especially that in the elementary school, which since the Education Act of 1870 had become the scene of a heated controversy over religious instruction. The popularly elected school boards, whose creation had been sanctioned by this Act, became the focus of this controversy. At the London School Board election held in November

[1] Marx to Liebknecht, 11 Feb. 1878, Liebknecht, *Briefwechsel*, 245.
[2] Eleanor Marx to Natalie Liebknecht, 1 Jan. 1875, Liebknecht, *Briefwechsel*, 422.
[3] Eleanor Marx to Natalie Liebknecht, 23 Oct. 1874, ibid. 419.

1876 Eleanor worked for the candidature of a certain Mrs. Westlake who had been prominent in hospital work and had also shown some interest in the question of higher education for women. 'Our aim is above all to work against the self-styled "Church Party" who want absolutely to abolish compulsory instruction', she wrote to Hirsch. Mrs. Westlake, 'though bourgeois at heart like almost every Englishwomen, is at least very much of a free thinker and is in any case worthier than the men who offer themselves as candidates'.[1] Maltman Barry, an old friend of her father from the days of the International, was one of those men, and he stood in the same constituency, Marylebone, describing himself in his election address as 'the only Radical candidate'. But he was completely ignored by Eleanor, who now went from house to house canvassing for Mrs. Westlake. 'You cannot imagine the strange things which I see and hear', she wrote in the same letter:

In one house they ask that 'religion above all other things' should be taught—in another house I am told 'education is the curse of the country' and 'education will be our ruin', etc. etc. Finally it is amusing but also sad now and then when you go to the house of a working man who tells you that he wants to 'consult his employer' first.

On polling day the novelty of voting by women attracted curious attention. 'Now and again', reported a Marylebone newspaper:

an elderly lady, descending hastily from a cab, would fix her eyes on the handle of an inside door, and make for the spot, as if she feared the blandishments which surrounded her: or a young member of the sex . . . impressed with the dignity of woman, her wrongs, her rights, her aptitude for all kinds of public business, and her peculiar fitness for School Board administration, moved firmly and deliberately through the group, probably to 'plump'.[2]

[1] Eleanor Marx to Karl Hirsch, 25 Nov. 1876, Ohara Institute, Society for the Study of Labour History, loc. cit.
[2] *Borough of Marylebone Mercury*, 2 Dec. 1876.

Mrs. Westlake was elected at the top of the poll in this largest
metropolitan division, while Maltman Barry was miserably
defeated. In the new London School Board there were thirty
supporters of the School Board policy against twenty Church
members, and the elections, according to the Radical
Reynold's Newspaper, proved that the large majority of
Londoners were 'not parson-ridden'.[1]

*   *   *

Meanwhile, the trade depression of the latter half of the
seventies was accompanied by a severe agricultural depression, which hit Ireland especially hard. The agitation for
Irish Home Rule was now combined with agrarian revolt,
and in October 1879 the Irish National Land League was
formed with the Fenian Michael Davitt, who had spent
seven years in prison, among its leaders. Evictions of poverty-
stricken tenants and acts of outrage against landlords and
their agents both multiplied in the following year or two;
the Land League was prosecuted for conspiracy; and in 1881
Gladstone's new Government proceeded with a Coercion
Act which suspended habeas corpus in Ireland. Now
Eleanor found herself once more drawn emotionally to the
cause of the Irish. 'And what Coercion!' she wrote to
Liebknecht:

After all, Library, we English people are thorough. Let Bismarck
do what he will, even in his own field of despotism we beat
him! . . . In utter meanness too I think we can—to say the least of
it—hold our own. As an act of cowardly retaliation and petty
spite the arrest of Michael Davitt is unparalleled.—The House of
Commons too is now most effectively gagged, and liberty of
speech is a thing of the past. . . . The English workmen—than
whom (between you and me) a worse crew does not exist—even
are beginning to think that Gladstone is 'coming it strong'—as a
Yankee would say—and they are beginning to hold meetings
all over London and the provinces to 'protest against the Irish
Bill'.

[1] *Reynold's Newspaper*, 3 Dec. 1876.

She recounted a scene she had made outside Bow Street
Police Court, whither she had gone to see Davitt:

I asked a Policeman with a very hibernian countenance if Davitt
were still there. 'No' said he 'its meself put him in the van'. From
his brogue I of course knew the man was Irish, so, as our American
Cousins say, I 'went for him'. I asked him if there were n't
enough Englishmen to do such dirty work that an Irishman must
help 'put in the van' a man who like Davitt had done so much for
his country etc. etc. Some other policemen present scowled at
me, but said nothing.[1]

To her sister Jenny, who was as much interested in the Irish
question as Eleanor herself, she wrote:

Never—even in '67 during the Fenian rising—has the Government tried so hard to drive the people into a revolt. Therein lies
the great danger—for an open rising would be crushed & the
movement thrown back for years. Notice the conduct of the
police in Dublin, Limerick etc.—It is simply outrageous.—If
only the people will keep firm but quiet the Government will
find its hands full.[2]

*   *   *

In the meantime the vigorous agitation put up by the
radical working men against Irish Coercion had provided
H. M. Hyndman, a well-to-do City man with Radical Tory
sympathies, with an opportunity to try to form a new party
with a policy of imperial federation and social reform. Early
in 1880 he had made the acquaintance of Marx through the
ubiquitous Hirsch, and had since more than once invited
Marx and Eleanor to dinner at his own house. Eleanor
formed the same critical opinion of Hyndman as her father,
who found him 'self-satisfied' and 'a weak vessel'. Nevertheless, Hyndman went ahead with his political plans and
managed to hold a preliminary conference in March 1881
with a view to forming a 'New Party', the object of which
he now defined as 'the direct representation of labour'.

---

[1] Eleanor Marx to Liebknecht, 12 Feb. 1881, Liebknecht, *Briefwechsel*,
428–9.
[2] Eleanor Marx to Jenny Longuet, 18 Oct. 1881, Bottigelli Collection.

Thereafter he suffered a temporary set-back, as some of his colleagues hesitated or even withdrew on account of his 'ultra-Jingo' views. 'We've not heard much more about the newest "New Party",' wrote Eleanor in April, 'but I don't think it will come to much.'[1] About the same time George Shipton, the secretary of the London Trades Council, and Adam Weiler, a German carpenter who was a member of the same body, were making arrangements for the publication of a working men's paper, the *Labour Standard*. 'The spirit of the paper, I daresay, [may] be willing, but the pens, so far as I can see, will be decidedly weak', commented Eleanor.[2] Shipton, however, gained the collaboration of Engels, who wrote leading articles for the paper, including one calling for an independent working men's party. There were several attempts to organize a 'democratic' or 'social-democratic' party at this time, and Robert Banner, a young Edinburgh Socialist, who was convinced that the 'see-saw policy' of the trade unionsts would 'never settle the labour question' and who had come into contact with Marx and Engels, helped to found a Scottish Labour party.[3] These ventures did not come to anything permanent, and it was only Hyndman's Democratic Federation, founded in June 1881, that came to be regarded as the pioneer body in the Socialist revival in England in the early eighties. Marx and Engels, however, continued to disavow its chief promoter. Indeed, shortly after the inaugural meeting at which Hyndman had distributed to the delegates a booklet he had written entitled *England for All*, Marx wrote to Hyndman saying that the two chapters dealing with labour and capital, a summary of his *Capital*, were 'altogether out of place in a commentary on a Program with whose professed aims they are not at all connected'. In fact, Hyndman's brochure was a textbook

---

[1] Eleanor Marx to Jenny Longuet, 7 April 1881, Bottigelli Collection.
[2] Ibid.
[3] Siegfried Bünger, *Friedrich Engels und die britische sozialistische Bewegung* (Berlin, 1962), 18, 27.

of English 'Tory Democracy', written as it was for a party led by middle-class democrats, and Marx's analysis of capitalist exploitation would, as he himself said, have had 'some fitness in the Exposé of a Program for the foundation of a distinct and independent Working Class Party'.[1]

In spite of such apparent political discrepancy between the two, however, Marx's objection to Hyndman was generally understood to be due to his disapproval of the fact that the latter dared not mention the author of *Capital* in his book. Hyndman was not the only British 'philistine' who fell into bad odour with Marx for such a reason. J. S. Stuart-Glennie, a barrister who was a member of the Marylebone Democratic Association and who later joined Hyndman's 'new party', had written a book entitled *Europe and Asia* in which he pleaded that the solution of the Eastern question should be found in a readjustment of the relations between Europe and Asia—a readjustment involving especially that of European states, by which he meant an internal reorganization with Nationalism, Socialism, and Secularism as its guiding principles. Socialism, in his view, was 'the project . . . to put the Means of Production at the command of the Labourer'. 'If there is any truth whatever in the theory of the new, the scientific, or the historic school of Socialism', he went on, Capitalism in England was 'nearest the point of natural transformation', but a settlement with respect to landed property, he thought, should be attained 'without a smack of confiscation'.[2] Apparently he sent a copy of the book to Marx, whom he admired, but again an intrusion of Marxist analysis into a book which emphasized 'an imperial policy' displeased Marx. 'I am . . . left as unable as ever to guess even what was the cause of offence', wrote Stuart-Glennie to Eleanor, who acted as her father's secretary in his dealings with the author: 'You say—"His only objection

[1] Marx to Hyndman, 2 July 1881, in 'La rupture Marx-Hyndman', Feltrinelli Institute, *Annali*, iii (1960), 626–7.
[2] J. S. Stuart-Glennie, *Europe and Asia* (1879), 527, 538–9.

EEM

to your book rests on your treatment of his scientific theories".
But, the special theories of Dr Marx's great work on Capital
I have not treated at all.'[1] In another letter to Eleanor he
said that a friend of his had told him that 'he "believed Dr.
Marx thought that I had picked his brains, & made no
sufficient acknowledgement of my obligations to him in my
book . . . ." I was exceedingly surprised at this information.'[2]
This friend may have been Hyndman himself. At any rate,
Eleanor shared her father's and especially Engels's intense
dislike of the founder of the Democratic Federation, and it
was only after Marx's death, when some of Engels's followers
sought to capture the Federation, that she came into any contact with this organization.

*   *   *

Several Socialist leaders of international fame had met
Eleanor at her father's house and later wrote their impressions
of this attractive girl. Bernstein, on his visit to London in
1880, was duly impressed by Tussy, who was then 'a bloom-
ing young maiden of twenty-four summers, with the black
hair and black eyes of her Father, and an exceptionally
musical voice. She was unusually vivacious, and took part,
in her sensitive and emotional manner, in our discussions
of party matters.'[3] The Russian revolutionary Morozov
found in her 'a slim attractive girl of the German type'. 'She
reminded me', he added, 'of the romantic Gretchen, or
Margaret, in *Faust*.'[4] Hyndman was somewhat critical of her
close resemblance to her father. In appearance Eleanor
resembled Marx, he later wrote,

as much as a young woman could. A broad, low forehead, dark
bright eyes, with glowing cheeks, and a brisk, humorous smile,
she inherited in her nose and mouth the Jewish type from Marx
himself, while she possessed a physical energy and determination

[1] Stuart-Glennie to Eleanor Marx, 27 Nov. 1881, IISH.
[2] Ibid., n.d., IISH.
[3] Bernstein, *My Years of Exile* (New York, 1921), 159.
[4] Morozov in *Reminiscences of Marx and Engels*, 302–3.

fully equal to his own, and an intelligence which never achieved the literary or political success . . . of which she was capable. Possibly, she felt herself somewhat overshadowed by her father's genius, whose defects she was unable to see.[1]

Eleanor herself in a moment of playful reflection wrote in a similar vein: 'I, unfortunately only inherited my father's nose—(I used to tell him I could sue him for damages as his nose had distinctly entailed a loss on me)—& not his genius.'[2]

Yet she inherited a wealth of Socialist ideas and sentiments from her father. In a way Marx's house was the cradle of the European Socialist movement, and prominent Socialist leaders of major European countries came and sought his counsel. In this house Eleanor grew up with open eyes, being often called upon to act as her father's secretary. Thus at the beginning of the 1880's she was well versed in the problems of the Socialist movement in various countries, and also personally knew many of its leaders. It is true that her devotion to her fiancé had not been weakened, but she was almost equally attached to her father and his cause. At the same time, many other interests began to attract her attention, and her increasing absorption in acting and the drama now intensified the conflict that had been going on in her mind between love and politics.

[1] H. M. Hyndman, *Further Reminiscences* (1912), 139.
[2] Eleanor Marx Aveling to Karl Kautsky, 28 Dec. 1896, IISH.

III ~ LOVE AND DRAMA

'Eleanor Marx was an inspired worshipper at the shrine of the dramatic Muse', wrote Bernstein many years later.[1] In fact, her interest in drama and literature, as we have seen, was partly hereditary, and had been cultivated and encouraged by her family. As early as 1874 Marx suggested to her that she should publish a criticism of Tennyson's new poem entitled 'A Welcome to Her Royal Highness Maria Alexandrovna, Duchess of Edinburgh', the model of which Marx found in an obscure poem written by a member of the French Academy for the Comte du Nord, later the Czar Paul I.[2] Apart from such a reference as this to be found in her father's voluminous correspondence, there is not much evidence of Tussy's literary activities, although Liebknecht claims that she made herself independent by her own work early in the seventies and in due time established herself as a dramatic and literary critic comparable to George Sand or George Eliot.[3]

In earlier days the whole Marx family would often take the long walk from Haverstock Hill to Sadler's Wells Theatre to see Samuel Phelps, the Shakespearean actor, from the pit, which was usually crowded with working men. In the seventies their enthusiasm for Shakespeare went further with the 'Hamlet fever' which set in when Henry Irving

[1] Bernstein, *My Years of Exile*, 159.
[2] Marx to Mrs. Marx, April or May 1874, 'Lettres et documents de Karl Marx 1856–1883', *Annali*, i (1958), 197.
[3] *Social-Democrat*, Sept. 1898.

acted 'the most human Hamlet', electrifying the spectators at the Lyceum in the autumn of 1874. It was a revolutionary performance, as it broke definitely with the declamatory convention and helped to revive an interest in the actor's art. Irving's attempt to follow up the success with a performance of *Macbeth*, however, brought in its train a series of bitter criticisms, in the course of which the 'fashionable tragedian' was made the object of ridicule. Eleanor and her parents were as much partisans of the new Shakespearean actor as they would have been if he had been a Socialist agitator. She sent Hirsch, who was then in Paris, a review of Irving written by her mother, to be inserted in the *Frankfurter Zeitung*, with which Hirsch had certain connexions. 'If he had time,' she wrote, 'Papa himself would have done a review on Mr. Irving who interests us very much (although we do not know him personally) firstly because he is a man of rare talent and secondly because all the English press, in consequence of the most miserable intrigues, set itself furiously against him and has got up a cabal.'[1] On Shakespeare's birthday in 1877 Marx, on behalf of Tussy, sent a ticket for a performance of *Richard III* at the Lyceum to Peter Lavrov, a Russian Populist and idealistic Socialist in exile. Lavrov, who had come near accepting Marxist views and had defended the position of the General Council in the International, had been a minor poet himself and kept up regular correspondence with Tussy for some time.[2]

In the meantime Eleanor joined the New Shakespeare Society, a literary body founded by Frederick James Furnivall, who sought to promote the study of the great Elizabethan dramatist and to print texts of his works. Furnivall, through his early contacts with John Malcolm Ludlow, had been drawn into the group of Christian Socialists and

---

[1] Eleanor Marx to Karl Hirsch, 25 Oct. 1875, Ohara Institute, Society for the Study of Labour History, *Bulletin*, no. 8 (Spring 1964).

[2] Marx to Lavrov, 23 April 1877, 23 Jan. 1882, *Revue Marxiste* (May 1929).

had taught English grammar and literature at the Working Men's College, though he soon turned agnostic. He had been a prominent member of the Philological Society and for several years undertook the compilation of the *New English Dictionary*. He himself founded a succession of literary societies, the Early English Text Society in 1864, the Chaucer Society in 1868, the New Shakespeare Society in 1873, the Sunday Shakespeare Society in the following year in conjunction with the National Sunday League, an attempt to present dramatic performances for its members on the Sabbath, the Browning Society in 1881, and finally the Shelley Society in 1886. Eleanor took an active part in most of these societies, did certain researches for them at the British Museum, and developed a close acquaintance with Furnivall himself. For the New Shakespeare Society, for instance, she translated a lecture by Professor Delius of Bonn University on 'The Epic Element in Shakespeare', which flattered the German professor.[1]

*   *   *

Towards the end of 1880 Eleanor gave a recitation, probably one of her first public appearances, at an evening entertainment held at a north London hall for the benefit of the widow of a Communard. According to an account given by Bernstein, who was present, Eleanor read 'The Pied Piper of Hamelin', the children's story by Robert Browning— she was 'full of life', 'spoke with a great wealth of modulation and earned a great deal of applause'.[2] Encouraged by a sympathetic reception, she was now determined to go on the stage. She was no longer a girl—25 years old in 1880—and she had no clear prospect of marriage in spite of her prolonged engagement to Lissagaray. She might gain independence or even success in a career which, she thought, was

[1] Mrs. Marx to Sorge, 20 or 21 Jan. 1877, partly quoted in Marx Memorial Library, *Quarterly Bulletin*, no. 26 (Oct.–Dec. 1965).
[2] Bernstein, op. cit. 160.

somehow cut out for her. Moreover, through her connexions with literary societies she was finding new friends who shared her dramatic interest and with whom she now tried the fortune of her ambition.

'The day before yesterday the Dogberry Club were here', wrote Marx to Jenny in April 1881. Among the guests on this occasion whom he compared to the Shakespearean constable, there were two young people, Ernest Radford and Dollie (Caroline) Maitland, who also belonged to the literary circle around Furnivall. 'Tussy has discovered a new *Wunderkind* among the Dogberries, a certain Radford', Marx went on: 'This youth is already a barrister at law, but despises the *jus* . . . He looks well, a cross between Irving and the late Lassalle . . . an intelligent and somewhat promising boy.'[1] Apparently Tussy found some attraction in this well-educated young Englishman, with whom she now gladly went out, for instance to see Irving in *Hamlet*. 'He is a very nice young fellow', she wrote to Jenny: 'We all like him very much—& he has one great virtue—he is wonderfully like Irving!'[2] In the same letter she revealed to her sister her determination to become an actress and to take lessons under Mrs. Vezin, a dramatic teacher:

Till Monday I could not write to her [Mrs. Vezin] as Papa hadn't the necessary money—but then I wrote & I have received a nice letter in reply. . . . I feel sorry to cost Papa so much, but after all very small sums were expended on my education, compared at least to what is *now* demanded of girls—& I think if I do succeed it will have been a good investment. I shall try too, to get as much work as I can so that I may have a little money by the time I need it.

She also informed Jenny that she was going to take a new job as a 'préer', one who summarized books and articles. 'You see, dear, I've goodly number of irons in the fire, but I feel I've wasted quite enough of my life, & that it is high time I did something.'

[1] Marx to Jenny Longuet, 11 April 1881, Marx-Engels, *Selected Correspondence* (1936), 389–90.
[2] Eleanor Marx to Jenny Longuet, 18 June 1881, Bottigelli Collection.

Tussy's first serious attempt to take part in a dramatic performance came on 5 July 1881, when she, together with Radford, Miss Maitland, and a few others, got up two little pieces at the Dilettante Theatre—a French comedy in one act entitled *First Love* written by Eugene Scribe, and another one-act French drama called *At a Farm by the Sea*.[1] Engels was among the spectators and wrote in a letter to Marx, who had gone to Eastbourne on his doctor's advice,

Both Tussy and D. Maitland have played very well; the little girl showed much self-possession and looked most charming on the stage. Tussy was very good in the passionate scenes and it was easily perceived that she took Ellen Terry for model while Radford took Irving, yet she will soon use it up; if she wants to make a public impact, she must absolutely strike out a line of her own, and there is no doubt that she will.[2]

She was probably more than passionate in playing her part, and Radford himself later recalled that on this or some other occasion he had played very badly 'through over-excitement because I thought Eleanor Marx did not take her part quietly enough'.[3]

*   *   *

It must have been hard on her to be asked to create a distinctive style of acting when she had not been allowed to start lessons. She had been doing all she could to earn a little money. She thought, as it seems, of happy days she had spent with Lissagaray and of objections from her parents. As a result of physical and mental exhaustion she was taken ill in the summer. Marx, who had gone with his wife to Argenteuil near Paris to stay with Jenny and her children, received a letter from Dollie Maitland, telling him that Tussy was very ill, but that she would not allow Miss Maitland to attend her and had called no doctor. He hurried back to London to find Tussy 'pale and emaciated'. 'For some weeks she has

[1] Handbill in Radford Papers.
[2] Engels to Marx, 7 July 1881, Marx-Engels, *Briefwechsel*, iv. 590.
[3] Ernest Radford to Dollie Maitland, 24 Dec. 1882, Radford Papers.

eaten nothing (literally)', he wrote to Jenny: 'Her nervous
system is in a pitiable state, whence continual insomnia,
tremblings of hands, neuralgic convulsions of the face, etc.'[1]
Dr. Donkin was called in but found no organic trouble except
a stomach upset and over-excited nerves. Tussy, however,
promised to follow his advice, and the danger of a complete
breakdown was avoided.

Now the shadow of death again lingered over the family.
Frau Marx had been unwell for several years, and her trouble
was diagnosed as a cancer in the liver. 'I cannot, my dearest
Di, give you a bright account from home', wrote Eleanor
to Jenny: 'Dear Mama is very ill—the worst is we can do
absolutely nothing. It is a beastly illness—the worse too that
in all other respect Mama is, Dr. Donkin says, so strong.'[2]
Marx, too, took to his bed with a severe attack of pleurisy
complicated by bronchitis. His doctor considered his case
almost hopeless. 'That was a terrible time', she recalled later.
'Our dear Mother lay in the big front room, Moor in the
small room next to it. They who were so used to each other,
whose lives had come to form part of each other, could not
even be together in the same room any longer.'[3] 'Since
Saturday I have not left Papa's room, day or night', she
wrote to Jenny: 'Tonight however Helen will be with him
as the doctor wants me to have a night's rest. . . Engels is
of a kindness & devotion that baffle description. Surely
there is not another like him in the world—in spite of his
little weaknesses.'[4] Some of her friends, such as Mme.
Lormier and Miss Clementina Black, the novelist, offered
to look after Frau Marx. 'Isn't it kind of people to take such
an interest?' she added in her letter to Jenny. By the end of
October Marx had somewhat recovered and was allowed to
go next door to see his ailing wife. 'Unfortunately I'm

---

[1] Marx to Jenny Longuet, 18 August 1881, *Nouvelle Revue Socialiste*
no. 27 (Dec. 1928–Feb. 1929). See also *Familie Marx in Briefen*, 150.

[2] Eleanor Marx to Jenny Longuet, 7 Oct. 1881, Bottigelli Collection.

[3] Quoted in Liebknecht in *Reminiscences*, 127.

[4] Eleanor Marx to Jenny Longuet, 18 Oct. 1881, Bottigelli Collection.

beginning to feel very seedy—now the excitement is over a reaction is setting in', she wrote again to Jenny: 'The doctor has given me iron to take, ordered me to go on more regularly again with my Turkish Baths & get out more.'[1] She wanted to work at the British Museum if she went out, for she thought she could not afford to lose her job.

On 2 December 1881 Frau Marx died. 'I do *so* miss you just now', Eleanor wrote to Jenny:

I send you, dear, some of her dear hair—it is as soft & beautiful as a girl's—If you could but have seen her face at the last—the look in her eyes was simply indescribable. Not only that they were so clear—clear as one only sees *children's* eyes—but the sweet expression as she saw & recognized us—which she did to the end. The last word she spoke was to Papa—'good' . . . Oh! Jenny she looks so beautiful now. Dollie when she saw her said her face was quite transfigured—her brow was *absolutely smooth*—just as if some gentle hand had smoothed away every line & furrow, while the lovely hair seems to form a sort of glory round her head.— Tomorrow the funeral will be. I do dread it—but of course Papa cannot go—He must not yet leave the house—& I am glad of this in every way.[2]

Engels came and 'said something that nearly made me wild at him', she wrote later: '"Moor is dead too". And it was true.'[3] Though Marx tried hard to stick to life in order to do something to complete his unfinished *Capital*, he was now a broken man and survived his wife only fifteen months.

'Of my father I was so sure!' wrote Eleanor some years later:

For long miserable years there was a shadow between us . . . yet our love was always the same, and despite everything, our faith and trust in each other. My mother and I loved each other passionately, but she did not know me as father did. One of the bitterest of many bitter sorrows in my life is that my mother died, thinking, despite all our love, that I had been hard and cruel, and

[1] Eleanor Marx to Jenny Longuet, 31 Oct. 1881, Bottigelli Collection.
[2] Ibid., 3 Dec. 1881, Bottigelli Collection.
[3] Liebknecht in *Reminiscences*, 127.

never guessing that to save her and father sorrow I had sacrificed the best, freshest years of my life. But father, though he did not *know* till just before the end, felt he must trust me—our natures were so exactly alike! . . . Father was talking of my eldest sister and of me, and said: 'Jenny is most like me, but Tussy . . . *is* me'.[1]

Reconciliation with her father, however, was attained in a tortuous way. Eleanor had to go through many trials, which culminated in a severe mental crisis, before reaching an understanding with him.

*　　　　*　　　　*

Indeed, when her mother died a hopeless feeling of remorse and sorrow overwhelmed Eleanor. Moreover, the dramatic lessons had to be postponed, probably because her parents, especially her mother, had hesitated to approve of her choice of a course of life which was fraught with all sorts of uncertainties. The same conflict that she had felt for many years—between filial duty and her own independence —again tormented her over-sensitive mind, and tension resulting from a dreary accumulation of bitterness and resignation now grew to a dangerous point. During the first two weeks in January 1882 when she was staying with her father at Ventnor on the Isle of Wight she fell seriously ill again. The same symptoms were repeated: she ate almost nothing, suffered from nervous convulsions, and read and wrote the whole day, neglecting everything else. She 'is very laconic, and seems indeed to endure the sojourn with me only out of the sense of duty as a self-sacrificing martyr', wrote Marx to his daughter Laura Lafargue, who was still in London.[2] Moreover, the weather was very depressing—rain almost every day—and the view of the sea and cliffs failed to distract Eleanor from her morbid melancholy.

She wrote a letter to Miss Black and a note to Ernest

[1] Eleanor Marx Aveling to Olive Schreiner, 16 June 1885, in Havelock Ellis, 'Eleanor Marx', *Adelphi*, Sept. 1935.
[2] Marx to Laura Lafargue, 4 Jan. 1882, *Annali*, i. 208.

Radford,[1] telling them respectively that she was very ill
and was afraid of breaking down altogether as she was
anxious to be able to look after her father. This alarmed her
friends so much that after a hurried consultation Radford
sent Dollie Maitland off to Ventnor. 'A very foolish thing to
do—as had I really needed some one Dollie would have
been worse than useless', Eleanor wrote to Jenny at the time:

. . . I'm grateful to Clemmie [Miss Black] & Mr. Radford &
Dollie—but I wish they had let me alone. It only made Papa
angry & anxious—& can do me no good. He was angry that I
had written I was ill & not told him.—It was rather hard—for
of course I'd only said nothing (& as I am really ill it was, to
say the least, trying) in order to save him from any anxiety!
Moreover I do not even like to complain—& I hate to do so to
Papa—He bitter scolds me—as if I 'indulged' in being ill at the
expense of my family—or gets anxious & that worries me most of
all. What neither Papa nor the doctors nor anyone will understand is that it is chiefly *mental worry* that affects me.—Papa talks
about my having 'rest' & 'getting strong' before I try anything &
wont see that 'rest' is the last thing I need—& that I should be
more likely to 'get strong' if I have some definite plan & work
than to go on waiting & waiting.[2]

As her father had by now tolerably recovered from his own
serious illness, she thought that he did not want her any more
as a nursing companion, and at the same time she feared that
her 'last chance of doing something' was going. 'If I only
had a *little* money', she went on in the same letter:

I should distinctly say this; go in for hard work with Mrs. Vezin
—& then *see* (you may be sure I will make no rash plunge) what
I can do. . . . You know, dear, I'm not a bit vain—& that if I err
it is not from over confidence but from distrust in myself—but
in this I think I could get on. I have seen too often—& with such
different people—that I can *move* an audience—& that is the
chief thing.

[1] Ernest Radford had wanted to dedicate his *Translations from Heine
and other Verses* to Marx, and had consulted Eleanor about his intention.
Presumably her reply was not encouraging, for the book was finally
inscribed to his own sister.
[2] Eleanor Marx to Jenny Longuet, 8 Jan. 1882, Bottigelli Collection.

Her condition, however, was serious. She slept only six hours in a week, and had taken various drugs without improvement. Dollie Maitland, who had of course no training as a nurse and groaned positively, as Tussy said, when she was five minutes unentertained, soon left Ventnor. Before she went, however, she had told Marx that she believed Tussy had been 'secretly married' and 'a lot of other coarse & dull stories'—complained the sick girl.[1] Two nights that she spent with Tussy, Dollie informed her father, were 'horrible', as her symptoms were 'of a hysterical nature'.[2] On her return to London, Dollie received a letter from Radford in which the generous young man expressed his hopes:

I must believe that now Eleanor will get this sickening weight off her mind . . . a load of trouble that has made her life miserable & made her act often wrongly & unjustly & that we shall somehow be able to stand round her & help her to lead a happier life perhaps in years to come than she has enjoyed in the past.[3]

It is not known whether he approached Marx at the time on Tussy's behalf, but her sister Jenny, on receiving her letter, immediately wrote to her father. Marx now realized, as he wrote to Engels, that the only thing he could do for his daughter was 'to do as she wishes and to let her go through her theatrical lessons at Madame Jung [Mrs. Vezin]'. 'I would not for anything in the world wish that the child should imagine herself to be sacrificed on the family altar in the form of the "nurse" of an old man.'[4] Thus father and daughter at Ventnor came to an understanding and reconciliation.

Marx allowed her to proceed with her plans for independence, and this, it appears, at last enabled Tussy to put an end to her long engagement with Lissagaray. It was a hard bargain for her to make, but as the obstacles in the way to

[1] Eleanor Marx to Jenny Longuet, 15 Jan. 1882, Bottigelli Collection.
[2] Marx to Engels, 12 Jan. 1882, Marx-Engels, *Briefwechsel*, iv. 620.
[3] Ernest Radford to Dollie Maitland, 11 Jan. 1882, Radford Papers.
[4] Marx to Engels, 12 Jan. 1882, Marx-Engels, op. cit. 619–20.

consummation of her love had been very great and her fiancé had actually returned to Paris, she finally decided to accept the inevitable. 'The chance . . . of independence is very sweet', she now wrote to Jenny:

But if all this has been troubling me it is not all. There has been much else. For a long time I have tried to make up my mind to break off my engagement. I *could* not bring myself to do it—he has been very good, & gentle, & patient with me—but I have done it now. Not only that the burden had become too heavy—I had other reasons (I can't write them—it would take so long; but when I see you will tell you)—& so at last I screwed my courage to the sticking place. And now, dear, I have a great favour to ask of you—namely that you will if possible see Lissa sometimes, & treat him just as an old friend. Remember *he* is blameless in this. I hope we shall continue the best & most intimate of friends—& to do this nothing will help so much as if you & Longuet continue to see him. You will, I am sure, understand my feeling in this!—Ah! it has been a terrible struggle. I sometimes wonder how I have lived through it all. I firmly believe that owing to my long intercourse with cats I have acquired, like them, nine lives instead of one.[1]

Jenny, who seems to have had enough trouble with Longuet, at once approved of her decision, saying that 'these Frenchmen at the best of times make pitiable husbands'.[2] Eleanor, in solitude, felt deserted by all her friends. Indeed, even Radford was to marry Dollie Maitland shortly afterwards.

*   *   *

It now appeared to Tussy that her only salvation lay in hard work. 'After all *work* is the chief thing. To me at least it is a necessity. That is why I love even my dull Museum drudgery. You see I'm not clever enough to live a purely *intellectual* life; nor am I dull enough to be content to sit down & do nothing.'[3] On her twenty-seventh birthday she left Ventnor in order to take part in a dramatic performance

---

[1] Eleanor Marx to Jenny Longuet, 15 Jan. 1882, Bottigelli Collection.
[2] Jenny Longuet to Eleanor Marx, n.d., photocopy, IISH.
[3] Eleanor Marx to Jenny Longuet, 15 Jan. 1882, Bottigelli Collection.

in London. A week later she wrote to Jenny: 'I must tell you that I got on capitally on Tuesday, & was "called" after the first thing (the Pied Piper) but as that is very long—it takes 25 minutes to do & [I] only bowed & would not take an encore (it is rather a tiring thing, you know) but after the "Bridge of Sighs" I had to take one & did.'[1] She was perhaps at her best when she recited the tragic story of a homeless girl who despaired and drowned herself—'The Bridge of Sighs' by Thomas Hood. By this performance, Eleanor earned £2, and Jenny rejoiced at her sister's prospect of 'living the only free life a woman can live—the artistic one'.[2]

In February Eleanor made a short visit to Paris and Argenteuil to see Jenny and her children. In March she took part in a discussion held at a meeting of the New Shakespeare Society, and 'Miss Marx' was reported to have 'insisted that Cordelia must have been beautiful, or else her sisters would not have hated her so'.[3] In the same month she wrote to Jenny on a performance of *Romeo and Juliet* at the Lyceum:

I've never seen a Shakespearian play so satisfactorily played 'all round'. The most disappointing feature is the 'Juliet'—charming in the early scenes—comedy scenes so to say—Ellen Terry gets weaker & weaker as the tragic element appears till in the potion scene she collapses altogether. It is of course very interesting to me; as since my return from Paris I've been grinding at Juliet with Mrs. Vezin. She seems extremely pleased with it—& says, despite my absolute ignorance of stage business she would like me to try it publicly.[4]

Eleanor was very critical of a Shakespearean actress: Mary Anderson, who was then creating a sensation in London, was 'a real fraud', 'exquisitely lovely—& voilà tout'.[5]

[1] Eleanor Marx to Jenny Longuet, 23 Jan. 1882, photocopy at IISH.
[2] Jenny Longuet to Eleanor Marx, n.d., photocopy, IISH.
[3] At its 77th meeting, 10 March 1882, *New Shakespeare Society's Transactions* (1880–6).
[4] Eleanor Marx to Jenny Longuet, 25 March 1882, Bottigelli Collection.
[5] Eleanor Marx to Laura Lafargue, 9 May 1884, photocopy, IISH.

Meanwhile, 'our Browning affair', as she put it, came off. At the annual entertainment of the Browning Society held at University College on 30 June, Eleanor gave two recitations, 'Count Gismond', an epic of chivalry, and again 'The Pied Piper of Hamelin'.[1] 'The place was crowded', she wrote to Jenny next day:

> & as all sorts of 'literary' & other 'swells' were there I felt ridiculously nervous—but [got] on capitally. Mrs. Sutherland Orr (the sister of Sir Frederick Leighton, the president of the Royal Academy) wants to take me to see Browning & recite his own poems to him! I have been asked to go this afternoon to a 'crush' at Lady Wilde's. She is the mother of that very limp & very nasty young man, Oscar Wilde: who has been making such a d-d ass of himself in America. As the son has not yet returned & the mother is nice I may go—that is if I have time for I am also going to Toole's benefit; where the beloved Henry recites. Ellen Terry does the 'Bridge of Sighs' which I look upon as a personal injury that being one of my stock pieces.[2]

These were probably the happiest days in her life. Emboldened by the prospect—perhaps a little too rosy—of establishing herself among the literary celebrities, she devoted herself more than ever to her daily work. It was also about this time that she went for a picnic down the Thames with Furnivall, now the chairman of the Browning Society.

*   *   *

In the meantime her father, in an attempt to restore his health, had gone to Algiers and thence to Monte Carlo, but the Mediterranean winter and spring in that year were unusually cold and wet. He suffered from fresh attacks of pleurisy, and his health improved only a little when he came to Argenteuil to spend the summer with Jenny and her children. During all this time Eleanor frequently wrote to her father, telling him how things went with herself and her friends. On one occasion she described the 'British

---

[1] *Browning Society's Papers* (1881–4).
[2] Eleanor Marx to Jenny Longuet, 1 July 1882, Bottigelli Collection.

Philistines' who, while glancing callously at the reported cases of starvation in London, were moved to tears by the removal of an elephant from the Zoo to a circus—'Shakespeare already declared that your Englishman would not "give a doit to relieve a lame beggar, but lay out ten to see a dead Indian"'.[1]

She was very fond of Jenny's children and sent them petticoats, saying that 'if the button holes are weak the spirit has been willing'.[2] Jenny, after her return to Paris, had been overburdened with the care of her growing family—she had given birth to three boys, Jean, Edgar, and Marcel, in the last six years, and another child was then expected. At Marx's wish Tussy came to Argenteuil towards the end of July to assist her sister. 'Tussychen helps Jennychen extraordinarily', wrote Marx to Engels: 'and her stay could hardly be regarded as a stage of convalescence, even if Tussy were not so good to the children and to the poor Jennychen, and she has under the specific circumstances developed special qualities which are dormant in London.'[3] Amidst a family of small children with another expected, Tussy must have felt motherly instincts and impulses in herself. She was 'an excellent disciplinarian' and brought the wild Johnny (Jean) to order. To save Jenny as much trouble as she could, in the middle of August she took Jean over to England.[4] They stayed for a while with Engels, who was on holiday at Great Yarmouth. Meanwhile, Marx, after having spent several weeks with Laura at Vevey on the shores of Lake Geneva, returned to London early in October to find Johnny well and lively under Tussy's motherly care—a cold wash every morning. 'I have just put my boy—(I am getting so used to & so fond of Jack [Jean] that I forget he is *your* boy) to bed',

[1] Eleanor Marx to Karl Marx, 23 March 1882, Bottigelli Collection.
[2] Eleanor Marx to Jenny Longuet, 25 March 1882, Bottigelli Collection.
[3] Marx to Engels, 3 August 1882, Marx-Engels, *Briefwechsel*, iv. 652.
[4] Eleanor wrote that she had spent three months about this time in Italy with Jean. Liebknecht in *Reminiscences*, 128.

she wrote to Jenny.[1] Marx, shortly after his return, left London again on Dr. Donkin's advice to spend the autumn and winter at Ventnor, where Tussy and Johnny visited him in November. In spite of all her care for Johnny, however, Tussy did not neglect her own work—she was given permission to read at the British Museum even during the 'closed-week', an immense favour accorded to no one else, she claimed, since Gladstone had been allowed there to finish his pamphlet on the Bulgarian atrocities. She worked for the Early English Text Society and also taught at a school conducted by a certain Mrs. Bircham at Kensington.[2] Indeed, hard work was her creed of life, but it was once again interrupted by the misfortunes which fell mercilessly upon her family.

Jenny had not been well, especially after a daughter had been born to her in the summer. Apparently she was suffering from certain symptoms of serious disease, presumably tuberculosis. From Ventnor Marx sent Tussy letters full of 'anxiety for Jennychen's sake', though even now he was able to indulge in abuse against 'the Hyndmanish English political dreams of the future'.[3] Then came the news of Jenny's death: Marx's first-born died on 11 January 1883. Eleanor immediately left for Ventnor. 'I felt that I was bringing my father his death sentence', she wrote later. On her father's strong wishes she at once went to Paris to look after the children left behind. Marx himself returned to London suffering from a fresh attack of bronchitis, and his condition grew worse. On 14 March 'he went out of his bedroom to his study in Maitland Park, sat down in his armchair and calmly passed away', recorded his daughter.[4] 'The greatest brain in the second half of our century had ceased to think', wrote Engels to Liebknecht.[5]

*   *   *

[1] Eleanor Marx to Jenny Longuet, 2 Oct. 1882, Bottigelli Collection.
[2] Ibid., 9 Jan. 1883, Bottigelli Collection.
[3] Karl Marx to Eleanor Marx, 8 Jan. and 9 Jan. 1883, *Annali*, i. 216–17
[4] Quoted by Liebknecht in *Reminiscences*, 128–9.
[5] Engels to Liebknecht, 14 March 1883, Liebknecht, *Briefwechsel*, 281.

Warm sympathies were now pouring in. Mrs. Hyndman invited Eleanor to come and stay with her—'You could have a room quite to yourself & see none not even ourselves unless you liked my husband joins [*sic*] with me in dinner'. 'One can not really help any one in trouble. . . . We can only give love', wrote Miss Black. Maltman Barry wrote in an apologetic tone: 'He was more than my master, he was my political maker. I don't know who was instrumental in keeping me from him. . . . I cannot believe it was yourself.' Furnivall hoped that her father had made some life-provision for her and that she would not out of generosity give it up to some other member of the family.[1]

On 18 August administration of the personal estate of Karl Marx, 'Gentleman', was granted to Eleanor: it amounted to £250. However, it was not his personal property but his literary remains that were really worth inheriting. 'This sorting of the papers will be terrible work', wrote Tussy to her sister Laura Lafargue:

. . . Of course I cannot sit down & do *only* that. I must keep up my lessons, & get all the work I can. I know Engels is goodness itself & that I shall always have all I want, but I think you will understand that I am more anxious than ever to earn my own living . . . I suppose Engels has told you that we have at *least* 500 pages of the 2nd Vol. [of *Capital*]—probably the whole. That is good isn't it?[2]

The immediate question, however, was publication of an English edition of *Capital*, which Marx had so long wished to see. To his alarm Engels discovered that nobody could now stop its unauthorized translation and that there were already several people in the field. Sam Moore, Engels's legal adviser and intimate friend from Manchester days,

---

[1] Matilda Hyndman to Eleanor Marx, 17 March 1883; Clementina Black to Eleanor Marx, 15 March 1883; M. Maltman Barry to Eleanor Marx, 20 March 1883; F. J. Furnivall to Eleanor Marx, March 1883, IISH.

[2] Eleanor Marx to Laura Lafargue, 26 March 1883, Bottigelli Collection.

was chosen as the official translator, and Tussy went to see the London publisher Kegan Paul, who, Engels thought, would be the best man for the project.

Laura in Paris, however, felt that she was left out in all this, and asked Engels 'whether Papa told you that he desired Tussy to be, with you, his literary executrix'.[1] Her father, she said, when she was with him at Vevey, had asked her to undertake a translation of the *Capital*, and she added with a certain spite: 'Papa, in health, would not have made of *his eldest and favourite daughter* [Jenny] his sole literary executrix, to the exclusion of his other daughters—he had too great a love of equality for that—let alone the last of his daughters.'[2] Laura's morbid jealousy must have astonished Engels and Tussy. Engels immediately replied to her:

After poor Mohr's death, on my inquiry, Tussy informed me that he had told her, she and I were to take possession of all his papers, and procure the publication of what was to be published, especially the 2nd vol. and the mathematical works. . . . According to English law . . . the only person living who is the legal representative of Mohr, in England, is Tussy.

He said that he would not wish to interfere in any way between two sisters, but asked Laura, in view of serious competition from the publisher Reeves, 'the most undesirable man of all', whether she could bind herself to the hard task of translation in a given time. What they should all aim at, he concluded, was 'a befitting monument to the memory of Mohr. . . . Let us then all contribute what we can towards that end.'[3] At Eleanor's ardent desire Laura paid a visit to London in the summer when an understanding was finally reached and fresh unpleasantness was avoided. Laura withdrew her claim, though the work of translation dragged on for several years.

[1] Laura Lafargue to Engels, 2 June 1883, Engels-Lafargue, *Correspondance*, i (Paris, 1956), 126.

[2] Ibid., 20 June 1883, Engels-Lafargue, *Correspondance*, i. 132.

[3] Engels to Laura Lafargue, 24 June 1883, photocopy at IML (Berlin).

Engels now acted as Tussy's guardian, and Helena Demuth, Marx's faithful maid, came to join Engels's household. Mary Ellen Burns, the gay and somewhat frivolous 'Pumps', was married to a business man, Percy Rosher, though her patron was still very much absorbed in her. Tussy thought the festivities at the Engels's grew odder every year. 'The good old General is prouder of Pumps than ever', she wrote to Laura: '"There never was *such* a woman!" he informed me the other day!!'[1] In fact Tussy inherited her parents' prejudices against Engels's character in her relations with his female companions. Referring to them in a letter, she said that both Mary and Lizzie Burns 'drank to excess: but my parents always said this was as much the fault of Engels as of the two women'.[2] When she began sorting the papers left by her father, she wrote to her sister: 'I shall take the *utmost* care to prevent our good General from seeing anything that is likely to give him pain.'[3] When she wrote this, she may have had in her mind Frederick Demuth, the illegitimate son of Helena, for whom, she somehow believed, Engels was responsible. At any rate, this shows that her trust in her guardian was not without serious reservations.

Eleanor now gained the independence which she had desired so long, and thought that she could brave all the risks involved in her own decisions. Indeed her independence, though financially more or less secure, was of a solitary nature, but she now found a congenial companion in Dr. Edward Aveling, who had invited her to write an obituary of her father in *Progress*, a Secularist monthly of which he was then acting as editor. He was a keen student of Shakespeare and aspired to become a dramatist, producer, and actor

[1] Eleanor Marx to Laura Lafargue, 27 April 1883, Bottigelli Collection.
[2] Eleanor Marx Aveling to Kautsky, 15 March 1898, IISH.
[3] Eleanor Marx to Laura Lafargue, 26 March 1883, Bottigelli Collection. It has been suggested that Laura and Eleanor destroyed some of Marx's letters which contained lines that would injure Engels's reputation. Mayer, *Engels*, ii. 356.

himself. He was quite prepared to learn Socialism from his new acquaintance. Through him Eleanor thought that she might be able to fulfil her own theatrical ambitions and at the same time to do something for the cause to which her father had devoted his whole life. Her future became inseparably united with Aveling's, and their life, dedicated as it was to the dramatic Muse, was woven into a drama of its own. Before the start of its first act, however, the actor Dr. Aveling has to be properly introduced and his earlier life to be examined.

4. Edward Aveling

IV ~ DR. AVELING

In 1851, when the Marx family was undergoing all the miseries of an *émigré* life in one of the poorer quarters of London, this mightiest and wealthiest city in the world was celebrating the opening of the Great Exhibition, the symbol of bourgeois prosperity, peace, and contentment. The Crystal Palace, a structure of glass and iron, was 'an eighth wonder of the world' and marked 'the triumphs of industry, ingenuity, and taste—of mind in its highest achievements in connection with matter'. Such, at any rate, was the solemn opinion of the Rev. Thomas William Baxter Aveling, a Congregational minister, when giving a discourse entitled 'Great Sights' at his chapel at Kingsland in East London. In this vast exhibition hall, as he pointed out, there was a stand set up by the British and Foreign Bible Society displaying copies of the Scriptures in more than 150 different languages and dialects of the world. 'The heart will thrill', he went on, 'as it reflects that by these the Church shall conquer the world for Christ.'[1]

In this same year the fifth son of this God-fearing minister was born. This was not Edward Aveling, who is to be our subject in this chapter, but his younger brother Frederick Wilkins, who later obtained a London B.Sc. and became a Nonconformist minister and an enthusiast for free trade, which must have been in accord with the highest expectations of his father. Edward Bibbins Aveling, who later

[1] Thomas Aveling, *Great Sights* (1851), *passim*.

claimed to have been born in 1851,[1] was in fact born on 29 November 1849 at Nelson Terrace, Stoke Newington, where his parents then lived. He was their fourth son. He later asserted that he could trace his ancestors back to the time of the Crusades and that many of them 'richly deserved hanging'.[2] The family was of Irish extraction with an admixture of French blood. His mother, Mary Ann Goodall, was a daughter of Thomas Goodall, a farmer and innkeeper of Wisbech, Cambridgeshire. She was known for her Irish 'bulls' and is said to have taken to drink. From his father Edward no doubt inherited his oratorical power; from his mother he may have acquired something of his wit and humour as well as the habit of excessive drinking. The latter, according to Havelock Ellis, was the key to his moral unsoundness.[3]

Edward Aveling grew up, then, in a large family. His three elder brothers were called Thomas Goodall, Charles Taylor, and William Arthur, and his two younger brothers were Frederick Wilkins and Ernest Henry. There were also two sisters, Mary Elizabeth and Alice Amelia De Rippé. Edward does not appear to have been a particularly attractive child. Already he insisted on the best of everything, and when he was asked whether he would take peas *or* potatoes at dinner he promptly replied 'Both please'.[4] In a charming story he wrote many years later entitled 'In Search of Happiness', he described the journey of a small child through a beautiful wood called 'Mother's Care' and along a clear and musical brook named 'Sister's Love', but in another and equally sentimental story he gave an account of a secret love of his mother and the thrill he felt when he discovered it, which may well have contained at least

---

[1] See Joseph McCabe, *A Biographical Dictionary of Modern Rationalists* (1920), and biographical accounts in *Republican* (Dec. 1881) and *Socialiste* (20 Feb. 1886).

[2] *Republican*, Dec. 1881.

[3] *Adelphi*, Sept. 1935.

[4] Eleanor Marx Aveling to Liebknecht, 2 June 1897, Liebknecht, *Briefwechsel*, 454.

something of personal reminiscence. Certainly he was very attached to one of his sisters, probably the only one of his family to whom, years later, he was still able to express kindly feelings.[1] He was a sickly, delicate child, and, worse still, careless nursing caused an injury to his spine which had lasting effects in a slight stoop. As a result he spent his early years mostly at home, reading Shakespeare, Bunyan, Defoe, and Fielding in his father's splendid library, though he was not allowed to read anything except *Pilgrim's Progress* on Sundays. A visit to the theatre was supposed to be out of the question, but he defied the ban and would sneak out to see a pantomime at the Drury Lane.

At a certain stage of his education he was sent to Harrow, and from there was moved to Taunton, where he studied medicine under a tutor for a year and a half. He was apparently intended for the medical profession. It was probably about this time that he visited Jersey—'I think Jersey hellish', he later wrote: 'Once there as a boy with a tutor & a hatred of him.'[2] His tutor, however, was a capable man, and he was a clever pupil. In 1867 when he became a student at University College, London, registering himself in the Faculty of Medicine, he was awarded an Entrance Exhibition of £25. Thereafter he gathered medals and awards like a child plucking flowers: a gold medal for chemistry, a First Certificate for practical physiology and histology, and a silver medal for botany. At the Intermediate Science Examination for 1869 he won an Exhibition of £40 in zoology, and in the following year he obtained a B.Sc. and a Scholarship of £50 per annum for three years in zoology. He continued his hard work, and spent some time at Cambridge as an assistant in the laboratory of Professor Michael Foster, an eminent physiologist. When he returned

[1] Edward Aveling, *The Bookworm and other Sketches* (c. 1878); Eleanor Marx Aveling to Kautsky, 8 Jan. 1898, IISH.
[2] Edward Aveling to Laura Lafargue, 30 Aug. 1887, Bottigelli Collection.

to London he began teaching at the North London Collegiate School for Girls, a pioneer institution for the higher education of women. In 1876 he took a D.Sc. at London and shortly afterwards was elected a Fellow of the Linnean Society. He was appointed Lecturer in Comparative Anatomy at London Hospital and for a while held a teaching position in science at King's College, London. He was also elected a Fellow of his alma mater, University College, a position which he held for life. He appeared to be safely embarked on a promising career which would have secured him at least a respectable social position, if not the reputation of a Huxley or a Tyndall.

*　　　　*　　　　*

Edward had been given a religious upbringing, but his training as a natural scientist took place in a period when theories of evolution as formulated by Darwin in his *Origin of Species* had almost conquered both religious and scientific opposition. He now emerged as an enthusiastic Darwinian, and yet in his naturalist studies he seems to have been encouraged rather than discouraged by his father. At a time when science was making converts even among the clergy, it would not be surprising if his father, a dissenting minister who firmly believed that the word of God 'does not come to us to expound any science at all, except that of salvation', appeared quite receptive to Darwin's theory, no matter how much it had alarmed orthodox theologians.[1] Although his son's faith in salvation was now rapidly receding, there seemed no immediate cause for serious disagreement between Edward and his family.

While he was an undergraduate, Edward had already begun 'coaching' in order to earn extra money. In 1874 he published *Botanical Tables* for the use of his pupils, and this was followed by *Physiological Tables* in 1877, when his classes had considerably expanded and he was preparing his pupils

[1] Thomas Aveling, *Christ and Christianity* (1851), 50.

for definite examinations held by the various medical bodies, particularly by the Department of Science and Art in South Kensington. The latter body, which owed its existence to the Great Exhibition itself, had been concerned with the expansion of technical education and the training of qualified teachers, and its work in this direction assumed greater importance as competition from foreign countries with superior technical education began to have adverse effects upon British trade. Coaching like that conducted by Aveling also became a thriving business, and in view of his 'prodigious intellectuality' it was said that he 'could have earned a thousand pounds a year' at this profession.[1]

By this time Edward was assuming family responsibilities of his own. In July 1872 the young science graduate was married to Isabel Campbell Frank, daughter of a poulterer. The marriage did not last long, but it is not known when and how he separated from his wife. She was apparently deeply religious, and according to Engels she ran away with a priest and began spreading insulting rumours about her husband.[2] Meanwhile, Edward's mother died of apoplexy in August 1877, and in the following year his father, who was then 63 years old, married a certain Miss Joscelyne, whose brother was also a minister. It was probably shortly after the death of his mother, to whom he was devoted, that Edward made up his mind to declare himself an atheist. When he announced the fact in July 1879 he said that his decision was 'some two or three years old'. It may be assumed that his separation from his wife and the beginning of rumours, which do not appear to have been altogether groundless, especially with regard to girl students, also occurred in the same period. How far Edward broke with his family is not clear. One view was that 'his heretical opinions have in no way interfered with his family relations'.[3] But

---

[1] Thomas Okey, *A Basketful of Memoirs* (1930), 62.
[2] Engels to F. A. Sorge, 4 June 1887, photocopy at IML (Berlin).
[3] *Republican*, Dec. 1881.

Charles Bradlaugh, President of the National Secular Society, stated that Aveling's participation in the free-thought movement had 'caused him the loss of many old friendships and severed for him life associations'.[1]

*   *   *

It was through one of his students at King's College that he was introduced to Mrs. Annie Besant, Vice-President of Bradlaugh's Society. Annie, who was two years older than Aveling, had separated from her husband, a clergyman, mainly as a result of her unorthodox views on religion. She was then determined to matriculate at London University, whose degree courses had lately been made available for women, and she became Aveling's pupil as well as a colleague in the Secular Society. Secularism as an organized movement had its origin in the last phase of Owenism, and in a faith in reason and science. A conception of utilitarian morality and a belief in the possibility of the improvement of human conditions in this world constituted the core of its principles. In the matter of politics Bradlaugh's followers formed a wing of the Radicals, and they had various associated bodies, such as a Republican Club, which took sustenance from the establishment of the Third Republic in France, and a Malthusian League, which conducted a campaign for birth control. In the course of the 1870's the Society gained some ground: its membership increased from about 1,000 in 1871 to nearly 6,000 in 1880.[2] When Aveling joined the movement, the Society was in a flourishing state under the vigorous leadership of 'C.B. and A.B.', who were obviously in love, and the new recruit was welcomed as a man of intellect who would bring scientific knowledge to the work of agitation.

In January 1879 Aveling started serializing a piece entitled 'Darwin and his Views' in the Society's organ, the *National Reformer*, under the signature 'E.D.'. It was an attempt to

[1] *National Reformer*, 23 May 1880.

[2] John Edwin McGee, *A History of the British Secular Movement* (Girard, Kansas, 1948), 73.

give an outline of the theory of natural selection, and in its
conclusion it stated: 'With the acceptance of this view there
is no loss of the beautiful—nay, in every truth a new loveli-
ness is added to all Nature as we study her with this for
guide.'[1] In July 1879 he published a statement entitled
'Credo Ergo Laborabo' ('I believe, therefore I shall work'),
in which he openly declared that he had become a freethinker. 'I desire, therefore,' he said, 'to labour for freedom
of thought, of word, of act, for all men and women. . . .
Beautiful Nature, the eternal comforter, is with us.'[2] Hereafter the need for some form of integration of science and art,
both dedicated to the shrine of Nature, became one of the
main themes of his frequent contributions to the *National
Reformer* as well as of his lectures.

On 10 August Aveling delivered his first lecture at the Hall
of Science, the focus of the free-thought movement, with Mrs.
Besant in the chair. His subject was 'Shelley'. In an essay
which he wrote on the poet—probably an amplification
of this lecture—he emphasized as Shelley's central idea 'the
unity of all forms of sensation', which, he said, was pointing
to 'the kinship that exists between two orders of thought . . .
the scientific and the poetical'. Yet he made no attempt to
go into the meaning of this 'kinship' except by a reference
to the similarity of the feelings provoked by the various
senses. Indeed, this was an application of his crude materialism, which he obviously derived from an apparently easy
victory of science over religion within himself. Apart from
this, his effort to integrate science and art was little more than
the seemingly scientific method of mechanically arranging
and classifying Shelley's views under various heads, a treatment singularly well suited for a man whose profession was
coaching.[3]

[1] *National Reformer*, 2 March 1879. His summary of Darwin's theories
was later published as *Student's Darwin* (1881).
[2] Ibid., 27 July 1879.
[3] *Modern Thought*, Dec. 1880.

After the lecture the chairman of the meeting, Mrs. Besant, whose self-sacrificing devotion to successive causes verged on the pathological, declared that 'our mistress Liberty has won this new knight'. To her, Aveling was more than the knight of Liberty. She was enraptured by the 'mere music' of his speech, the 'artistic charm' of his language, which was 'exquisitely chosen' and 'polished to the highest extent'.[1] It seems that the two of them went on holiday together among the mountains and dells of north Wales and exchanged love poems which were more directly personal than allegorical.[2] It is not known how Annie's new discovery affected her relations with Bradlaugh, but 'the great Trinity in Unity', as they were called, extolled each other's faculties as they carried on their Secularist agitation.

Aveling began a series of weekly Sunday lectures all over the country, and travelled from Cornwall to Scotland, complaining of the difficulties of the railways and of hotel life. Apparently his greatest objection was to 'the man that disputes his hotel bill' and 'the non-tipper' who defied 'all the laws and customs of the kingdom of waiterdom'.[3] He presumably preferred, as it later turned out, to ignore the bill entirely rather than to dispute its details. His devotion to the Secularist cause showed that he was capable of no small sacrifice for the cause in which he believed. Yet there was an element of aesthetic hedonism in his beliefs, shared by many other cultivated intellectuals at the time, who somehow imagined themselves to be witnesses of a turning-point in history and civilization, and this seems to have been at least partly responsible for his personal degeneration.

Indeed, the reason for his objection to Christianity was itself hedonistic. In one of his earliest lectures, entitled 'The Sermon on the Mount', he declared: 'With the unhappy he

---

[1] *National Reformer*, 17 Aug. 1879.

[2] N.S.S. *Almanack for 1880*, quoted in Arthur H. Nethercot, *The First Five Lives of Annie Besant* (1961), 167.

[3] *National Reformer*, 12 Sept. 1880.

[Christ] would sympathise. But the joyousness of life he seems not to have been able to understand . . . . We are told that he wept. It is in no place recorded of him that he smiled.'[1] An incorrigible optimist, he glorified the pleasure of being alive. In fact, when he delivered the above lecture he took advantage of the Secularist rite which had been designed to replace baptism, and named a child of one of its members 'Aveling Hope'.[2] In a lecture entitled 'Why I dare not be a Christian', he gave, as one of his reasons, the pain—the agony of moral uncertainty—which he had suffered while he had held the Christian faith, but he said: 'In this, our creed, we have not to concern ourselves with the will of a hypothetical being. . . . There is for us the simple question ever recurring, will this act, or word, or thought of mine add to the sum of human happiness or of human misery?'[3] It was Utilitarianism undiluted: Aveling now firmly believed that Secularism would provide the conditions in which everyone would have the right to every pleasure in this world.

*   *   *

He soon began to play a prominent role in the political agitation of the National Secular Society. In February 1880 —at the time of the Irish agrarian war—when the Society held a meeting in London to demand a land law reform, he was in the platform party and declared in his speech: 'The Irish blood that moves in my own veins makes me cry for Ireland . . . "more freedom".' He advocated the extension of the borough franchise to the counties. It might be true that agricultural labourers were not taxed directly, he said, but 'there is taxation upon human strength, taxation upon human labour, upon human blood and, . . . taxed person has right to representation'. Michael Davitt also spoke, and denounced landlordism as 'a huge robbery'. It was decided

---

[1] Aveling, *The Sermon on the Mount* (n.d.), 3.
[2] *National Reformer*, 18 Jan. 1880.
[3] Aveling, *Why I dare not be a Christian* (n.d.), 5–6.

to set up a Land Law Reform League, whose object, in Bradlaugh's words, was to work for the establishment of 'a land-crushing machine, the handle to be turned by the tax-gatherer, until the estates were squeezed into reasonable size'. Mrs. Besant in her concluding speech stated that the new League was the child of the Corn Law League of Cobden: 'of what use to free the corn if you do not free the land upon which it has to grow?'[1] In practice, however, the land reform agitation, which was soon reinforced by Henry George's spectacular campaign for his Single Tax panacea, provided a political education for those who later became prominent in the Socialist movement, including Aveling himself.

At the General Election of 1880 Bradlaugh, who had been a parliamentary candidate for Northampton (a two-member constituency) since 1868, was elected with Henry Labouchere, a leading Radical and critic of Royalty. Now a new subject was added to Aveling's Sunday lectures—'Representation of the people'—but, as he pointed out, Bradlaugh, 'the most real representative of the people of England', was allowed neither to take the parliamentary oath nor to make affirmation, a privilege that had been given to the Quakers and others. When Bradlaugh claimed the right to be sworn and refused to withdraw from the House, he was removed by the Serjeant-at-Arms to the Clock Tower of the House for custody. In the following year he was unseated, sought re-election, and was successful, but the struggle went on till January 1886, when, having been elected five times by his Northampton supporters, he was at last allowed to take his seat. The political struggle became to Aveling 'that which religion is supposed to be to the Christians', and he went for it with the single-minded devotion of a religious crusader. Through Bradlaugh's 'constitutional struggle' he came into direct contact with the workers in London and the provinces. In March 1881, together with Mrs. Besant and

[1] *National Reformer*, 15, 22 Feb. 1880.

George William Foote, the veteran Secularist and journalist, he founded a League for the Defence of Constitutional Rights, and organized a series of 'Constitutional Rights meetings' with the support of various working men's clubs and trade unions. On 3 August 1881, when Bradlaugh was again forcibly ejected from the House, Aveling reported the scene for the *National Reformer*. He reminded readers of 'the ominous roar' of the Northampton voters whom he had addressed, 'the shouts of Lancashire men' which were 'ringing in my ears' and 'the miners by their thousands who would cast aside to-morrow pick and lantern and journey south for him'. He concluded with an implied threat: 'Thousands of wronged working men are growing angry and these may not be so patient. . . . And then—who knows?'[1] Yet he knew that Bradlaugh's Northampton supporters were mostly Nonconformists and that those working men's clubs in London who assisted the campaign were in religious matters 'wholly opposed' to the junior Member for Northampton.[2]

* * *

Aveling intensified his anti-religious agitation with the aid of his scientific knowledge. During the first ten months of his Secularist work he gave 116 lectures, mainly on science and religion. At the 1880 annual conference of the National Secular Society, at which he was elected one of its vice-presidents, he read a paper 'On the Relationship between Science and Secularism' in which he claimed that most of the scientists were wittingly or unwittingly atheists.[3] In a new lecture which he started early in 1881 entitled 'The Wickedness of God', he went so far as to call the Christian God an 'encourager of polygamy' and an 'instigator to theft'. In September 1881, when the International Federation of Freethinkers, which had been founded in the previous year

---

[1] *National Reformer*, 14 Aug. 1881.   [2] Ibid., 12 June, 6 Nov. 1881.
[3] Ibid., 23 May 1880.

at Brussels, held its second annual congress at the Hall of Science with Prof. Ludwig Büchner, one of the popularizers of Darwin in Germany, in the chair, Aveling read a paper on the origin of religion and its climatic environment after the fashion of Montesquieu.[1] Soon after the congress, Prof. Büchner and Aveling paid a visit to Darwin at his secluded home at Downe, Kent. On the host's inquiry about atheism, the two visitors pointed out that the Greek *a* was privative, not negative, and 'whilst we did not commit the folly of god-denial, we avoided with equal care the folly of god-assertion'. Darwin replied: 'I am with you in thought, but I should prefer the word Agnostic to the word Atheist.' Now Aveling suggested that 'after all, "Agnostic" was but "Atheist" writ respectable, and "Atheist" was only "Agnostic" writ aggressive'. Darwin's confession that 'I never gave up Christianity until I was forty years of age' and that Christianity 'is not supported by evidence' delighted the two visitors.[2]

Indeed, Darwin kept silence in public on this question in order not to offend his wife, who was a regular church-goer, and there were also persistent attempts among certain Churchmen to effect a compromise between the *Origin* and the Bible. In order to prove their irreconcilability, Aveling invoked the authority of Darwin himself. In September 1882, five months after the death of Darwin, a letter from him to a student at Jena was given publicity in Germany. Darwin wrote that science and Christ had nothing to do with each other and that he did not believe that any revelation had ever been made. The letter was also published in England by the *Pall Mall Gazette*, the *National Reformer*, and the *Spectator*, but *Nature*, the leading scientific journal, ignored it. Thereupon Aveling sent a letter of regret to Prof. Ernst Haeckel of Jena, who had been responsible for the original publication of the letter. He gladly published Haeckel's

[1] *National Reformer*, 2, 9, 16, 30 Oct. 1881.
[2] Aveling, *The Religious Views of Charles Darwin* (1884), *passim*.

reply that the German scientists, unlike the English, had liberated themselves from the bonds of medieval prejudice.[1]

Aveling remained in occasional correspondence with Haeckel, translated his *Pedigree of Man* and other essays, and was only too glad to endorse his monistic view of the universe based on a kind of metaphysical materialism. In fact, the culmination of Aveling's Secularist thinking was what he called 'the gospel of Evolution', which was to replace that of Christianity. Evolution here was explained in Haeckel's sense as the idea of unity and continuity of phenomena: matter and motion were 'all in all', and even life itself was reduced to 'a mode of motion'. 'The preachers of this new gospel', he declared:

are nature herself and all her children. Thus the history of man, all science, all human lives, we that live and love, are the apostles of the new evangel. And its temples ... are the halls of universities, the state-schools, the science classes for our young men and maidens, the laboratories, and the studies of the philosophers, the hearts of all that seek for truth.[2]

Aveling had started two science classes in the autumn of 1879—one for inorganic chemistry and the other for animal physiology—under the auspices of the National Secular Society. The Rev. Stewart Headlam, founder of the Guild of St. Matthew, agreed to act as chairman of the Society's school committee in order to satisfy the regulations of the South Kensington authorities. In the course of three years, the original two classes were expanded to eleven (fourteen at the fourth session), and the number of students—mostly skilled artisans—increased from 115 to 214. Mrs. Besant and the Misses Hypatia and Alice Bradlaugh, the daughters of Charles Bradlaugh, who had all achieved remarkable successes in the South Kensington examinations, were added to the teaching staff. The classes were held at the Hall of Science, and in the summer of 1881 Aveling acquired a

[1] *National Reformer*, 1, 22 Oct. 1882.
[2] Aveling, 'The Gospel of Evolution', *Atheistic Platform* (1884), 48.

laboratory in Newman Street off Oxford Street which he named the 'Practical Science Laboratory'. Here he conducted some of the advanced and practical classes.[1] But the classes soon became the target of an anti-Secularist campaign led by Sir Henry Tyler, a Conservative M.P. In August 1881 Tyler asked a question in the House as to whether the classes at the Hall of Science and their teachers, in view of their known associations, were entitled to Government grants. He especially objected to Aveling, who, he said, had stated that 'the attributes of the Cross are condemnatory of God'. A. J. Mundella, who was in charge of education in Gladstone's Government, replied that her Majesty's inspectors had reported very favourably of the instruction given there and that was all the Government was concerned with.[2] Tyler raised the same question again in the following year but failed to disqualify Aveling's classes, which were said to have gained a higher percentage of prizes and passes for their students than most other schools.[3]

The pressure of what Aveling called 'Christian bigotry' was felt in many other directions. In June 1881 he was dismissed from the London Hospital for the technical reason that he had not lectured on the days chosen by the Hospital Board. In fact, after certain inquiries in which some of his colleagues assisted, the Board had to admit that his duties had been discharged 'with punctuality and ability.'[4] It seems that he had many profitable teaching positions, and the arrangement of the timetable of lessons always gave him trouble, which could easily be taken advantage of by his opponents both public and private. Aveling, however, defied the Hospital Board and at once announced that he would start a course of lectures on comparative anatomy at the Hall of Science. In view of a serious illness—an attack

[1] *National Reformer*, 12 June, 31 July, 23 Oct. 1881, 1 Oct. 1882.
[2] *Daily News*, 25 Aug. 1881; *Evening News*, 23, 24 Aug. 1881.
[3] *National Reformer*, 28 May 1882.
[4] Ibid., 18 Dec. 1881, 8 Jan. 1882.

of typhoid—from which he suffered shortly afterwards, it is doubtful whether he actually gave the lessons he had thus advertised.

The struggle between the militant atheists and the self-appointed guardians of Christian morality reached its highest point in the trial of G. W. Foote, the editor of the *Freethinker*, which he had founded as an 'aggressive' 'anti-Christian organ' in May 1881. It was a lively paper featuring, besides Foote's trenchant articles, a series of 'Comic Bible Sketches' and 'Profane Jokes'. Aveling contributed several articles on religious and scientific topics. Now at the behest again of Tyler, Foote and his publisher and printer were prosecuted on the charge of 'blasphemous libel' published, as it was asserted, in an article entitled 'What Shall I do to be Damned!' in its number of 28 May 1882. Aveling denounced Tyler and his friends as the 'nineteenth century Pharisees, Hypocrites', and made a curious remark: 'The earlier Christians were persecuted, and now it is our turn.'[1] While the trial dragged on, another prosecution was started against the Christmas number of the paper, and in March 1883 Foote was sentenced to twelve months' imprisonment. Aveling became its interim editor and advocated 'the right to blaspheme'. Indeed, he went further and pointed out the class nature of the prosecution, which, in fact, had been started by the Corporation of the City of London, saying that 'prosecution only comes when the blasphemy in which the rich delight is brought to the poor in penny numbers every week'.[2] By this time he had obviously come under Socialist influence.

*   *   *

One of Aveling's atheist principles was the importance of education. 'By this, and this only', he said, 'can we hope to raise all men', and he added: 'The Board Schools of this century will be to the generations that succeed us as the

---

[1] *Freethinker*, 30 July 1882.   [2] Ibid., 1 April 1883.

churches were to those before our time.'[1] At the London School Board elections held in November 1882 Aveling stood for the Westminster Division, and through his campaign he was initiated into the organized Socialist movement, for his candidature was supported not only by the Westminster branch of the National Secular Society, but also by Hyndman's Democratic Federation, which had its headquarters at Westminster. In his election address he declared himself in favour of 'free, secular, compulsory education'. The Rev. Stewart Headlam, Alsager Hay Hill, editor of the *Labour News* who also sat on the committee of Aveling's science classes, Hyndman himself, W. J. Morgan, then secretary of the Federation, and James and Charles Murray, the veteran Chartists, also members of the Federation, assisted his campaign. He was nominated by 'two working-men friends', one of whom was H. W. Lee, a young clerk, who became secretary of the Westminster branch of the Federation and in due course of the Federation itself. Various working men's clubs in the district also worked for him. At the election he polled 4,720 votes and was the fourth of the five successful candidates in this division. Mrs. Besant called his election 'a sore blow to the Church and Tory party', but Aveling was no longer a mere Secularist, and in an address he issued after the election he pointed out the class divisions of his constituency. Mayfair and Belgravia he would not represent, but, he said:

Westminster includes Soho, Peabody Buildings, Seven Dials, and the voices of the dwellers in such places as these are faintly heard; for over-work and under-pay, hardship and sickness, stifle them. I want to speak especially for such as these. The poor, the wronged, the untaught are, above all, my constituents.[2]

He was already well on the road to Socialism, and it was in the name of the working class that at the meetings of the

[1] Aveling, *The Creed of an Atheist* (n.d.), 7.

[2] *National Reformer*, 3 Dec. 1882. See also *National Reformer*, 29 Oct., 5, 12, 19, 26 Nov. 1882, and *School Board Chronicle*, 2 Dec. 1882.

School Board he supported the cause of higher education
and especially technical education. He also moved a resolution in favour of free, compulsory elementary education,
which was defeated, though supported 'with great warmth'
by Miss Helen Taylor, the stepdaughter of John Stuart Mill
and herself a member of the Democratic Federation. From
the beginning he vehemently criticized religious influence
and pressure on the management of Board schools, and it
was only to be expected that several attempts by his sympathetic colleagues to add his name to the School Management Committee were constantly barred. When Mrs. Fenwick
Miller, a pioneer woman journalist, proposed social economy
as a new subject to be taught at schools, he supported the
motion on the ground that economics would provide a link
between various branches of science and a basis for their
practical application for the use of the community. Yet, as
the nature of 'Social Economy' became clear—according to
Mrs. Fenwick Miller, it was to be focused upon capital, the
source of all production—Aveling objected to its adoption. He
was 'in favour of teaching the facts of social economy, but not
the dogmas'.[1] Indeed, his election to the School Board with
the overwhelming support of the Democratic Federation,
and his work at its meetings, led him to believe, as Hyndman
said, that Socialism was 'the necessary constructive corre-
lative of the purely negative and destructive Secularism'.

Yet Aveling was an enigma to many of those who came
into contact with him. Hyndman added to the above comment on Aveling's conversion to Socialism:

I did not like the man from the first. 'Nobody can be so bad as
Aveling looks' was a remark which translated itself into action
in my case. In spite of the most unpleasant rumours about his
personal character, alike in regard to money and sexual relations, I put compulsion on myself and forced myself to believe
that . . . his forbidding face could not in truth be an index to his
real character.

[1] *School Board Chronicle*, 13, 20 Jan., 3 Feb., 21 July, 6 Oct. 1883.

'Aveling was one of those men', he went on, 'who have an attraction for women quite inexplicable to the male sex. Like Wilkes, ugly and even repulsive to some extent, as he looked, he needed but half an hour's start of the handsomest man in London.'[1] Such an allegation may baffle an attempt to analyse the charms of Aveling's personality, but one of the clues to his attractions could be found in the 'exquisite' manner, as Mrs. Besant said, in which he treated artistic subjects.

*   *   *

Along with science, politics, and education, he emphasized the importance of Art. 'As our aim is to gladden the life of man, and to remove all that saddens it', he would tell his audience, 'we love all forms of art. Free as children we can laugh, and sing, and dance to our heart's content.'[2] He could implant the feeling of exhilaration and even intoxication in the minds of his hearers, who could not detect any signs of affectation or even sentimentality in his flowing passion, in which he often lost himself as he spoke. He was a born entertainer, a preacher dedicated to the gospel of *joie de vivre*. In fact, he had attempted a theatrical career before he became an atheist lecturer, and for a while acted as the manager of a travelling dramatic company.[3] It is characteristic of this semi-professional entertainer that the occasion for his first public appearance in the Secularist movement was an entertainment organized by the London Secular Choral Union. His 'Recitations from Poetry and Prose', covering a wide range from Shakespeare to Francis Bret Harte, the American humorist, given at Steinway Hall, Portman Square, were described as an 'unqualified success'.[4] At a meeting of the Hall of Science Students' Association, Aveling, its president, gave 'Readings, Grave and Gay',

[1] Hyndman, *Further Reminiscences*, 140–2.
[2] Aveling, *The Creed of an Atheist* (n.d.), 7.
[3] Bernstein, *My Years of Exile*, 161.
[4] *Republican*, May 1880. See also Nethercot, op. cit., 162.

featuring Edgar Allan Poe's 'Bells', his favourite piece. He
was perhaps at his best when he read the story of the bells
tolled by ghouls. He was to repeat this on many other occasions; it was said to have been his best performance, for
there was 'something rather uncanny and impish in his
nature which doubtless made him a good interpreter of the
weird'.[1] Yet at the same time he asserted that plays and
poems, as well as men and women, their loves, fears, and
aspirations, were one and all 'so much matter in certain
conditions of motion'.[2] The seemingly facile combination of
materialism and aestheticism must have made him appear
more attractive and even profound to many of his audience.
He could sing of a 'maiden's love' in a sort of trance, and at
the same time could write an essay on Malthusianism from
the biological point of view.

When he gave a series of lectures on the works of Shakespeare at the Hall of Science towards the end of 1881, he
again emphasized the need for unity between 'the scientific
mind' and literature and dealt with the subject in the manner
of a textbook, as he had done with Shelley, but suggested that
the deepest meaning of Shakespeare's works, 'like the thought
that lies behind a woman's eyes', was not meant for all men.
He warned against what he called 'affectation of Shakespeare
comprehension', but was delighted to find in Swinburne's
Study of Shakespeare a presentation of the dramatist as a
free-thinker, a Republican, 'a spiritual if not a political
Democrat and Socialist'.[3] He was a regular theatre-goer
and would treat distinguished guests and special friends to a
dinner and a box at the Criterion. He took charge of the
'Art Corner' in the columns of *Our Corner*, a Secularist
publication founded by Mrs. Besant in January 1883, in
which he wrote monthly reviews of drama and music,

[1] Henry Salt, *Seventy Years among Savages* (1921), 81; *National Reformer*,
20 Feb. 1881.

[2] *National Reformer*, 7 Aug. 1881.

[3] Ibid., 9, 30 May 1880; Aveling, 'Plays of Shakespeare', *Hall of
Science Thursday Lectures* (1882).

focusing his attention upon Irving at the Lyceum. Here he attempted a detailed analysis of Shakespeare and in an introductory essay declared that 'our idle class', who had never produced artists like Shakespeare or men of science, would one day be ousted even from politics, their traditional field of work, 'by the more vigorous, if less favoured toilers'.[1]

*   *   *

A popular atheist lecturer, a coach of science classes, a member of the School Board, an entertainer, and an art critic, who had already shown interest in Socialism—such was Dr. Aveling when Eleanor Marx came into contact with him in the early eighties. Aveling, however, had met Eleanor once before, when he gave a lecture at the Orphan Working School, Hampstead, quite near Marx's residence. He was at the time a young man of 21 or 22 and it was long before he became a Secularist lecturer. His subject was 'Insects and Flowers', a charming illustration of the theory of natural selection. After the lecture he was introduced to a man 'with a tremendous leonine head' who had come to hear his talk with his wife and daughter. It was, however, only the man, Karl Marx, who spoke to him and congratulated him on his achievements.[2]

After this he apparently had no contact with the Marx family for years, as Marx distrusted Bradlaugh, with whom Aveling soon associated himself. At an earlier date some of Marx's followers in London had joined Bradlaugh's movement, and even his wife and children attended his lectures. But after the Paris Commune, when Bradlaugh assisted those French refugees who were opposed to the General Council of the International, Marx attacked him as 'a courtesan of Plon Plon [Prince Napoleon, the leader of the

[1] *Our Corner*, March 1883.

[2] Aveling, 'Charles Darwin and Karl Marx—III', *New Century Review*, April 1897. According to the authors of *Die Töchter von Marx*, Aveling made the acquaintance of Marx and his daughter in October 1873, see p. 154.

'Left' Bonapartists]' and later, with regard to the controversy over the Eastern question, denounced him as 'one of
the noisiest demagogic supporters of Gladstone's pro-Russian
campaign against Disraeli'. 'The utter meanness of Bradlaugh shines most', he wrote to Charles Longuet,

in the manoeuvres by which he has succeeded to oust [*sic*] all the
other popular preachers of free thought (the scientific preachers
address themselves to other couches sociales) such as Mrs. Law
[Mrs. Harriet Law, the only woman member of the General
Council of the International], who wanted not to be his personal
séides, by appropriating to himself all the funds of the party.
He even succeeded to have all lecturing halls in London shut to
them, while he built out of the party's funds a lecturing hall for
his own personal use.[1]

This was long before Aveling's affiliation with the free-
thought party, but Bradlaugh continued to attract the attention of the Marx family, though his name was always
received with disparagement and contempt. Eleanor herself
wrote in a letter to her mother shortly after the famous scene
that Bradlaugh had made in August 1881: he 'is just now
the hero of the day here. The papers [are] full of him; crowds
follow him about—& wherever one goes one hears only of
him—considering what a hash he made of the whole business
at first he ought to feel he has been very lucky.'[2] It is not
impossible that she was already taking an interest in Aveling,
who was then making a tremendous effort to support
Bradlaugh in his constitutional struggle.

The members of the free-thought party, for their part, had
also been attracted to some form of Socialism. In 1877, they,

---

[1] Karl Marx to Charles Longuet, 4 Jan. 1881, written in English,
photocopy at IML (Berlin). Marx denounced the Universal Federalist
Council of the International, which was hostile to his own General
Council, as an assembly of 'free rogues and fools'. The Federalist Coun-
cil had its headquarters at Bradlaugh's Hall of Science. Marx on the
Federalist Council quoted in Engels to Maltman Barry, 15 Sept. 1872,
B.M.Add.MSS. 46288.

[2] Eleanor Marx to Mrs. Marx, 7 Aug. 1881, Bottigelli Collection.

together with the remnants—mostly English and French—
of the old International, set up a short-lived 'International
Labour Union' with a provisional council including Mrs.
Law herself. The two streams of progressive thought,
Radicalism and Socialism, converged in a highly intellectual
monthly paper called *Modern Thought* which was founded
by J. C. Foulger, an enterprising publisher, in February
1879. Among thirty articles on 'Leaders of Modern Thought'
serialized in the paper, there was one on Karl Marx, written
by E. Belfort Bax, a young journalist who had studied
philosophy and music in Germany. Bax presented a short
biography of his subject and a summary of *Das Kapital*.
The article was highly pleasing to Marx, and Eleanor sent
an appreciative letter to the author on behalf of her father.[1]
Aveling contributed an article on Shelley to the series, and
he was also connected with the *Republican*, the Secularist
monthly, which on several occasions drew attention to 'the
modern scientific teaching of Karl Marx' and reproduced an
article by Mrs. Law on 'Dr. Karl Marx' a few months before
his death.[2] It is not known exactly when and how Aveling
and Eleanor were drawn to each other, but there were many
occasions at this period when the two could meet. The
British Museum was certainly one possible location. Mrs.
Besant was of the opinion that about 1882 Aveling took to
reading at the British Museum, where he joined the company of 'the Bohemian Socialists'.[3] Aveling himself wrote a
humorous account of the meeting of the sexes at the Museum
and recommended their segregation for 'there would be less
talking and fewer marriages'.[4] It was probably sometime in
1882 that they met, but till after the death of her father, it
appears, she kept quiet about her new association in view of

[1] *Modern Thought*, Dec. 1881; Marx to Jenny Longuet, 17 Dec. 1881;
Nouvelle Revue Socialiste, Dec. 1928–Feb. 1929; Bax, *Reminiscences and
Reflections of a Mid and Late Victorian* (1918), 45.
[2] *Republican*, Nov. 1882, originally published in *Secular Chronicle*,
7 July 1878.
[3] *National Reformer*, 4 May 1884.   [4] *Progress*, May 1883.

her father's hostility to Aveling's colleagues in the Secularist movement.

* * *

'Karl Marx, foremost of the Socialist party, has passed away', read a short notice published in *Progress*, a monthly magazine of 'advanced thought':

The best comment on his many-sided nature is furnished by the names of those present by his grave-side. His daughter Eleanor, his two sons-in-law, his friend of forty years, Herr Engels, Herr Liebknecht . . . , Professor Schorlemmer of Owen College, Professor Ray Lankester of Oxford and University College, London, Dr. Edward B. Aveling, and Mr. Ernest Radford.[1]

The magazine, which had been founded three months before by G. W. Foote, was now edited by Aveling, who gained the co-operation of Eleanor and her friends. Radford wrote many poems, and one of them entitled 'For ever and a Day' could be meant for the new lovers:

> He murmured, 'Love, for ever!'
> And she whispered, 'and a day';
> And I whose pain ends never
> Saw her stand in her bright array
> And knew that her love was for ever,
> And his false love for a day.[2]

Aveling, too, produced poem after poem, and appeared to answer Radford and establish his new love:

> I tore at her robe till the breast outburst,
> And knew with a secret laughter
> His counterfeit lips had touched her first,
> Then mine in the real thereafter.[3]

Then, towards the end of 1883, he wrote: 'They met, changed eyes. Changed hearts? Who knows? Turned, met again, again, were married. . . . That fatal day! Love comes and goes.'[4]

[1] *Progress*, April 1883. [2] Ibid., April 1883.
[3] Ibid., June 1883. [4] Ibid., Dec. 1883.

Eleanor herself wrote an obituary of her father and an account of the theory of surplus value for *Progress*, and she asked the Lafargues to send something for the paper, which, she said, 'is beginning—to the great annoyance of Bradlaugh —to have a really good circulation.'[1] Her association with Aveling, however, led her to believe more than ever that 'atheism and socialism are one'. She took strong exception to Radford, who had declared himself 'little in sympathy with that raucous atheism', and denounced him for his 'respectability', 'superiority', and 'great fellow feeling for donkeys'.[2] When Beatrice Potter, later the wife of Sidney Webb, met her at the refreshment room of the British Museum in the spring of 1883, she was 'very wrath' about the imprisonment of Foote for blasphemy. She was of the opinion that ridicule was a perfectly legitimate weapon, of which Voltaire had made full use. 'We think the Christian religion an immoral illusion', she told Miss Potter: '. . . The striking difference of this century and the last is, that free-thought was the privilege of the upper classes then, and it is becoming the privilege of the working classes now.' Her description of Christ as 'a weak-headed individual' deeply shocked Miss Potter, who had already been pained by her appearance. 'In person', wrote Beatrice,

she is comely, dressed in a slovenly picturesque way, with curly black hair flying about in all directions. Fine eyes full of life and sympathy, otherwise ugly features and expression, and complexion showing the signs of an unhealthy excited life, kept up with stimulants and tempered by narcotics.[3]

It appears that Eleanor now found a refuge in Aveling's aggressive atheism and was leading a sort of constantly agitated life.

[1] *Progress*, May, June 1883; Eleanor Marx to Laura Lafargue, 14 Sept. 1883, Bottigelli Collection. She also wrote an article on Russian prisons and a review of Stepniak's *Underground Russia*, *Progress*, May, Aug., Sept. 1883.

[2] Ibid., Dec. 1883.

[3] Beatrice Webb, *My Apprenticeship* (1962), 258–9n.

About this time she often stayed and worked with her suitor at his Practical Science Laboratory at Newman Street, and it was to this retreat that she invited Karl Kautsky, who was then in London. He had met Aveling shortly before at Engels's birthday party and had found him simply 'repulsive'. He, like Hyndman, tried to overcome his first impression and unlike him succeeded.[1] Indeed, Aveling's reputation was already a chequered one, and Eleanor was fully aware of it. But she recalled calumnies against her father and also the excuses which he had been accustomed to make for Heine: 'Poets, Mohr maintained', she later wrote to Kautsky, 'were green kittle-cattle, not to be judged by the ordinary, or even the extra-ordinary standards of conduct.'[2] 'The worse the reputation, the brighter the merit', wrote Liebknecht, 'and it is not saying too much that just the badness of Dr. Aveling's reputation helped to gain him Eleanor's sympathy.'[3]

Tennyson, in a dramatic monologue entitled 'Despair', described the tragedy of a man and his wife who, having lost faith in God, resolved to end their life, which was utterly miserable; the woman was drowned, but the man was rescued by a minister of the sect he had abandoned. But according to Aveling, the atheist was:

not inclined to be miserable in this his only life. He loves it, joys in it, revels in it. He is not blind to its pains and sorrows. Bearing these cheerfully as he may, he concentrates his attention on the pleasures and sweetness of life, and on . . . the task of lessening the aggregate of the world's misery.[4]

Eleanor, whose worries and sufferings had many times driven her to the brink of nervous collapse, now threw in her lot with Aveling. She accepted his hedonistic appreciation of this life and his emphasis on the importance of the utilitarian

---

[1] Eleanor Marx to Kautsky, 4 Dec. 1883, IISH; Kautsky, *Engels' Briefwechsel mit Karl Kautsky* (Wien, 1955), 88.

[2] Eleanor Marx Aveling to Kautsky, 7 Sept. 1895, IISH.

[3] *Social-Democrat*, Sept. 1898.   [4] *Modern Thought*, Jan. 1882.

task of social amelioration, which for her meant simply a devotion to the cause for which her father had worked all his life. Yet all through the ups and downs of her subsequent life, dedicated though it was to Socialism and Art, the spectre of Tennyson's 'Despair' seemed constantly to cast its sombre shadow.

V ~ SOCIALISM AND FREE LOVE

'I T is a curious fact', wrote Engels in an article he contributed to Aveling's *Progress*, 'that with every great revolutionary movement the question of "free love" comes in to the foreground.'[1] Indeed, Socialism would involve a rejection of the bourgeois conventions, including 'property marriage', but the Secularists would also ignore the religious restraints of conventional marriage. The problem of free love cut across the two systems of thought, and Aveling's estrangement from the Secularist chiefs was as much personal as it was ideological.

At a time when Eleanor was seeking to identify her lover's cause with her father's, Mrs. Besant wrote in the *National Reformer*: 'My name is being used by a Miss Eleanor Marx . . . to give authority to a gross and scandalous libel on Dr. Edward Aveling. . . . Warning should be given of strangers who try to creep into our movement with the object of treacherously sowing discord therein.'[2] Some months later when a sympathetic working man, J. L. Mahon, a young Scottish engineer, drew Eleanor's attention to this note, she replied:

I do not think it necessary that *I* should answer such a person as Mrs. Besant, from whom I consider abuse the best compliment. . . . The reason of this—'lady's' animosity is not far to

[1] *Progress*, Aug. 1883.   [2] *National Reformer*, 23 Dec. 1883.

HEM

seek. The one clear thinker and scientific student whose popularity *in the Secularist Party* almost equals Mr. Bradlaugh's—Dr. Edward Aveling, has joined the ranks of the Socialists, & Mrs. Besant does me the honour to make me responsible for this. I am very proud of Dr. Aveling's friendship for myself, but I hope I need not tell you that his conversion to Socialism is due to a study of my Father's book & not to me.[1]

A new monthly journal, *To-Day*, which had attempted a partial translation of *Das Kapital* shortly after the death of its author, now declared itself 'the exponent of scientific Socialism'. In the first number of its new series (January 1884), Aveling wrote his first Socialist article entitled 'Christianity and Capitalism', in which he declared that 'the class-supremacy of to-day is due partly to capitalistic influence, partly to clerical' and denied the title of Socialist to any avowed Christian. In this same number, Eleanor started a 'Record of the International Popular Movement' and held in derision 'the teachings of Parson Malthus', in which the Secularists firmly believed: 'The French are practical Malthusiasns—and the French working-class is even more wretched than are their prolific English brethren'.

To-Day was in fact an independent organ of Hyndman's Democratic Federation, which had committed itself to Socialism with the publication of a manifesto, *Socialism Made Plain*, in the previous summer, and both Eleanor and Aveling seem to have joined the body by this time. They attended a special meeting of the Federation held at Anderton's Hotel, Fleet Street, on 11 January 1884, at which Hyndman announced the publication of its weekly organ *Justice* and skilfully conducted a heated debate on the question of political action by Socialists. Aveling was in favour of 'political movements', and supported 'payment of members, even of the London School Board'. Speaking as a scientific student, he believed Socialism to be based on science, and urged each of the participants to become 'a missionary of

[1] Eleanor Marx to J. L. Mahon, 8 May 1884, E. P. Thompson, *William Morris*, 858–9.

Socialism'. An anti-parliamentary amendment proposed at the meeting which declared that 'all means are justifiable' to achieve the emancipation of the workers gave a cue for Mrs. Besant to issue another warning in the *National Reformer* directed chiefly to her former protégé against the 'Marxist views'.[1] Indeed, she and Bradlaugh were, as Engels said, 'furious at the new Socialist "rage" in London which threatens to cut short their wittles'.[2] Aveling immediately replied that the revolution sought by Socialists might be 'one of thought', but she mercilessly cut his long letter, especially the section dealing with 'the school of Karl Marx', of which he now declared himself to be 'certainly one'.[3] Eleanor was indignant at Mrs. Besant's 'characteristic dishonesty and cowardice' and especially her 'chaste style', and 'wished like Beatrice [in Shelley's *Cenci*] that "I were a man" & that I could inflict on Mr. Bradlaugh the sound thrashing he deserves'.[4]

Meanwhile Aveling, now President of the North-Western (London) Branch of the National Secular Society, made Milton Hall, Kentish Town, his headquarters for a new campaign for which the branch alone was made responsible. Every Sunday was devoted to a morning lecture on a scientific or political subject, to afternoon science classes, and to an evening performance of music and recitations, for which he even issued a season ticket. His first Socialist lecture recorded was the one he gave for the N.S.S. branch at Ball's Pond, North London, on 2 March 1884, where he predicted that 'within a few years' time the name of Karl Marx would be in sociology honoured as that of Charles Darwin in biology'.[5] Mrs. Besant for her part, in a report

[1] *Justice*, 19 Jan. 1884; *National Reformer*, 3 Feb. 1884.
[2] Engels to Laura Lafargue, 5 Feb. 1884, Engels-Lafargue, *Correspondance*, i. 164.
[3] *National Reformer*, 10 Feb. 1884; *Justice*, 9 Feb. 1884.
[4] Eleanor Marx to Laura Lafargue, 13 Feb. 1884, Bottigelli Collection.
[5] *Freethinker*, 16 Dec. 1883, 17 Feb. 1884; *Justice*, 15 March 1884.

on the much advertised debate between Bradlaugh and
Hyndman on Socialism, contemptuously wrote: 'Socialism
is just now fashionable. . . . It suits those who like to play in
artistic, dainty, dilettante fashion with problems of life and
death, which they have not the earnestness, the courage, nor
the self-sacrifice to solve.' She even indulged in personal
acrimony by criticizing an article by Aveling entitled 'Mental
Revolution in Animals', which, she said, was 'written by
such a slovenly amanuensis that I have had to make the best
of it throughout'.[1] Aveling was then in Birmingham, where
he opened a local Darwin Institute and gave a lecture on
'Socialism and Freethought' in which he stated: 'It took
seven years before I declared my adhesion to Freethought
and five years of deep study and close reading before I
became a Socialist.'[2] He certainly exaggerated his Socialist
training, and this, in the eyes of his former lover, added
insult to injury. 'It is less than five years since Dr. Aveling
joined the Freethought party', she now retorted:

. . . As his own friends closed their doors against him, I opened
mine, and save for the time that he was with his pupils and at
night time, he made my house his home. All his work was carried
on with me. During all that time he never uttered a word on
Socialism, nor studied it in any way. He and Mr. Bradlaugh and
myself were constantly discussing politics, and he was quite at
one with us, though his political knowledge—like that of most
purely scientific and literary men—was very small. He had not
a single Socialistic book in his library, which was entirely literary
and scientific. In fact, he never touched Socialism in any way,
or knew anything about it, until in 1882 he took to reading at the
British Museum, and unfortunately there fell into the company
of some of the Bohemian Socialists, male and female, who flourish
there.[3]

Aveling, nevertheless, was allowed to continue his missionary work for Socialism among the Secularists, and in May

[1] *National Reformer*, 20 April 1884.
[2] *Justice*, 26 April 1884; *National Reformer*, 20 April 1884.
[3] *National Reformer*, 4 May 1884.

he delivered a Socialist lecture at their headquarters, the Hall of Science. The Secularist leaders were now clearly on the defensive. Indeed, it was not so much due to Hyndman's debate with Bradlaugh, as is often claimed, as to Aveling's persistent work among Bradlaugh's followers that Socialism made considerable progress among the ranks of the free-thought party. At the annual conference of the N.S.S. held in June at Plymouth, he, though an avowed Socialist, was again elected one of its vice-chairmen. But the final breach soon came, as their campaign to calumniate him and to deprive him of a place in the party bore its fruits. In July Mrs. Besant made a handsome acknowledgement to Aveling and to his efficiency as the director of science classes. But in August Aveling's 'Art Corner' in her paper came to an end. Although the hostility of the Secularists was to endanger his position in the Socialist party, it failed to win him back from the daughter of Karl Marx.

*   *   *

The house at Maitland Park Road where Marx had spent his last years was vacated in March 1884. Tussy was then living at Great Coram Street, not far from the British Museum, and from there she wrote to her sister Laura in June: 'You must have known, I fancy, for some time that I am very fond of Edward Aveling—& he says he is fond of me. So we are going to "set up" together. You know what his position is—& I need not say that this resolution has been no easy one for me to arrive at.' She added that she would give her friends 'a chance of cutting us or not'.[1] She gave such a choice to the Radfords: 'I am going to live with Edward Aveling as his wife', she wrote to Dollie:

You know he is married, & that I cannot be his wife *legally*, but it will be a *true* marriage to me—just as much as if a dozen registrars had officiated . . . Edward had not *seen* his wife for many, many years when I met him, & that he was not unjustified

[1] Eleanor Marx to Laura Lafargue, 18 June 1884, photocopy, IISH.

in leaving her you will best understand when I tell you that Mr. Engels, my father's oldest & dearest friend, & Helen, who you know had been as a mother to us, approve what I am about to do, & are *perfectly* satisfied. . . . If love, a perfect sympathy in tastes & work, & a striving for the same ends can make people happy, we shall be so. . . . Yet I can understand that people brought up differently, with all the old ideas & prejudices will think me very wrong, & if you do I shall not mind it, but simply 'put myself in your place'—You know I have the power very strongly developed of seeing things from the 'other side'.[1]

On 1 July Aveling's father died after a year's illness. Though the legacy he received was not much, he was at last freed from concern about his own family.

Eleanor now 'set up' with Edward in a flat in Fitzroy Street. One of the first visitors at her new home, however, was Bradlaugh, who arrived in a cab and demanded the return of Mrs. Besant's letters to her former lover.[2] It was probably the shock she received from his visit that made her confess her uneasiness in a letter to Dollie, who had apparently decided not to 'cut' her: 'I have thought of you very much, & often longed for you. For I am *very* lonely, Dollie, & I never felt lonelier than I do just now. . . . I have been seriously unwell for the last two weeks, & as I was threatened with an absolute breakdown I am just resting.'[3] Engels, for his part, commented on Eleanor's decision in a letter to Bernstein, saying that 'my London is a little Paris'.[4] He had his own misgivings. 'In fact had Tussy asked my advice before she leaped', he wrote to Laura, 'I might have considered it my duty to expatiate upon the various possible and unavoidable consequences of this step'.[5] Yet he, too, had come to like Aveling, who, he said, had 'a good foundation of solid studies'. He therefore chose to give his blessing to the newly established couple with a gift of £50 for their 'honeymoon'.

[1] Eleanor Marx to Dollie Radford, 30 June 1884, Radford Papers.
[2] Havelock Ellis in *Adelphi*, Sept. 1935.
[3] Eleanor Marx to Dollie Radford, 2 July 1884, Radford Papers.
[4] Bernstein, op. cit. 162.
[5] Engels to Laura Lafargue, 22 July 1884, *Correspondance*, i. 216.

On 24 July they left for the Derbyshire dales and lodged at an inn at Middleton near Wirksworth. On the same day they paid a visit to Olive Schreiner, who was staying at Bole Hill near by. Olive had been one of their closest friends since Aveling had written a sympathetic review of her first novel, *The Story of an African Farm*, which he praised for its 'bold outspeaking' about the relations between men and women.[1] At Bole Hill, however, Olive detected certain forebodings of disaster. In a letter to Havelock Ellis, her intimate friend, whom she had introduced to Eleanor, she wrote: 'Dr. Aveling and Miss Marx have just come to see me. She is now to be called Mrs. Aveling. I was glad to see her face. I love her. But she looks so miserable.'[2] About ten days later she wrote again:

I am beginning to have such a *horror* of Dr. A. [Aveling], other-self. To say I dislike him doesn't express it at all; I have a fear and a horror of him when I am near. Every time I see him this shrinking grows stronger . . . I love her, but *he* makes me so unhappy. He is so selfish, but that doesn't account for the feeling of dread. Mrs. Walters [a woman suffragist and a friend of Olive's] has just the same feeling. I had it when I first saw him. I fought it down for Eleanor's sake, but here it is, stronger than ever.[3]

At her suggestion Ellis came up to spend a week with them early in August. During the long walks they took together in this delightful country, he closely observed Eleanor:

She was then in full physical, mental, and emotional maturity. It is perhaps a bodily trait of her powerful personality that I have never known a woman who on a long summer's day ramble diffused so potent an axillary fragrance. She was none the less always a delightful personality, intelligent, eager, full of enjoyment, whatever the moods and melancholy she may privately have been subject to.

[1] *Progress*, Sept. 1883.
[2] Olive Schreiner to Havelock Ellis, 24 July 1884, S. C. Cronwright-Schreiner (ed.), *The Letters of Olive Schreiner* (1924), 34.
[3] Ibid., 2 Aug. 1884, ibid. 36–37.

He found Edward an agreeable companion, though he thought him odd when he disregarded notices against trespassers 'with immense gusto' and 'trampled ruthlessly over everything in his path'. At times he read aloud to his companions, and the passionate intensity with which he recited some of Ellis's own poems, probably one on 'Sophia Perovskaia' published in *To-day*, astonished Ellis. Olive and Ellis soon left Bole Hill, and the Avelings stayed on a little longer. Ellis heard later that Aveling, who had lived freely at the inn and ordered drinks without stint, had absconded without paying the bill.[1]

Eleanor's close friends now began to realize his short-comings, but she clung to him with devotion and loyalty. Their union, at least to her, was not one of free love—neither an attempt to justify easy relations between man and woman nor an act of defiance and challenge against conventional morals. She would have formally married him if he had not already been married. Free union was a necessity and she simply accepted the fact. When she wrote to Mahon from Derbyshire, saying that 'we were justified in setting aside all the false & really immoral bourgeois conventionalities',[2] she was addressing herself to a Socialist worker. Free love was a justification rather than a cause, and to some extent she was making a virtue of a necessity. Nonetheless it gave her strength to bear the consequences of her decision. Indeed, she took the matter of principle so seriously that she went so far as to cut herself off from the philistine world and wrote a letter of resignation to the principal of a boarding school—presumably one at Kensington—where she, as a much esteemed teacher, could have been allowed to go on teaching.[3] On the other hand, Aveling, who had completely neglected his work on the School Board for the last few

[1] *Adelphi*, Sept. 1935.
[2] Eleanor Marx Aveling to J. L. Mahon, 1 Aug. 1884, Thompson, op. cit. 860.
[3] Bernstein, op. cit. 161.

months, apart from writing a frivolous account of its members for *Progress*, sent in his resignation in October, giving the reason, characteristic of him, that 'the work entails too great an expenditure of time, and therefore, indirectly, of money, for a poor man'.[1]

Upon their return from Derbyshire they settled in rooms they had rented at 55 Great Russell Street, opposite the British Museum. 'Edward is the very devil for untidiness', she now wrote to Laura, '& I'm a good second. . . . I swear at myself all day. . . . If scrubbing "is my vexation", cleaning knives is "twice as bad", joints "puzzle me" & potatoes "drive me mad".' But her real worry was not that of a house-wife. 'We are having a lot of trouble & worry I must tell you about, through Bradlaugh', she went on: 'You can imagine how wild he is about Edward & he is doing all he can to ruin him.'[2] Bradlaugh's attempt to prevent the weakening of the Secularist party by railing at the chief deserter to Socialism was in fact taken advantage of by Aveling's opponents within the Socialist movement.

* * *

The small group of British Socialists who had associated themselves in the Democratic Federation were already showing signs of a serious internal dispute. One faction, in which Bax, the militant internationalist, was most prominent, rallied round *To-Day*, which he edited with J. L. Joynes, formerly a master at Eton. The other, led by Hyndman, editor of *Justice*, was more or less committed to parliamentary politics. William Morris, the poet and medievalist, divided his affections between the two, though he was coming under the anti-political influence of Andreas Scheu, an Austrian Socialist. Engels, the arch-enemy of Hyndman, declined an invitation to collaborate in *Justice*, though he was ready

[1] *School Board Chronicle*, 11 Oct. 1884; *Progress*, July 1884.
[2] Eleanor Marx Aveling to Laura Lafargue, 22 Sept. 1884, Bottigelli Collection.

to help *To-Day*, to which Eleanor and Aveling were now regular contributors. Eleanor formed a high opinion of Bax, but distrusted Joynes and regarded Morris as 'a sentimental Socialist'.[1] In an article published in *To-Day* she exposed how *The Times* had suppressed her letter defending her father against the charge of an inaccuarate quotation.[2] Hyndman, pretending superior knowledge, now intervened, and his *Justice* published what Engels called 'almost a declaration of war', criticizing *To-Day* for burdening itself with such a dispute as the one between Eleanor and her father's critic, which was 'scarcely suited', and also with a 'wearisome controversy' over 'Christian' Socialism in which Aveling indulged.[3] In fact, in the eyes of the parliamentary Socialists Aveling's militant atheism, which *Justice* called 'dogmatic', constituted a liability rather than an asset for the Federation. On the other hand, *To-Day* was quick to point out the 'racial predilections' in Hyndman's *Historical Basis of Socialism in England*, a daring work with which he sought to consolidate his leadership.[4]

The tension came into the open for the first time in March when a demonstration was scheduled at Highgate Cemetery for the commemoration of the death of Marx and the proclamation of the Paris Commune. Hyndman had been asked by the German Communist Workers' Educational Association of Tottenham Street to speak at the graveside, but he declined and stated in *Justice* that 'an English working

---

[1] Kautsky to Engels, 12 March 1884, Kautsky, *Briefwechsel*, 104–5.

[2] In the 'Inaugural Address' of the International Working Men's Association, Gladstone was made to have said that the growth of wealth in the fifties had been confined to classes of property, but this was exactly opposite to what he actually meant. The issue on this question, which had been raised in the seventies by Lujo Brentano, the German critic of Marxist economics, was now brought out again by Sedley Taylor, an economist at Cambridge, who skilfully handled Eleanor's passionate refutation. *To-day*, Feb., March 1884.

[3] *Justice*, 8 March 1884; Engels to Bernstein, 24 March 1884, *Labour Monthly*, Sept. 1933.

[4] *To-Day*, April 1884.

man was the proper person to speak'. Now Aveling was
chosen as the speaker, and Eleanor and her friends sought to
make Hyndman declare either for or against the demonstration. At Bax's suggestion she and Aveling attended a
committee meeting of the Federation. 'Owing to my being
there Hyndman only said the Federation should take part, &
even had to declare that Dr. Aveling would have their
"entire sympathy".'[1] Hyndman, who declared himself
against the 'canonisation of individuals', which, he said, was
'contrary to the principle of Socialism', was doubly humili-
ated, as the demonstration proved to be a great success. As
the Highgate Cemetery Company did not allow a huge
crowd of nearly 5,000 bearing red flags and singing the
'Marseillaise' to pass the gate, which was defended by a
force of 500 policemen, and even refused a request that
Eleanor alone should be allowed to go and place flowers
on her father's grave, the demonstrators moved to the top
of the hill at Dartmouth Park, where, according to Eleanor,
Aveling delivered a 'splendid speech' which 'touched the
hearts of all his hearers'.[2] Eleanor and Aveling apparently
won the first round in the battle with Hyndman.

Another bone of contention aggravated the ill feeling
between Hyndman and his opponents. The two divisions of
the French Socialists—the reformists or Possibilists led
by Paul Brousse and the revolutionary Marxists under the
leadership of Guesde and Lafargue—were both seeking
international support, especially in view of the growing
interest among the European workers in an international
eight-hour movement. The Possibilists had held an international conference in 1883 which was attended by a group
of British trade unionists led by Henry Broadhurst, M.P.,
Secretary of the parliamentary committee of the T.U.C., and
now the Marxists wanted to make their annual conference

[1] Eleanor Marx to Laura Lafargue, 17 March 1884, Bottigelli Collection.
[2] *To-Day*, April 1884.

at Roubaix a preparatory meeting for a new International and invited the Democratic Federation to send delegates. At the same committee meeting of the Federation at which Eleanor was present, the question was brought up. 'Hyndman', she wrote to her sister:

—who Bax afterwards told me had intended making a violent attack on the suggested Conference as a 'family measure' of ours —did not dare to say much—but nevertheless objected to the Federation taking part or lot in the Congress. This was opposed by most present—& I gave him his coup de grâce by explaining, so far as I was able, the position of the Roubaix people vis-à-vis of the Broussists, & carried all the committee with me by saying this was a necessary protest against the Broadhurst Congress.[1]

When the question of delegates came up, Hyndman tried to keep Bax out on the old ground of his not being a 'working man'. 'Well', she continued in another letter to Laura: '[James] Murray is blindly devoted to Aveling, & obeys him like a child. Aveling—not being of the Executive—could not himself propose Bax. So he got Murray to do so. . . . I "worked" Scheu who seconded Murray's proposition.' Thus Bax was elected together with Harry Quelch, a follower of Hyndman. 'I can always "work" some of the Committee, & Aveling & I together can do something', and she would do her best 'to keep the English connected with the right side'.[2] At Roubaix the English were the only foreign delegates, and Quelch, 'a "genuine" working man, and no "ouvrier pour rire"', delighted the Frenchmen, while Bax, elected to the chair, condemned colonialism, both English and French. London was chosen for an international congress in 1885, which was to 'revive' the International, Eleanor triumphantly reported in *To-Day*.[3]

The rivalry between the two factions was further intensified when the rumour reached Engels that Hyndman was busy

[1] Eleanor Marx to Laura Lafargue, 17 March 1884, Bottigelli Collection.
[2] Ibid., 19 March 1884, ibid.
[3] *To-Day*, May 1884.

translating *Das Kapital*. As an English translation by his friend Samuel Moore had been making only slow progress, Aveling was adopted as a co-translator, though he was allowed at first only to try the chapter on 'Der Arbeitstag', 'this being chiefly descriptive', wrote Engels, 'and free, comparatively, from difficult theoretical passages for which A[veling] is totally unfit *as yet*'.[1] Eleanor undertook to look up the quotations from Bluebooks in order to avoid errors in re-translation. Hyndman, for his part, apparently needed a monthly journal for his own translation, and the one stone with which he could kill two birds was obviously *To-Day*, which was in financial distress. He offered it funds on condition that Bax should be replaced by H. H. Champion, an invalided artillery officer who was a follower of his. This proposal was accepted. The rival translations, however, were further delayed. At any rate, Eleanor and Aveling ceased to write for *To-Day* after July.

They still had *Progress*, which Aveling had been editing jointly with Foote since the latter's release in February. Here Eleanor wrote an article on the 'Irish Dynamiters', disowning the 'foolish utterances' made by O'Donovan Rossa, whom she had once admired.[2] *Progress*, in which Bax also collaborated, might have become a substitute for *To-Day*. Foote, the chief editor, however, was no Socialist, and had been criticizing all 'proud schemes of social reorganisation' in his *Freethinker*, for which he had assumed sole responsibility. After a period of uneasy alliance Aveling finally left *Progress* in November. In fact, Hyndman had things much his own way, but, as Eleanor wrote to Laura, 'he is playing his cards very badly—irritating everyone'. 'His little game will soon be

[1] Engels to Laura Lafargue, 18 April 1884, *Correspondance*, i. 193. As late as February 1886 Engels felt that Aveling's translation of *Capital* was not satisfactory. 'Both the economic theories and the language of the author are rather new to him and I know the portion done by him will give me more work.' Engels to Danielson, 8 Feb. 1886, photocopy, IML (Berlin).
[2] *Progress*, May 1884.

HUNT LIBRARY
CARNEGIE-MELLON UNIVERSITY

played out', she said: 'The sooner the better for our move-ment. It has *every* chance here at this present time if only we had better leaders than Hyndman & his henchmen.'[1]

On 4 August 1884 the fourth annual conference of the Federation was held at its headquarters at Westminster. The party changed its name to the Social Democratic Federa-tion (often abbreviated to S.D.F.). Aveling attended the conference as the delegate of the newly created Westminster branch, but Eleanor stayed behind in Derbyshire. Both she and her husband were elected to the new executive council, and Aveling contributed to the success of the anti-Hynd-manite faction by persuading the party to accept the spirit of the anti-political programme of the Labour Emancipation League, an affiliated body.

Preparatory work for a new programme dragged on, and at one stage Aveling's proposal for the Disestablishment of the State Church, which Morris regarded as an 'ineptitude', appeared much favoured, but the final draft adopted at an executive meeting in October seemed to satisfy everybody, though it was certainly less parliamentarian than before.[2] Morris, so far, had been playing the role of a conciliator, and wrote to Scheu: 'I think that the days of personal dictation are over. . . . What do you think of Mrs. Aveling in the Chair, as she was last Tuesday?'[3] It was probably under pressure from the Avelings that an executive manifesto issued shortly before the Trades Union Congress of that year urged the unions to throw in their lot with the S.D.F. as they had previously done with the International.[4]

*   *   *

It was at this juncture that Bradlaugh's vendetta against

[1] Eleanor Marx to Laura Lafargue, 21 July 1884, Bottigelli Collec-tion.
[2] Morris to Scheu, 13 Aug. 1884, Philip Henderson (ed.), *The Letters of William Morris* (1950), 211; *Justice*, 25 Oct. 1884.
[3] Ibid., 28 Aug. 1884, Henderson, op. cit. 212.
[4] *Justice*, 6 Sept. 1884.

Aveling was carried into the executive council of the S.D.F. According to Engels, 'the sly Bradlaugh—a former attorney's clerk' had made arrangements so that Aveling alone was legally liable for the Practical Science Laboratory, which seems to have gone bankrupt. In this and other money matters, believed Engels, his protégé was 'as easily cheated as if he were a three-year old child'.[1] Bradlaugh now accused him of not paying his debts and other 'irregularities' with regard to the accounts of the N.S.S. and demanded that Aveling should be deprived of his vice-presidency in the Society. Aveling had no alternative but to resign. Moreover, when Bradlaugh issued a circular against him, he did not answer it and even undertook to pay him £200, though in instalments.[2] Aveling's embarrassment gave Hyndman an opportunity to try to get rid of his chief adversary in the Federation. He insisted that Aveling should also resign from the S.D.F. executive unless he could clear his character. At the executive meeting held on 2 September, the matter was formally raised by John Burns, a young engineer and follower of Hyndman, but Aveling said very little in reply. 'I want to keep Aveling if we can', wrote Morris, 'the worst of it is that A[veling] is much disliked by many of our best men . . . I fear Bradlaugh in his character of solicitor's clerk will have been careful not to bring a quite groundless charge against A.'[3] At the following meeting, held one week later, Aveling explicitly denied malversation of the N.S.S. funds, and told his colleagues that Bradlaugh refused to give him any details of the accusation and that he would press him on this point. 'We all agreed', wrote Morris, 'that if the latter could not give definite details he (Aveling) would come off with flying colours. So I hope all will be right. Aveling is undoubtedly a man of great capacity, & can use it too.'[4] Aveling, who was

[1] Engels to F. A. Sorge, 4 June 1887, photocopy, IML (Berlin).
[2] Engels to Bebel, 1 Oct. 1891, Bebel, *Briefwechsel mit Friedrich Engels* (The Hague, 1965), 444.
[3] Morris to Scheu, 8 Sept. 1884, IISH.
[4] Ibid., 13 Sept. 1884, IISH.

too ill to attend the next meeting of the executive, was finally persuaded to issue a public statement. 'I am at the present time', he wrote in *Justice*, 'indebted in many sums to many persons. But I wish to say that to the best of my knowledge and belief all monies received by me as funds in trust for others have been fully accounted for. My monetary difficulties have to do with my poverty and my want of business habits alone.'[1] The funds entrusted to him included a collection made for Mme Olga Novikoff, a Russian lady who was an effective mouthpiece of the cause of the Slavs in English society.[2] At any rate, with this letter for exoneration which was as vague as Bradlaugh's accusations, the Aveling matter had apparently 'blown over'. Indeed, such unconfirmed or unfounded accusations gave his friends the impression that he might after all be 'the victim of malicious tongues'.

George Bernard Shaw, still comparatively unknown, who had just made his début in the literary and Socialist world in this year, observed the affair of Aveling, who, he said, was 'a man to be thrown out of the window or shaken hands with cordially, as the case might be, but not such a fool as to let himself be elbowed out'. 'On one point Aveling is far sounder than Hyndman', he said: 'He sees the importance of educating the party, whereas Hyndman seems to be too impatient to do anything but ply them with stimulants—stories of capitalist greed and oppression & so forth.'[3] Aveling began his work of education at his own branch at Westminster, of which he was chairman. The branch had its headquarters at a tavern called 'Salutation', which, as its secretary, H. W. Lee, later recalled, had probably been acquired through the influence of Aveling, who was then a member of the School Board and was very fond of drink. They were, however, soon

[1] *Justice*, 27 Sept. 1884.

[2] Nethercot, op. cit. 214. For Mme Novikoff, see W. T. Stead, *The M.P. for Russia, Reminiscences and Correspondence of Madame Olga Novikoff*, 2 vols. (1909).

[3] Shaw to Scheu, 26 Oct. 1884, IISH.

evicted and moved to a nearby 'Blue Ribbon Hall', which was associated with teetotalism of the strictest kind. Early in September Aveling announced his intention of starting a series of lessons in 'Scientific Socialism', but it was not till the middle of October when he had barely cleared himself from disgraceful charges that the executive council approved the action of the Westminster branch in establishing 'gratuitous Social Science classes'. On the first night the Blue Ribbon Hall was packed, but Aveling treated the audience like scholars at school, and the working men, who were not used to coaching, stealthily crept out of the hall.[1] Lee, who worked closely with Aveling about this time, left an account of this man of pleasure, who, he said, was 'utterly unscrupulous about the way in which he satisfied his desires. . . . The best was good enough for him—at no matter whose expense.' One day he gave an order to a German tailor, who belonged to the Communist Workers' Educational Association, for a velvet jacket and waistcoat. The tailor, who could not get his money, was further grieved when he went to the Lyceum Theatre and saw Aveling in the stalls, 'attired in the unpaid-for velvet jacket and waistcoat, and accompanied by a lady'.[2]

Aveling the entertainer was also conspicuous in his Socialist work. He gained the co-operation of Morris, Bax, and Shaw in an Art Evening held at Neumeyer Hall, Bloomsbury, on 21 November under the sponsorship of the S.D.F. Here Eleanor and Aveling played in a piece entitled *In Honour Bound*, a one-act comedy by Sidney Grundy, which, according to Helena Demuth, who was among the audience, was 'more or less their own history'.[3]

Aveling indeed was an excellent actor off the stage. He was good at playing the part of a victim of pettiness and

---

[1] Lee and Archbold, *Social-Democracy in Britain* (1935), 67–68; *Justice*, 25 Oct. 1884.

[2] Ibid., op. cit. 87.

[3] Engels to Laura Lafargue, 23 Nov. 1884, *Correspondance*, i. 244.

jealousy, and he evoked sympathy from his friends. Early in December, when Hyndman visited Scotland, he stated that Morris's cashier had declined to join the party on the ground that he would have been compelled continuously to draw cheques in Aveling's favour. The latter brought the matter up at an executive meeting, and Morris emphatically denied that any money had been lent to Aveling. 'This was, of course, a great triumph for Aveling', wrote Bax, 'who obtained credit and loans in various quarters in consequence.'[1]

*   *   *

Meanwhile the future of *Justice*, whose weekly loss had been covered by Morris, was discussed by the S.D.F. leaders. It seems that Aveling and Bax suggested that the paper should be edited jointly by themselves and Morris.[2] Hyndman now wrote to Morris, protesting against any such scheme. 'It is worth notice', he said, 'that the change is especially wanted by the very persons—Dr. Aveling & Mrs. Aveling—who, owing to Bax's disastrous weakness, ruined *To-Day* by their prejudices and advertising puffery of themselves.'[3] He even threatened to hand over the paper to a wealthy supporter.

The crisis of the S.D.F., as has often been recounted, came to a head as the immediate result of the mutual hostility between Hyndman and Andreas Scheu, the Austrian exile, who had set up a semi-independent Scottish Land and Labour League at Edinburgh. Scheu regarded Hyndman as a 'chauvinist', while the latter denounced Scheu as a friend of Most's and an Anarchist during his visit to Scotland, although he knew that Scheu had severed his connexion with his former chief.[4] Those who had grievances against

[1] Bax, *Reminiscences and Reflections*, 109; Aveling in *Sozialdemokrat*, 26 March 1885.

[2] C. Varenholz in *Sozialdemokrat*, 26 Feb. 1885.

[3] Hyndman to Morris, 27 Nov. 1884, B.M.Add.MSS. 45345.

[4] Aveling in *Sozialdemokrat*, 26 March 1885.

Hyndman now met at the Avelings' house and invited Scheu to come to London to state his case before the executive.

Yet this was not all, and Eleanor herself had been drawn into the atmosphere of suspicion and bitterness. Hyndman had been opposed to the plan to revive a Marxist International. Mme Lafargue, who was on a visit to London, attended an executive meeting of the Federation in October. 'They were squabbling over some trifle', wrote Engels, 'but so furiously that the words "damned liars" were scattered freely about.'[1] In November the executive council decided to start preparations for an International Socialist Conference to be held in London in the spring of 1885, though the decision soon melted away in the heat of the party crisis. It was probably in connexion with this controversy over a new International that Hyndman received two mysterious letters from the same person in Paris but in different hands. He was puzzled, but soon convinced himself that these letters had been forged by Mrs. Aveling and Mme Lafargue in order to entice him over to Paris for some sinister purpose.[2]

Now, at the executive meeting held on 23 December at which Scheu was present, Eleanor challenged Hyndman. 'I "went" for Hyndman & his creatures about that', she wrote to her sister:

After trying, without exactly asserting it, to insinuate that the letter was forged, he was forced to withdraw his statement. I read your letter on the subject—& then told Mr. H. what I thought of him.—Oh dear! is not all this wearisome & stupid! But . . . I suppose this kind of thing is inevitable in the beginning of any movement.[3]

At this same meeting a vote of confidence in Scheu and of no confidence in Hyndman was hotly discussed, but the meeting adjourned till the 27th. In the meantime Morris and Aveling

[1] Engels to Kautsky, 20 Oct. 1884, *Labour Monthly*, Oct. 1933.
[2] Aveling in *Sozialdemokrat*, 26 March 1885.
[3] Eleanor Marx Aveling to Laura Lafargue, 31 Dec. 1884, Bottigelli Collection.

visited Engels, who gave them further advice on the course
for them to take. He thought that 'Hyndman handled the
Committee as Bismarck did the Reichstag', but 'the only
honest men among the intellectuals'—Aveling, Morris, and
Bax, 'two poets and one philosopher'—were utterly 'unprac-
tical'.[1] He probably judged that they were not capable of
carrying out a revolution in Hyndman's 'Reichstag'. Now,
at the close of the adjourned meeting on 27 December, where
the above motion was adopted by 10 votes to 8, the majority,
including the Avelings, Morris, and Bax, issued a statement
criticizing Hyndman's 'arbitrary rule' and announcing their
resignation. Indeed, their majority was a precarious one, for
they had won over at least one executive member at the
eleventh hour, and they had certainly no hopes of winning
the majority of the rank and file to their side of the dispute.
'The personal question . . . is after all very secondary to the
principle(al (Ed. A.)) one', wrote Eleanor, '—that of whether
we were to sink into a merely Tory-democratic Party or to
go on working on the lines of the German Socialists & the
French Parti Ouvrier.' The principle which had in fact
been submerged under the more interesting question of
personality was not necessarily guaranteed to convince the
average S.D.F. member, who had his own loyalties and
prejudices. 'Our majority was too small', said Eleanor, 'to
make it possible for us to really get rid of the Jingo Faction, &
so, after due consultation with Engels we decided to go out,
& form a new organisation.'[2]

*   *   *

The new body, the Socialist League, was founded on 30
December, and its monthly organ, *Commonweal*, was launched
in February 1885 with Morris as editor and Aveling as
sub-editor. In its manifesto it declared for 'Revolutionary

[1] Engels to Bernstein, 29 Dec. 1884, *Labour Monthly*, Oct. 1933.
[2] Eleanor Marx Aveling to Laura Lafargue, 31 Dec. 1884, Bottigelli
Collection.

International Socialism', rejecting 'mere politics' as well as 'certain incomplete schemes of social reform' such as co-operation, nationalization of the land 'alone', and State Socialism. Education, organization, and party democracy were the means by which to attain its end, 'the realisation of complete Revolutionary Socialism'.[1] The handful of revolutionary Socialists now began an active campaign to set up branches. In February Morris and the Avelings visited Oxford to address a group of undergraduates at a hall in Holywell. 'They had really listened to me', wrote Morris, 'even the noisy ones: but it seems they had agreed that A[veling] at any rate should not be allowed to speak; but he began very cleverly and won their ingenuous hearts so that they listened to him better than they did to me.' Although the meeting was spoiled by a stink-bomb which was suddenly let off, Morris and the Avelings spent a pleasant evening, visiting New College cloisters with sympathetic students who formed the Oxford Socialist Association as a branch of the League and later a Marx Club.[2]

Meanwhile Eleanor appealed to her friends abroad to support *Commonweal*, and with their cordial responses she started a monthly 'Record of the Revolutionary International Movement'. Engels contributed an article on the 'privileged position' lost by the English working class which was later incorporated in the oft-quoted preface to the English edition of his *Condition of the Working-Class in England*. Eleanor also addressed League branches at Mile End and other parts of London on 'The Factory Acts', the subject on which she was assisting her husband in translating the *Capital*. Aveling wrote an article entitled 'The Factory Inferno' for *Commonweal*, and together with Eleanor published a pamphlet under a similar title, both based on the factory reports of 1884, which, they said, 'might be that of 1864. The

[1] *Commonweal*, Feb. 1885.
[2] Morris to Mrs. Burne-Jones, Feb. 1885, Henderson, op. cit. 231–2; *Commonweal*, April, Aug. 1885.

same disease, accidents, prosecutions. . . . Our factory-chimnies that Radical politicians call "the glory of England" are in truth, the curse of England.'[1]

Aveling now began what he had tried with the Westminster S.D.F.—instruction in Socialism—under the auspices of the League. He gave his first lesson in February, and 'it was very successful, 150 audience all attentive, many taking notes and answering very well'.[2] He also serialized his lectures in *Commonweal* with a concise definition of each of the terms mentioned. Profits, if any, were to be devoted to the League's Propaganda Fund, but Aveling objected to the suggestion of a collection to be made after each lecture, which he considered 'very undignified'.[3] Indeed, monetary trouble soon arose, and Morris reported in the summer that nearly £40 were still due to the South Place Institute, the 'rather expensive' lecture hall, 'because of certain disputed items in the bill'. There were even 'censures and reproofs' in connexion with his lessons, which apparently stuck in the financial bog. Instead he now started science lessons at the Hall of the Socialist League in a more congenial line—for South Kensington examinations—'under his control and for his own benefit'.[4] He later acquired a hall in Tottenham Court Road where he gave a course of lectures 'to an attentive and on the whole well paying audience', though it interfered with his after-dinner port.[5] Another fad of his also emerged in connexion with his Socialist lessons: a social entertainment was held in June at the conclusion of his lectures, which was opened with Morris's prologue 'Socialists at Play' and was enlivened as usual by recitations by Eleanor and Aveling. The League also organ-

[1] Edward and Eleanor Marx Aveling, *The Factory Hell* (1885), *passim*.
[2] Morris to May Morris, 20 Feb. 1885, Henderson, op. cit. 230.
[3] Aveling to the Lessons Committee, Socialist League, 6 April 1885, IISH.
[4] Eleanor Marx Aveling to Secretary, Socialist League, 6 April 1885, IISH; *Commonweal*, Aug., Sept. 1885.
[5] Engels to Laura Lafargue, 9 Feb. 1886, *Correspondance*, i. 337.

ized a series of 'free evenings for the people' to which the Avelings invariably contributed their artistic talents.[1] Eleanor, however, deplored a certain degeneration of these entertainments and especially objected to Charles Theodor or Theodor 'Reuss', an executive member and a musician, whose 'comic songs' she thought 'a dull piece of vulgarity'. 'I like fun—any fun no matter how rough as [sic] it be wholesome—as well as any', she wrote in a letter to the League Secretary: 'but I fail to see fun in pure (or impure) & simple vulgarity. Brainless middle class cads may like this sort of things: I don't believe working-men who have a real sense of humour do.' The Socialist education, she said, meant 'Art Education' as well, and the executive council which had rejected boxing and other vulgar forms of entertainment should always try to keep up its standard.[2] Eleanor was also much interested in entertainment for children and took the initiative in getting up a Christmas tree for the children of the League members. 'We cannot too soon make children understand that Socialism means *happiness*', she wrote to the League council, pointing out also that the origin of the Christmas festival was 'the beautiful old Pagan feast that celebrated the birth of light'. 'Is not Socialism the real "new birth", & with its light will not the old darkness of the earth disappear?'[3]

Socialism might also be a means of salvation for the unfortunate women of the streets. In July 1885 W. T. Stead, editor of the *Pall Mall Gazette*, published a series of sensational articles entitled 'The Maiden Tribute of Modern Babylon: the Report of Our Secret Commission' in which he cited shocking cases of sexual criminality in 'the London Inferno'. Although 'the maw of the London Minotaur' seemed insatiable, he protested against 'the continued immolation

[1] *Commonweal*, July, Sept. 1885, Jan. 1886.
[2] Eleanor Marx Aveling to Secretary, Socialist League, 1 March 1886, IISH.
[3] Eleanor Marx Aveling to the Council, Socialist League, 5 Oct. 1885, IISH; *Commonweal*, Dec. 1885.

of the daughters of the people as a sacrifice to the vices of the rich' and even went so far as to declare that 'the future belongs to the combined forces of Democracy and Socialism'. His practical proposals were less sensational. He had carried out his investigations with the assistance of the Salvation Army and several philanthropic bodies, and his proposed remedy actually amounted to the raising of the age of consent from 13 to 16.[1] Although Stead suffered a short term of imprisonment as a result, his campaign was vigorously supported by 'the Women of England', nearly 200 strong, including women suffragists and the wives of certain prospective Liberal candidates. The passage of the Criminal Law Amendment Bill in the course of 1885 satisfied most of his demands. The Socialist League endorsed the *Pall Mall* campaign with certain reservations, and Eleanor made these clear in her article in *Commonweal*. The age of consent had little to do with sexual crimes, she said, and so long as there were two classes, 'the one literally in a position to buy, and actually buying, the *bodies* of the other', the crimes would continue. 'We, the women, must, above all the rest, bestir ourselves. . . . We need a deluge—aye! though it were one of blood—to wipe out our sin and wickedness of this society of ours. It is with those who would revolutionise society that our work as women lies.'[2] The martial vigour of her appeal indeed resembled that of a religious crusader.

In fact she treated the whole woman question as the problem of 'sex-rule', the solution of which was entirely subordinated to 'the abolition of class-rule'. This was the position Bebel had recently enunciated in his book, *Women in the Past, Present, and Future*. An English translation by Dr. Harriet B. Adams Walther was published in this year, and Eleanor reviewed it in *Commonweal* and also in a pamphlet entitled *The Woman Question*, a joint work with her husband.

[1] *Pall Mall Gazette*, 6, 8, 9, 13 July 1885; J. W. Robertson Scott, *The Story of the Pall Mall Gazette* (1950), 281.
[2] *Commonweal*, Aug. 1885.

All the ideas of 'our "advanced" women', including woman suffrage and higher education for women, the Avelings declared, were 'based either on property, or on sentimental or professional questions'. 'Our weddings' were 'business transactions', and 'marriages thus arranged . . . seem to us . . . worse than prostitution'. Chastity was 'unhealthy and unholy', and 'we regard chastity as a crime'. 'Personally, we believe that monogamy will gain the day', but when? They suggested that it would be only after a Socialist revolution, when 'love, respect, intellectual likeness and command of the necessaries of life' would be assured for a harmonious blending of two human lives. As Ibsen stated in his *Doll's House*, their favourite play, 'home life ceases to be free and beautiful directly its foundations are borrowing and debts', but until the abolition of the capitalist society there would always be 'borrowing and debts'.[1] All this was a curious confession of Aveling's weaknesses in matters of money and sex as well as an attempt to justify them with reference to high ideals. Eleanor appears to have acquiesced in the fatal logic for the sake of the revolutionary principles which now became, as it seemed, almost the only source of strength to sustain her in her by no means happy relationship with Aveling. Moreover, it was only reasonable to conclude from their argument in *The Woman Question* that under capitalist society 'free marriage' could be as much encumbered with the nuisance of adultery and debts as was bourgeois marriage, of which it was merely an artificial variety.

*　　　*　　　*

In April 1885 Aveling was taken ill with an inflammation in the kidney and had to break off his Socialist classes. On receiving an urgent message from Eleanor, her friend, Olive Schreiner, wrote: 'If he gets dangerously ill I must go. If the Avelings are very hard-up I must try to send them

[1] Edward and Eleanor Marx Aveling, *The Woman Question* (1886), *passim*.

something.'[1] A few days after this Eleanor informed her sister that Aveling had gone off to Ventnor for a few days' rest. 'We could not possibly afford to go away together', she wrote: 'it was as much as I could do to get him off. He has been *really* very ill.'[2] Her cares and sacrifices, however, meant very little to her husband, who was either utterly insensitive or else simply self-indulgent, or both. In June she felt so miserable that she revealed her bitterness in a letter to Olive. 'I have such a terror of losing your love', she wrote:

. . . You do not know, Olive, how my whole nature craves for love . . . Edward is dining with Quilter and went off in the highest of spirits because several ladies are to be there (and it just occurs to me you may be one! How odd that would be!) and I am alone, and while in some sense I am relieved to be alone, it is also very terrible . . . I am so tired, Olive. The *constant* strain of appearing the same when nothing *is* the same, the constant effort not to break down, sometimes become intolerable. How natures like Edward's (i.e. pure Irish and French . . .) are to be envied, who in an hour completely forget anything. If you had seen him, for example, to-day, going about like a happy child with never a sorrow or sin in his life, you would have marvelled. Yet apart even from all the other troubles, we have mere money troubles enough to worry an ordinary man or woman into the grave. I often don't know where to turn or what to do. It is almost impossible for me now to get work that is even decently paid for, and Edward gets little enough. And while I feel utterly desperate he is perfectly unconcerned! It is a continual source of wonder to me. I do not grow used to it, but always feel equally astounded at his absolute incapacity to feel anything unless he is personally much incommoded by it—for twenty-four consecutive hours. I said just now such natures were to be envied, and there are moments when I think it. But only moments. We, into whose hearts joy and sorrow sink more deeply, are better off after all. With all the pain and sorrow (and not even you, my Olive, know quite how unhappy I am), it is better to have these stronger feelings than to have practically no feelings at all.

[1] Olive Schreiner to Havelock Ellis, 8 April 1885, *Letters of Olive Schreiner*, 69.

[2] Eleanor Marx Aveling to Laura Lafargue, 12 April 1885, Bottigelli Collection.

'No one but you and possibly Dollie', she added, 'should ever hear a word of [my trouble] if I could help.'[1] Bernard Shaw, who was a frequent visitor at her house about this time, recorded in his diary in August that there was a 'rumour of split between the Avelings'.[2] They managed, however, to spend a week or so at Deal in the summer, and the following spring obtained a workroom at Kingston-on-Thames. Eleanor had apparently got over the terrible shock of knowing what Aveling really was, but the latter was as cheerful as ever and sometimes 'clean forgot' his duty to attend a council meeting of the Socialist League because of 'those money-making engagements that lead to more other money-making'.[3]

*   *   *

In the meantime the animosity between Hyndman and Aveling continued and came into the open again in the free-speech fight, which the S.D.F. and later the Socialist League, with the aid of the Fabian Society and the radical clubs, carried on at Dod Street, East London, in the summer of 1885. Aveling, who was then working for the Leicester branch of the League, wrote to its council: 'If you think it is worth while for the question to be fought out & some of us to go to prison . . . will you give clear instructions to that effect?'[4] On 20 September both Aveling and Eleanor were among the speakers who defied a police ban at Dod Street. 'He had a voice like a euphonium', wrote May Morris, daughter of William Morris, 'and by a stupendous effort he made it reach to the ends of the solidly packed street between the tall warehouses.' At the Thames police court, where some of the League members but not Aveling were charged, he appeared in the witness box and answered the

[1] Eleanor Marx Aveling to Olive Schreiner, 16 June 1885, *Adelphi*, Sept. 1932.
[2] Shaw Diary, 24 August 1885, BLPES.
[3] Edward Aveling to Secretary, Socialist League, 13 April 1886, IISH.
[4] Edward Aveling to Council, Socialist League, 14 Sept. 1885, IISH.

magistrate's warning against speaking at the meetings by exclaiming 'I shall speak till I am locked up', and Eleanor followed suit. The harsh sentence imposed on the accused called forth cries of 'Shame' from the angry spectators which, according to Aveling, gave the signal for the constables to launch 'an assault upon all and sundry'. They tore Eleanor's cloak and 'thumped her at large'; 'William Morris, remonstrating at the hustling and the thumping, became at once the chief thumpee.'[1] On the following Sunday a vast crowd filled Dod Street, and the police discreetly took no action. Aveling was the first speaker, and in fact he and the League were now in the forefront of the successful campaign. Hyndman, deeply wounded in his pride, alleged that Aveling had committed a 'breach of faith' by speaking at the meeting before the Radical speakers. Both the League and the joint vigilance committee denied the existence of such an arrangement, and Eleanor was convinced that it was 'simply his impotent rage and jealousy' that 'induced him [Hyndman] to make an ass of himself'.[2]

Indeed, Hyndman committed a series of blunders about this time. First came the scandal of 'Tory gold' which he and his colleagues in the S.D.F. had accepted in order to finance some of its parliamentary candidates at the General Election of 1885. It was probably by the instrumentality of the Avelings that the news was sent abroad in a letter by Hubert Bland which appeared in *Le Socialiste*, the organ of the French Marxists.[3] Then in the famous West End Riot, into which an S.D.F. demonstration of the unemployed deteriorated on 8 February 1886, Aveling remarked that 'such unsystematic, isolated action . . . is to be deprecated. . . . We must have an organisation co-extensive with the working-classes.'[4] In August of the same year when Hyndman held out an olive

---

[1] May Morris, *William Morris* (1936), ii. 226; *Commonweal*, Oct. 1885; *Daily News*, 22 Sept. 1885; Thompson, *William Morris*, 468–9.
[2] Eleanor Marx to Laura Lafargue, 13 Oct. 1885, photocopy, IISH.
[3] *Socialiste*, 12 Dec. 1885.   [4] *Commonweal*, March 1886.

branch to Morris, he cited as an instance of their past discord
the case of Aveling, who had 'never lost a chance of vilifying
members of our body in the American & other foreign
press'.[1] Aveling's difficulty, however, was not with Hyndman
alone, for he was increasingly estranged from a good many
members of the Socialist League.

Early in 1885 the provisional council of the League
adopted a draft constitution, most likely the work of the
Avelings, incorporating Engels's views on correct Socialist
policy, such as the conquest of political power by securing
the election of Socialists to various administrative bodies and
the encouragement of trade unions, co-operatives, and other
genuine working-class organizations.[2] Yet, as we have seen,
the manifesto of the League, published in February, was
diametrically opposed to this line of policy. The Avelings,
nevertheless, worked hard for the League, speaking for its
branches and writing for *Commonweal*. 'There is the *constant*
worry from the "Socialist League"', Eleanor wrote to her
sister in April: 'From childhood we have known what it is to
devote oneself to the "proletaire".' But, she continued,

the Anarchists here will be our chief difficulty. We have many on
our Council, & by & by it will be the devil to pay. Neither
Morris, nor Bax, nor any of our people know really, what these
Anarchists are: till they *do* find out it is a hard struggle to make
head against them—the more that many of our English men taken
in by the foreign Anarchists (half of whom I *suspect* to be police
agents) are unquestionably the best men we have.[3]

The first battle against the Anarchist influence in the
League was fought at its General Meeting held in July 1885,
at which a proposal was made by Joseph Lane of the Labour
Emancipation League, an affiliated body, to make branches
less dependent upon the central council. Lane regarded 'free
federated Communes' as the best basis for society in the

[1] Hyndman to Morris, 21 Aug. 1886, B.M.Add.MSS. 45345.

[2] Thompson, op. cit. 448–9; Bünger, op. cit. 82.

[3] Eleanor Marx Aveling to Laura Lafargue, 12 April 1885, Bottigelli
Collection.

future. But his proposal was just defeated, the opposition being led by Aveling.[1] There was already a manifest hostility to the Avelings within the League, and Theodor (Reuss), the musician, objected to more than one member of the same family sitting on the council on the ground that this might lead to personal bias in voting. Although his suggestion was voted down, Eleanor was not re-elected to the council at this meeting.[2]

Anarchism was in fact rapidly infiltrating the League. Mrs. Charlotte M. Wilson, the wife of a stockbroker and a member of the Fabian Society, who had organized a study circle with Shaw and others to examine the work first of Marx and then of Proudhon, and who was soon to co-operate with Kropotkin, began to be advertised in *Commonweal* as a lecturer on Anarchism. From 1 May 1886 the paper became a weekly, declaring itself against 'all meddling with the parliamentary method of "reform"'. Aveling resigned as sub-editor and Bax took his place. Eleanor and Engels had persuaded him to give up the position, for 'there is no one here really dependable to work with', wrote Eleanor: '... Bax—reasonable on many points is quite mad on others, & both he & Morris are just now more or less under the thumb of the Anarchists. We should therefore have been held responsible for a paper that will certainly do things we should be bound to condemn.'[3] Even her 'Record' of the international movement soon came to an end and was succeeded by contributions by May Morris and others. Meanwhile, she wrote an open letter to Bismarck, protesting against his remark that a certain Ferdinand Blind, who had made an attempt on his life, had been a disciple of Marx.

[1] An appeal to the members of the League on suggested alterations of rules issued by the Avelings and others. I owe this to the kindness of Mr. C. Abramsky.

[2] *Commonweal*, August 1885. Reuss was later expelled from the League as a police spy. *Commonweal*, 22 May 1886.

[3] Eleanor Marx Aveling to Laura Lafargue, 23 April 1886, Bottigelli Collection.

Although her sister Laura, whose name had been attached to the letter without her consent, did not wish to 'contribute to M. Bismarck's waste-paper basket', Eleanor and Engels were eager to clear the name of Marx from any association with terrorism.[1]

It was about this time that the old enmity of Mrs. Besant was again aroused. Mrs. Besant, who had joined the Fabian Society through her friendship with Shaw, reported on her lost lover, who had attended a Fabian conference on Socialism as a delegate of the League. 'The Marxian metaphysics', she wrote, 'occasionally throw a mist over his own naturally clear and acute expositions. He would be more useful to Socialism in England if he trusted more to himself.'[2] An anonymous writer, probably Mrs. Besant herself, reviewed the Avelings' *Woman Question*, saying that 'the construction of some of the sentences suggests a drunken compositor and a hurried proof-reader'.[3] Even without the personal spite of this passionate woman the Avelings' position in the British Socialist movement was becoming increasingly vulnerable.

Eleanor's Socialist conviction was then stated in a preface to her translation of Lissagaray's *History of the Commune*. She simply followed her father's views in presenting the Commune as 'the first attempt of the proletariat to govern itself'. The Commune meant or could have meant 'the substitution of true co-operative, *i.e.*, communistic, for capitalist production', but, she added, it also meant 'the internationalising, not only the nationalising, of the land and of private property' by virtue of 'the participation in this Revolution of workers of all countries'.[4] What actually amounted to international collectivism, however, does not appear to have

---

[1] Laura Lafargue to Engels, 13 April 1886, *Correspondance*, i. 350. The open letter was published in *Sozialdemokrat*, 15 April 1886 and *Socialiste*, 24 April 1886.

[2] *To-Day*, July 1886.   [3] Ibid.

[4] Eleanor Marx Aveling, Introduction to Lissagaray's *History of the Commune of 1871* (London, 1886), vii–viii.

gained support among the followers of Hyndman or Morris or Kropotkin. She and Aveling found it difficult to maintain their position in the movement and sought an opportunity to escape from the impasse in which they found themselves both on political and personal grounds. They were soon preparing themselves for a transatlantic propaganda tour which might improve their reputation and perhaps enable them to take the leadership of the movement at home.

VI ～ AN AMERICAN
INTERLUDE

The persecuted and impoverished European Socialists had been attracted to the idea of collecting money in America, where the kinship ties of immigrants seemed to assure an easy access to her great wealth. When the German party began to suffer under Bismarck's Anti-Socialist law, Eleanor urged Liebknecht to undertake a speaking tour in the New World: 'I have spoken on the subject to several people who know America *well* and all say you would "make plenty of money" there. . . . Parnell made thousands on thousands—why should you not at least make *something*—If you go I'll go as your "secretary".'[1] A German attempt in 1881 brought in a considerable amount of money, and now in 1886 Liebknecht was at last persuaded to go himself. The Avelings for their part had been in correspondence with a group of American free-thinkers in the hope of arranging their own tour in the States, which, they hoped, might be combined with Liebknecht's.[2] Finally it was decided by the Socialistic Labor Party of America that Aveling as well as Liebknecht should be formally invited and that his expenses should be met by the party. The American Socialists, who were predominantly German in their origins, now apparently

[1] Eleanor Marx to Liebknecht, Nov. 1880, Liebknecht, *Briefwechsel*, 425.
[2] Engels to Bebel, 20 Jan. 1886, Engels, *Briefe an Bebel*, 125, Bebel, *Briefwechsel mit Engels*, 255.

KEM

wanted to take advantage of the great upsurge of the labour movement in that year in order to strengthen their own party.

The 'great upheaval' of American labour, as it was called, was centred on a nation-wide strike for the eight-hour day declared for 1 May 1886, and the initiative in the movement had been taken by the Knights of Labor, a powerful organiz- ation of the unskilled workers. The Socialistic Labor Party, on the other hand, had suffered a set-back because of the splitting away of a revolutionary wing that had formed an Anarchist organization with Most as its acknowledged leader, and those Anarchists who had been active in the trade union movement were now in the thick of the eight-hour struggle, especially at its storm centre, Chicago. A bomb exploded in that city on 4 May which killed and wounded several police- men and was attributed to the Anarchists. But this served to precipitate the defeat of the workers' cause. The eight- hour movement, after its initial successes, met a determined counter-offensive from employers, and failed in the end. Industrial action was superseded by the growing interest in the political struggle among the workers, who now formed an independent labour party. Both Socialists and trade unionists joined the United Labor Party, as it was called, and invited Henry George to fight the New York mayoralty campaign in the autumn. The Avelings' tour coincided with this phase of the American movement, which appeared to confirm the correctness of their views on Socialist tactics. In fact, Aveling, in one of his last contributions to *Common- weal* before his departure, had just advocated the formation of such an independent party of the workers.[1] The Socialist League, now largely under the Anarchist influence, however, took little interest in his American tour, and seems to have declined his request to speak in America as its representative.[2]

*   *   *

[1] *Commonweal*, 26 June 1886.
[2] Edward Aveling to Secretary, Socialist League, 26 July 1886, IISH.

'I look forward to this journey with no little anxiety. We shall have a difficult time of it in many ways, especially since this Chicago business', wrote Eleanor to her sister on 31 August, a few hours before embarking on the *City of Chicago*, an Inman liner at Liverpool. 'If we make millions of dollars', jokingly added her husband, 'we will send some of the very first of them in a Cook's ticket to [you].'[1] During their voyage across the Atlantic they observed their fellow passengers, many of them wealthy Americans on their way home from a European holiday, who, Eleanor indignantly reported, 'could laughingly look at the poor emigrants lying on the deck in their wretched clothes . . . without the least sign of sympathy'.[2] Edward recorded his impression of 'the travelling American'—'He is too palpably the creator of commerce she is too palpably its creature. It is all business and success, business and success.'[3] On 10 September the steamer entered New York harbour with the almost completed Statue of Liberty standing under the blue sky. A reporter of the *New Yorker Volkszeitung*, to which Aveling had been an occasional contributor, came on board and met 'a man . . . with long, black hair, clean shaved, and with distinguished features, and a young lady'.

The man wore a grey travelling costume and a broad, black felt-hat. Hastily observed, he made the impression of a Quaker. Briskly flashed his dark eyes. The young lady, who leaned on his arm, had rich, glossy, black hair, dark-brown eyes and a not unlovely, oval face. Her complexion was heavily browned by the sun during the voyage. The cotton garment which the young lady wore, was gathered together at the waist by a black girdle, above which a kind of blouse with delicate creases fell and from there a steel watch-chain stretched towards the girdle. The intelligent face of the lady was covered by a large, white straw hat with a white bow.

[1] Eleanor Marx Aveling to Laura Lafargue, 31 Aug. 1886, Bottigelli Collection.
[2] *New Yorker Volkszeitung*, 11 Sept. 1886.
[3] Edward Aveling, *An American Journey* (New York, n.d.), 14.

Aveling told the reporter that on his tour he would speak on 'Socialist science' as against Anarchism, because 'the Chicago story had terribly damaged us in England'. Eleanor recounted 'the rudeness and brutality of the so-called "better" classes' on board.[1] At the dock they were met by W. L. Rosenberg, secretary of the National Executive Committee of the Socialistic Labor Party, and were taken to a hotel in the German quarter of the city. 'I rather regret this', wrote Eleanor to Laura, 'for the Vaterland like the poor is always with us here.'[2] Moreover, the vulgarity of the growing city, typified as it seemed by a policeman who made a rude passing remark about Eleanor: 'Say, what the blank is that?', deeply shocked the visiting Socialists from the Old World.[3]

On the 14th they made their first public appearance at a mass meeting held at Bridgeport, Connecticut, one of the strongholds of the S.L.P., and especially of its American section. Here Aveling emphasized the necessity for strengthening the native section, which was still weak, by gaining recruits from various American organizations such as the Knights of Labor, trade unions, and Central Labor Unions. And Eleanor urged the women to join the movement. On the 16th they visited New Haven, where they addressed an audience including students and some professors from Yale University. Two days later they were invited to Meriden in the same state, where they had an interview with some of the leaders of the Knights and were assured by them that their organization would soon unite with the Socialist party, a pledge which was never fulfilled. The Avelings took the co-operative principles of the Knights for a manifestation of 'pure and unadulterated Socialism' and hoped for the replacement of its more conservative leaders.

---

[1] *New Yorker Volkszeitung*, 11 Sept. 1886.

[2] Eleanor Marx Aveling to Laura Lafargue, 14 Sept. 1886, Bottigelli Collection.

[3] Aveling, *An American Journey*, 37.

'In the Knights of Labor', they wrote later, 'we have the first spontaneous expression by the American working people of their consciousness of themselves as a class.'[1]

On the 19th a huge demonstration took place at Brommer's Union Park, New York, where Liebknecht, who had just arrived, addressed his German 'comrades', whose honour as the initiators of Social Democracy in America, he said, 'history can never withhold' from them. But the movement, he added, needed to grow beyond the circle of the German-speaking Americans. Aveling in his speech stressed the same point, which was in fact the keynote of their campaign, on which they had consulted Engels before their departure. The successful demonstration, however, was marred towards its close by police intervention in which Eleanor was roughly handled.[2] Late in September—by which time they had spoken at several towns near New York—the Avelings met Henry George, already the labour candidate for Mayor of New York. The meeting took place at the house of John Lovell, a Fourierist and publisher. Although their conversation with Henry George on this occasion was merely social, they formed the impression that he would soon come to the parting of the ways between Land Reform and Socialism.

On 2 October they set out for a twelve weeks' tour, visiting thirty-five towns in all. The first place where they spoke was Rockville, a factory town in Connecticut, where 'a female "hand"' told them how she had been mulcted of her wages by her employer. At Manchester, New Hampshire they saw women trudging to their work with greater marks of famine and degradation 'in their cheeks' than were to be found on their sisters in Lancashire. Their observations of the factory towns in New England were on the whole

---

[1] *New Yorker Volkszeitung*, 15 Sept. 1886; *Socialiste*, 23 Oct. 1886; Edward and Eleanor Marx Aveling, *The Working-Class Movement in America* (1888), 139–40.

[2] *New Yorker Volkszeitung*, 20 Sept. 1886.

isolated and fragmentary, though they obtained statistical evidence to reinforce their impressions from Carroll D. Wright, the head of the Federal Bureau of Labor, whom they visited at his office in Washington towards the end of their tour. In New England they made excursions to Harvard, to the celebrated Custom House at Salem, and also to a 'delectable mansion' at Fieldingham where they were guests of Mrs. Isabella Beecher Hooker, a woman suffragist and sister of Mrs. Harriet Beecher Stowe. During the first eight weeks Aveling visited at least ten theatres, as he was also working for several literary journals. He was rather amused by what he called 'hypocrisy in abstinence': when he ordered a bottle of champagne at an inn in Rhode Island, a prohibition state, 'in ten minutes a bottle of Heidsieck was before me', he triumphantly wrote, 'and, soon after, within'.[1]

Early in November they moved to the Middle West, and Aveling, accompanied by Liebknecht, paid a visit to Cook County Jail, where the condemned Chicago Anarchists were held. One of them, Samuel Fielden, an Englishman, with whom Aveling spoke with fingers interlocked, clung to him 'as a fragment of his own land'. At Milwaukee, the stronghold of the German Socialists, the Avelings parted company with Liebknecht, and after a visit to Minneapolis-St. Paul they proceeded to Kansas City. The Pullman palace car which they took on the way passed through Iowa, another prohibition state, but Aveling 'hoarded up' a bottle of white wine and drank it with great deliberation. At Kansas City, still a boom town in the Western prairie, they found the price of land 'so wickedly exorbitant that the shanties are mortgaged up to the roof'. Here they were able to recruit forty new members for the American section of the S.L.P., probably the greatest single success they had in their tour.[2] At Cincinnati on their way back to the East they were impressed by a cowboy who made a violent denunciation

---

[1] Aveling, *An American Journey*, 109.
[2] *The Working-Class Movement in America*, 32, 210; *An American Journey*, 62.

of the ranch-owners for their exploitation of his fellow workers. Thence they made a circuit to Baltimore and Washington and returned to New York on 19 December. The tour was on the whole successful, and they apparently enjoyed it. Many of the hotels where they stayed were of the the first class, though Aveling never ceased to complain about the facilities, inadequate as they certainly were for his almost insatiable desire for comfort.

They also kept sending encouraging letters to London and Paris. Already in September Lafargue wrote: 'This journey will have a great repercussion in America and in England. It will . . . establish Tussy and Aveling's reputation in England. They will, on their return, be able to have a greater influence on the Socialist League and lead it into the correct track.'[1] 'Our people have indeed hit upon a lucky moment for their journey', wrote Engels in November:

> it coincides with the first formation of a real American working men's party and what was practically an immense success, the Henry George 'boom' in New York. . . . And considering that the Germans in America are anything but a fair and adequate sample of the workmen of Germany, but rather of the elements the movement at home has eliminated—Lassalleans, disappointed ambitions, sectarians of all sorts—I for one am not sorry that the Americans start independently of them, or at least of their leadership. . . . The unavoidable starting point, in America, are the Knights of Labour, who are a real power, and are sure to form the first embodiment of the movement.[2]

The Americans, however, did not live up to his expectations: George, after he had been narrowly defeated in the mayoralty election, was soon to quarrel with the Socialists, and the Knights of Labor never recovered from the failure of their eight-hour campaign. Moreover, the Avelings' tour ended in a serious dispute with the national executive of the S.L.P. in the course of which Edward's reputation was badly

---

[1] Paul Lafargue to Engels, 30 Sept. 1886, *Correspondance*, i. 389–90.
[2] Engels to Laura Lafargue, 24 Nov. 1886, *Correspondance*, i. 407–8.

damaged by sensational accusations made by his hosts.

*   *   *

On 21 December a mass meeting was held in New York under the auspices of the S.L.P. to protest against an attempt to set up a workhouse for tramps. Aveling, one of the speakers, condemned the system which created the tramps, and urged the Socialists to join the Knights of Labor in order to hasten the overthrow of that system.[1] Two days later a general meeting of the party members took place, at which the Avelings presented a report on their tour. 'The movement, if it were to succeed', Edward now declared, 'must become American and pass from the hands of the German over to those of the English-speaking people.' On the practical problems of organization he remarked:

If I were a domiciled worker here, I would join the Knights of Labor and the Central Labor Union so as to spread and assert my Socialist doctrines in those circles. In no State, with the exception of New York, have I found Socialists or otherwise sensible people who did not agree with me. (Mrs. Aveling, correcting her husband: 'Only the Anarchists'.)

This was a direct challenge to the party leadership, which was mostly German and sat in New York. Indeed, one member drew his attention to the fact that the opposition to the Knights of Labor came largely from the German elements in the party. Thereupon remarked Aveling: 'Only the stupidity and egoism of an individual should be blamed, if he puts up such an opposition.' By this he obviously meant Rosenberg, the party secretary. The executive felt the discussion had gone too far, but Aveling kept on expounding his views on relations with the Knights.[2]

Early in December Rosenberg had already informed Aveling that the party had been too short of money to accept his proposal to hold a conference of English-speaking Socialists in New York, and two weeks later he again

[1] *New Yorker Volkszeitung*, 22 Dec. 1886.   [2] Ibid., 24 Dec. 1886.

expressed regret about this, as 'the expenses of the tour have swallowed up more than we expected'. The executive was apparently preparing to deal a blow at the eloquent critic of its leadership by calling in question the financial accounts of his tour. He and Eleanor were invited to attend an executive meeting held after the conference on the same day, and at this meeting Aveling's statement of expenses was discussed. H. Walther, an executive member, 'declaimed against my reckonings as excessive from end to end', wrote Aveling, and 'denounced us both as aristocrats living on the money of the workers, as not worthy to belong to the party, &c.'.[1] Aveling, as we have seen, had been working not only for the S.L.P. but also for several journals, for which he had to write dramatic criticism. And he had been slovenly enough to put together all his and his wife's expenses 'down to every cent. to every glass of beer' in a weekly statement he had sent to the executive, and thoughtless enough to ask it to decide for which items it would feel the party was responsible.[2] He had often been too generous and had paid all the expenses for Liebknecht and his daughter while they were together in Boston. All the wines Liebknecht had consumed with him during the journey, it was said, had been paid for by him.[3] This was the reason for the statement of the executive that Aveling had spent nearly twice as much as Liebknecht had.

According to the original agreement between him and the executive, the latter undertook to pay all his travelling expenses, his hotel bills, Eleanor's railway expenses, and in addition $3 a day. Now, Aveling's list of expenditure in his weekly reports amounted to $2,050, of which he had actually received $1,364. Part of his daily stipend to the amount of $176 was still in arrears and was offered to him at this meeting. In view of the charges against him, however, he

---

[1] Circular issued by Edward Aveling to the Sections of the S.L.P., 26 Feb. 1887, photocopy, Illinois State Hist. Lib.

[2] Ibid.

[3] Engels to Sorge, 16 March 1887, Marx-Engels, *Letters to Americans* (New York, 1953), 179.

could not accept the money. He returned $76 at once, and the rest, which he needed for his and his wife's journey back to England, he decided to return from London.[1] On the eve of their departure Aveling sent a protest to the executive complaining of the 'brutal treatment' he and Eleanor had received from the party leaders. Rosenberg, for his part, regarded Aveling's action as 'presumptuous', for he felt that the Avelings had had a good time in America at no expense of their own.[2]

They left New York on the 25th and arrived in London early in January 1887 with 'many, delightful reports' of America.[3] Yet the hostility of the S.L.P. executive against Aveling did not end with the unpleasant meeting of 23 December. The story had been leaked by a certain Herbert Eaton, an executive member, to the *New York Herald*, which in its issue of 30 December published a sensational account of the meeting.[4] Two weeks later the *Herald* article was extensively quoted by the *Evening Standard* of London, which reported that the New York Socialists were determined 'nevermore to import a professional agitator from the effete monarchies of Europe. The luxury is too expensive.' 'Dr. and Mrs. Edward Aveling', it went on,

are the two luxuries whom the Transatlantic upsetters of society have found too dear. The lady and gentleman lectured for thirteen weeks and charged 1300 dollars for it. It was pointed out that this was 'rather stiff for a Socialist who professed to have the welfare of the poor at heart'; but Dr. Aveling playfully replied, 'Well, it's English, you know, quite English'; and intimated that another bill of 600 dollars was coming . . . There was one item of 25 dollars for 'corsage bouquets' for Mrs. Aveling . . . Fifty dollars were put down for cigars for the doctor, and cigarettes

[1] Aveling's Circular to the S.L.P. Sections.

[2] *New York Daily Tribune*, 31 Dec. 1886.

[3] Engels to Domela Nieuwenhuis, 11 Jan. 1887, photocopy, IML (Berlin).

[4] Bernstein in *Sozialdemokrat*, 26 April 1890; Dorothy Rose Blumberg, 'Florence Kelley: the Early Years', M.A. thesis, Columbia University (1963), 85.

for his emancipated wife; a two days' wine bill at a first-class hotel was 42 dollars; and, though Dr. Aveling had been accustomed to gain free admission into New York theatres by modestly representing himself as the dramatic critic of the *Saturday Review*, theatres were summarised at 100 dollars—a nice round sum . . . Altogether, delivering lectures on Socialism seems a lucrative business.[1]

This was a terrible accusation. Moreover, the S.L.P. executive issued a circular on 7 January, repeating its charges against him and calling upon the local sections of the party to pass a resolution against the 'swindler'. It also complained that Aveling, 'instead of working for the extension and strengthening of our Socialist organisation', had adopted the slogan: 'All Socialists must be the Knights of Labor.'[2] Apparently this was the real grievance, but the whole issue was turned into an attack upon Aveling's personal character, which was indeed vulnerable. He and Eleanor now had to fight a rearguard action against the New York leaders in order to save their own honour, which was at stake. Their efforts met with a sympathetic response in some quarters, especially in the Middle West, where the need for a mass organization was better appreciated than in New York. A circular in which they explained their position, arguing that they had worked more for the interest of the party than for that of the executive, was published by a St. Paul Socialist in the *Chicagoer Arbeiter-Zeitung*.[3] In February, when they received from Rosenberg a copy of the original circular of the executive, Aveling issued a second circular directed to the sections of the S.L.P. in which he contradicted every item of the accusations and declared in conclusion:

It is an attempt to introduce into the Socialistic Labor Party judicial methods that are a mockery even of the ordinary bourgeois ideas of justice and equity . . . and this at the very time when

---

[1] *Evening Standard*, 13 Jan. 1886.
[2] Quoted in Aveling's Circular, 26 Feb. 1887; see also Bernstein in *Sozialdemokrat*, 26 April 1890.
[3] *Chicagoer Arbeiter-Zeitung*, 17 Feb. 1887, newspaper cutting at IISH.

we are all protesting against the verdict in the Chicago trial, in which the accused did at least have a hearing. If this is the kind of judicial procedure to be introduced into the Socialistic Labor Party, I for my part, should ask to be tried before a Chicago Jury.[1]

Upon their return from America the Avelings had stayed for a while at Engels's residence at 122 Regent's Park Road, and all their attempts to vindicate their position were made in close consultation with him. Indeed, Engels himself was much annoyed by the extent to which the charges against them had been given publicity. Mrs. Florence Kelley Wischnewetzky, the American translator of his *Condition of the Working-Class in England*, accepting the executive version of the Aveling affair, urged Engels to boycott him by 'giving Kautsky a hint, not to let the letters appear which are advertised in the name of Dr. Aveling'. Thereupon Engels wrote her a long letter of eleven pages, defending the Avelings and their attitude in America. 'That great national movement', he said, 'was the real starting-point for the work-ing-class movement in America, and if the Germans stood aloof, they would only become a dogmatic sect. 'Mrs. Aveling who has seen her father at work, understood this quite as well from the beginning, and if Aveling saw it too, all the better.' 'I have known Aveling for four years', he went on:

I know that he has twice sacrified his social and economical position to his convictions, and might be, had he refrained from doing so, a professor in an English university and a distinguished physiologist instead of an overworked journalist with a very uncertain income. I have had occasion to observe his capacities by working with him, and his character by seeing him pass through rather trying circumstances more than once.

So he could not believe the mere allegations spread by hostile people in New York. With anger and scorn he rejected the charge that Aveling had tried to 'swindle' the party.

[1] Aveling's Circular to the Sections of the S.L.P., 26 Feb. 1887.

How could he do that during all his tour without his wife being cognizant of it? And in that case the charge includes her too. And then it becomes utterly absurd, in my eyes at least. Her I have known from a child, and for the last seventeen years she has been constantly about me. And more than that, I have inherited from Marx the obligation to stand by his children as he would have done himself, and to see, as far as lies in my power, that they are not wronged. And that I shall do, in spite of fifteen Executives. The daughter of Marx swindling the working class—too rich indeed![1]

The defamatory charges, which in Engels's view were 'nothing but the usual complaint of Knoten against Gelehrte greatly disturbed the Avelings, however. 'Poor Edward had an awful shock about these ridiculous accusations, so soon after his quinsy', wrote Engels to Laura: 'He is not over endowed with power of resistance to malady, and so this threw him back very much. He has been off and on at Hastings.'[2] Eleanor must have gone through a trying time, and her public silence was an indication of the depth of her anxiety.

Aveling's quarrel with the New York executive provided Hyndman with a new weapon with which to start another campaign to discredit him in English Socialist circles. *Justice* published a notice entitled 'A Costly Apostle' and declared that 'the S.D.F. had every reason for repudiating any connection with Dr. Aveling'.[3] The latter replied that the sections of the S.L.P. to which both he and the executive had appealed had decided largely in his favour, and the Board of Supervisors of the party to which the executive had been obliged to put the dispute had begged him to allow the matter to drop.[4] In a further communication which Hyndman's organ refused to publish, he sought to quote a letter from Liebknecht in which his travelling companion

[1] Engels to Mrs. Wischnewetzky, 9 Feb. 1887, photocopy, IML (Berlin), published in Marx-Engels, *Letters to Americans*, 169–71. See also Dorothy Rose Blumberg, 'Dear Mr. Engels', *Labour History* (Spring 1964).
[2] Engels to Laura Lafargue, 24 Feb. 1887, *Correspondance*, ii (1956), 17.
[3] *Justice*, 30 April 1887.   [4] *Justice*, 14 May 1887.

objected to an attempt to create 'an artificial antagonism' between himself and Aveling and said: 'I know Aveling sufficiently to assert that he is incapable of cheating the party.'[1]

The National Convention of the S.L.P. held at Buffalo in September 1887 put an end to the whole dispute. It adopted an executive report which simply stated that 'Aveling's first bill was too exorbitant'. This was quite true, and so 'a reparation of his honour' was refused.[2] Meanwhile *To-Day*, now a Fabian journal, blamed Aveling for the 'unbusiness-like arrangements' that had been the root of the whole trouble. 'The Socialist Labor Party', it said,

found the task of deciding whether this or that particular cigar or bottle of soda water was 'a means of production' of lecturing or of dramatic criticism, invidious and impossible. Dr. Aveling took a high tone, and told them, in effect, to pay what their conscience told them they ought to pay. They then lost their tempers; accused him of 'trying it on'; and expressed their belief that if they had paid the amount in full without remonstrance he would have pocketed the total without a word. Obviously this could neither be proved nor disproved.[3]

Engels now more or less agreed with this view and wrote in a letter to Sorge:

The youngster has brought it all on himself through his complete ignorance of life, people, and business, and through his weakness for poetic dreaming. But I have given him a good shaking up, and Tussy will do the rest. He is very gifted and useful, and thoroughly honest, but as gushing as a boy, and always inclined to some absurdity. Well, I still remember the time when I was just such a noodle.[4]

*   *   *

Meanwhile the Avelings were making an effort to attract the Radical workers in London, and in this task they met a

[1] Aveling to editor of *Justice*, n.d., IISH.

[2] *Report of the Proceedings of the Sixth National Convention of the Socialistic Labor Party* (1887), 21.

[3] *To-Day*, Aug. 1887.

[4] Engels to Sorge, 8 Aug. 1887, *Labour Monthly*, Feb. 1934.

similar pattern of opposition from the Anarchist majority in their own body, the Socialist League. In January, Aveling had spoken on 'Socialism in America' and Eleanor on 'The Relative Position of English and American Workmen' for the Clerkenwell branch of the League.[1] In March Engels wrote to Mme Lafargue that Aveling 'is making a very useful and probably successful campaign amongst the East End Radicals to engage them to cut loose from the Great Liberal Party and form a working men's party after the American fashion'.[2] They also wrote a series of articles on 'The Labour Movement in America' for the monthly *Time*, in which they placed special emphasis on the United Labor Party as an example to be followed in England, for it was, as they saw it, a distinct political party of the working class, opposed to the two great traditional parties, 'taking its stand on the doctrine of unpaid labour'.[3] The Avelings were also prominent among the speakers at a huge demonstration of Radical working men held in Hyde Park on 11 April to protest against Coercion in Ireland. 'Considerable interest was naturally taken', wrote a reporter of the *Daily Telegraph*,

in the speech delivered with excellent fluency and clear intonation by Mrs. Marx Aveling, who wore beneath her brown cape, a dress of green plush with a broad hat trimmed to match. The lady has a winning and rather pretty way of putting forth revolutionary and Socialistic ideas as though they were quite the gentlest thoughts on earth.[4]

Engels now expected the emergence of a new working-class party with the Avelings in its leadership. 'Aveling is carrying on a very successful agitation in the East End of London', he wrote in May:

[1] *Commonweal*, 29 Jan., 5 Feb. 1887.
[2] Engels to Laura Lafargue, 21 March 1887, *Correspondance*, ii. 25.
[3] *Time*, May 1887; see also *Time*, March–June 1887. These articles were later incorporated in their joint work, *The Working-Class Movement in America*, published in 1888.
[4] *Daily Telegraph*, 12 April 1887.

The Radical clubs, to which the Liberals owe the twelve seats they hold out of the 69 [*sic*] in London, have approached him with the proposal to lecture to them on the American movement, and he and Tussy are very busy in the work. It is now an immediate question of organising an English Labour Party with an independent class programme. If it is successful, it will relegate to a back seat both the Social Democratic Federation and the Socialist League, and that would be the most satisfactory end to the present squabbles.[1]

Engels was now despairing of the Socialist League, although that body had come into existence with his blessing. An attempt by the Anarchists to revise its constitution had been defeated in the previous summer at its second annual conference, but their hold on the League had been considerably strengthened during the Avelings' absence. It was about this time that Mrs. Wilson started *Freedom*, a small monthly paper, for Kropotkin, who had recently arrived in England. Moreover, Aveling had resigned from the League's executive council before his departure for America, and upon his return he found his influence further weakened. Though Bax had joined the 'parliamentary' group, he was somewhat estranged from Aveling, and Morris had also apparently come to distrust his former ally. Even with the support of the Bloomsbury branch, of which he was a member, Aveling failed to persuade the council to ensure that his reply to *Justice* about his American tour should be published in *Commonweal*.[2] On this 'Aveling stir' May Morris wrote in a letter to Andreas Scheu: 'Of course Father is not going to have any personal nonsense of that sort flaunted in the "Weal".'[3]

At the third annual conference of the League held on 29 May 1887, an amendment from William Morris upholding 'the policy of abstention from parliamentary action' was

---

[1] Engels to Sorge, 4 May 1887, *Labour Monthly*, Feb. 1934, also in Marx-Engels, *Letters to Americans*, 185.

[2] Aveling to the Council of the Socialist League, 16 May 1887, IISH.

[3] May Morris to Andraes Scheu, 5 May 1887, IISH.

carried by 17 votes to 11, the minority including Eleanor, who represented the Bloomsbury branch.[1] The 'parliamentary' faction which was thus defeated held a private meeting next day, at which Aveling, who was in the chair, was reported to have said: 'Sorry we left the S.D.F. Reverse our blunder made there, and get the League in our own hands. . . . Make W. Morris give up the paper.'[2] On the same day one of the Anarchist members of the League, Mme Gertrude Guillaume-Schack, a friend of Mrs. Wischnewetzky's who had been active in the women's movement in Germany, wrote to Engels announcing her intention not to visit him any more. The reason she gave was that she could not meet Aveling, as he had committed disreputable acts, far more serious than his conduct in America, and also had been slandering his own wife, intimating that Eleanor had been extremely jealous. Neither Engels nor the Avelings, who went to see her, however, managed to obtain any particulars of her accusation.[3] Engels thought that Mme Schack received all the gossip about Aveling from 'the pious bourgeois women' of the Anti-Contagious Diseases Acts Agitation with which she was associated and also from the Anarchist elements in the League.[4] At that time she was sharing a house with Scheu and the Kautskys, who were again in London, and it is quite likely that her strong views about Aveling were shared by Scheu's friend, Morris, who denounced 'that disreputable dog Aveling' for his part in the factional struggle of his own party.[5]

Aveling's reputation thus fell very low indeed: he was even 'cut' by an active member of his own 'parliamentary'

---

[1] Socialist League, *Conference Report* (1887), 12–13.
[2] To the Members of the Socialist League, handbill issued by Joseph Lane and F. Charles, quoted Thompson, *William Morris*, 536n.
[3] Engels to Laura Lafargue, 7 June, 11 June 1887, *Correspondance*, ii. 44–45, 47.
[4] Engels to Sorge, 4 June 1887, photocopy, IML (Berlin).
[5] Morris to John Glasse, 23 Sept. 1887, R. Page Arnot (ed.), *Unpublished Letters of William Morris* (1951), 7.

group, J. L. Mahon. Mahon, whom Eleanor had regarded with favour, was now forming a North of England Socialist Federation among the miners and ironworkers around Newcastle. He had the grandiose scheme of founding a united Socialist party by organizing the provincial workers, urging them to exert pressure upon the squabbling London leaders, and thus promoting an atmosphere of unity among the latter in the direction of political action. Engels, who regarded his attempt as premature, nevertheless offered to assist him in his propaganda work in the provinces through 'some *English* Committee', possibly 'a *London* Committee', actually, however, through the Avelings, to whom he said he would give his contribution.[1] In fact, he attached conditions to his financial help, and asked Mahon to 'treat Aveling with the fullest confidence, consult him in all party matters & regard him as an essential person in the movement', but Mahon bluntly declined these conditions.[2] When Aveling wanted to know the reason for his refusal, he was given a curt reply: 'It cannot be of much consequence to you what I think of you. We were never very close comrades or friends and often, perhaps generally, very much the opposite.'[3] In the early days of the Socialist League, when Mahon acted as its secretary, Aveling had treated him in a high-handed manner and had often criticized him for his 'unpunctuality' and other minor offences.[4] He may well have come to believe the rumours about Aveling's misconduct. For his new Socialist campaign he had been in close touch, among others, with Ernest Radford, then a popular figure in the League, who was often elected chairman of its conferences and who knew Aveling's personal history quite well. Mahon, however, soon came under the influence of Champion, who was then preparing a revolt against Hyndman within the S.D.F. by

[1] Engels to Mahon, 23 June 1887, Thompson, *Morris*, Appendix II, 864.

[2] Mahon to Engels, 21 July 1887, ibid. 866.

[3] Mahon to Aveling, 31 July 1887, ibid. 868.

[4] Aveling to Mahon, 24 March, 27 April 1885, IISH.

attempting to broaden its appeal to labour as a whole. Mahon therefore rejoined the S.D.F. and put an end to his own venture for an independent Socialist party.

*   *   *

The English translation of the first volume of *Capital*, for which the Avelings, in addition to Samuel Moore, the chief translator, had worked for many years, appeared shortly after their return from America. The first English reaction took the form of a friendly review published in the *Athenaeum* in May. In this review Marx was described as 'the prophet of the working class' who came 'at a time that, to all appearance, and especially in the country which he has selected as the principal field for his inquiries, that class is attaining the dominant political influence in its turn'. He was valued chiefly as a social historian who made an empirical study of factory legislation. 'It is much owing to his influence', continued the review, 'that this benevolent kind of legislation has of late spread so much in other countries. If Europe is to be saved from the social revolution that he believes to be impending, it will only be, he thinks, by taking prompt action in this and similar directions.'[1] Engels welcomed this article, which, he believed, had given 'the key-note' to the reviews that would follow.[2]

Engels was soon disappointed, for the prevailing tone of the English reaction turned out to be that of the Fabians, who concentrated upon Marx as an economist and a philosopher rather than a historian. Bernard Shaw demurred when the *Pall Mall Gazette* called *Capital* 'the text-book of modern Socialism'. Socialism, he declared, 'is not based on Marx's theory of value', and 'does not stand or fall with either Mr. Wicksteed's theory or Marx's.'[3] The defence of

[1] *Athenaeum*, 5 March 1887.
[2] Engels to Laura Lafargue, 10 March 1887, *Correspondance*, ii. 20.
[3] *Pall Mall Gazette*, 6, 7, 12, 13 May 1887. P. H. Wicksteed was an economist of the school of W. S. Jevons and one of the first critics of Marxian economics in England.

Marxian economics was left to Hyndman, while Aveling was expostulating with Shaw in 'a friendly letter'. Shaw in reply asked Aveling to tell him how he was to face Mrs. Aveling after his 'blasphemy'. 'Remember', he added, 'that Newton was wrong about light—that Goethe was wrong about colors —that Darwin clearly overstressed natural selection, and then ask yourself whether it isnt at least possible that Marx was wrong about value. Even I had erred in my time.'[1] Aveling, for his part, indulged in rather heavy humour on the subject, calling the four protagonists of the Jevonian theory of utility—Shaw, Webb, Sidney Olivier, and Mrs. Besant—'a noble & most economical (shall we omit the letters underlined?) quartet'.[2] Yet it was Mrs. Besant who had the last word in this *Pall Mall* controversy. Marx, according to her, entered the region of 'pure metaphysics', for his concept of labour value was 'analogous to the tabularity which is present in all tables'. 'I make bold to say', she concluded, 'that this quagmire of contradictions and bad metaphysics is no safe foundation for modern Socialism.'[3]

Apparently *Capital* fell on stony ground as far as its theoretical aspect was concerned. It is true that the book made a good start: the first impression of 500 copies was almost sold out in the first two or three months, though

[1] Bernard Shaw to Edward Aveling [17 May 1887], Shaw, *Collected Letters 1874–1897*, ed. by Dan H. Lawrence (1965), 168. According to the editor, Aveling under the pseudonym of 'T. R. Ernest' had written a reply to Shaw's earlier criticism of the Marxian theory of surplus-value (ibid. 81). In a letter published in *Justice* (15 March 1884) G. B. S. Larking (i.e. Shaw) maintained that the thief who robbed the workers was not the capitalist alone, but that the consumer who bought the product of labour as cheap as possible from the capitalist was as great a thief as the latter. 'T. R. Ernest' replied that 'society at large are the thieves'—this view was to become the basic tenet of Fabian Socialism —and consequently 'a reorganisation of the whole system' was needed. ('How is the Thief to be caught', *Justice*, 22 March 1884.) Shaw agreed with 'T. R. Ernest'. Was Aveling responsible for Shaw's Fabianism?

[2] Edward Aveling to Bernard Shaw, 22 May 1887, Shaw Papers, British Museum.

[3] *Pall Mall Gazette*, 24 May 1887.

nearly half the number went to America. But soon the sales slackened: only sixty-five copies were sold for one year from July 1887.[1] This was the time when Aveling's reputation remained badly injured, and the sale of *Capital* may well have been affected by the opprobrium to which one of its translators had been subjected, as well as by the critical and unfavourable reviews by the Fabians.

* * *

Meanwhile the fate of the condemned Anarchists in Chicago aroused much excitement among the Socialists, who saw a miscarriage of justice in the harsh judgement passed upon them. This judgement was finally confirmed by the Supreme Court of Illinois in September 1887; and the Avelings, who had kept in touch with Captain William Black, the advocate for the Anarchists, now appealed to the working men's clubs in London to pass resolutions protesting against 'this murder' and send them to the President and the Supreme Court of the United States.[2] The *Pall Mall Gazette* published an 'interview' with Eleanor, who drew the attention of the middle-class Londoners to the facts of the case. 'There really was not enough evidence to hang a dog upon,' she declared. Yet the State Attorney had elevated the case from the question of guilt or innocence of the accused into the wide issue of one's attitude towards anarchy and assassination. The jury was 'admittedly prejudiced', and the judge 'unblushingly partisan'. It was, she said, 'just as if you were to hang Michael Davitt and John Dillon if some tenants threatened with eviction were in a sudden access of passion to kill an emergency man'.[3] Eleanor and her husband also

[1] Engels to Laura Lafargue, 10 March 1887, 13 Oct. 1888, *Correspondance*, ii. 20, 171. Royalties for this year amounted to £12 3s. 9d. (3s. 9d. per copy).

[2] Typescript copy of an Appeal on the Chicago Anarchists issued by Edward and Eleanor Marx Aveling, BLPES.

[3] *Pall Mall Gazette*, 8 Nov. 1887.

wrote in the Socialist *To-Day*, declaring that 'our position
of antagonism to the teachings of Anarchism strengthens our
position in asking justice for the condemned men'. The eight-
hour movement, they argued, lay at the bottom of the whole
affair, and thus 'the sentence is a class-sentence; the execu-
tion will be a class-execution'.[1] Many of the Radical clubs
in London subscribed to a cablegram asking for mercy, and
according to Eleanor 'a second petition signed by at least a
few well-known names, was also cabled'. In spite of all their
protests, however, on 11 November four of the condemned
men were hanged. Even from this work for 'common justice'
Aveling did not emerge unscathed. Hyndman alleged that
the second cablegram had never been sent and that 'Aveling
pocketed the money'. It is again difficult to prove or disprove
this categorical charge, as there was no protest from the
accused, except for the equally categorical assertion by
Engels that the whole affair was 'from A to Z fabricated' by
Hyndman.[2]

   In the wake of the 'legal murder' of the Chicago Anarchists
came the incident known as 'Bloody Sunday' of 13 November
when an Anti-Coercion demonstration held in Trafalgar
Square was broken up by police on foot and on horseback.
The demonstration was organized by the Metropolitan
Federation of Radical Clubs as a protest against the police
decision to forbid the holding of public meetings in the
square. When the demonstrators tried to force their way into
the square, fighting broke out, and over 100 casualties were
reported as a result. John Burns and Cunninghame Graham,
the Radical M.P. for North-west Lanark, were arrested and
later sent to prison. The Avelings also took part in the
demonstration. 'I have never seen anything like the brutality of
the police', wrote Eleanor in a letter to the *Pall Mall Gazette*,

----

[1] *To-Day*, Nov. 1887.
[2] Hyndman, *Further Reminiscences*, 142. Eleanor Marx to Laura
Lafargue, 16 Nov. 1887, photocopy, IISH. Engels to Bebel, 1 Oct. 1891,
Bebel, *Briefwechsel*, 444.

and Germans and Austrians, who know what police brutality
can be, have said the same to me. I need not tell you that I was
in the thick of the fight at Parliament-street, and afterwards in
Northumberland Avenue I got pretty roughly used myself. My
cloak and hat (which I'll show you) are torn to shreds; I have a
bad blow across the arm from a policeman's baton, and a blow
on the head knocked me down—but for a sturdy old Irishman (a
perfect stranger to me) whose face was streaming with blood,
I must have been trampled on by the mounted police. But this is
nothing to what I saw done to others.[1]

Engels however said, 'Tussy . . . was not the attacked but
the attacker'.[2] On the initiative of W. T. Stead, the editor
of the *Pall Mall Gazette*, a Law and Liberty League was
formed with the task of helping the victims of the free speech
fight, and Eleanor was among those who went bail for them.
She and Aveling also dealt with 'Despotism from a Socialist
standpoint' in their lectures. 'Why should language that is
not tolerated in Ireland be allowed here . . . ?' asked a
correspondent in the *Globe* who had heard Eleanor recom-
mending a boycott against the police at two successive meetings held on Clerkenwell Green.

On each occasion Mrs. Aveling said (at least the words were to
this effect):—'You must make social war on the policeman. If
you see a policeman go into a shop, do not go into it. . . . don't
enter the doors of a public house where a policeman goes. Avoid
these perjurers and murderers, and mind you force them to be on
duty on Christmas Day. Even if we can't get into square, we can
spoil their Christmas dinners for the fat specials and for the
murderous ruffians of Sir Charles Warren [the Commissioner of
Police]'.[3]

On 18 December the Law and Liberty League organized a
public funeral for a workman, by name Alfred Linnell, who
died of injuries received during the demonstration. 'The

[1] *Pall Mall Gazette*, 14 Nov. 1887.
[2] Engels to Natalie Liebknecht, 29 Nov. 1887, Liebknecht, *Briefwechsel*, 301.
[3] *Globe*, 22 Dec. 1887.

Linnell funeral was *very* fine, & a great success. The streets were a wonderful sight especially as we neared the East End', wrote Eleanor. She was still in a militant mood and added: 'If only the Radicals were not so many of them cowards we could carry the Square. As it is they are all "funking" more or less.'[1] Engels now looked with satisfaction on the widening gap between the working-men Radicals and the middle-class Liberals and Radicals as a result of the whole affair. He saw a great future for the Law and Liberty League, 'the first organisation in which Socialist delegates as such are seated at the side of Radical delegates'.[2] But he was not in a position to exert much influence on the League, for its Socialist side was represented on its executive by Morris for the Socialist League, Mrs. Besant for the Fabians, and one or two from the S.D.F., and the utmost the Avelings could do was to organize an entertainment on its behalf.[3]

There was a slackening of tension, albeit of short duration, among the quarrelling Socialist bodies in the following spring. The Socialist League, the S.D.F., and the Anarchists held a joint meeting in commemoration of the Paris Commune at which Hyndman and Morris, John Burns and Mrs. Wilson, Kautsky and Kropotkin all spoke. On this occasion Eleanor delivered what Hyndman called 'one of the finest speeches I ever heard'. 'The woman', he said, 'seemed inspired with some of the eloquence of the old prophets of her race, as she spoke of the eternal life gained by those who fought and fell in the great cause of the uplifting of humanity: an eternal life in the material and intellectual improvement of countless generations of mankind.'[4]

[1] Eleanor Marx Aveling to Laura Lafargue, 31 Dec. 1887, Bottigelli Collection.
[2] Engels to Mrs. Wischnewetzky, 22 Feb. 1888, *Labour Monthly*, Feb. 1934, also in Marx-Engels, *Letters to Americans*, 197.
[3] *Justice*, 14 April 1888.
[4] Hyndman, *Record of an Adventurous Life* (1911), 346–7; see also *Commonweal*, 24 March 1888 and *Justice*, 24 March 1888.

Soon, however, dissension between the two factions of the Socialist League again came to the fore. The Bloomsbury branch, to which the Avelings belonged, had carried on an active agitation among the Radical workers and had increased its membership from 50 to 110 during the year preceding the annual conference of 1888. Even before the conference the Anarchist elements in the League urged the branch's expulsion on the grounds that it had nominated a candidate for the Board of Guardians elections in April and had induced 'very many members of the S.D.F.' to join it in order to attempt to subvert the League. The branch was also blamed for having aided Mahon's north of England campaign, which was 'largely political'.[1] At the fourth annual conference of the League held on 20 May, the Bloomsbury branch put forward a motion demanding an alteration in the League constitution so that branches might 'be empowered (if so disposed) to run or support candidates for all the representative bodies of the country', but this was defeated by a wrecking amendment moved by Morris which was carried by 19 to 6.[2] Shortly after the conference, when the League council received notice from the Bloomsbury branch claiming complete autonomy and intimating its determination to form another organization for the purpose of running candidates at elections, the branch was formally dissolved.[3] In August an independent Bloomsbury Socialist Society was formed, but it was not before the rise of 'New Unionism' in the early nineties that the Society under the leadership of the Avelings played any significant role in the Socialist movement.

[1] Annual Report of the Bloomsbury branch of the Socialist League, May 1888; 'Parliamentarism in the Socialist League', a suppressed letter from a member of the Bloomsbury branch to the editor of *Commonweal*, 16 May 1888, IISH; a draft resolution for disaffiliation of the Bloomsbury branch, n.d., IISH.

[2] Socialist League, *Conference Report* (1888), 12–13.

[3] Decision of the executive council of the Socialist League to dissolve the Bloomsbury branch, n.d., IISH.

The Avelings' propaganda tour in America had strengthened their belief in an independent labour party, and this they sought to organize on their return by trying to convert the Radical working men's clubs to Socialism and by consolidating the 'parliamentary' group within the League. They continued their work among the Radical clubs— Eleanor spoke, for instance, on 'Working men and Politics' for the Central Croydon Liberal and Radical Club towards the end of the year.[1] But it now became clear that there was no prospect of immediate success in their attempt to form a working-class party in which they could exert decisive influence. Moreover, as we have seen, the serious charges made by the American Socialists against Aveling's personal character, exaggerated though they were, only served to weaken his already damaged popularity among the English Socialists, and as a result he was boycotted by most of them. The more Socialist politics disappointed the Avelings, the greater the interest they took in their other field of enthusiasm, the theatre, and Edward now seriously tried his luck as a dramatist and Eleanor hers as an actress.

[1] *Commonweal*, 15 Dec. 1888.

VII ∿ WOOING THE
DRAMATIC MUSE

AVELING was not destined to become a successful dramatist in spite of his repeated attempts to win the favour of
the Dramatic Muse, and Eleanor's theatrical ambition
faltered at an early stage. Yet their combined efforts provided
an element of the new driving force in what was called 'a
veritable revolution' in the theatrical world in England at
the time. A new era was dawning: technical innovations
allowed greater exploitation of the possibilities of the stage;
a boom in theatre construction had begun; audiences grew
more respectable, and even the Nonconformists were losing
their old antipathy towards the theatre. The emergence of the
leisured class led to the development of the modern matinée,
which in its turn allowed a playwright to experiment with
new plays and new ideas. Dramatic criticism became an
acknowledged profession, and the stage not only catered for
entertainment but also began to express views on serious
issues of public moment. Indeed, 'the Renaissance of the
drama', as it was called, brought with it a revolt against the
predominance of conventional middle-class opinion in the
theatre. Naturalism began to assert itself on the English
stage, and young and daring dramatists launched an attack
upon accepted standards of morality and respectability.
They dealt above all with marriage and property, the two
bulwarks of bourgeois supremacy. Adultery for obvious
reasons became one of their favourite subjects. The whole

tendency curiously suited the taste of the Avelings, especially of Edward, as it provided a vehicle both for the expression of their Socialist views and for the explanation and justification of their personal relationship, which was anything but conventional.

*   *   *

The new dramatic movement owed much to the influence of Henrik Ibsen, whose idea of asserting one's own personality by defying convention greatly strengthened the revolt against bourgeois morality. The Avelings were among the pioneers who introduced the Norwegian dramatist to the English public. Ibsen and his works had been known to a limited circle of English readers since the seventies, but it was William Archer, a Scottish journalist, who became the principal propagandist of the cause for which Ibsen's name stood in the dramatic world. During a visit to Italy he met his hero, who was then living in Rome, and was delighted to discover that Ibsen had 'the most vivid sympathy' for Bradlaugh.[1] Archer himself was a Secularist and was a friend of G. W. Foote. When the latter was sent to prison for blasphemy and Aveling took charge of his journal, *Progress*, Archer assisted the interim editor as best he could. In consequence the magazine devoted considerable attention to contemporary Scandinavian literature and published among other things a short story by Anne Charlotte Edgren, a Swedish authoress of the new school. Mrs. Edgren was then on a visit to England, and Eleanor was introduced to her, probably through Aveling. In a letter to her sister Laura, Eleanor wrote how she had been 'struck' by Mrs. Edgren's stories and asked Laura to introduce the novelist to the Socialist circle in Paris, where she was shortly to be. 'It is strange how immensely rich Scandinavia is just now in authors!' she wrote: '. . . I send you an English translation of the Norwegian (this is rather Irish!) Ibsen's splendid play—"Nora". I don't say

---

[1] Lieut.-Colonel C. Archer, *William Archer* (1931), 113.

anything about it, because I know *how* you will appreciate.'[1]

Nora was the title under which the play *A Doll's House* was first translated into English. It had created a sensation in Scandinavia and in Germany, but when it appeared in English in 1882 in Miss Frances Lord's translation, it attracted little attention outside the small circle of 'advanced' dramatists. In the spring of 1884 an adaptation by the young playwright Henry Arthur Jones and his friend Henry Herman was produced at the newly opened Prince's Theatre under the title of *Breaking a Butterfly*, but it was much reconstructed to suit the English taste. In this version Helmer, the husband, was introduced as an ideal hero who took his wife's crime on his shoulders—the forged note was stolen from the villain and destroyed—and the crisis in their married life ended in reconciliation and happiness. Jones later admitted that this was a 'transgression' of his early career.[2] Aveling denounced this version as 'a mutilation' which evaded the tragic problem, 'emasculated' Ibsen, and rendered him 'commonplace'. Ibsen, he wrote, 'sees our lop-sided modern society suffering from too much man, and he has been born the woman's poet. He wants to aid in . . . revolutionising . . . the marriage relationship.'[3] Aveling, whose relationship with Eleanor Marx would be regarded as 'revolutionary', spent part of his honeymoon in Derbyshire reading a section of Ibsen's *Ghosts*, which was still in manuscript form. His effective rendering of the piece impressed Olive Schreiner, who was with the couple: 'It is one of the most wonderful and great things that has long, long been written', she wrote to Ellis, '. . . I cried out aloud. I couldn't help it.'[4]

[1] Eleanor Marx Aveling to Laura Lafargue, 18 June 1884, photocopy, IISH. *Progress* serialized 'The Doctor's Wife', a short story by Mrs. Edgren, in its issues of July–September 1884.

[2] Quoted in Miriam Alice Frank, *Ibsen in England* (Boston, 1919), 78.

[3] *To-Day*, June 1884; *Our Corner*, 1 May 1884.

[4] Olive Schreiner to Havelock Ellis, 29 July 1884, *Letters of Olive Schreiner*, 36. The English translation by Miss Ford was to appear in *To-Day* in 1885.

Bernard Shaw, who was then on friendly terms with the Avelings, recorded in his diary on 30 January 1885 that he played in 'a third rate comedy' with them at the Ladbroke Hall, Notting Hill. This was *Alone* by Palgrave Simpson and Hermann Merivale.[1] Shaw and Aveling soon joined the staff of the *Dramatic Review*, which was founded in February by an Irishman named Edwin P. Palmer. Archer also wrote for this journal. Shaw often had talks with the editor and Archer about Aveling, who was then grumbling that he was being boycotted by the *Review*.[2] Aveling was soon allowed to write occasional criticisms of drama and music under the name of Alec Nelson. This *nom de plume* was certainly a convenience for a man suffering from so much unfavourable comment, both on the grounds of his political and religious attitude and because of his personal behaviour and private life. His contributions were not very remarkable, except for his repeated objections to 'disturbing coin of the realm for a programme' in the theatre.[3]

He was, however, more serious and up to his mark when he wrote for the *Neue Zeit*. The majority of the pieces played in London, he said, were of the kind that a businessman would want to see when his day's work was done, and consequently most of the dramatists failed to understand the advice of Shakespeare, who put into Hamlet's mouth the view that the stage ought to 'hold as it were, the mirror up to nature: to show virtue her own feature, scorn her own image, and the very age and body of the time his form and pressure'. ' "The body of the time" is exactly what our modern writers dare not touch', he said: 'Real problems, life questions (I speak always of England) are just as much tabooed on the stage as on the academic platform.' Thus 'our modern dramatists . . . are not in a position to understand the sham

---

[1] G. Bernard Shaw, Diary & Notes, 1885, BLPES; Shaw, *Collected Letters 1874–1897*, 115.

[2] Shaw, Diary & Notes, 1885.

[3] *Dramatic Review*, 15 Feb., 6 June 1885.

civilisation at the end of the 19th century. . . . They do not appear to see the fact that we live in a transition stage.'[1] It was only to be expected that Aveling should bitterly criticize the Church and Stage Guild for imposing morality and new respectability upon the drama. The Guild was making efforts, he once declared, to 'link the rising fortunes of the drama on to the decaying fortunes of religion'. 'In art, as in science', he said, 'the best work of to-day, and the only work of the future, will be that which deals with the natural, and the natural alone.'[2] Indeed, the English drama itself was on the threshold of a great revolution, and Aveling aspired to play his part as a playwright in the new epoch of naturalism.

*   *   *

Eleanor did all she could to assist her husband in his effort to set himself up as a dramatist. She begged Olive Schreiner to try and induce some of her influential friends to read his play. Aveling, in collaboration with Philip Bourke Marston, a blind poet, had just written a one-act play entitled *A Test*. They had already approached Beerbohm Tree, the celebrated actor, but there was no reply. 'This is a sore disappointment to Edward, and will be equally a sore one to poor Philip', she wrote to Olive. 'If I did not feel that from the *actor*'s point of view the play would "go", I should not speak of this at all', she added.[3] Aveling also asked Wilson Barrett, manager-actor at the Royal Princess's Theatre, whom he had called 'far and away the best of our romantic melodramatic actors', to consider the play. But Barrett replied that one-act plays were not wanted.[4] Aveling finally managed to present *A Test* under his own direction at the

[1] Edward Aveling, 'Das Drama in England', *Neue Zeit*, iii Jahrgang (1885), 171.

[2] *Freethinker*, 27 April 1884.

[3] Eleanor Marx Aveling to Olive Schreiner, 16 June 1885, *Adelphi*, Sept. 1935.

[4] Wilson Barrett to Edward Aveling, 29 Aug. 1885, B.M.Add.MSS. 45345.

Ladbroke Hall on 15 December. The work was preceded by
To Oblige Benson, a comedy by Tom Taylor, who was good at
anglicizing French melodramas, and in this piece both
Aveling and Eleanor played 'pleasingly enough'. In his own
play he played the part of a country doctor, Eleanor his
wife, and May Morris also took part. The whole play,
according to a review, was crudely constructed, and its
unhappy ending was merely 'painful without being really
dramatic'. 'Dr. Aveling was manifestly out of his depth;
but, on the other hand, Mrs. Aveling, as his wife, displayed a
quite surprising amount of force and feeling.'[1] The reception
of *A Test* was thus not encouraging, though Eleanor found
consolation in the kind remarks about her acting.

Eleanor, as we have seen, had long desired to establish
herself as an actress, and in her ambition she was encouraged
by Bernard Shaw, who was a frequent visitor at her house.
On 25 February Shaw wrote in his diary: 'Mrs. Aveling
asked me to call in the afternoon & have a chat. Went at
5 & stayed until 8 nearly. Aveling absent at Crystal Palace
Concert. Urged her to go on the stage. Chatted about this,
death, sex, & a lot of things.'[2] In May he discussed with her
and Aveling a project to read *Nora* for a private circle. A
performance of this play had just been attempted by a group
of 'rash amateurs' at the School of Dramatic Art, and even
Archer had relegated Ibsen to the category of the 'theâtre
impossible'.[3] The Avelings now felt that they ought to do
something to 'make people understand our Ibsen'. In June
Eleanor wrote to Shaw, asking him to call on her to save her
'from a long day & evening of tête-à-tête with myself—
the person of all others I am most heartily sick of'. She said
they should try to get May Morris for their projected reading

[1] *Dramatic Review*, 19 Dec. 1885; Handbill of Dramatic Entertainment
at Ladbroke Hall, 15 Dec. 1885, Kautsky Archives, IISH.

[2] Shaw, Diary & Notes, 1885, BLPES.

[3] William Archer, 'Ibsen in England', *Dramatic Review*, 4 April 1885;
a review of the presentation of *Nora* at the School of Dramatic Art,
ibid., 28 March 1885.

of *Nora*. 'She was here yesterday', she went on, 'looking as sweet & beautiful as the flower she is called after. It was like a breath of fresh air to look at her. I wonder whether all people enjoy beauty as intensely as I do. It always makes me for a time at all events, believe there must also be some good in the world somewhere.' She urged Shaw to take up the part of Krogstad, the blackmailer, and said:

It is not in the least necessary that you should be sane to do that. Au contraire. The madder the better . . . I wish some really *great* actors would try Ibsen. The more I study the greater I think him. How odd it is that people complain that his plays 'have no end' but just leave you where you were, that he gives no *solution* to the problem he has set you! As if in life things 'ended' off either comfortably or uncomfortably. We play through our little dramas, & comedies, & tragedies, & farces & then begin it all over again. If we *could* find solutions to the problems of our lives things would be easier in this weary world.[1]

Nearly six months later Eleanor was at last able to invite 'just a few people *worth* reading "Nora" to' to the reading of the play. It took place at her house at Great Russell Street on 15 January 1886. She read the part of Nora, Aveling Helmer, Shaw Krogstad, and May Morris Mrs. Linde. 'It is . . . a real duty', she wrote to Ellis, 'to spread such great teaching as his [Ibsen's] and my little effort is just a poor beginning.' 'There are some people one gets to know *at once*', she added in her letter: '. . . and others that one is a stranger to after a lifetime passed together.'[2] This latter category seemed to include her husband as well. She must often have felt as if she were a Nora—a stranger to her husband—but she also felt she was bound to Aveling by her own free will, and she tried to be loyal to him. Just as she had protested against the idea of filial duty and yet had

[1] Eleanor Marx Aveling to G. Bernard Shaw, 2 June 1885, Shaw Papers, B.M.
[2] Eleanor Marx Aveling to Havelock Ellis, December (1885), quoted in *Adelphi*, Oct. 1935; letter of invitation to Ernest and Dollie Radford on the occasion of 'A Reading of Nora', Radford Papers.

MEM

succumbed to it, so she now more or less resigned herself to the fate that united her with her husband. Yet Aveling had none of her father's warm, human affection and was in many ways irresponsible and unscrupulous.

*   *   *

Eleanor was then on friendly terms with George Moore, whose 'strong' and 'bold' novels she highly valued, and it was through him that she obtained the profitable work of translating *Madame Bovary*, Flaubert's masterpiece. It was 'to the eternal honour of Flaubert', as Eleanor herself wrote in a preface to her translation, that this book had been prosecuted by the Government of Napoleon the Third. M. l'avocat, the Imperial prosecutor, objected less to the conception of adultery in itself, she remarked, than to the fact that Flaubert, 'with the calm of a doctor describing a disease', said that 'the fig-leaf morality of the avocat revolts'. True to the Shakespearian ideal of a dramatic work, Flaubert held up a mirror, and it was only natural that 'some, recognising their own image, should be shocked'. Eleanor, for her part, was fascinated by the character of Emma Bovary, which presented the problem of self-deception and falsification of one's personality. 'Her life is idle, useless', she wrote in her preface:

And this strong woman feels there *must* be some place for her in the world; there *must* be something to do—and she dreams. Life is so unreal to her that she marries Bovary thinking she loves him . . . She does her best to love 'this poor wretch'. In all literature there is perhaps nothing more pathetic than her hopeless effort to 'make herself in love'. And even after she has been false, how she yearns to go back to him, to something real, to a healthier, better love than she has known.[1]

This analysis of Emma's personality reflected Eleanor's own aspirations and anxieties. She felt the same longing for a

[1] Eleanor Marx Aveling, introduction to her translation of *Madame Bovary* (London, 1886), xx. See also Eleanor Marx Aveling to Laura Lafargue, 27 April 1886, photocopy, IISH.

healthier love. Yet with Emma, adultery was the beginning and life-negating nihilism was the end. The subject must have had a tremendous appeal for Eleanor, who had not the courage of Ibsen's Nora. She could share Emma's intense feeling of 'the misery of earthly affections and the eternal isolation in which the heart remains entombed'.[1] She might be able to end her life as Emma did, accusing no one. Emma's tragedy was that she was ever in search of an ideal and yet became corrupt and base. 'But for her surroundings', said Eleanor, 'she would be a monster and an impossibility.' Given the surroundings, Emma was only inevitable. No doubt Eleanor saw in the heroine's fate an image of her own married life. Flaubert's 'mirror' reflected her own striving for an ideal and her husband's corruption and degeneration. Emma combined these two opposite qualities in one personality, and the result was her destruction. Eleanor seems to have felt that she had a full presentiment of the life to come. She devoted herself to the work of translation, which was completed in May 1886, and her work, though not faultless, remained for many years the only English version available.

*　　　*　　　*

Early in 1887 'Dr. Edward Aveling' returned from his American trip 'with a few dollars and an intense disgust for the American stage', according to the *Dramatic Review*; 'He says dramatic work in the States is all imported, and that when the Yankees are left alone with their own plays, the result is too painful for contemplation.'[2] Soon the American accusation against him as a 'swindler' found wide circulation, and he was obliged to conceal himself as 'Alec Nelson' in the *Review*. One of the plays Nelson reviewed the following season was *As in a Looking Glass*, a naturalist drama by F. C. Grove, which dealt with an adventuress hankering after better things. 'Temptations to good and

[1] Gustave Flaubert, *Madame Bovary*, tr. by Eleanor Marx Aveling (Everyman's Library, 1957), 192.

[2] *Dramatic Review*, 15 Jan. 1887.

temptations to evil' in the play, Nelson wrote, 'are as rife and as evenly balanced as in real life'; to betray one's friend and to lie to one's spouse, 'these are questions as large as those that you and I, my reader, have to solve and live. The stern, tragic end, the suicide, when the game is up, is in keeping . . . with the strong tone of the play.'[1] The problem of man's alienation and the resulting struggle of good and evil provided Aveling with food for reflection.

Eleanor, after her return from America, was looking for a job and was only too glad to accept an offer of collaboration from Ellis, who was then planning a 'Mermaid Series' of selected plays of the Elizabethan dramatists. 'Among actors the Series *should* be much read', wrote Eleanor, '. . . I shall be glad to get any work I am capable of doing. I need work much, and find it very difficult to get. "Respectable" people won't employ me.'[2] Ellis's plan matured only slowly, and it was not till the following year that she was given any work for the series.

Shortly after their American tour the Avelings settled in a flat of three large rooms on the fourth floor at 65 Chancery Lane, and in the summer they acquired a cottage at Dodwell near Stratford-on-Avon. They were not, however, as well off as this may at first suggest. They visited the Shakespeare country with the two passes for the North-Western Railway which Aveling had obtained for his article for the *Dramatic Review*, and on a stroll around Stratford they came across a farm with two cottages, one of which they discovered they could rent for two shillings a week. There was a garden of a quarter of an acre which was 'not only ornamental but useful'. Eleanor arranged the sub-letting of the cottage for the period of their absence. 'I can't tell you how charming this country life is after the hurry & worry & wear & tear of London', wrote Eleanor to her sister:

[1] *Dramatic Review*, 28 May 1887.
[2] Eleanor Marx Aveling to Havelock Ellis, March 1887, *Adelphi*, Oct. 1935.

It is . . . essentially English . . . as it becomes Shakespeare's home
to be. Think of it, Laura, Shakespeare's home! We work two
or three times a week at his 'birth place' (by permission of the
Librarian of the place) . . . Now that I have been in this sleepy
little Stratford, & met the Stratfordians I know where all the
Dogberries & Bottoms & Snugs came from.[1]

Here Eleanor worked hard, translating short stories by
Alexander Kielland from the Norwegian, and Aveling was
'writing no end of things', dreaming of the days when, in his
own words, 'the plays begin acting & royalties roll in'.
They returned to London in September, to their 'teaching
and usual dreary round of work'. Eleanor still 'devilled' for
her employer, a certain Miss Zimmern; 'necessity knows no
laws, 25/ is 5/', i.e. Miss Zimmern paid her 5 out of her
earning of 25 shillings.[2]

*   *   *

On 25 November 1887 Aveling's second play, *By the Sea*,
was performed at the Ladbroke Hall. It was an adaptation
from a French piece, *Jean-Marie* by André Theuriet, and was
founded on the old Scottish ballad 'Auld Robin Gray',
which, as we have seen, Eleanor had acted with the Radfords. Once again Eleanor played Jeannie, the heroine, who
lost her lover, a sailor, in a shipwreck and married an elderly
suitor, Robin Gray. The sailor, however, returned, and a
struggle began between Jeannie's youthful passion and her
loyalty as a wife. The latter won and the sailor consented to
leave the country. Aveling's adaptation was called 'a pretty
little drama', but the acting was severely criticized. 'Miss
Eleanor Marx', wrote a critic in the *Dramatic Review*,

. . . is said to be a pupil of Mr. Herman Vezin, and it must be
admitted that some of her elocution was worthy of her distinguished tutor. But small though the theatre was, she was frequently inaudible, even close to the stage, and never for a moment

[1] Eleanor Marx Aveling to Laura Lafargue, 30 Aug. 1887, Bottigelli
Collection.
[2] Ibid, 9 May 1884, 24 June 1888, photocopy, IISH; Edward Aveling
to Laura Lafargue, 30 Aug. 1887, Bottigelli Collection.

seemed to understand that she ought to be heard by anybody more than a few feet off. Some of her lines were prettily spoken, but she did not rise to the height either of the repentant wife, who grieves to have offended against her husband even in thought, or the loyal wife who repulses the still-loved lover of her childhood . . . The part of the husband was played by the adapter himself. Mr. Nelson has done the literary part of the work so well, that we do not like to compare the two efforts.[1]

The review was a harsh blow to Eleanor. It was for the sake of her theatrical ambition that she had had a long struggle with her father and had more or less forsaken her first lover. It was again the same aspiration for dramatic success that had sustained her in every subsequent hardship and in every disappointment with Aveling. Her long cherished hopes were now dashed all at once, dashed to the ground. Moreover, Herman Vezin wrote up to deny that she had ever been a pupil of his, and this seemed to suggest that she had been carrying on a deception.[2] In fact she had been a pupil of Mrs. Vezin, and it was indeed the carelessness of the critic that was responsible for the error. She must have been mortified by the incident.

This humiliation was also accompanied by a growing sense of isolation in both the dramatic and the political sphere. She began to feel that because of her husband she was being boycotted even by some of her close acquaintances. In March 1886 F. J. Furnivall, her old friend, had founded the Shelley Society, which came to notice by sponsoring a private performance of *The Cenci*, which had been banned by the Lord Chamberlain. Yet even with this organization trouble occurred when Aveling applied for membership. Henry Salt, one of its active members, later recalled ironically that the majority of its committee decided against him because of 'his marriage relations being similar to Shelley's', and its decision was withdrawn only through pressure from the chairman, W. M. Rossetti, who threatened to resign.[3]

[1] *Dramatic Review*, 3 Dec. 1887.   [2] Ibid., 10 Dec. 1887.
[3] Henry S. Salt, *Seventy Years among Savages*, 95.

But in fact Eleanor herself would have been welcome in the Society, and the antipathy to Aveling was probably due to a deeper cause than mere prudish objections to the informal nature of their union. Aveling, for his part, launched an attack on what he called Furnivall's 'intense vulgarity and egotism' in his review of the performance of *The Cenci*, while he defended the play as 'a moral play' permeated with the spirit of rebellion against 'all forms of tyrants'.[1]

At a meeting of the Society held in April 1887 an attempt was made to dissociate Shelley from 'the blatant and cruel socialism of the street'.[2] The Avelings prepared a reply which Edward turned into two lectures and which was later published for private circulation as a booklet entitled *Shelley's Socialism*. It was an attempt to present Shelley as a Socialist who condemned commercial morality and who believed in the inevitability of a clash between the two classes of society. Godwin's influence on Shelley was stressed and Marx's authority was invoked to designate him as 'one of the advanced guard of Socialism'.[3] Meanwhile, a lecture given by Aveling in December—possibly the one on Shelley —elicited an 'exasperating' comment from Shaw. 'I am glad you thought the lecture "superior" (hideous words!)', wrote Eleanor to Shaw,

---

[1] *Progress*, June 1886.

[2] Shelley Society, *Notebook* (1888), 190.

[3] Edward and Eleanor Marx Aveling, *Shelley's Socialism* (1888), *passim*. Also published as an article 'Shelley and Socialism' in *To-Day*, April 1888. Shelley's writings, wrote Eleanor in a letter to Salt, had exerted 'enormous influence' on leading Chartists: 'I have heard my father and Engels again and again speak of this; and I have heard the same from the many Chartists it has been my good fortune to know— Ernest Jones, Richard Moore, the Watsons, G. J. Harney, and others.' Salt, op. cit. 90. The Avelings were then so much preoccupied with the Socialist Shelley that in a comic sketch of a Socialist House of Lords 'Baron Aveling' was described as giving a recitation from Shelley for the House where the 'Bishop of Merton' (William Morris), Lord Chief Justice of Blackfriars Bridge (Hyndman), Archbishop of Canterbury (Stewart Headlam), and others were debating a bill for renewing carpets in coal mines. *To-Day*, April 1888.

for I can lay claim to a fair share of it—Yes—the boycotting was rather mean. But I am getting so used to being boycotted that it is no longer a novelty. I marvel much more now when I am not boycotted. You never come to see us now, & I have sometimes wondered whether you were boycotting us too![1]

It was probably sometime in 1887 that Eleanor made an attempt at suicide, though it is not known exactly when it was. Ellis, speaking of his invitation to Eleanor to work for the Mermaid Series already referred to, tells us that 'it may have been not so very far from this period' that she did this. 'It was by deliberately taking a large overdose of opium', he wrote: 'But by administering much strong coffee and making her walk up and down the room the effects of the poison were worked off. I never knew what special event in her domestic life it was which led to this attempt. Her friends were grieved; they were scarcely surprised.'[2] Indeed, several incidents that took place about this time can be pointed to as possible causes for the attempt: the controversy with the American Socialists; Mme Shack's accusation; her own failure as an actress; and the growing consciousness of being boycotted. An equally likely cause would be her discovery of some fresh infidelity by her husband. This, however, was not novel, nor was ostracism by others. The American charge of 'swindling' the working class had been vigorously refuted by Engels as well as by Aveling, and she was more angry with than hurt by Mme Schack, from whom she even tried to extract an elaboration of her charges. The collapse of her theatrical ambition was probably the most serious set-back she suffered, though each of her misfortunes or a combination of some of them would have been enough to drive her to desperation, especially in her often sickly state of health.

*   *   *

[1] Eleanor Marx Aveling to Bernard Shaw, 16 Dec. 1887, Shaw Papers, B.M.
[2] *Adelphi*, Oct. 1935.

While Eleanor felt miserable after her failure on the stage, Aveling was happy and elated because a play of his had for the first time been given a favourable review. Towards the end of the year he left for Torquay to superintend the production of this—*By the Sea*—and another play of his, called *The Love Philtre*; these were produced at the Torquay Theatre for the matinée on 7 January 1888. Miss Frances Ivor, the wife of Leonard Outram, a well-known actor, played the part of Jeannie. It was a great triumph for 'Mr. Alec Nelson', 'a London journalist who is rising into repute as a dramatist', and the audience called for the author, who was 'received with warm plaudits'. The plot of the second play was an ingenious story about a love potion which made a girl love its possessor for the sake of duty rather than of love. It was equally successful.[1] In March it was reported that Nelson's 'poetical comedy' *By the Sea* had been reproduced at the Lyric Hall, Ealing, 'with the success which attends this piece wherever it is played'.[2] All this success made Aveling very cheerful. He gave publicity to 'the Asphaleia stage' with new devices for a safety theatre, a model of which had been exhibited at the Society of Arts by Karl Kautsky, the Austrian Socialist, and his brother Hans. The two brothers had come to England to introduce the invention, which was the work of their father, the chief painter to the Imperial Court of Berlin.[3] It was also about this time that Aveling got up an entertainment for the Law and Liberty League with Eleanor, John Burns, and others. He also invited Burns to play a part, 'a strong character part with a dash of pathos in it', in his new drama *The Bookworm*, which was produced at the Athenaeum in April.[4]

Aveling was preparing another series of plays for the stage. Engels, who took an interest even in this aspect of his

[1] *Dramatic Review*, 14 Jan. 1888.
[2] Ibid., 24 March 1888.   [3] Ibid., 28 Jan. 1888.
[4] Edward Aveling to John Burns, 7 April 1888, B.M.Add.MSS. 46288.

activity, was exultant at his 'remarkable *preliminary* successes'.
'He has sold about half a dozen or more pieces which he
had quietly manufactured', he wrote to Laura in May:

Some have been played in the provinces with success, some he
brought out here himself with Tussy at small entertainments, and
they have taken very much with the people that are most
interested in them, viz such actors and impresarios as will bring
them out. If he has now one marked success in London, he is
a made man in this line and will soon be out of all difficulties.
And I don't see why he should not, he seems to have a remarkable
knack of giving to London what London requires.[1]

The 'one marked success' Engels hoped for was then expected from his adaptation of Hawthorne's *Scarlet Letter*, in
which the actor Charles Charrington and his wife, Janet
Achurch, had taken much interest. But he was not alone
in the field, for a rival version, which made things end
happily, was played about the same time and promised to
be a financial success. Aveling's adaptation, which retained
the tragic ending of the original, was performed at the
Olympic Theatre at the matinée on 5 June. 'Mr. Nelson's
dialogue is powerful', read a note in the *Dramatic Review*,
'and his language replete with the grim poetic spirit of the
book, but there is too much of it—that is, for an acting
play'. The play was not a marked success. Miss Achurch's
Hester was said to have been 'full of mannerisms' and
Charrington's Dimmesdale 'far from forcible'.[2] Aveling,
however, still had several other pieces to try his luck with.
On 22 June his new one-act play, *For Her Sake*, was produced at the Olympic matinée. It was called 'a clever, well
written *lever de rideau* of pathetic interest, exhibiting neat
construction and sound literary style', and 'the piece had
the support of a painstaking and able cast'.[3] Another *lever
de rideau* by Nelson was played at the Strand Theatre a week
later. In July Eleanor and Aveling retired to their 'castle'

---

[1] Engels to Laura Lafargue, 9 May 1888, *Correspondance*, ii. 127.
[2] *Dramatic Review*, 9 June 1888.   [3] Ibid., 7 July 1888.

at Dodwell, but Aveling came up to London to read two plays to 'speculative actors (Alma Murray is one) who intend to invest in a bit of novelty', wrote Engels.[1] Miss Murray, 'the poetic actress without a rival' as Robert Browning called her, had played the part of Beatrice in *The Cenci*, and Aveling had admired her as 'an artist and a thinker'.[2] It looked as if he was attracting sufficient popular notice to give him, if not financial security, at any rate a good many fresh opportunities.

In the same month Engels informed Laura that Tussy and Edward were expecting to sail sometime in August for America, 'where Edward is to superintend the mise en scène of three of his pieces, to be played simultaneously in New York, Chicago and God knows where besides. . . . If his dramatic success goes on at this rate, maybe he will have to go next year to Australia, at the expense of some theatrical impresario.'[3] They had been in touch for their second American trip with John Lovell, who had just published Aveling's *American Journey*. Engels himself was planning a holiday in America in order to convalesce from his eye trouble. His companion was to be his old friend Schorlemmer, but he wanted to keep his plans secret to avoid 'the delicate attention of the German Socialist Executive, etc. of New York'.[4] Early in August the four of them left for New York on board the *City of Berlin*, the same steamer which had carried the Avelings back from their first American trip. 'We've *such* a lot of priests, & clergymen on board, & some babies & no end of Amurken twang', Eleanor wrote to Laura from the ship: 'Both our old men seem to be enjoying themselves & eat, drink & are as merry as possible.'[5] 'The General & Jollymeyer [Schorlemmer] are

[1] Engels to Laura Lafargue, 15 July 1888, *Correspondance*, ii. 150.
[2] *Progress*, Dec. 1885.
[3] Engels to Laura Lafargue, 6 July 1888, *Correspondance*, ii. 148.
[4] Ibid., 6 Aug. 1888, *Correspondance*, ii. 163.
[5] Eleanor Marx Aveling to Laura Lafargue, 9 Aug. 1888, Bottigelli Collection.

staying at Hoboken (Engels at Sorge's, Jollymeyer next door) & we came to this hotel', she wrote from St. Nicholas Hotel, Broadway: 'The city of iniquities strikes me as more hideous than ever—& yet it might be so beautiful. I dont believe there is any large town in the world so exquisitely situated as New York—& commerce has made of it a very hell. . . . Edward . . . will have to spend the next few days seeing after rehearsals.'[1] They made a tour to Boston and Niagara and up to Montreal, but there was no mention of Aveling's achievements on the American stage. On 19 September they sailed for Liverpool by the S.S. *City of New York*. Apparently Aveling's attempt to build up his dramatic reputation in America was a failure, but he refused to give up his hopes and tried his luck once more on the English stage.

*   *   *

All this while Eleanor remained acutely unhappy, but she kept her worries to herself. In December 1887 when Aveling was away at Torquay, Eleanor kept herself busy by decorating her rooms and sending Christmas presents to Longuet's children in Paris, but she confessed to her friend Dollie that 'Christmas without children is a mistake'.[2] In February 1888 when she heard the death of a certain 'Louie', apparently a close friend, she again wrote to Dollie: 'She was one of those who *ought* to live. But all things are contrary, & at times like this the sense of the sadness of life comes upon us almost too painfully for endurance'.[3] Her consolation, as it appears, always lay in her work. She was then finishing a translation of Ibsen's play, *An Enemy of the People*, which was published early in the summer under the slightly different title of *An Enemy of Society* in a volume edited by Ellis. The volume,

[1] Eleanor Marx Aveling to Laura Lafargue, 21 Aug. 1888, Bottigelli Collection.

[2] Eleanor Marx Aveling to Dollie Radford, 28 Dec. 1887, Radford Papers.

[3] Ibid., 23 Feb. 1888, Radford Papers.

which also included Archer's translation of *Pillars of Society*
and Miss Lord's *Ghosts* revised by Archer, gained an immediate success. All the three translations it contained were
recognized as far superior to any previous translation of
Ibsen's work. Indeed, it is said to have been 'the first English
translation of Ibsen that gained for the Norwegian any
adequate recognition'.[1]

Eleanor wished to go on working on Scandinavian literature. From Boston she had written to Ellis, urging him to
edit another Ibsen volume. This suggestion did not mature,
and instead of an Ibsen drama Ellis offered her an Elizabethan play, *A Warning to Fair Women*, to be edited for his
Mermaid Series. The plot of this play had certain affinities
to Hamlet. Eleanor accepted with enthusiasm and even
paid a visit to Oxford to look up the original manuscript.
'I give the locality of the Scenes', she wrote in a letter to
Ellis. 'Why, the *social* interest is the only real one of these
plays. . . . I have become much interested in the subject
as a whole. I used to know the individual plays well enough.
I don't think I before realized their value as "documents".'[2]
She was so much enchanted by the Elizabethan drama that
she even shocked A. H. Bullen, the Elizabethan scholar, by
the freedom with which she referred in conversation to the
less decorous aspects of her subject. But her labour was
wasted, for after a prosecution of the publisher of the Series
for issuing Zola's 'obscene' novels, his business was ruined,
and the Mermaid Series was taken out of Ellis's hands.

*   *   *

Eleanor and, to some extent, Aveling soon became
involved in the preparatory work for founding the Second
International, but this did not mean that she became freer
of domestic worries. On New Year's Eve she wrote to

[1] Miriam Alice Frank, *Ibsen in England*, 64.
[2] Eleanor Marx Aveling to Ellis, December 1888, *Adeplhi*, Oct. 1935.

Laura: 'Tomorrow Edward is going to Cornwall to stay with some friends of his who are also very anxious for me to go down. I am not. I dont care for rich folk, tho' I fear I shall have to go. But certainly I shall put it off as long as possible.'[1] There were as always many rumours about Edward's personal character. Bernstein, who came to stay in London in the autumn of 1888, one day received a social invitation from the Fabian Hubert Bland and his wife Edith 'Nesbit', later well known as a writer of children's books. The Blands were on friendly terms with Olive Schreiner and Havelock Ellis, and certainly were not conventional people. This was particularly true of Edith, an 'advanced' woman who cut her hair short, wore all-wool clothing, and smoked heavily, and who used to visit Eleanor at her flat at Great Russell Street. It was while he was receiving the Blands' hospitality that Bernstein let drop reference to the Avelings. Then 'there was suddenly a suspiciously unanimous chorus of praise of them', he recalled:

'Oh, the Avelings are very clever people'. 'Oh, everybody must admit that they have been of great service to the movement', and so forth, in the same key, so that it was at once clear to me that there was something in the air. I diverted the conversation to politics. But a judge of human nature might have blurted out the question: 'What's the truth about them, really? Have they murdered their children, or what?'[2]

Bernstein was apparently shocked, but the question he raised, though it sounded serious enough, only illustrated the extent to which distrust and disapproval of Aveling had grown even in 'advanced' circles. Shortly before her departure for South Africa in 1889, Olive wrote to Ellis:

You can't understand that to feel any human creature hopelessly false is more terrible to me than all poverty, all loneliness, all

[1] Eleanor Marx Aveling to Laura Lafargue, 31 Dec. 1888, Bottigelli Collection.
[2] Bernstein, *My Years of Exile*, 203–4.

death. The fact of such a nature as Edward Aveling's, for instance,
is more terrible to me, does more to cripple my power of life and
work, than all the close personal sorrows of my life.[1]

Yet Engels, living in seclusion like a 'Grand Llama', as
Hyndman called him, refused to hear anything that would
place his favourite disciple in an unfavourable light. 'We
have got hold of another Mother Schack in Miss Harkness',
he wrote to Laura in the autumn of 1889.[2] This was because
Miss Margaret Harkness, who had often gone 'slumming'
with Eleanor and had written several novels on the condition
of the unemployed workers in the East End of London under
the pseudonym of 'John Law', had now voiced her disapproval of Aveling. It did not matter that Engels had praised
one of her books as 'a masterpiece' and had given her his
advice on realism in literature. When she sent him a note
that their friendship must end on account of Aveling, and, like
Mme Schack, refused to give him any further reason for
avoiding his protégé, he at once reacted against her. 'One is
forced to suppose', wrote Berstein, 'that Aveling had been
guilty of some insult of a kind that a refined woman would
not willingly speak of.'[3]

*   *   *

Meanwhile Alec Nelson worked hard as a dramatist. On
4 April 1889 his new comedietta, *The Landlady*, was played
at a matinée at the Shaftesbury Theatre. It was the story of
a couple of young lovers whose future was threatened by the
drunkenness of an uncle, and the play was fairly well
received, as it was 'prettily told'.[4] On 16 May a dramatic
sketch by Nelson called *Dregs* was produced at the Vaude-
ville matinée. 'Although Aveling has not conquered the
public in a full assault', wrote Engels, 'the critic is occupied
with him, even those people who have till now kept a

---

[1] Olive Schreiner to Ellis, 6 July 1889, *Letters of Olive Schreiner*, 165.
[2] Engels to Laura Lafargue, 16 Nov. 1889, *Correspondance*, ii. 357.
[3] Bernstein, op. cit. 202.   [4] *Dramatic Notes* (1890), 40.

conspiracy of silence.'[1] The piece, a duologue between a degenerate young man and his heart-broken sweetheart, which ended 'à la Ibsen—without solution', fared better than Engels had hoped. Its comparative success was largely due to the performance of Miss Rose Morreys or Norreys, whom Eleanor had called 'a very popular and "rising" young actress' and with whom Edward had been in touch for the past few years.[2] His next play, *The Jackal*, a comedy in three acts which was produced at the Strand matinée on 28 November, was of a kind that would suggest parallels with the personal life of its author. A hard-drinking, dissolute man, who obtained credit for having written plays which were the work of another man, attempted to seduce this other man's lover, an actress. The girl was rescued by the injured dramatist, but she turned out to be henceforth a debauchee.[3] The play was not a success, and it was nearly a year later before another piece of his was performed. This was *Madcap*, a comedietta, in which the main characters were a young girl and her lover, a tutor. It was performed at the Comedy on 17 October 1890 and met with a good reception.[4] 'Edward's "Madcap" is still running at the Comedy', wrote Eleanor in December: '& he has hopes of other things. The devil of it is hopes wont pay bills.' 'I am doing hack translations (very bad) for a new magazine', she went on, '. . . Edward writes all sorts of things—good, bad & indifferent. We both have meetings & work of that sort in every spare hour. There's really no time to consider whether life is worth living or is a most unmitigated nuisance.'[5]

From January 1890 'Alec Nelson and E.M.A.' had been

[1] Engels to Paul Lafargue, 16 May 1889, *Correspondance*, ii. 263.

[2] *Dramatic Notes* (1890), 59; Engels to Paul Lafargue, 17 May 1889, *Correspondance*, ii. 265; Eleanor Marx Aveling to Laura Lafargue, 30 Aug. 1887, Bottigelli Collection.

[3] *Dramatic Notes* (1890), 148.   [4] Ibid. (1891), 135.

[5] Eleanor Marx Aveling to Laura Lafargue, 19 Dec. 1890, Bottigelli Collection.

writing 'Dramatic Notes' for *Time*, then edited by Belfort Bax or, according to Shaw, 'run' by the Avelings for Bax.[1] Eleanor published in this magazine two stories by Alexander Kielland which she had earlier translated.[2] In a dramatic review also published there the Avelings wrote:

The only essential modern lines along which a dramatist can work are the economic, the religious, the sexual, i.e. from our point of view, as the greater includes the lesser, the economic only. The really great modern play, when it comes, will deal not with the struggle in two human lives only, but with that class-struggle which is the epic of the nineteenth-century also. And thus far, even Ibsen has failed us.[3]

There were several 'problem plays' produced about this time, and Wilson Barrett, for instance, sought to deal with the problem of capital and labour in *The People's Idol*. There was even a burlesque of the workers on strike, though the piece was soon withdrawn owing to what the Avelings called 'the pit and gallery objection'. 'Working men', they said,

have no objection to good-humoured fun . . . But they do not forget that the theatre, as at present constituted, is like the rest of our institutions, on the side of the classes, not of the masses. They looked upon the burlesque of the strikers . . . as a distinct weapon in the warfare of the classes against them.[4]

'Alec Nelson', however, who must have hoped to become a playwright for the masses, made no attempt to live up to the high standard which he set for modern dramatists. At any rate, he and Eleanor remained staunch partisans of Ibsen, defending him in the great controversy on his merits which had then just begun.

*   *   *

The controversy had been provoked by a performance of *A Doll's House* in June 1889, and Miss Achurch, the weak

---

[1] Bernard Shaw to Charles Charrington, 28 Jan. 1890, Shaw, *Collected Letters 1874–1897*, 241.
[2] 'A Good Conscience', *Time*, Feb. 1890; 'A Ball-Mood', *Time*, May 1890.
[3] Ibid., July 1890.   [4] Ibid., Feb. 1891.

Hester, who now played Nora, was at one stroke placed in the front rank of rising actresses. The influential critics were now divided between the Ibsenites, led by Archer, who saw in their master an eloquent apologist for the emancipation of women and for true morality, and the anti-Ibsenites, led by Clement Scott of the *Daily Telegraph*, who found Ibsen's work inimical to decency and destructive of family life. The polemic even took the form of writing rival sequels to *A Doll's House*. Walter Besant, an Anti-Ibsenite, described the hopeless state of the family deserted by Nora, with her husband now addicted to drink, her son engaging in forgery, and her daughter committing suicide.[1] Bernard Shaw wrote a sequel in opposition to this 'representative middle class evangelical verdict on the play'.[2] Eleanor for her part, in collaboration with Israel Zangwill, the well-known Jewish novelist, wrote another sequel entitled ' "A Doll's House" Repaired', with the express purpose of complying with the demands of English common sense. In this Nora was represented as a repentant woman listening obediently to her husband's exhortations on ideal womanliness, and Helmer as a considerate husband who might have left her as an act of punishment but who chose to live with her like brother with sister in order to keep up appearances.[3] Shaw also gave a Fabian lecture on Ibsen which started a controversy over the 'Socialist' Ibsen.[4]

In January 1891 the first issue of *Playgoers' Review* was published. This was a new dramatic magazine edited by J. T. Grein, a young Dutch enthusiast for the drama. In it was an article by 'Alec Nelson' on 'The Ibsen Influence', which tried to show how his 'treatment of that great problem of speaking out the whole truth' had affected two English

[1] *English Illustrated Magazine*, Jan. 1890.
[2] Bernard Shaw to Charles Charrington, 28 Jan. 1890, Shaw, *Collected Letters*, 239; Shaw, 'Still After the Doll's House', *Time*, Feb. 1890.
[3] Israel Zangwill and Eleanor Marx Aveling, '*A Doll's House' Repaired*, reprinted from *Time*, March 1891.
[4] Shaw, *The Quintessence of Ibsenism* (1891).

dramatists of the first rank, H. A. Jones and Arthur Pinero. The Playgoers' Club, which had been in existence since 1884, now renewed its activities. At its meeting on 10 February Aveling gave a reading from *Ghosts*, and it was reported that he had been at his best in bringing out the hypocrisy of Parson Manders and the cynicism of Engstrand.[1] He opened the next meeting of the club with a paper on Ibsen's plays, and Eleanor, Shaw, Grein, Zangwill, and others took part in the discussion that followed at this and also at the following meeting. According to one report of these meetings, Aveling 'has Ibsen at his fingers' ends':

... it would be, we should say, impossible to find a more enthusiastic exponent . . . He defended Ibsen from the charge of being unsympathetic . . . from the charge of dwelling exclusively on the gloomy and morbid side of life . . . He remarked that Ibsen, in exposing the evils from which society suffers, was doing great good, inasmuch as he made us think and ask ourselves how far we are or are not responsible.[2]

Bernard Shaw described these meetings of the club as the sittings of 'an assemblage of barloafing front-row-of-the-pit-on-a-first-night dilettanti'. He attended on two nights when they discussed Aveling's paper. 'Mrs. Aveling and I, being of course seasoned socialist mob orators, were much in the position of a pair of terriers dropped into a pit of rats', Shaw exclaiming that 'Ibsen would be the end of Scott'.[3]

Aveling's reading of *Ghosts* was only a preliminary to the production of the play in March at the Royalty Theatre. The producer was Grein, who now founded an Independent Theatre Society after the fashion of the Théâtre Libre in Paris and the Freie Bühne in Berlin. The presentation of *Ghosts* (which came after the performance of *Rosmersholm* in February), and that of *Hedda Gabler* which followed in April, stirred up the passions of the controversialists, and the

[1] *Playgoers' Review*, 16 March 1891.
[2] Ibid.
[3] Bernard Shaw to Charles Charrington, 30 March 1891, Shaw, *Collected Letters*, 288.

hostility of the anti-Ibsenite newspapers was so menacing that the lessees of the Royalty Theatre insisted that the plays to be produced should be censored beforehand.[1]

On 4 May Aveling, who had almost lost his voice at an eight-hour day demonstration the previous afternoon, gave a lecture on Ibsen's *Lady from the Sea* at a meeting of the Playgoers' Club. Eleanor, who was also present, contributed a 'fervent defence' of the play.[2] In fact her translation of the play had come out in the previous year, and it was about to be performed under Aveling's direction at Terry's Theatre for a matinée on 11 May. The story, which had many points of similarity to that of 'Auld Robin Gray', was a familiar one, but it emphasized the freedom of choice with which a married woman finally overcame her dissatisfaction with the real. Eleanor apparently shared the heroine's conviction that 'a freely given promise is just as binding as a marriage', and she probably acquiesced in the distasteful reality, which was indeed the result of her own free choice. At any rate, 'this play, that promised more than any other if it were put upon the stage', according to a review, 'proved in representation the most disappointing of any of Ibsen's yet seen in England'.[3]

*   *   *

Eleanor's literary activities now began to show signs of flagging, but Edward still remained active in the theatrical world. On 16 July 1892 his new piece, *A Hundred Years Ago*, a pastoral operetta, was produced at the Royalty Theatre with music composed by Henry Wood, who was to inaugurate the Promenade Concerts a few years later. Wood had taken an interest in physiology and anatomy, and this may have drawn him into Aveling's acquaintance. The operetta was 'a pleasant little work reflecting credit on both

[1] C. Archer, *William Archer*, 174.
[2] *Playgoers' Review*, 15 May 1891.
[3] *Dramatic Notes* (1892), 103.

author and composer', read a review.[1] In the summer
Eleanor and Aveling spent a holiday in Norway, and from
Faleyde she wrote to her Italian friend: 'Your beautiful
Italy could scarcely be more beautiful.'[2] It was the influence
of Ibsen as much as the scenic beauty of the country that had
attracted her to the Norwegian coasts. Towards the end of
this year (1892) Eleanor read a paper on 'Immorality on
the Stage' at a meeting of the Playgoers' Club.[3] In October
in the following year Aveling's new comedy, *The Frog*, was
played at the Royalty Theatre, but it was a complete
failure, 'a result I fully expected', wrote Eleanor to her
sister, 'because it was *not* a good play. He knew that too,
but thought *that* might save it. He is out supping with some
theatrical friends.'[4] He made one more effort to gain recognition as a playwright with a new piece, *Judith Shakespeare*,
which was produced at the Royalty in February 1894, but
the dramatic Muse now definitely forsook the would-be
playwright.[5] It had been a long struggle, and his constant
labour had exhausted his modest creative powers.

In their dramatic efforts the Avelings had pursued one
theme—the clash between love and duty, freedom and convention. It was to be expected that Ibsen would become their
favourite master. The conflict that Ibsen described on the
stage also affected Eleanor in her private life. She was
inclined to believe that her love and her duty were not of
this world of conventions, and she found it difficult to
accept the excess of freedom with which Aveling, happy and
insensitive like a small child, went on satisfying his desires.
Her salvation appeared to lie only in her Socialist work.

[1] *Dramatic Notes* (1893), 107; Henry J. Wood, *My Life of Music* (1938),
43, 71.
[2] Eleanor Marx Aveling to Anna Kuliscioff (Mrs. Turati), 21 Aug.
1892, IISH.
[3] *Dramatic Notes* (1893), 172.
[4] Eleanor Marx Aveling to Laura Lafargue, 11 Nov. 1893, Bottigelli
Collection.
[5] *Judith Shakespeare* was also performed at Stratford-on-Avon during
Shakespeare's birth-week in 1895. *Justice*, 8 Feb. 1896.

Moreover, the development of the working-class movement had altered the scope of Socialist action. From its modest beginnings in the eighties it had grown into real attempts to form a mass organization, both national and international, with which the Avelings also could throw in their lot.

VIII ⌁ NEW INTERNATIONAL
AND NEW UNIONISM

B Y the end of the 1880's European Socialists, in spite of serious internal dissensions, had sufficiently consolidated their strength to feel competent to launch an international organization. Bismarck's Anti-Socialist law and his extensive plan for social insurance had failed to weaken the German Social Democrats, who emerged as the largest Socialist body in Europe with the impressive vote of three-quarters of a million at the Reichstag elections of 1887. The French Socialists, though numerically much weaker and divided among themselves, still enjoyed the prestige of their revolutionary tradition. The smaller parties, such as the Belgian, Dutch, Swiss, and Italian, also aspired to play an international role. At the same time the process of industrialization, which created the urban proletariat, had gone so far in most of the major European countries that international labour legislation became a subject to be considered even by Governments. Trade unionism had by now become a power, especially in England, where the movement to organize the unskilled workers was now beginning. The foundation of 'New Unions' gave a great impetus to the recruitment of workers to all existing unions as well. It was under these auspicious circumstances that the Avelings sought once more to assume a place of leadership in British Socialism and to form a mass labour party recruited from the new unions with the backing of a new International.

*   *   *

There were certain serious difficulties in the path of attempts to form a new International. The Marxists of Hyndman's S.D.F. were allied with the French Possibilists, the arch-enemies of the French Marxists. The rival Socialist factions in France, as we have already seen, were in competition in their efforts to take the initiative in founding a new International. In England the man who worked as the principal champion of the Possibilist cause was Adolph Smith Headingley, a writer in *Lancet*, who had engaged in ambulance work during the Franco-Prussian war and also in the Paris Commune and had since sided with those refugees of the Commune who resented the Marxist or German domination in the International.[1] It was he who persuaded British trade unions to send delegates to the Possibilist international conferences held in the eighties and acted as their interpreter. At the conference held in August 1886 it was decided to hold an International Workmen's Congress in 1889 with the Possibilists as its conveners. The T.U.C. for their part called for an International Trade Union Congress in London in November 1888. The British delegates at this congress, as might be expected, were definitely opposed to a resolution in favour of eight-hour legislation, but 'amid shouts of laughter from the foreign delegates' they actually voted for an Anarchist amendment which stated that the workers could only 'rely on their own strength' to achieve their emancipation. 'So anxious were the English to avoid Socialism', reported Headingley, 'that they fell into the arms of the dynamite party.'[2] At this congress the mandate given to the Possibilists for an international congress in 1889 was confirmed.

---

[1] Headingley together with certain French refugees had served on the executive of the Universal Republican League and also on the Universal Federalist Council of the International in the seventies. See *Justice*, 29 Dec. 1921; Engels to Maltman Barry, 15 Sept. 1872, B.M.Add.MSS. 46288; Bax, *Reminiscences and Reflections*, 53–55.

[2] Adolph Smith (Headingley), *A Critical Essay on the International Trade Union Congress* (1888), *passim*.

The London congress, however, had been boycotted by the German party, which had appealed to European Socialists to do the same because the T.U.C. had declined its demand for alterations in the organization of the congress to suit the special conditions in Germany. Hyndman and the S.D.F. were naturally irritated by these demands, which they regarded as 'dictatorial'. Moreover, when the *Sozial-demokrat*, the organ of the German party, was expelled from Switzerland and moved to London, the centre of the controversy about the proposed International also shifted to the British capital, where Engels, Eleanor, and Bernstein, the editor of the paper, now tried their best to secure a Marxist leadership at the forthcoming congress.

'To play off the French Possibilists against the English Marxists', Eleanor later recalled, 'was a very clever dodge on the part of that most artful dodger, Hyndman. That the whole (practically) of the French provinces were Marxist didn't count. To the Englishman Paris is still France, and Paris in the hands of the Possibilists meant to them a Possibilist France.'[1] Yet Hyndman, apart from his old grudge against the Marx family, had reason to support the Possibilists. They had formed an alliance with the Radicals in an attempt to prevent General Boulanger from seizing power, whereas some of the Blanquists, the allies of the Marxists, flirted with 'Boulangism' under the pretext of destroying opportunism, and Lafargue, in spite of repeated warnings from Engels, persisted in 'tender treatment' of the General, whom he regarded as 'the man of the people'.[2]

Engels, at this stage, supported a German attempt to overcome dissensions within the Socialist ranks. He even criticized a Marxist conference held at The Hague in February 1889 for inviting the Socialist League but not the

[1] Eleanor Marx Aveling to Laura Lafargue, 30 May 1892, Bottigelli Collection.
[2] Paul Lafargue to Engels, 24 April 1888; Engels to Laura Lafargue, 2 Jan. 1889, *Correspondance*, ii. 123, 197; Alexandre Zévaès, *Les Guesdistes* (Paris, 1911), 50.

S.D.F.[1] The Possibilists, however, went ahead and issued formal invitations, while Hyndman and the S.D.F. attacked the Hague conference as 'a sort of private caucus' which would repeat 'the wretched intrigues that broke up the old "International"'.[2] The point at issue now became clear. On Engels's suggestion, Bernstein published 'A Reply', stating the Marxist case and denouncing the Possibilists as 'Ministerial Socialists', and the *Sozialdemokrat* criticized *Justice* for its 'national' attitude towards an international congress.[3] Hyndman now hesitated and showed signs of seeking reconciliation, expressing hopes for a united congress. 'Hyndman had meantime practically caved in', wrote Eleanor to Laura, '& as after all, a single Congress is desirable we must do our best for that.' For this purpose she and Bernstein paid a visit to Hyndman early in April. 'Hyndman looked green when he saw me', she went on:

& knowing what an awful temper I had did [his] best to irritate me. But tho' I'm a bad temper I'm not a fool. I saw his game & would not play up to it. I remained quite polite & amiable, even when he began with the usual calumnies against us & Paul. I only remarked (I could n't for the life of me resist *that*) that if Lafargue was accused of all manner of sins to the party, he, Hyndman too was so accused, & that it all came to a question of personalities rather than facts. . . . Then came up the old sore of our *family*. You & I should feel proud. *We*'re supposed to be doing it all! About 20 times Hyndman informed Bernstein & me that I was a 'bitter partisan'. I am, & I'm not ashamed of it. However the upshot of it all is (you could trust me & Bernstein, Jews that we are, to drive a bargain) that Hyndman will, we think, do all he can to bring about some sort of 'conciliation'. . . . We have worked hard, but it all has to be done under the nose [*sic*]. If we, just now, come out too much, the cry of 'Marxist intrigue' would go up at once.[4]

[1] Engels to Paul Lafargue, 12 March 1889, *Correspondance*, ii. 219. The League, however, was unable to send delegates.

[2] *Justice*, 9, 16 March 1889.

[3] Bernstein, *The International Working Men's Congress of 1889: A Reply to 'Justice'*, 1889; *Sozialdemokrat*, 30 March 1889.

[4] Eleanor Marx Aveling to Laura Lafargue, 11 April 1889, Bottigelli Collection.

Hyndman put some pressure on the Possibilists to secure a compromise, but his French allies remained adamant in their refusal to accept the Hague conditions, which, if accepted, would allow the French Marxists a prominent place at the congress.

It was probably at this stage that Eleanor and Engels definitely gave up hopes of a single congress. However, Liebknecht, the sponsor of the Hague conference, in view of the growing demand for unity among the smaller parties, and especially among the Belgians, waited till the end of April before finally deciding to launch a rival congress. Engels blamed him for 'the loss of time' and appeared jealous of what he considered to be Liebknecht's ambition to figure as the centre of the international movement.[1] Eleanor too thought that 'our good friend Liebknecht' was 'responsible for the whole affair' caused by the delay, for the *Star*, the Radical newspaper edited by H. W. Massingham, from which she expected support, now sided with the Possibilists.

The *Star* published what Eleanor called 'a disgraceful Paris article' in its issue of 7 May. Massingham was then in 'gay Paris', reporting the opening ceremonies of the centenary exhibition of the French Revolution. He was met, Eleanor believed, by A. S. Headingley and was 'held captive', for he sent a glowing account of the 'practical Socialists at the Hôtel de Ville' in which he stated that their plan for a workers' exhibition had failed because of the Blanquists' association with the Boulangist movement. Thereupon Eleanor and Aveling, with 'Bax who is keeping fairly straight in this matter', went to the *Star* office to protest against this and also against a previous *Star* article on the congress, and at the same time Eleanor urged Laura to 'bombard' Massingham's paper with letters—'A la guerre comme à la guerre'.[2] But in spite of all her efforts the *Star*

[1] Engels to Laura Lafargue, 7 May 1889, *Correspondance*, ii. 246.

[2] Eleanor Marx Aveling to Laura Lafargue, 8 May 1889, Bottigelli Collection; Engels to Paul Lafargue, 11 May 1889, *Correspondance*, ii. 251; *Star*, 4, 7 May 1889.

was now lost, and among the known opponents of Hyndman she failed to find any reliable ally. As for Morris, she thought, 'his army is one that would have put even Falstaff to the blush. He himself blushes at it. Morris is personally liked, but you would not get a ½ dozen workmen to take him seriously'. And Champion was 'quite gone over to the Tories. He tried to get a small party of Socialists to back him. Edward very nearly walked into the spider's parlor. I kept away carefully.'[1]

In the meantime the Amalgamated Society of Engineers and several other individual unions decided to send delegates to the Possibilist congress, though the parliamentary committee of the T.U.C. refused to associate itself with international Socialism. In this field, too, Eleanor tried hard to win support for the Marxist congress and invited John Burns, one of the A.S.E. delegates, and his colleague in the same union, Tom Mann, to meet Bernstein at her house, where Burns, though 'a rather uncertain quantity', promised to co-operate with her side. Keir Hardie, secretary of the Ayrshire Miners Union, whom Eleanor had taken to see Engels at the time of the International Trade Union Congress the previous November, was getting constant counsels from Engels. 'Hardie, who is a splendid fellow, has helped us immensely in Scotland', she wrote to Laura: 'I hope he may get money to be at the Congress. He would interest you. Till recently he worked in the mines (now he gets £80 a year as sec. of his Union—not much for a man with a wife & four children!) & is quite self-educated.'[2] She deplored Liebknecht's 'blundering' of hesitation, which would deprive the Marxist congress of the support of other trade unionists whose sympathy, she believed, she had won. 'I've today sent off 500 copies of the last invitation, & some 100 letters & post cards, & am dead tired', she wrote in the same letter

---

[1] Eleanor Marx Aveling to Laura Lafargue, 11 April 1889, Bottigelli Collection.
[2] Ibid., 1 June 1889, Bottigelli Collection.

to Laura: '. . . I've to see half a dozen Trade Unionists tonight about the Congress . . . We've lectured at Radical Clubs steadily, & now I hope to turn our work to some account.'

    *   *   *

Engels had come to the view that the two rival congresses, 'the one of Socialists and the other chiefly of *aspirants* to Socialism', thus different in character, 'might sit side by side without any harm'. Now two International Socialist Congresses were to be opened on 14 July, the centenary of the storming of the Bastille, and naturally there was a widespread demand for the achievement of unity on this question. But Engels would have none of it and was extremely suspicious of Liebknecht's 'fusion mania'.[1]

About a week before the congress the Avelings arrived in Paris to assist in preliminary meetings, and Edward with notebook in hand attended most of these gatherings. He was working as a correspondent for the *Sun*, the newly founded Radical paper, and attended the Marxist congress as delegate of the East Finsbury Radical Club. The congress was opened at the Salle Petrelle, Rue Petrelle, and soon moved to the nearby Salle des Fantasies Parisiennes, Rue Rochechouart, as the original hall was found too small for its more than 400 delegates. 'The most ticklish' business, according to the *Sun* correspondent, was brought about by an attempt to unite 'the Socialist Congress' with 'the more reactionary Trades Union one', i.e. the Possibilist congress.[2]

Actually both the Belgian and the Italian delegates had been instructed by their parties to strive for the unity of the two congresses. Among the British delegates Morris was against *rapprochement*, for he was convinced that 'the Possibilists foster only election-opportunism and no Socialism'. Hardie was for the merger, as he believed that there were Socialist trade unionists at the Possibilist congress with

[1] Engels to Laura Lafargue, 28 June 1889, *Correspondance*, ii. 293.
[2] *Sun*, 21 July 1889.

whom one could easily come to an understanding. In the end a resolution proposed by Liebknecht was adopted. This rejected unconditional fusion but invited the other congress to declare for unity under conditions satisfactory to the Marxists. As the other congress still insisted on strict examination of the credentials of all the delegates, negotiations finally broke down.[1] According to Aveling, the union of the two congresses would have taken place 'but for Mrs. Besant', who as a delegate at the Possibilist congress demanded a scrutiny of the mandates of the Marxist delegates. It was already the fourth day of the congress, and eloquent reports from Bebel, Guesde, and other Socialist leaders now began and took three more days.

Meanwhile Eleanor, together with Morris and Cunninghame Graham among the English, served on a standing committee of the congress, and she was very busy as an interpreter from French and German into English. Her translation of a speech by Dr. Saverio Merlino in which the impetuous Italian Anarchist attacked both labour legislation and Marxism was criticized by his supporters for being incomplete.[2] When, however, she translated into French and English a speech by Clara Zetkin, the delegate of the women workers in Berlin, on the question of female labour, there was lively acclamation.[3]

It was only on the afternoon of the last day, 20 July, that the congress began tackling its real business. It passed a series of resolutions in favour of international eight-hour legislation and other measures for the protection of the workers, disarmament and 'general arming of the citizens', universal suffrage and the conquest of political power, and an international labour demonstration for 1 May. The significance of the congress, as has been pointed out, lay not so much in its practical achievements as in its symbolic

---

[1] *Protokoll des Internationalen Arbeiter-Congresses zu Paris* (1889), 11–23 24, 30; *Justice*, 3 Aug. 1889.
[2] *Protokoll*, 65.   [3] Ibid. 84.

value.[1] The Second International, which was to emerge
from the rivalry of the two Socialist congresses in Paris, and
also the annual May Day demonstration, virtually the only
tangible result of the Marxist congress, were to provide
occasions for displaying the potential strength of international labour, though not always its unity. The Avelings,
especially Eleanor, who had come into contact with trade
union elements in the course of preparations for the congress, now sought to avail themselves of this in their attempt
to return to the forefront of Socialist politics in England.

*   *   *

The Avelings left Paris on 29 July, too late to attend a
demonstration held in Hyde Park on the previous day to
celebrate the success of the Gasworkers in obtaining the
eight-hour day. The Gasworkers' Union had been started
in March on the initiative of Will Thorne, a stoker then
employed at the Beckton Gas Works and an active member
of the S.D.F., and it had won its demand for the eight-hour
day in London almost without a fight. With Socialist support, mainly from the S.D.F., the National Union of Gas
Workers and General Labourers of Great Britain and
Ireland, as it was officially called, developed into a fighting
union whose benefits were at first limited to strike pay and
legal assistance. It was probably on account of the Gasworkers' close association with the Hyndmanites at an early
stage that the Avelings appeared to keep aloof from their
struggle, and it was only after the S.D.F.'s hold on them
weakened, as a result of the spread of New Unionist activity,
that they began to play a decisive role in this union.

After the Gasworkers' success the next major event was
the great Dock Strike. This arose from a pay dispute in the
South Docks, Milwall, on 12 August. It was led by John
Burns and Tom Mann, 'our men' as Engels was quick to
point out, and there were indeed no Hyndmanites among its

[1] James Joll, *The Second International* (1955), 39.

leaders.[1] Eleanor soon found herself 'doing a drudgery of clerical work' at the headquarters of the strike committee at the Wade's Arms at Poplar. 'A most capable woman', as Tom Mann called her, who possessed 'a complete mastery of economics', she could tease him for his exploit of having 'heaved a struggling barmaid clean over the counter into the august parlour, where the strike leaders were having their drinks'.[2] The strike was well organized, and the open-air propaganda of the strikers—especially their processions round the City—attracted wide attention and considerable sympathy. 'It is the movement of the greatest promise we have had for years, and I am proud and glad to have lived to see it', wrote Engels at the time: 'If Marx had lived to witness this!' In this great strike he saw signs of 'the abdication of the middle class', which had in his view resigned its 'proper' function of attacking the medieval monopoly of the dock companies into the hands of the exploited dock labourers, 'the poorest of the poor'. This, thought Engels, was the reason for the extraordinary public sympathy shown for the dockers.[3] When the strike committee issued a manifesto calling for a general strike throughout London, he at once wrote to Eleanor asking her to oppose 'such a desperate game', as it would alienate the support of 'the great mass of the bourgeoisie who all hated the dock monopolists'.[4] It is not known whether Eleanor exerted any pressure on the committee, but the manifesto was immediately withdrawn. Shortly afterwards, early in September, when a demonstration was held in Hyde Park in support of the 'docker's tanner', Eleanor figured among the speakers. 'Curious to see Mrs. Aveling addressing the enormous crowds', wrote

[1] Engels to Laura Lafargue, 27 Aug. 1889, *Correspondance*, ii. 312.
[2] Dona Torr, *Tom Mann and His Times* (1956), 291; *Tom Mann's Memoirs* (1932), 92; Ben Tillett, *Memoirs and Reflections* (1931), 134.
[3] *Labour Elector*, 31 Aug. 1889. Engels, 'The Abolition of the Middle Class', *Labour Elector*, 12 Oct. 1889, originally published as 'Die Abdankung der Bourgeoisie' in *Sozialdemokrat*, 5 Oct. 1889.
[4] Engels to Laura Lafargue, 1 Sept. 1889, *Correspondance*, ii. 317.

Cunninghame Graham, himself a voluntary helper at the strike committee, 'curious to see the eyes of the women fixed upon her as she spoke of the miseries of the dockers' homes, pleasant to see her point the black-gloved finger at the oppressor, and pleasant to hear the hearty cheers with which her eloquent speech was greeted.'[1] By this time the Australian contribution, amounting to £30,000, had begun to pour in, and mediation by Cardinal Manning and the Lord Mayor soon brought the strike to a successful issue for the men.

*   *   *

Of the Socialists, it was Champion and his friends who supplied the leadership for the dockers' struggle. His *Labour Elector* had supported the Marxists in their struggle against the Possibilists, and Cunninghame Graham had attended the Marxist International Congress as the delegate of the Labour Electoral Association, a Championite body. The *Labour Leader*, the organ of the Scottish Labour Party, of which Keir Hardie was secretary, had been incorporated with Champion's paper, which was now adopted as the organ of the newly founded Dockers' Union. It is true that the *Labour Elector*, quite possibly financed by Tory funds, had been partisan in tone, and for this reason Eleanor, as we have seen, hesitated to associate with Champion.[2] But now a committee of management for the paper was set up with Burns, Mann, and Hardie among its members, and Champion assured Eleanor that the paper belonged to this committee and that he was no more than its editor and liable to dismissal. Eleanor, therefore, agreed to contribute translations from the Continental Socialist papers, and these were published in its columns under the heading 'Labour Movement Abroad' or 'Foreign Notes'. But Engels was still suspicious of Champion, who, he noted, had formed a

[1] *Labour Elector*, 7 Sept. 1889.
[2] Eleanor also protested against the critical comments on Irish Home Rule which were published in this paper. *Labour Elector*, 22 June 1889.

OEM

'Women's Trades Association' with the support of middle-class philanthropists and 'took good care to exclude' Eleanor.[1] Furthermore, the committee of management soon found it difficult to swallow the editor's obvious inclinations for the Tories, and so it broke up. The result was that Eleanor decided to put an early end to her co-operation with Champion.

In the meantime she was closely associated with John Burns, by now a member of the newly created London County Council. Burns had formed the Battersea Labour League, and Eleanor supported his candidature for Parliament. But her chief concern at the time was for the new labourers' union that had sprung up after the Dockers' Strike, and she had become 'quite an East Ender' herself.[2] She played a leading part in the strike of the workers employed at the India Rubber Works at Silvertown which took place in the autumn. Clara Zetkin, who visited London at the time, saw Eleanor mounting on tables and chairs to harangue the women strikers.[3] 'For ten mortal weeks', wrote Eleanor, 'I travelled daily to that end-of-the-world place; speaking every day—often twice a day, in all weathers in the open air.'[4] She founded and acted as secretary of a women's branch of the Gasworkers' Union at Silvertown, but she coud not prevent the Silvertown strike, a bitter and long-drawn-out struggle, from ending in a defeat for the workers.

By this time the Gasworkers were on the defensive, and at the South Metropolitan Gas Works non-unionists effectively replaced the 2,000 stokers who were out on strike in the winter. It was probably about this time that by dint of sheer hard work the Avelings secured a considerable influence over this union. Eleanor, who served on the strike committee at the South Metropolitan, noticed that 'the

[1] Engels to Laura Lafargue, 17 Oct. 1889, *Correspondance*, ii. 342; *Labour Elector*, 12 Oct. 1889.
[2] Engels to Laura Lafargue, 17 Oct. 1889, *Correspondance*, ii. 342.
[3] Laura Lafargue to Engels, 14 Nov. 1889, *Correspondance*, ii. 352.
[4] Eleanor Marx Aveling to Laura Lefargue, 25 Dec. 1889, photocopy, IISH.

public & the police are not so "enthusiastic" as they were for the Dockers', and she was glad that 'the Gasworkers are saved from "patronage" of the bourgeoisie'.[1] In March 1890 Aveling was sent to Ireland, where the Gasworkers had organized several branches, and attended a labour demonstration held in Phoenix Park, Dublin, under the auspices of the union.[2] In April Eleanor visited Northampton as a delegate from the union in order to assist the local branch in organizing the unskilled workers in the district. Bradlaugh, her personal foe, had declared himself against legislative intervention in determining the length of the working day, and she was glad to report that ' "Charlie" is by no means the popular idol he once was'.[3] She also gave assistance to Will Thorne, the general secretary of the union, who found the task of keeping accounts and preparing reports beyond his capacity, and she did much to improve his reading and writing, which were rudimentary.[4]

'Tussy leads the gasmen (under cover) and this union certainly seems to be by far the best', wrote Engels in April. The Dockers' Union, on the other hand, had, he thought, been 'spoilt by the assistance of the respectable citizen'. Indeed, the Gasworkers had gained the valuable assistance of the daughter of Karl Marx. Eleanor served on the council of their union as delegate from the Silvertown women, and she was so popular on the council that she was invariably called 'our mother'.[5]

*   *   *

[1] Eleanor Marx Aveling to Laura Lafargue, 25 Dec. 1889, photocopy, IISH.

[2] The demonstration was boycotted by Michael Davitt, who insisted that the principle of 'Home Rule' should be thoroughly recognized in all relations between British and Irish labour bodies. In a reply Aveling stressed 'complete autonomy' enjoyed by individual branches of his union. *People's Press*, 12 April 1890; Aveling in *Freeman's Journal*, 8 April 1890, quoted in *People's Press*, 19 April 1890.

[3] *People's Press*, 19 April 1890.

[4] Will Thorne, *My Life's Battle* (1925), 117.

[5] Engels to Sorge, 19 April, 30 April 1890, *Labour Monthly*, May 1934.

Meanwhile the unusually successful record of the Gas-workers, who had obtained an eight-hour day for 80,000 men in the East End alone by the end of the previous year, was now threatened by the employers' counter-offensive. Legislative intervention seemed desirable for preserving the gains. At a delegate meeting of the union held in January it was unanimously decided, on Eleanor's proposal, that in accordance with the resolutions adopted at the Paris con-gress a May Day demonstration should be held for a legal eight-hour day. For this purpose they got in touch with the Bloomsbury Socialist Society, which had been represented at the congress. At first Eleanor favoured holding the demon-stration on 1 May, the date originally proposed at Paris. There were practical difficulties in holding it on a working day, but these, she thought, could be overcome by adopting the expedient of the German party, which was to permit celebrations in the evening if necessary.[1] But at a meeting held early in April at the Workmen's Club, Vauxhall, pre-sided over by the Rev. William Morris, an Anglican clergy-man and a member of the Gasworkers' Union, it was decided that the demonstration should be on the first Sunday in May instead. A central committee with Aveling acting as chairman was appointed to make the necessary arrange-ments, and the support of smaller unions and Radical clubs was secured. A serious complication, however, arose as the Dockers' Union refused to co-operate with the committee. Tom Mann, the dockers' delegate on the London Trades Council, persuaded the latter body to hold a demonstration on the same day for a non-legal eight-hour day. This was upsetting to the Socialists, who wanted to commit the trade unions to winning the legal eight-hour day as a step on the road to Socialism. In addition, the Trades Council obtained permission to use Hyde Park for Sunday, 4 May, and allo-cated two of its seven platforms to the S.D.F., which had been denouncing the Paris resolution as a 'foolish' attempt

[1] *Sozialdemokrat*, 1 Feb. 1890; *Labour Elector*, 5 April 1890.

by the 'Marxist clique'. Thereupon Aveling went to the office of the Commissioners of Works and by threatening trouble in the park obtained a further seven platforms for the central committee. Now 'the tables were turned', as Engels wrote in a letter to Sorge, and after 4 May, he said, 'the movement here will take on quite a different aspect, and you will then hear more of Tussy publicly'.[1]

On Sunday two processions, the one 'legal' and the other 'non-legal', started from the Embankment and marched by different routes to Hyde Park, where there assembled a vast crowd of 250,000–300,000—of whom, according to Engels, three-quarters were actual demonstrators. At a platform presided over by a member of the Gasworkers' Union Eleanor spoke as a trade unionist and a Socialist, declaring that 'the unemployed both at the top and at the bottom of society would be got rid of'. At another platform, where Aveling was chairman, Lafargue spoke as a representative of the French workers, who had celebrated 1 May by a stoppage of work. Engels, who was present as an observer, wrote to Laura a few days later: 'I can assure you I looked a couple of inches taller when I got down from that old lumbering waggon that served as a platform—after having heard again, for the first time since 40 years, the unmistakable voice of the English Proletariat.' He thought that the Avelings, and especially Eleanor, who had 'done the whole thing', now acquired quite a different standing from the one they had held before, and 'the real socialistic mass movement has begun with 4 May'.[2]

In fact the 'legal' platforms far surpassed their rivals in the size of the crowds that gathered around and in the popularity

[1] Engels to Sorge, 30 April 1890, *Labour Monthly*, May 1934; Aveling, 'The Eight Hours' Working-Day', *Time*, June 1890; *People's Press*, 19 April 1890.

[2] Engels to Bebel, 9 May 1890, Bebel, *Briefwechsel mit Engels*, 390–1; Engels to Laura Lafargue, 10 May 1890, *Correspondance*, ii. 396; *People's Press*, 10 May 1890.

of the speakers who addressed them.[1] The success of the May Day demonstration enhanced Eleanor's reputation and influence among the New Unionists, and at the first annual conference of the Gasworkers held at the Workmen's Club in May shortly after the demonstration, she acted as secretary and was elected to the executive committee without opposition, 'on the ground that the feeling that she should be on the Executive was unanimous'.[2]

At this conference of the Gasworkers a new set of rules was adopted—mostly Eleanor's work, as she confessed in a letter to Kautsky: 'I am on the Executive of this Union and drew up their address, and the Rules for the most part.'[3] According to the new address the hope of the workers lay in trade unionism, which recognized the class struggle. The immediate object of the union, which was to admit all workers, women as well as men, on an equal footing, was to raise its members 'from mere beasts of burden to human beings' by improving their material conditions and by 'dividing more equally between all men and women the tears and laughter, the sorrow and the joy, the labour and the leisure of the world'.

It added that the interests of all workers were one and that 'victory or defeat of any portion of the Army of Labour is a gain or a loss to the whole of that Army, which by its organisation and union is marching steadily and irresistibly forward to its ultimate goal—the Emancipation of the Working Class'. The new rules included a clause for

[1] The speakers included such well-known figures as John Burns, Will Thorne, Cunninghame Graham, Michael Davitt, and Bernard Shaw. There were also representatives of the Shop Assistants' Union, for whom Eleanor had worked, advocating 'exclusive dealing' against those shops that had refused to give up 'scandalously long hours of labour'; and of the newly-founded General Railway Workers' Union, whose demand for a nine-hour day she supported, though she thought it a very modest aspiration for a union capable of paralysing the entire industry of the country. *People's Press*, 15 March, 17 May 1890.

[2] *People's Press*, 31 May 1890.

[3] Eleanor Marx Aveling to Karl Kautsky, 22 Sept. 1890, IISH.

equal pay for women and another for 'legislation for the bettering of the lives of the Working Class'.[1]

She was then involved in a new struggle of the Gasworkers at the Beckton Works, where the men went on strike, objecting to a reduction in wages for those working on a new machine and also to a proposed new agreement which involved forfeiture of arrears of pay on dismissal.[2] Her devoted work helped the men to win the strike. She was, indeed, very much in demand as a speaker and an organizer, and at Chatham in June she assisted women workers in various trades, especially tailoring, to form a branch of the Gasworkers.[3] She also organized those whom she called 'the unhappy human machine', namely typists, whose occupation she herself had recently taken up.[4]

Meanwhile the Gasworkers fought another battle, this time in Leeds, where the Gas Committee of the city corporation, with the aid of 'black-legs' introduced from outside, made an attempt to take back from the men their newly-won rights and concessions. Aveling was a witness of what he called a 'Homeric fight': it was fought, he said, in heavy rain between thirty Gasworkers led by Will Thorne on the one hand and some 200 police guarding blacklegs on the other in the small hours of a Tuesday morning early in July. According to him, the whole body of police was thrown into confusion by the unexpected assault, and refused to escort

[1] The new Address and Rules were later published as ordered by the second annual conference of the Gasworkers held in May 1891, *Revised Rules of the National Union of Gasworkers and General Labourers*, 1892. See also Eric Hobsbawm, *Labour's Turning Point* (1948), 100–1.

[2] Believing that the men's grievances had been misrepresented, Eleanor wrote a detailed account of the strike in the *People's Press*, 7 June 1890. They were not opposed to the introduction of machinery as such, she declared, but to the sweating system designed with it.

[3] *People's Press*, 28 June, 5 July 1890.

[4] Ibid., 5 July 1890. 'I'm going in for a new business—type-writing', she wrote about a year before: 'I'm buying a machine, & as soon as I've learnt the work—which is very easy, I shall set up, & issue a prospectus!' Eleanor Marx Aveling to Laura Lafargue, 10 April 1889, Bottigelli Collection.

any more blacklegs after this. The Leeds corporation had to accept the demands of the men. 'Our soldiers and our police should remember, like Nora', wrote Aveling, 'that they are human beings first and officials afterwards.'[1] Engels, with his interest in strategy, was very much fascinated by the story of the street battle, 'this mode of *lawful* resistance' as he put it, and gave Thorne a copy of *Capital* as testimony of his admiration.[2]

* * *

With the prestige of having been the real sponsors of the May Day demonstration, and with their growing influence among the new unions, especially the Gasworkers, the Avelings now started a campaign to set up a new independent working-class party. Already in May it was decided on the initiative of the Bloomsbury Socialist Society to reconstruct the central committee which organized the demonstration in order to form a permanent body. Among its new members was Friedrich Lessner, the old veteran of the German revolution of 1848, who had been active in the Socialist League. He represented the German Communist Workers' Educational Club of Tottenham Street, with which the Bloomsbury Society had been closely associated.[3] Engels gave his blessing to the new committee, which he regarded as 'a representative body which will serve as the nucleus for the movement, en dehors de toute secte'.[4] The Bloomsbury Socialist Society now for the first time proclaimed its existence publicly by issuing a manifesto giving a brief history of its work, which was mostly educational.[5]

There was, however, a good deal of obstruction from

---

[1] *People's Press*, 12 July 1890.

[2] Engels to Laura Lafargue, 30 July 1890, *Correspondance*, ii. 401; Thorne, op. cit. 128–32.

[3] *People's Press*, 17 May 1890.

[4] Engels to Laura Lafargue, 10 May 1890, *Correspondance*, ii. 396.

[5] *Manifesto of the Bloomsbury Socialist Society*, May 1890, also published in the *People's Press*, 31 May 1890.

Aveling's adversaries. Ferdinand Gilles, a German journalist who was a member of the Communist Club and also of the S.D.F., and who had been at loggerheads with those controlling the official organ of the German party, helped to found an International Labour League and Federation in East London, and invited Aveling's new body to amalgamate with it. Gilles was a man of sanguine nature, chatty and light-hearted. It is almost certain that he was in liaison with Hyndman, who was obviously determined to do something to frustrate Aveling's new party. Gilles's proposal was naturally rejected, but he managed to dissuade the Communist Club from joining the new party by means of his first 'unmasking' of Aveling, whom he called 'the mysterious gentleman and the party's sacred man'. Aveling denounced Gilles as 'a spy', and his quarrel with Gilles, as we shall see, was to handicap his later activities as a Socialist leader.[1]

Meanwhile Aveling's organization was launched in July under the title of the Legal Eight Hours and International Labour League. It had the support of the Gasworkers, the General Railway Workers, and other smaller unions, and also of the Metropolitan Liberal and Radical Federation and the Scottish Labour Party. Its aims were 'to educate, agitate and organise' for a legal eight-hour day and other resolutions of the Paris congress, and for the formation of 'a distinct Labour Party'. It promised to bring forward labour candidates for parliamentary and other elections wherever desirable and possible. A provisional executive committee, including the Avelings, was set up. The *People's Press*, a weekly paper that had been started as the organ of the Gasworkers and several other new unions, was adopted as the League's organ.[2]

In September the Avelings went to Liverpool for the

[1] Ferdinand Gilles, '*Sozialdemokratische*' *Ketzerrichterei*, 1892; *Justice*, 26 Sept. 1891; *People's Press*, 7 June, 28 June 1890; *Sozialdemokrat*, 28 June, 19 July 1890. For Gilles, see also a brief account of his life by 'Social-Democrat' in *Workman's Times*, 4 Feb. 1893.

[2] *People's Press*, 19 July 1890.

annual meeting of the Trades Union Congress. 'The great struggle will be upon the 8-hour question, but the whole of the Congress will, practically, resolve itself into a struggle between the "Old" & "New" Unionists', Eleanor wrote to Kautsky from the congress hall.[1] She had been elected to attend the congress as one of the Gasworkers' delegates, but was refused admittance on the ground that she was not a working woman. Yet Lady Dilke and Miss Clementina Black, an old friend of Eleanor's, both active in the women's trade union movement, were allowed to take seats. Eleanor protested that she was in fact a worker herself—'I work a type-writer'. She added: 'Miss Black, who has never done a day's manual labour, is admitted. I am boycotted!'[2] Cunninghame Graham soon found her, 'thoughtful and short-sighted', sitting at the reporters' table along with Maltman Barry and Adolph Smith Headingley.[3] A resolution in favour of the legal eight-hour day was carried by 193 votes to 155, and Eleanor hailed this as 'an immense success for the New Unionism'. 'The immense political power' of the working class, she declared, 'must be used henceforth . . . to form a labour party opposed to . . . all the old political parties.'[4] This was the tenet of their whole campaign. Both Eleanor and Aveling had a busy time at Liverpool. They wrote letters to local newspapers advocating the cause of their own League and also found time to watch a performance by Beerbohm Tree at a local theatre, where they were able to study the reactions of a provincial audience.[5]

The Avelings' International Labour League was apparently intended as a link between the new unions and the newly created Marxist International. They were hoping to organize the political aspirations of the New Unionists into

[1] Eleanor Marx Aveling to Karl Kautsky, 1 Sept. 1890, IISH.
[2] *People's Press*, 6 Sept. 1890.   [3] Ibid., 13 Sept. 1890.
[4] *Time*, Oct. 1890.
[5] *Liverpool Daily Post*, 5 Sept.1890; *People's Press*, 20 Sept. 1890; *Time*, Oct. 1890.

an independent party that could represent British Socialism
in the International.

*   *   *

Meanwhile, a new situation had emerged in Germany
with the downfall of Bismarck. The rejection by the Reichstag of his attempt to renew the Anti-Socialist law, which
was soon to expire, was followed by remarkable successes of
the Social Democrats at the General Election of February
1890. Engels had laid in a huge cask of German beer for his
friends, who gathered with him as the election results came
in. According to Aveling, it was quite a party: as telegrams
began pouring in from all parts of Germany, 'if it was victory
we drank, and if it was defeat we drank'. But there was an
impressive proportion of victory. 'We are in a constant
intoxication of triumph', wrote Engels, and the triumph was
as real as the intoxication, for the party had won 1,300,000
votes at the first round of elections.[1] In September, when
the *Sozialdemokrat* wound up its heroic career of twelve years'
illegal life in defiance of the Imperial Government, Aveling
interviewed its editor for the *Star*, giving an account of how
the paper had been smuggled across the frontier. He also
published an extract from its last number in which Engels
declared that the German party would now fight 'with the
legal means which, by our strong use of illegal methods, we
have reconquered'.[2]

In spite of the successes in Germany, however, Engels felt
uneasy about the future prospects of the International. The
Belgian party, which had been given a mandate by the
Possibilists to convene the second International Congress at
Brussels in 1891, had issued its invitations, and the Liverpool
T.U.C. had answered favourably. The Marxists, on the
other hand, had entrusted a Swiss commission with the

[1] Aveling in *Labour Prophet*, Oct. 1895; Engels to Laura Lafargue, 26
Feb. 1890, *Correspondance*, ii. 382.

[2] *Star*, 29 Sept. 1890; *Daily Chronicle*, 25 Sept. 1890; *Sozialdemokrat*,
27 Sept. 1890.

responsibility of deciding whether to hold their next congress in Switzerland or in Belgium, but the commission, apart from publishing one or two issues of an international journal, the *Eight Hours Working Day*, had done little. Engels, upon receiving news from Eleanor and Aveling that English trade unionists would go to the Brussels congress 'with the enthusiasm of neophytes', now persuaded the French and German leaders to favour Brussels and to try to achieve a fusion on conditions of complete equality.[1] It was obviously for the purpose of ensuring foreign support for Brussels by explaining the situation in England that Eleanor left London early in October to attend the party congresses of the French and the German Socialists as a fraternal delegate from the Legal Eight Hours and International Labour League.

At the Lille congress of the Parti Ouvrier, held on 11–12 October, Eleanor was much impressed by the unusual sight of sixty-four Frenchmen sitting quietly and voting almost unanimously on many questions such as the decision to go to Brussels and the recommendation to transfer municipal funds that had been used for the 'bourgeois' fête of 14 July to the workers' demonstration of 1 May. She took part in a debate on the general strike—'Happily the "Revolution" was not declared', she wrote to Engels. 'But think of my horror, General', she went on, 'when huge placards on the Lille walls calling a meeting with a large white slip pasted across stared me in the face with the following announcement "Sous la presidence de Eleanor Marx Aveling"!' This meeting, however, was a success; she was 'very sure of herself', and Aveling, who also addressed the packed audience, made a good impression, though his report of the congress published in the *Daily Chronicle* was criticized by Lafargue for the lack of 'liberté d'esprit'.[2]

[1] Engels to Paul Lafargue, 15, 25 Sept. 1890, *Correspondance*, ii. 410–11, 418.

[2] Eleanor Marx Aveling to Engels, 14 Oct. 1890, photocopy, IISH; Aveling in *Daily Chronicle*, 14 Oct. 1890; Paul Lafargue to Engels, 16 Oct. 1890, *Correspondance*, ii. 427–9; Claude Willard, *Les Guesdistes*, 115.

While Aveling remained there a few more days to attend the Calais congress of those French trade unionists who were allied with the Marxists, Eleanor set out with Guesde and two other Frenchmen on a journey to Halle, where the German party was meeting to deliberate on its party programme. 'The great quarrel that was supposed to be raging between the "old" leaders and the "new" men never came off', wrote Eleanor in a report to the *People's Press*. Discontent among the young members of the party had attracted considerable attention, as they had bitterly criticized the 'old' leaders for their 'opportunism', which was said to have been particularly evident in their opposition to a stoppage of work on May Day. A certain Wilhelm Werner, their spokesman, however, made a poor showing at the congress, and the overwhelming majority rallied round the 'old' leaders. Yet the party was 'making a mistake', she informed Engels, 'in not sufficiently realizing the danger of Vollmar . . . a very clever intriguer'. Indeed, George von Vollmar, the Bavarian Socialist, who had been a member of the Reichstag since 1881, was already advocating coalition with other parties in securing protective measures for the workers, and was soon to represent the growing tendency towards reformism within the German party. '*Entre nous*', she wrote to Engels, 'I can't deny that the Germans are too much like the majority of the Liverpoolers—i.e. painfully respectable & middle-class looking. There *must* be a strong sprinkling of philistines among them'. As to Bebel, she thought that the party owed much of its success to his 'really incredible work', but she hardly saw him at Halle because he was busy all day. Liebknecht was the *rapporteur* of the new party programme, and 'talked an awful lot of nonsense'. 'All of these men', she complained, 'are worried about their own home affairs, and are hardly in the humour to realize the importance of external questions.' But an international meeting was held at which all the foreign visitors to the congress were present, and it recommended that the Swiss commission should invite the Belgian party to summon the second International Congress on the Marxist terms of complete equality. The Belgians had no objection, and the Swiss commission acted accordingly.[1]

This paved the way for the establishment of a Marxist leadership in the International, and some of the new union leaders in Britain were invited to co-operate with it. In November Bebel and Liebknecht came to London to celebrate Engels's seventieth birthday, and they met Burns and Thorne at Eleanor's home. Thorne took Aveling and Lafargue, who was on holiday in London at the time, to the East End on Christmas Eve to show them the poverty of the slums and 'the mysteries of Chinatown'. Personal contact between British New Unionism and Continental Marxism was thus effected through the mediation of Engels and the Avelings, who were still working hard to expand their Legal Eight Hour and International Labour League.

* * *

But these signs of their ascendancy in the British movement were not overlooked by Hyndman, who was on the watch for every opportunity to foil their ambitions. In January 1891 the Northampton branches of the Gasworkers and of the S.D.F. invited Aveling to stand as a labour candidate at a by-election which had been occasioned by the death of Charles Bradlaugh, one of the sitting members for the town. Early in the following month the Avelings visited Northampton and started to campaign, but when they discovered that the money advanced for the Returning Officer's fees had come from a Tory agent, Aveling withdrew his candidature.[2] Hyndman was apparently shocked by the

[1] Eleanor Marx Aveling to Engels, 14, 16 Oct. 1890, photocopy, IISH. For the German translation of these two letters, see Heinrich Gemkow, 'Zwei Briefe Eleanor Marx-Avelings an Friedrich Engels über den Pareitag der deutschen Sozialdemokratie zu Halle 1890', *Zeitschrift für Geschichtswissenschaft*, xii (1965), Heft 7, 1194–205. See also *People's Press*, 1 Nov. 1890.

[2] *People's Press*, 14 Feb. 1891.

'insubordination' of one of the S.D.F. branches, and *Justice* denounced Aveling as a man totally unfit to serve as a Socialist representative.[1] There were many Gasworkers within the S.D.F., and for them, thought Engels, 'to touch Aveling and Tussy meant war'.[2] Both sides, however, wanted a war. Aveling sent a reply to *Justice*, stating that he had earned his living 'as a general labourer, teacher, and journalist', and had 'never made or lost one farthing by Stock Exchange speculations', a reference to Hyndman's own financial activities. Hyndman now posed a series of questions to Aveling to which he demanded an answer before being prepared to accept him as a Socialist candidate:

1. Why was he forced to leave the National Secular Society?
2. What were the proceedings in regard to his classes in Newman Street, Oxford Street, which occasioned so much talk?
3. What sort of bills did he run up for Mrs. Eleanor Marx Aveling and himself when the Socialist workers of the United States (all poor men) paid the expenses of his tour? . . .
4. What did he do in relation to the money collected to send a cable despatch . . . to the Governor of Illinois, when the fate of the Chicago Anarchists were trembling in the balance?
5. What was his action in regard to a certain family whose children he undertook to educate?[3]

As we have already seen, there was some substance in each of these charges, though it is not clear what was implied by the last one. In his attack Hyndman did not spare Engels, his chief adversary, whom he called 'the head of the Marxist clique' and 'a disruptive personality', pointing to the fact that Marx's old criticisms of the Gotha Programme and the Lassalleans had been published by Engels in an attempt to influence the new party programme then under discussion in Germany.[4]

Aveling retaliated by virtually excluding the S.D.F. from

---

[1] *Justice*, 14 Feb. 1891.
[2] Engels to Paul Lafargue, 10 Feb. 1891, *Correspondance*, ii. 18–19.
[3] *Justice*, 21 Feb. 1891.
[4] *Justice*, 21, 28 Feb. 1891.

the second May Day demonstration. The London Trades
Council, with an accession of New Unionists to its ranks,
had come round to the 'legalist' view on the question of an
eight-hour day, and had agreed to set up a joint demonstration committee with Aveling's organization. On Sunday
3 May, when the demonstration took place in Hyde Park,
the S.D.F. had to hold its own meeting 100 yards away from
the main body of the demonstration, with Hyndman as a
main speaker railing at 'the calculated moderation of an
Eight Hours Legalist'.[1]

In May the Avelings went to Ireland to attend the second
annual conference of the Gasworkers, which was held in
Dublin. ' "We fight the employers!" was the general cry',
wrote Eleanor in *Le Socialiste*, the new organ of the French
party, 'and Orangists and Nationalists united in applauding
these sentiments'.[2] She was elected together with Thorne to
represent the union at the Brussels congress of the International, scheduled for August. *Justice*, however, published
satirical comments on the Gasworkers' conference, and
especially on 'Brother Aveling', its chairman. It referred to
Eleanor as 'Miss Marx'—an appellation that revealed,
according to the indignant Engels, 'the degree of lowness'
Hyndman had come to.[3]

*   *   *

As the Brussels congress approached, the problem of a
challenge from the Possibilists again worried Engels and
Eleanor, although the French Possibilists had split and the
dissident elements led by Jean Allemane took a more independent line of Socialist policy than the followers of Brousse.
Engels suspected that the Belgian leaders, who were Possibilists 'in their inmost hearts', were paying court to the

[1] Engels to Laura Lafargue, 4 May 1891, *Correspondance*, iii. 44;
Justice, 9 May 1891.
[2] *Socialiste*, 3 June 1891.
[3] *Justice*, 4, 11 July 1891; Engels to Laura Lafargue, 12 July 1891,
Correspondance, iii. 79.

Marxists in their ambition to become the General Council
of a new International.[1] 'The Possibilists—our London ones,
at any rate—mean to kick up a row, if they possibly can',
wrote Eleanor to her sister.[2] She was then preparing a joint
report to be presented to the congress by the Gasworkers, the
Legal Eight Hours and International Labour League, the
Bloomsbury Socialist Society, and the Battersea Labour
League. She sent a copy to Laura, asking her not to be too
censorious, for, she said, 'I had to write it while I was
terribly worried, & not very well, & constantly interrupted.
It had to be so long because we have not *one* Party here to
report for—but a dozen.'[3] In her report she emphasized that
the Socialist bodies in England were 'sects rather than a
party', but Socialism had impressed itself upon the workers,
as could easily be seen from the 'Address' attached to the
rules of the Gasworkers (which was her own work). This
union, she declared, could now boast of 25,000 members in
Ireland alone, and that both in north and south. She was
critical of the Dockers' Union, which, she said, 'has hindered
instead of helped in bringing about the federation of all
unskilled Unions'. She commended the work of John Burns
on the London County Council, which together with other
local administrative bodies would form 'the centre of future
communes'.[4] John Burns was then still on friendly terms
with the Avelings, and his 'right-hand man', William
Sanders, later secretary of the Fabian Society, who had on
several occasions taken part in Aveling's play, *By the Sea*,
attended the Brussels congress as a delegate from the Legal
Eight Hours League.[5]

[1] Engels to Sorge, 9 Aug. 1891, *Labour Monthly*, June 1934.
[2] Eleanor Marx Aveling to Laura Lafargue, 6 July 1891, Bottigelli
Collection.
[3] Ibid., 6 Aug. 1891, Bottigelli Collection.
[4] *Report from Great Britain and Ireland to the Delegates of the Brussels
International Congress, 1891* (London, 1891).
[5] Bernstein, *My Years of Exile*, 165; William Sanders, *Early Socialist
Days* (1927), 91.

PEM

HUNT LIBRARY
CARNEGIE-MELLON UNIVERSITY

Neither Hyndman nor Brousse attended the second congress of the Second International, which was held at the Maison du Peuple, Brussels, on 16–23 August. Frau Liebknecht, who accompanied her husband, found Eleanor 'unrivalled as a translator' and described Aveling as 'a typical Englishman'.[1] The Anarchists were formally excluded from the congress, but the door was held wide open for the trade unions. An important topic debated at Brussels was that of the Socialist attitude towards war. Domela Nieuwenhuis, in the name of the Dutch delegation, proposed a general strike in the event of war, and was supported by the French and also by many of the British delegates, Ferdinand Gilles, Aveling's personal enemy, now acting as their spokesman.[2]

The presence of Gilles was ominous enough. He had made an attempt only a few months before to wreck a meeting of the German Communist Club addressed by the Avelings by asking Edward to answer the notorious five questions put by Hyndman. Now at Brussels he circulated a German translation of the same questions among the German delegates. A correspondent of the *Kölnische Zeitung* apparently took a hint from this *exposé*, and, while commenting on Eleanor's report to the congress, stated that 'her downright trade union opponents in England often call her "Miss Marx" intentionally because she merely entered a free-love union with Dr. Aveling who deserted his wife and three children'.[3] Aveling was very annoyed by this and other similar articles, and after the congress he wrote to several German papers to say that he was 'on the track of' the man who was responsible. On 8 September he visited Gilles at his North London home and 'gave him three or four blows in the face'. His

[1] Natalie Liebknecht to Engels, 26 Nov. 1891, Liebknecht, *Briefwechsel*, 383.

[2] Brussels International Socialist Congress, *Rapport* (Brussels, 1893), 62–77.

[3] *Kölnische Zeitung*, 18 Sept. 1891; see also Werner Blumenberg's note in Bebel, *Briefwechsel mit Engels*, 429–30.

impetuous act cost him dear, for he was summoned to appear at the North London Police Court, and further publicity was given to Hyndman's five questions in the course of the hearing of the case. He was fined 40s. with 23s. costs.[1] Gilles, for his part, started issuing fly-sheets denouncing Aveling as a 'mean swindler'. 'At present Gilles is said to be preparing a pamphlet', wrote Eleanor to Laura. 'Let him! The only difficulty here is that one never knows where one may be landed in a libel case, & every word of what we say would be, in a sense, libellous. And you know what that means here in the way of money. . . . As Bebel writes 20/- per "Ohrfeige [box on the ear]" is temptingly cheap.'[2] Gilles continued to serve Hyndman by attacking the German party for its 'narrow-minded reform policy' and especially for its expulsion of a 'revolutionary opposition' at the Erfurt congress in the autumn. He founded a co-operative bakery, which soon went bankrupt, he suffered a mental breakdown, and died a few years later.

*   *   *

The Avelings' attempt to organize the New Unionists into a mass party had already met serious obstacles. The early defection of the Dockers clearly showed that the new unions had their own sectional interests to serve. Among the thirty-three British delegates at Brussels, many of them trade unionists, only six were said to have belonged to the 'faction' led by Aveling.[3] It is true that Eleanor's popularity among the Gasworkers was genuine and well-merited, but her association with Aveling was always a drawback, for it constantly invited his opponents to resort to personal abuse.

[1] *Daily Chronicle*, 18 Sept. 1891; *Justice*, 12, 26 Sept. 1891; *Workman's Times*, 25 Sept. 1891; *Socialiste*, 3 Oct. 1891. When Aveling challenged Hyndman to debate with him on his personal conduct, the latter replied that 'the courts are . . . open to him'. *Workman's Times*, 9, 23 Oct. 1891.

[2] Eleanor Marx Aveling to Laura Lafargue, 25 Sept. 1891, Bottigelli Collection.

[3] Gilles, op. cit.

The Legal Eight Hours and International Labour League remained a small body almost unnoticed except at the time of a May Day demonstration. Engels often vilified the S.D.F. as a sect which turned Marxism into a fixed dogma, but Aveling's organization failed even more dismally to develop from the state of a sect into a party. But the Avelings were afforded one more opportunity to assume a place of importance in the British labour movement, and this was provided by the national movement to launch an independent labour party.

IX ❧ INTERNATIONAL AND INDEPENDENT LABOUR

T HE movement for an independent labour party was preceded by the employers' counter-attack on trade unions, which
became further intensified with the return of trade depression. The Avelings now sought to inspire some of the unions
with the spirit of international solidarity and to direct them
towards the acceptance of independent political action.
Already at the Brussels congress of the International,
Aveling, himself a delegate from the Gasworkers, recommended the creation of an international secretariat for trade
unions in each country, 'the thing already done in England'.[1]
In fact he and his wife had formed such a 'secretariat' by
themselves for the Gasworkers and had made attempts to
establish contacts between English and Continental trade
unions. Thus Eleanor was able to state in her report to the
congress that financial assistance had lately been sent by the
Nottingham lace workers to their co-workers at Calais, by
the English glass blowers to the French at Lyons, and by
Austrian to English brickmakers.[2] Their work in this field
was evidently not limited to the new unions, for the craft
unions had also become imbued with the new spirit.

The glass workers were particularly active in the international field. They set up an international organization in

[1] Brussels International Socialist Congress, *Rapport*, 53.
[2] Gasworkers *et al.*, *Report . . . to the Delegates of the Brussels International
Congress* (1891), 16.

1889, and during the bitter and prolonged strike of the Lyons flint glass workers in 1891 contributed more than £300 to the strike fund through Eleanor as intermediary.[1] In July 1892 the International Glass Workers' Union held its fourth congress in London; Eleanor served as secretary and translator and Aveling as the sole press reporter.[2] It was disclosed at this congress that a 'Masters' Association', consisting not only of the British glass makers but also of those from the Continent, had been formed, and a German delegate asserted that though the British trade unions were better organized than those in Germany, their political organization as an independent labour party was 'in its infancy'.[3] Indeed, the British masters soon launched an offensive against the union. The glass workers' lock-out which took place early in 1893 involving 5,000 men has been called 'the most important dispute among the minor crafts'.[4] The men resisted the employers' demand for a reduction in wages and the abolition of their restrictions on apprentices. The struggle spread from Yorkshire to Lancashire and continued for sixteen weeks. Shortly after its outbreak Eleanor sent her sister Laura an appeal from A. Greenwood, secretary of the Yorkshire Glass Bottle Makers, to be inserted in the French papers and also to be forwarded to a certain Clausse, the leader of the Lyons glass workers. 'The English [original]', she wrote:

must go to him as Clausse & Greenwood both are sticklers for etiquette & insist on having all the originals along with the translation . . . Don't be alarmed at the length of Greenwood's epistle, I get such to translate constantly. . . . Anyway I count on your help.—This fight means a life & death struggle here of

[1] *Workman's Times*, 2 Jan. 1892.

[2] Eleanor seems to have been paid for her work as a translator at international trade union congresses, though her demands, according to Bebel, were 'very moderate'. Bebel to Engels, 10 July 1894, Bebel, *Briefwechsel mit Engels*, 771.

[3] *Workman's Times*, 23 July 1892.

[4] H. A. Clegg *et al.*, *A History of British Trade Unions Since 1889*, i. (1964), 170.

the whole Glass Working industry. It is bound to last for months. What the end will be the Lord knows—& as Edward always says the Lord is *so* incommunicative.[1]

When the masters finally capitulated late in April, Aveling declared that the victory would have been unthinkable if the International Union had not stood up for their English members. In fact, contributions from glassworkers in France, Denmark, and Germany amounting to hundreds of pounds had flowed into the strike fund.[2]

Meanwhile another and considerably larger craft union, the Amalgamated Society of Engineers, had also been affected by a spirit of militancy, which arose in large part from the effect of technological innovation and heavy unemployment. The union was involved both in strikes against the introduction of machines and in a number of demarcation disputes with other unions. Eleanor wrote the 'inside story' of one of these strikes, which took place in the northeast in the spring of 1892, and published it in a German magazine, *Sozialpolitische Centralblatt*. The engineers' dispute with the plumbers on Tyneside was said to have been motivated by the 'true spirit of a mediaeval guild', but, she declared, it was in fact a genuine struggle against the employers, because the engineers did not wish to allow the plumbers—their rivals—to take their place and work for lower wages and overtime.[3] 'I know the facts from a delegate of the Tyneside engineers to the Executive of my Union [Gasworkers]', she wrote to Laura: '. . . You see our "unskilled" men being employed as "labourers" in every trade, we get to hear all the facts about *all* the "skilled" trades.'[4]

In May 1892 Eleanor made a flying visit to Cumnock on

[1] Eleanor Marx Aveling to Laura Lafargue, 7 Jan. 1893, Bottigelli Collection.

[2] *New Yorker Volkszeitung*, 21 May 1893.

[3] Eleanor Marx Aveling, 'Die letzten englischen Strikes', *Sozialpolitisches Centralblatt*, no. 20 (1892), 251–2.

[4] Eleanor Marx Aveling to Laura Lafargue, 30 May 1893, Bottigelli Collection.

behalf of the German party in order to see the German
miners working in the Ayrshire mines. They had become the
focus of ill-feeling among the Scottish miners. On her return
Engels informed August Siegel, the leader of the German
miners in Westphalia, that the matter had been set right as
a result of Eleanor's mission. He warned him, however, that
the Germans must come to terms with the Scotsmen and also
'with us' before accepting anything from the mine owners.
'The Germans are reputed here to be the greatest under-
cutters of wages and strikebreakers, and not entirely without
justice', he went on:

and Messrs. Burt, Fenwick, etc. wanted to provide you absolutely
with no work here for that reason. If, therefore, the Germans in
Muirkirk [near Cumnock] now gave the smallest pretext to
corroborate this old prejudice against the Germans, it would be
of the highest danger to the international relation between
Germany and England in general and indeed to the workers of all
trades, not only to the miners.[1]

Eleanor, for her part, noticed with regret that the 'darg'
system in the Scottish mines, a method of limiting output to
protect the slower workers, was being superseded by the
modern competitive method of the devil taking the hindmost.[2]
    The miners had also established an International, which
held its third congress in London in July 1892, and Eleanor
attended this congress and worked in a secretarial capacity
and as an interpreter. The question of eight-hour legislation,
which had divided the British miners, was brought up, and
the foremost opponents of this action, the Durham and
Northumberland miners led by Thomas Burt and Charles
Fenwick, both Liberal M.P.s, found themselves isolated.
Eleanor, in a report published in the *Arbeiter-Zeitung* of
Vienna, remarked that the privileged position enjoyed by
the Tyneside miners who worked only six hours and a half
had been secured at the expense of the children, who were

[1] Engels to August Siegel, 28 May 1892, photocopy, IML (Berlin).
[2] *Arbeiter-Zeitung*, 22 July 1892.

obliged to work ten to eleven long hours. Another question discussed at the congress was that of an international general strike to secure the eight-hour day. This was supported by the newly-founded Miners' Federation of Great Britain, which shared some of the militancy of the New Unionists. But the congress passed a moderate resolution in which all the miners were urged to strengthen their organizations and to prepare themselves for all possible situations.[1] The Miners' Federation fought a desperate struggle against a lock-out in the following year, which, however, ended in their accepting a board of conciliation.

The new unions, too, suffered under the employers' offensive. At a fierce struggle at Hull in 1893 when the Shipping Federation, an association of the shipowners, made full use of its 'free labour' registry, the Dockers and the Seamen received a crushing defeat. 'The cause of New Unionism has been badly injured by the fight at Hull and its result', wrote Aveling. He blamed the Dockers for having taken 'an unwise step' by closing their books. 'As Engels said at the time, they have raised their own blacklegs in this way, and I am of the opinion that many of these black sheep have appeared on the wrong side in the strike.'[2]

Even the Gasworkers, whom the Avelings had inspired with Socialist ideas, had been forced to reconsider their earlier militant tactics, and had begun to adopt the more cautious method of collective bargaining. Already in 1891 the union's rules had been altered so as to include the settlement of disputes 'by amicable agreement or arbitration wherever possible', and in the following year Thorne urged caution in negotiation with the employers.[3] In June 1892 the Avelings attended the Gasworkers' annual conference held at Plymouth, at which, as Eleanor reported, the principle of

[1] *Arbeiter-Zeitung*, 22 July 1892; R. Page Arnot, *The Miners* (1949), 158, 166f.

[2] *New Yorker Volkszeitung*, 4 June 1893.

[3] H. A. Clegg, *General Union in a Changing Society* (Oxford, 1964), 20.

economic emancipation through political action was upheld, for the conference unanimously recommended that all the district organizations and branches of the union should put forward their own candidates for all the municipal and parliamentary elections in opposition to the old parties.[1] On behalf of the union's general secretary and also of the women's branch of Silvertown and Canning Town, Eleanor sent fraternal greetings to the party congress of the Austrian Social-Democrats, in which she proclaimed that the English workers, like their Continental brothers, now recognized the necessity for obtaining political power.[2] In the meantime, she gladly gave publicity to the success of the Parti Ouvrier at the recent municipal elections in France, at which as many as 635 members of the Marxist party had been elected. 'They did not', she added, 'like some of our London "Labour Leaders", run with the Socialist hare and hunt with the Liberal hounds.'[3]

It was again the Gasworkers who took the lead in political action of an independent kind. By 1893 they had elected eighteen men and women to various local bodies,[4] their political sympathies being largely with the S.D.F. Thorne himself was elected as an S.D.F. town councillor at West Ham as early as 1891. Indeed, the S.D.F. had had some successes in organizing and influencing new unions in London, but it failed to penetrate sufficiently into the industrial north, which now became the centre of new independent labour politics.

*   *   *

Aveling, in an article on the Independent Labour Party written shortly after its formation, rightly stressed the unsectarian character of the new party by tracing its origins to 'the whole Socialist movement in England for the last few years'. The idea that the workers should renounce allegiance to the old parties had forced its way among 'the

[1] *Arbeiter-Zeitung*, 22 July 1892.   [2] Ibid., 10 June 1893.
[3] *Pall Mall Gazette*, 24 May 1892.   [4] H. A. Clegg *et al.*, op. cit. 88.

better elements' of the trade unionists, and this was due, he claimed, above all to the work of two organizations, the Scottish Labour Party led by Hardie and Shaw Maxwell and his own Legal Eight Hours and International Labour League. He was generous enough to give credit to 'the splendid effect of the educational work' carried on by the S.D.F. —this, he added, in spite of 'the lack of insight on the part of its leader'. He was also appreciative of the contribution made by the *Workman's Times* and its editor Joseph Burgess, formerly a cotton piecer from Yorkshire, who had launched a campaign for a national independent labour party. He considered it to be 'especially propitious' that the movement was much stronger in the north than in London.[1] This last statement, however, weakens his claims for the Legal Eight Hours League, which was confined to London. In fact, the League had made little progress even in London against the Progressives, who successfully combined the Liberals and the Radical workers in metropolitan politics. It is true that several new unions and Radical clubs continued to remain in the League, but they did so by no means in order to form the nucleus of a new Socialist party but, as has been pointed out, to work through it for limited purposes such as eight-hour agitation and May Day demonstrations.[2] The movement in the north and in Scotland drew its sustenance again from a variety of sources. Not only the 'Independents' campaign' conducted by Burgess and the activities of the Scottish Labour Party, which put forward eight candidates at the General Election of 1892, but also the Fabian propaganda in Lancashire, Robert Blatchford's popular Socialist journalism in his *Clarion*, and the political preoccupation of the Bradford Labour Union, which had been formed in 1891 as a result of a strike by textile workers, all contributed to its growth.

At the General Election of 1892 the movement showed

---

[1] *New Yorker Volkszeitung*, 5 Feb. 1893.
[2] Bünger, *Engels und die britische sozialistische Bewegung*, 190.

some signs of strength, for John Burns was elected at Battersea and Keir Hardie at South West Ham. They were the first M.P.s, declared the Avelings in the *Neue Zeit*, who had been elected 'on the ground of a definitely proletarian programme that will keep them distinct and separated from the two bourgeois parties'. The absence of a Liberal opponent in each case was due only to 'the pressure of the circumstances'. Burns secured the great majority of more than 1,500 votes, they explained, as a result chiefly of his admirable achievements on the London County Council and also of his efforts to organize the unskilled workers. Hardie's campaign had been splendidly organized, thanks above all to the Gasworkers' Union (West Ham was one of its citadels) and also to Robert Banner, who, as the son of a Chartist father and a Chartist mother, 'had Socialism in his blood'. The Avelings, however, regretted that the small group of labour representatives in the House had lost 'something more than a head—their heart' in the person of Cunninghame Graham, who had been defeated at Camlachie, Glasgow, by a Liberal-Unionist with two Liberal candidates running also against him. They regarded the Liberal's complaints of labour splitting their votes as mere hypocrisy. 'To talk to Shylock, we may very well say that "we have our masters on the hip". We consider it essential to knock the Liberal shadow-boxers out of the field, and so we split the Liberal Party. . . . Let them feel our fangs.'[1]

The candidatures of Burns and Hardie as well as of H. R. Taylor of the S.D.F. and another metropolitan candidate had been financed by H. H. Champion, who aspired to direct the independent labour movement on his own terms. He also made approaches to Aveling. 'Champion—of all people!—wrote & offered to get Edward all the money necessary if he cared to "run" anywhere!!!' wrote Eleanor to her sister:

[1] Edward and Eleanor Marx Aveling, 'Die Wahlen in Grossbritannien', *Neue Zeit*, x–ii (1891–2), Nr. 45, 596–603.

Of course Edward replied that first of all he had no desire to run, & secondly that he could only take money through a Committee—should he ever stand—of his constituents, but nothing privately. Of course everyone has not been so scrupulous. Other offers—direct & indirect—were made [to] Edward from other quarters too.

She apparently felt some pity for Hyndman, whose financial difficulties, especially after his losses in the Barings crisis of 1890, had damped his ambitious plans for the election. 'Of the large sums of money which Mr. Hyndman so bragged of in "Justice" nothing came', she went on:

He was promising the money—but gave none: not even to Taylor who was candidate in London. That too has led to all sorts of queer results—one of them being that the S.D.F. Branch in Taylor's constituency have called upon Hyndman to withdraw from the S.D.F. because of the treachery of his conduct!—This same Taylor actually wrote & begged Edward & me to go & help him—& as his programme was excellent, & as he was fighting that beast Howell [George Howell, Lib-Lab M.P.] we did help him. But he failed ignominiously—& that chiefly through the S.D.F. So you will understand that there are like to be more internal rows in the happy S.D.F. family.[1]

Obviously the Avelings shared the mixed feelings Engels had for the S.D.F., the only Marxist organization in England led by a man who refused to accept the 'family' influence of his master. Engels was puzzled when shortly before the election Hyndman placed the editorship of *Justice* in the hands of Bax, albeit only for seven weeks, for Bax, after he had rejoined the S.D.F., still kept in touch with Engels. The interim editor was even allowed to publish a flattering account of 'an important speech' delivered by Aveling in June for the Aberdeen Socialist Society, in which, according to another account, he 'thrilled' his audience by his recitations from Shelley.[2] Hyndman changed his tune somewhat,

[1] Eleanor Marx Aveling to Laura Lafargue, 26 July 1892, Bottigelli Collection.

[2] *Justice*, 18 June 1892: William Diack, *History of the Trades Council and the Trade Union Movement in Aberdeen* (Aberdeen, 1939), 105.

but it was never 'agreeable', wrote Engels at the time: 'I like Hyndman as enemy (where he is rather powerless) much better than as friend (where one must continually keep a strict eye upon him with a great loss of time).'[1] He was pleased when it was rumoured that the S.D.F. conference in the summer had decided to invite Hyndman to take responsibility for his failure to provide election funds and to withdraw from the leadership of his organization.[2] Hyndman firmly denied the truth of the allegation—'Taylor was not even present at the Conference'—and boasted that he was even more widely demanded as a speaker than before.[3] Old animosities between him and Engels persisted, but the S.D.F., which had gained some mass support through the spread of New Unionism, could no longer be treated by Hyndman as his personal fief. Consequently even the Avelings, it seemed, would stand a chance of reconciliation with the S.D.F. if they made an approach. The beginnings of such a reconciliation, however, were delayed by their support for the movement for an independent labour party, to which the S.D.F. displayed a grudging attitude amounting at best to 'benevolent neutrality'.

*   *   *

Aveling was present at the Trades Union Congress held in Glasgow in September 1892 as a reporter for the *Neue Zeit*. The lack of unity and common action on the part of 'the radical delegates' was to be ascribed, he remarked, largely to the fact that there was no one among them who could embody the movement in his own personality. Will Thorne was 'too modest to accept his proper place as a leader'; Hardie could 'scarcely succeed in holding together the heterogeneous elements'; and Burns did not even put in an appearance. Since the Liverpool congress two years before where the New Unionists had shown their strength

[1] Engels to Bebel, 20 July 1892, Bebel, *Briefwechsel mit Engels*, 546.
[2] Ibid., 11 Sept. 1892, ibid. 584.
[3] Hyndman to Wilhelm Liebknecht, 16 Sept. 1892, IML (Berlin).

for the first time, the T.U.C. had been divided on the question of a statutory eight-hour day, and soon a new issue was added, that of independent political action. Now in Glasgow, Aveling emphasized, the term 'independent' was introduced to describe labour representation.[1] After the close of the Glasgow T.U.C. an important meeting under the chairmanship of Hardie was held, attended by those delegates who would support the formation of an independent labour party, and arrangements made at this preliminary conference finally led to the foundation of the I.L.P. early in the following year.

Engels, however, remained cautious and did not want to burn his fingers by committing his followers to the new party projected in Glasgow, which, he said, was 'just now no more *the* independent Labour party than the S.D.F.'.[2] He was suspicious of Hardie, who, he said, was 'a Scot and indeed very shrewd in his diplomacy and had an impulse to exploit his new position as M.P. as much as possible' through the new party.[3] But soon he had to alter his attitude to the new movement, for the Glasgow T.U.C. had presented a serious challenge to the future of the International.

The T.U.C. was still dominated by the 'old' leaders, and its relations with the new International had been tenuous, though the latter was seeking the support of the British trade unions because of their great strength and organization. At the request of a Swiss committee charged with preparations for the forthcoming congress at Zurich, Eleanor had drafted a special invitation to be sent to the Glasgow T.U.C. However, it was decided in Glasgow to call an international congress to discuss the question of a legal eight-hour day, and the Zurich letter of invitation was not even acknowledged by the congress to which it was addressed. 'The

---

[1] Edward Aveling, 'Der Kongress der britischen Trades-Unions', *Neue Zeit*, xi–i (1892–3), Nr. 1, 20–28.

[2] Engels to Bebel, 26 Sept. 1892, Bebel, *Briefwechsel*, 591.

[3] Engels to Kautsky, 26 Sept. 1892, *Briefwechsel mit Kautsky*, 369.

T.U.C. in Glasgow has declared war against us the Continentals', wrote Engels to Bebel. 'The sudden awakening of the Eight Hours' enthusiasm . . . has almost succeeded in giving a reactionary character to that cry. . . . In fact the insult is complete', he wrote to Laura.[1] Eleanor urged her Italian friend Anna Kulischoff, the wife of Turati, to take steps for concerted action by the Continental Socialists to forestall the decision of the T.U.C., which, she said, was 'not only an imbecility but a malice'.[2] Aveling in a letter to the *Pall Mall Gazette* drew attention to a statement by Bebel in which the T.U.C. leaders were denounced for their 'old-world prejudices': they 'look at the world through spectacles "made in England", and with genuine British egotism wish to make the working-class movement of the rest of the world subservient to their particular interests'.[3] Aveling had just published an English translation of Engels's *Socialism Utopian and Scientific* with the author's special introduction in which it was suggested that 'Germany will be the scene . . . of the first victory of the European proletariat'. It was indeed an important task of the International to help the German party on to victory, and therefore the challenge from the T.U.C. was all the more serious.

The T.U.C.'s bid for leadership in the international working-class movement was nothing but an improvisation, but it caused a genuine panic among Engels's followers. It was probably at this point that Aveling decided, or it was decided for him, to approach the *Workman's Times*, virtually by now the organ of the movement for a national independent labour party, and advocate the cause of the Zurich congress through its columns in order to bring the new party in line with the International. In a series of articles he

[1] Engels to Bebel, 11 Sept. 1892, Bebel, *Briefwechsel*, 582; Engels to Laura Lafargue, 11 Sept. 1892, *Correspondance*, iii. 205–6.

[2] Eleanor Marx Aveling to Anna Kulischoff, 15 Sept. 1892, IISH.

[3] *Pall Mall Gazette*, 11 Oct. 1892. Bebel's statement, 'Ein internationaler Kongress für den Achtstundentag', was published in *Neue Zeit*, xi–i, Nr. 2, 38–42.

reported the reaction of the Continental Socialists to the Glasgow decision and described the spectacular achievements of the German Social Democrats as they had set them out at their party congress in November.[1] Eleanor, too, was actively engaged in agitation of a similar kind, and a speech she had delivered on 'Socialism, at home and abroad' was reported to have made an impression on local trade union leaders, who 'expressed their surprise at the state of the Labour movement in Germany'.[2] The T.U.C., however, went ahead, and its parliamentary committee, which included Ben Tillett among its New Unionist members, now issued a circular for an international eight-hour congress which was to be held in London in the summer of 1893 and to be attended only by those delegates who were 'bona fide workers' and 'legal members of Trade Societies'.[3] The T.U.C.'s challenge to the Continental Socialists had its repercussion on the formation of the I.L.P.

*   *   *

The national conference to form the I.L.P. was held at Bradford on 13 and 14 January 1893. In line with earlier suggestions by Hardie the structure of the new party was to be based on the model of the T.U.C., with a national executive and a considerable amount of local autonomy.[4] 'English trade unionism was the best sort of Socialism and Labourism', declared Ben Tillett, who now launched a violent attack on the Continental Socialists:

. . . With his experience of unions, he was glad to say that if there were fifty such red revolutionary parties as there was in Germany, he would sooner have the solid, progressive, matter-of-fact, fighting trade unionism of England than all the hare-brained chatterers and magpies of Continental revolutionaries.[5]

[1] *Workman's Times*, 15, 22, 29 Oct., 26 Nov., 3, 10 Dec. 1892.
[2] Ibid., 7 Jan. 1893.   [3] Ibid., 10 Dec. 1892.
[4] Henry Pelling, *The Origins of the Labour Party* (2nd ed., 1965), 113.
[5] *Workman's Times*, 21 Jan. 1893.

QEM

Aveling's credentials as the delegate of the Legal Eight Hours League had earlier been disputed, but he was accepted and allowed to introduce Bernstein, the London correspondent of *Vorwärts*, the organ of the German party, who occupied a seat on the platform as a guest. The German representative sought to answer Tillett's insinuations by pointing to the strength of his party—he mentioned its financial resources and its newspaper network as well as the past sacrifices of its pioneers.

During the conference a committee was appointed to draw up a programme, and Aveling was a member of this. He introduced a draft advocating 'less political reform and more social reform', and the conference accepted this with slight modifications. Aveling also helped to defeat the Manchester I.L.P. in its demand for abstention from voting in elections except when a Socialist candidate was standing. The German party, he informed the conference, had been opposed to 'the suicidal line of action advocated by the Manchester party. They had played off one party against another, and the consequence was that they had thirty-six members in Parliament.' Aveling was elected to the executive, though he was the only person chosen who did not yet belong to a local I.L.P. His Eight Hours League certainly intimated its desire to ally itself with the new party, but it was not prepared simply to become an I.L.P. branch.

Thus at Bradford Aveling made a successful return to Socialist politics. His efforts to bring the nascent I.L.P. into contact with the Continental Marxists seemed equally successful. In fact, he had come to Bradford 'in fear and trembling', as he confessed, 'afraid of the many and possibly conflicting personalities involved'. But he met decency and enthusiasm. He was so much impressed by 'the common-sense, earnestness, true comradeship of the mass of the delegates' that he even declared that 'the Bradford meeting will go down to history as a definite starting point in England of a movement akin to . . . that of the Social Democratic Party in Germany'.[1] Bernard Shaw, however, who had also attended the conference, was less optimistic. He pointed out that London had been practically unrepresented. The Fabian Society had decided to remain outside, and the absence of John Burns and his Battersea Labour League was conspicuous. 'Aveling alone was emphatically a London delegate', Shaw went on, 'but Aveling's peculiar Marxism has isolated him so completely that he is more out of the movement in London than any other equally well known Socialist.'[2] Engels, on the other hand, believed that Aveling had been right in joining the executive for the very reason that the strength of the new party lay outside London, 'the home of cliques', and also because of its programme, which in its main points was 'the same as ours'. He hoped the I.L.P. would succeed in detaching the masses from the S.D.F. and from the Fabians and thus in establishing a new unity.[3]

The Avelings now began writing regularly on the 'International Working-Class Movement' for the *Workman's Times*. They gave an account of the founding congress of the Italian Workers' Party which had been held at Genoa in the previous year and at which a Socialist programme for the conquest of political power was adopted in opposition to the Anarchist and '"old" English trade unionist' view of politics. They praised a Socialist speech delivered in the French Chamber by Lafargue, who had been elected while in prison; and they reported the results of the German elections, which 'concern the proletariat of the world.'[4]

They also undertook a propaganda tour immediately after the Bradford conference. They spent four days in the Black Country, visiting Dudley and Wolverhampton, where 'even blacker than coal and iron', wrote Aveling, was 'the black apathy and indifference of the masses of the workers'.[5]

---

[1] *Workman's Times*, 21 Jan. 1893.   [2] Ibid., 28 Jan. 1893.
[3] Engels to Sorge, 18 Jan. 1893, *Marx-Engels on Britain*, 531.
[4] *Workman's Times*, 18 Feb., 4 March, 24 June 1893.
[5] *New Yorker Volkszeitung*, 19 Feb. 1893.

'The Black Country is *too* horrible', Eleanor wrote to her old friend Dollie Radford: 'They talk of "Christian faith". I dont know how anyone with only *Christian* faith can bear to see all this misery & not go mad. If I had not faith in Man & *this* life I could not bear to live.'[1] From there Eleanor went to Edinburgh and proceeded to Aberdeen, where she gave two lectures on 22 January. 'At the close of her lecture', recalled William Diack, then the secretary of the Aberdeen Socialist Society, 'a Communistic critic . . . ventured to take Mrs. Aveling to task, and endeavoured to explain to her what Karl Marx really meant by Social Democracy. Eleanor Marx listened patiently to the luridly red exposition, then, rising from her seat, she said in tones of caustic solemnity: "Heaven save Karl Marx from his friends!"'[2] Shortly after her return to London she wrote to Diack: 'You said you were afraid of me. I didn't know I had such a formidable reputation (Friend Leatham [James Leatham, a Socialist pioneer in Aberdeen] said he expected an "intellectual iceberg", and seemed relieved to find I wasn't an iceberg or intellectual.)'[3] The warm reception she met with at Aberdeen was an indication of her popularity among the provincial Socialists, who had no doubt come under the spell of her personality, always friendly and unaffected.

*   *   *

Meanwhile the Avelings' relations with Hardie were by no means friendly, as they suspected his political integrity as the leader of an independent working-class party. When Hardie asked Eleanor for greetings from 'Lafargue & Liebknecht' to be sent to a meeting of the Scottish Labour Party, she urged her sister to send him a message and to lay stress on 'the independent side of the movement', because,

[1] Eleanor Marx Aveling to Dollie Radford, 25 Jan. 1893, Radford Papers.

[2] William Diack, op. cit. 62.

[3] Eleanor Marx Aveling to William Diack, 27 Jan. 1893, quoted in Diack, op. cit. 63.

in her opinion, 'Hardie has a *very* strong hankering after conservative flesh pots—which oddly enough he tries to mix up with the "support" of the "nonconformist conscience!"'[1] Information supplied by Aveling strengthened Engels's earlier misgivings that Hardie had cherished a secret desire to lead the new party 'in such a dictatorial way as Parnell led the Irish', with more sympathy for the Conservatives than for the Liberals.[2] Aveling severely criticized an amendment moved by Hardie to the address in reply to the Queen's speech in which the leader of the I.L.P. asked the sovereign to direct Parliament to legislate promptly in the interests of the unemployed. 'He should have known as a politician and tactician', he wrote, 'that the Government and its supporters would oppose. The worst of it, however, was that the proposition was not supported by the few members who actually or at least seemingly are the representatives of labour, but by a certain Mr. Howard Vincent, a rabid Tory and Protectionist'. He blamed Hardie for not having consulted the party executive beforehand as to his conduct in Parliament.[3] He told the readers of the *Workman's Times* that the problem of the unemployed could never be solved until the collectivist object of the I.L.P. was obtained and that the effect of Hardie's motion could 'painfully' be compared with that of a debate on the same question in the German Reichstag in which a long extract from the *Communist Manifesto* had been read out.[4]

When in February 1893 the I.L.P. fought its first parliamentary election—a by-election at Halifax—with John Lister, an executive member, as its candidate, Aveling went north and assisted his campaign. Lister was defeated, and a certain number of workers had voted against him because he

[1] Eleanor Marx Aveling to Laura Lafargue, 7 Jan. 1893, Bottigelli Collection.

[2] Engels to Bebel, 24 Jan. 1893, Bebel, *Briefwechsel*, 650.

[3] *New Yorker Volkszeitung*, 19 Feb. 1893. Vincent was Conservative M.P. for Sheffield Central, and a pioneer of Tariff Reform.

[4] *Workman's Times*, 18 Feb. 1893.

was a Catholic. Unfortunately, declared Aveling in a report to the *New Yorker Volkszeitung*, 'many Englishmen, who take a prominent part in the labour movement are still "religiously" minded. Among others we have Keir Hardie, whose religion and politics are mixed up with each other in a way that would make you Germans . . . stupefied.'[1] In the subtle rivalry and estrangement that characterized the relationship between Hardie and Burns, the Avelings' sympathies had always been with the latter, who, Edward said, had gone through 'an excellent school' on economic questions and was much clearer even on the problem of unemployment than Hardie, whose economic knowledge was 'deficient'.[2] The trouble with Aveling's criticism of Hardie, however, is that it was largely furtive and underhand, as it appeared for the most part in the German Socialist paper published in America.

Aveling's opposition to Hardie did not strengthen his position within the I.L.P.; nor did his unfavourable comments on the labour churches, which had a close association with the new party. At a meeting of the council of the I.L.P. held at Manchester in March, his plea for the affiliation of the Legal Eight Hours League failed to receive a favourable response, and it was pointed out that among its constituents were Radical clubs which should not be allowed to join the party. At this meeting he was appointed, along with Hardie and Shaw Maxwell, the party secretary, to represent the I.L.P. at Zurich.[3] His standing in the party now largely depended upon its relations with the International.

*   *   *

In the meantime, the parliamentary committee of the T.U.C. had decided to abandon the projected eight-hour international congress and to send delegates to Zurich.[4] The danger of a split was thus avoided, and the third Inter-

---

[1] *New Yorker Volkszeitung*, 12 March 1893.   [2] Ibid., 2 April 1893.
[3] *Workman's Times*, 25 March 1893.   [4] *Justice*, 11 Feb. 1893.

national Socialist Workers' Congress was held in August 1893 in the Concert Hall at Zurich. John Hodge, general secretary of the Steel Smelters, who had been president at the Glasgow T.U.C., took the chair when the congress discussed the steps for the international attainment of an eight-hour day and other topics. At this congress the I.L.P. was very poorly represented. Hardie did not come; Aveling appeared as a delegate from the Gasworkers, as did his wife, who again undertook the duty of acting as an interpreter. The expulsion of protesting Anarchists and the verification of mandates considerably delayed the proper business of the congress. On one of its main topics, that of the Socialist attitude towards war, Aveling criticized a Dutch motion demanding a general strike against war. 'When we are strong enough to carry through the military strike', he declared, 'then we can achieve quite a different thing. Then the question for us will be to dispatch capitalism either to heaven or to hell. (Loud applause.) Today, however, the question is . . . to create unity and clearness on this question.'[1] With a reference to a future revolution, he thus contributed to the adoption of a German resolution which was not so much revolutionary as realistic and even cautious. The Congress also passed a resolution which defined the May Day celebration as a 'cessation of work' (*Arbeitsruhe*) to be carried out on 1 May. The resolution impressed the English, who had held their annual demonstration on the first Sunday in May, whereas the German party, within three months after the congress, decided to interpret *Die Maifeier* more as a 'festival' than as a 'holiday', i.e. a stoppage of work.[2]

The congress itself provided an occasion for a holiday for many delegates. At a beer-garden in the town Eleanor met several English workers, Will Thorne among them, whom

---

[1] International Socialist Workers' Congress of 1893, *Protokoll* (Zurich, 1894), 27.
[2] Joll, op. cit. 53–54.

she knew to be teetotallers. She made scornful remarks on what she took to be their weak principles, but to her embarrassment Thorne assured her that lager beer was a temperance drink.[1] Engels surprised most of the delegates by his unexpected appearance in the congress hall on the last day when he took a place of honour and gave the closing speech. After the congress the majority of the delegates joined in a trip to the Isle of Ufenau on the lake of Zurich, which had a revolutionary record of its own. But the most important event for the British delegation was the decision to hold the next congress in London in 1896. As a result, an arrangements committee of ten, soon to be known as the Zurich Committee, was elected by the delegation. It consisted among others of Aveling, Thorne, Quelch of the S.D.F., and Maxwell of the I.L.P., and Aveling evidently formed the personal link between the committee and the Continental Socialists.[2] Hardie, who was annoyed by this step, declared in his *Labour Leader*: 'There was a tendency shown by a section of the delegates to boss the show at Zurich, and this will require to be carefully guarded against in the future.'[3]

*　　　*　　　*

Aveling had hoped to influence the T.U.C. through pressure from the International and also from the I.L.P., and to dominate the I.L.P. possibly by himself and at any rate with the aid of someone other than Hardie. Things looked propitious at least with the T.U.C., for the Trades Union Congress held at Belfast in September 1893 responded favourably to an approach from the Zurich Committee, and after the Norwich congress in the following year the parliamentary committee of the T.U.C. began an active collaboration in the preparation of the London congress. Moreover, the Belfast T.U.C. declared for 'Socialism pure and simple', wrote Aveling; a 'historical amendment' moved by James

[1] Bernstein, *My Years of Exile*, 209.
[2] *Workman's Times*, 26 Aug. 1893.　　　[3] *Labour Leader*, Sept. 1893.

Macdonald, a Socialist tailor, to request candidates to pledge themselves to support the principle of nationalization of the means of production and distribution was at last carried by 177 votes to 79 after it had been ignored or defeated for the previous three years. Macdonald's success, however, did not mean an acceptance by the T.U.C. of Socialism or even of the principle of independent labour politics. John Burns, who actually sat on the Government benches in Parliament, supported Macdonald's Socialist amendment.[1]

On the other hand, Aveling never felt secure in the I.L.P. At a meeting of the National Administrative Council of the I.L.P. held at Halifax in November 1893, he finally consented, in view of strong opposition, to withdraw the application for affiliation which he had pressed for on behalf of his Legal Eight Hours League. It was reported at the same meeting that the District Council of the London I.L.P. had declined to admit the Bloomsbury Socialist Society and had returned its affiliation fee.[2] At the second annual conference of the party held in Manchester in January 1894, Aveling, a delegate from the St. Pancras branch, proposed a series of political demands, ranging from adult suffrage to abolition of the monarchy, to be incorporated in the party programme. He added that these had been adopted not only by the S.D.F. but by the Continental Socialists. His motion, which was evidently intended to bar Anarchists from the I.L.P., would have removed at least part of the ground for objections to the Radical clubs inside his own League, but it was not even put to a vote. Moreover, he was defeated in the election for the new Administrative Council.[3] Shaw Maxwell, who had shown some interest in Continental Socialism, resigned his secretaryship, and was succeeded by Tom Mann, for whom the Avelings had no higher regard than for Hardie. Aveling was now virtually isolated in the I.L.P.

[1] *Workman's Times*, 16, 23 Sept. 1893.
[2] Ibid., 2 Dec. 1893. [3] Ibid., 3, 10 Feb. 1894.

Meanwhile the S.D.F., under the pressure of competition from the I.L.P., had been endeavouring to consolidate its strength. It approached Eleanor, asking her to write reports on the international movement in *Justice*, an offer which, according to Engels, 'she naturally refused as long as the infamous insults which *Justice* has made for years against her and Aveling are not officially revoked'.[1] To Aveling, however, the S.D.F. appeared to be 'setting aside its stony jealousy' when he found the Federation willing to co-operate with his demonstration committee for the May Day of 1893.[2] Early in the following year Eleanor spent a week in Lancashire, and seven of the eight lectures she gave were for the S.D.F. branches which organized her speaking tour.[3] There were even attempts to win the support of Engels for the S.D.F.: John Hunter Watts, an executive member who had come to Marxism, like Aveling, through his earlier activity as a Secularist, tried to secure the co-operation of Engels, whom he called the 'Nestor of our army'; Quelch, who represented the S.D.F. on the Zurich Committee, was soon to make personal contact with him; and Bax and Thorne apparently contributed to bring about an atmosphere of reconciliation.[4] Moreover the S.D.F., in accordance with the Zurich resolution, organized a May Day demonstration for 1894 in Hyde Park on 1 May, at which Aveling spoke along with Morris, Hyndman, Hardie, and even Ferdinand Gilles![5] Another and much larger May Day demonstration took place in the same park on the first Sunday of the month (6 May) under the auspices of a joint demonstration committee comprising delegates from the Legal Eight Hours League, the London Trades Council,

[1] Engels to Sorge, 18 March 1893, *Labour Monthly*, Dec. 1934, also in Marx-Engels, *Letters to Americans*, 249.

[2] *New Yorker Volkszeitung*, 19 March 1893.

[3] Eleanor Marx Aveling to Laura Lafargue, 22 Feb. 1894, Bottigelli Collection.

[4] Bünger, op. cit. 219–20.

[5] *Justice*, 5 May 1894; *Labour Leader*, 5 May 1894.

the S.D.F., and the Fabian Society.[1] A 'foreign' platform, noted the *Labour Leader*, was 'under the care of the erudite Dr. Aveling'.[2] In fact, the I.L.P. had not been represented in the demonstration committee, and Aveling, its secretary, had not taken the trouble to obtain a platform for the I.L.P.

Now the final rupture between Aveling and the I.L.P. came. Some time after the May Day demonstration he was expelled by the London District Council of the I.L.P. This expulsion, he later wrote, was done 'in my absence, without my being heard, without my witnesses being heard, without the names of my accusers being given to me'. But he was convinced that 'the sole reason' for it was his failure to accommodate the I.L.P. at the first Sunday demonstration in May 1894.[3] Bernstein, however, has suggested that there were graver reasons that 'would have sufficed to land him in prison'.[4] Aveling was then severely ill, and the *Labour Leader*, reporting his inability to undertake engagements, asked its readers to 'cease from troubling' him.[5] Probably this was the end of his attempt to secure predominance for himself within the I.L.P.

Hyndman, on the other hand, showed readiness to 'come to a close agreement with our German brethren, letting bygones be bygones on both sides', though he could not conceal his bitterness against 'Engels and the clique which surrounds him'.[6] Yet the Avelings formed a useful link with the Continental Socialists, with whom the S.D.F. was then anxious to come to terms, especially in view of the forthcoming London congress of the International.

Meanwhile the May Day demonstration of 1895 provided an opportunity for them to co-operate with Hyndman's organization. They now believed that 'the five years

[1] *Justice*, 12 May 1894.　　[2] *Labour Leader*, 12 May 1894.
[3] *Justice*, 8 Aug. 1896. See also *Social-Democrat*, Aug. 1898, and *Justice*, 10 Sept. 1898.
[4] Bernstein, *My Years of Exile*, 203.　　[5] *Labour Leader*, 20 Oct. 1894.
[6] *Justice*, 29 Sept. 1894.

of Sunday demonstrations have done their work', but they failed to induce the demonstration committee and the Legal Eight Hours League to accept 1 May. Thereupon they resigned from the committee and threw in their lot with a rival First of May Committee in which again the S.D.F. took the lead. This naturally led to the disintegration of the Eight Hours League, but Edward persuaded himself that his organization had fulfilled its historical task as an advance-guard of the working class. 'The first idea of every progress is always at first conceived by a small minority and rejected by the mass of the working-class', he declared: 'With energy and perseverance, however, the minority gradually overcome and in the end vanquish the opposition or, what is worse, the inertia of the majority.' Thus he summed up the earlier history of the May Day demonstration in England with an explanation that would even anticipate Lenin.[1]

The Avelings' agitation for a statutory eight-hour day and for an independent labour party had certainly influenced a large section of the working class, but they always belonged to a minority. When the I.L.P. shut its doors on Edward, he and Eleanor were obliged to co-operate with the S.D.F., which was aspiring to lead British Socialism possibly with the aid of the International. Yet Hyndman was never forgiven by Engels, not even at the very end of their guardian's life, which was now soon to come.

---

[1] Edward Aveling, 'Histoire des manifestations de mai pour la journée légale de huit heures en Angleterre', *Devenir Social*, May 1896. This article was also published in *Neue Zeit*, xiv–ii (1895–6), Nr. 31, 137–43, under the title 'Zur Geschichte der Mai-demonstration für den gesetzlichen Achtstundentag in England'. See also *Justice*, 23 March, 11 May 1895.

X ⬥ THE MARXIAN LEGACY

THE memory of her father sustained Eleanor in her devoted work for the cause of Socialism. Every spring on the anniversary of his death, she would make her way to the Highgate Cemetery with crocuses, primroses, and hyacinths. These blossoming spring flowers—and also a small cypress-tree—planted on her parents' modest grave would be there to impress Engels as he arrived at the grave to commemorate his dead friend.[1]

Marx once confided his affection for his youngest daughter: 'Tussy is me', and she remembered and cherished it. Indeed, it was Eleanor who personified the Marxian legacy more than anybody else. Yet she was only part of that great legacy, for the movement which owed its guiding principles to the doctrines taught by Marx had disseminated itself into most of the European countries. Moreover, his teaching itself was still in the process of enunciation and clarification in the hands of Engels, who was editing further volumes of *Das Kapital* from the notes and papers left by her father. Most of the books once owned by him as well as his book-cases had gone to Engels. So had Lenchen, Helena Demuth, who now acted for Engels, as she had done for Marx, 'as his housekeeper and as his trusted counsellor and advisor, not only in the matters of daily life, but even in politics'.[2] Engels,

[1] Engels to Laura Lafargue, 14 Feb. 1890, 14 March 1892, *Correspondance*, ii. 380, iii. 166.
[2] Edward Aveling, 'Frederick Engels at Home', *Labour Prophet*, Sept. 1895.

for his part, believed that he had inherited the duty to protect his friend's surviving children, while Eleanor and, for that matter, Aveling placed an almost unbounded trust in their guardian, the 'General'.

Eleanor, however, was not altogether uncritical of Engels, especially of his relations with his female companions, and in fact it was from her father that she had inherited these reservations about her protector. Mary Ellen or 'Pumps', the niece of his deceased 'wife' Lizzie Burns, acted as the queen of his household at the time, even though she had long been married to an accountant named Percy Rosher. Engels was fond of the merriment and good cheer which characterized his Sundays, his birthday, Christmas, and New Year's Day, to say nothing of the day of an electoral victory of the German Socialists, and 'Pumps' was always the centre of the joviality. Eleanor, accompanied by Aveling, took part in most of these special dinners, though she was not much attracted by the extent of the refreshment. 'Sunday, of course, we still spend with the General', she wrote to Laura in 1887, '& there is the usual round of dinner, drink, cards, supper & more drink. Pumps had a great excitement. . . .'[1] 'Pumps', however, was not politically interested, and Eleanor amusingly observed: 'All the German refugees were at the General's on Xmas day—to Pumps's disgust.'[2] His birthday spree would go on till the next morning to celebrate Aveling's own birthday, which conveniently fell on the following day.

Meanwhile, on 4 November 1890, Lenchen died after a period of illness. Engels declared at her funeral that Marx had taken counsel of this extraordinary maidservant 'even in respect to his economic writings' and that she had been 'the sunshine' of his home.[3] She was buried in her master's grave

[1] Eleanor Marx Aveling to Laura Lafargue, 30 August 1887, Bottigelli Collection.

[2] Eleanor Marx Aveling to Laura Lafargue, 31 Dec. 1888, Bottigelli Collection.

[3] *People's Press*, 22 Nov. 1890.

at Highgate, and with her departed a faithful woman who had often acted as 'a second mother' to Marx's children.[1] Eleanor's memories of her happy childhood were deprived of an important witness, but the loss was partially compensated for by the friendship she now formed with Lenchen's son, Frederick Demuth.

In the presence of Engels and the Avelings, Lenchen—on her deathbed—had made a will in which she made her son Frederick or possibly her grandson the sole legatee. The existence of this man 'Freddy', who was then living in Hackney as a manual worker, had been known to the Marx family, and Laura had discussed with Charles Longuet, her brother-in-law, 'the subject of Freddy' and his need for financial assistance.[2] The identity of his father was still shrouded in mystery, but Eleanor seems to have believed that Engels, whose relations with women were after all very unorthodox, was his father. 'Freddy has behaved admirably in all respects—& Engels' irritation against him is as unfair as it is comprehensible', she wrote to her sister shortly after Lenchen's death, 'we should none of us like to meet our pasts, I guess, in flesh & blood.—I know I always met Freddy with a sense of guilt & of wrong done. The life of that man! To hear him tell of it all is a misery & a shame to me.'[3] The fate of the poor man was indeed pitiable. At some time in 1892 his wife ran away, taking with her most of his money and belongings, including £24 that had been placed in his keeping by his fellow workers for a small benefit fund of theirs. Freddy asked Eleanor to try and obtain something from Longuet, who, it seems, had been acting as a sort of guardian for him. There was no response from Longuet, though Laura, who had transmitted her request to him, sent 50 francs for Freddy. 'Of course I have

[1] Liebknecht, *Karl Marx*, 123.
[2] Laura Lafargue to Engels, 1 Feb. 1887, *Correspondance*, ii. 10.
[3] Eleanor Marx Aveling to Laura Lafargue, 19 Dec. 1890, Bottigelli Collection.

not told all these facts [about his wife] to Longuet', wrote Eleanor to Laura:

as Freddy does not want anyone to know—particularly not Engels.—I think we shall pull through though, because Edward hopes to get something for a little operetta (don't be alarmed—he was only responsible for the words!) to-day or to-morrow, & with what Freddy has it will be all right.—It may be that I am very 'sentimental'—but I can't help feeling that Freddy has had great injustice all through his life. Is it not wonderful, when you come to look things squarely in the face, how rarely we seem to practise all the fine things we preach—to others?[1]

Indeed, Freddy was a thorn in the Marxian flesh, and Eleanor was acutely conscious of the shortcomings of the small circle who gathered around Engels—many of them, intellectually advanced as they were, curiously lacking in feelings of charity towards individuals.

*   *   *

Karl Kautsky and his wife, Louise, had spent a considerable time in London and had been counted among Engels's closest friends and disciples who were admitted to his Sunday dinners. In the summer of 1888 they left London together, but not long afterwards they finally parted. Kautsky fell in love with a girl in the Salzburg Alps and informed Louise of the fact, and the latter set him free. Engels, when he heard this, was indignant. 'We all of us here were very fond of Louise', he wrote to Laura, 'and could not make it out how K[autsky] could be such a fool—and such a mean one; except that an intrigue was at the bottom, planned by his mother and sister (who both hated Louise) and that he had fallen into the trap.'[2] Engels urged him to reconsider, reminding him that the effect of a divorce on the social standing of a woman was much more serious than on that of a man.[3] Eleanor fully shared Engels's view of the affair

[1] Eleanor Marx Aveling to Laura Lafargue, 26 July 1892, Bottigelli Collection.

[2] Engels to Laura Lafargue, 13 Oct. 1888, Correspondance, ii. 170.

[3] Engels to Kautsky, 17 Oct. 1888, Engels-Kautsky, Briefwechsel, 223.

and firmly sided with Louise, whose 'heroism' and 'woman-liness' she seems to have admired.[1] A small consolation for Kautsky was that Bernstein, who knew his wife more inti-mately than did Engels or Eleanor, approved of the divorce, which was now complete.[2] Kautsky formally married another Louise, Fräulein Louise Ronsperger, the girl of the Salzburg Alps and a friend of his mother's, in 1890.

In October 1890 Eleanor had 'a long talk' with Victor Adler at Hanover about Louise, who had been well received in Vienna by the Austrian party and had taken up a job as a midwife.[3] In the following month, shortly after the death of Lenchen, Louise came to London. She had received a flattering letter from Engels begging her to come and stay with the helpless old man.[4] Bebel and other German leaders also arrived in London to celebrate Engels's seven-tieth birthday. 'Louise Kautsky'—they still called her by her married name—'. . . made me extremely comfortable', wrote Engels when the usual spree was over. A fortnight later he wrote again: 'Louise Kautsky remains here for good. So my troubles are settled. She seems to like it better after all than setting other people's children into this world. And we get on capitally. She superintends the house and does my secretary's work which saves my eyes and enables me to make it worth her while to give up her profession, at least for the present.'[5]

The presence of Louise caused a sensation in Engels's household, where 'Pumps' had reigned. Pumps counted—so it was believed—upon a generous legacy in Engels's will, and Engels encouraged her selfish hopes. 'The history of the last week', as Eleanor put it in a letter to her sister, 'gives an insight into Engels's private life.' Laura had attended Lenchen's funeral but not his birthday party. 'The Saturday

[1] Engels to Kautsky, 15 Sept. 1889, ibid. 247.   [2] Ibid. 214.
[3] Eleanor Marx Aveling to Engels, 14 Oct. 1890, IISH.
[4] Mayer, *Engels*, ii. 475.
[5] Engels to Laura Lafargue, 1 Dec., 17 Dec. 1890, *Correspondance*, ii. 442, 446.

REM

to Sunday after your departure I spent with the General, & we "pumpsed" till 2.30', wrote Eleanor:

I was so sleepy that I hardly remember what we pumpsed. I have only a general impression of valiant defiance breathed against the redoubtable Pumps.—Well, that Sunday passed over in comparative quiet, but Pumps retired early & the General began to quake. Then things grew more exciting. There were many 'alarums & excursions'. Finally Louise arrived. Meantime the General had screwed his courage to the sticking point & Pumps had been informed that on *my*(!!) invitation Louise was coming over, & must be properly treated—on pain of a new testament being submitted for the old. Louise came.—She was, as you may suppose, dead tired: the journey straight through from Vienna, coming on the top of weeks of hard work is no slight affair. That very day Engels would have dragged her off to Pumps, but as (we had met Louise in the morning) I had said I would call in the afternoon, the visit was postponed till the next day. Then they called, & the first day Pumps deigned to return the visit she had champagne galore. Of course the 'head of the table' question cropped up. At first the General insisted, in spite of Louise's protests that she could not & should not 'carve', on the 'head of the table' being occupied by her, but at the last moment he funked, & so Pumps as usual presided.—To tell you all the ups and downs would be to write a volume. But you know what it would be. Only one thing is too charming to omit. On the General's birthday Pumps getting more drunk than usual confided *to Louise* that she 'knew she had to behave to her, or she'd get cut out of the will!'—I am sorry for Louise. Bebel & all the others have told her it is her *duty* to the Party to stop. It hardly seems fair to her. She was getting on so well at Vienna & to sacrifice her whole career is no trivial matter.—No one would ask a *man* to do that. She is still so young—only just 30. It seems not right to shut her up, & keep her from every chance of a fuller & happier life. And *you* know what her life here will be. Why our poor Nymmie [Lenchen] couldn't get out—unless she took Pumps. *Then* it was all right. Moreover, entre nous I don't think it will or can last. But I can, naturally, do nothing. But I see well that it will end in unpleasantness. And in any case it is hardly fair to Louise. A stranger like Marie Rosher [Pumps] would make her own terms. Louise can't. Well all one can do is to look on & wait. Meantime there has been any amount of comedy & farce—the General is more afraid of Pumps—or is it of her eye?

—than ever, and more abject. On one or two Sundays when Pumps has gone home he has sent her half the food in the house—not to mention the drinkables.[1]

Unpleasantness there was certainly to be, but Eleanor did not understand its real cause, for she did not take the trouble at that time to find out why it was Louise's 'duty to the Party' to remain with Engels. She was only kindly disposed to Louise, whom she regarded as a victim of the men's tyranny.

Yet Louise's mission in London was of a Machiavellian nature, for she was apparently asked to try and secure for the German party the literary remains of Marx, which, though in the possession of Engels, rightly belonged to his daughters. Bebel and Adler were the promoters of this scheme. Bebel, shortly after his return from London, told Adler that the plan, suggested by the latter, for publishing the 'Marxschen Nachlass' could not be carried out, as those papers were 'not at Louise's disposal', but that he had advised her to stay and 'come openly and frankly to an understanding with Engels'. 'I got an impression—entre nous—that it would not matter a great deal to Tussy if Louise remained there', he added: 'Lastly, Louise herself must know what she has to do.'[2] She soon established or was made to establish herself as a political journalist, continued to gain the confidence of Engels, and was able to act as the representative of Bebel and Adler in London. Eleanor was not aware at the time of Bebel's intention and even supported Louise in her struggle with the 'bellicose' Pumps.

The first issue of what Engels called 'Louise's Hyena paper' appeared in Vienna in January 1892.[3] Eleanor, too, was asked to collaborate in her *Arbeiterinnenzeitung* and sent a series of articles on the women's trade union movement in England, in which she dealt with its history and criticized

[1] Eleanor Marx Aveling to Laura Lafargue, 19 Dec. 1890, Bottigelli Collection.

[2] Bebel to Adler, 20 Dec. 1890, *Victor Adler Briefwechsel mit August Bebel und Karl Kautsky* (Wien, 1954), 66.

[3] Engels to Laura Lafargue, 2 Oct. 1891, *Correspondance*, iii. 101.

certain unions for their 'bourgeois' leadership. 'Such shameless exploiters of labour as the millionaire Lord Brassey,
such "ladies" as the wife of the arch-reactionary Sir Julian
Goldschmid', she wrote, 'hold salon meetings in order to
maintain the women's [Trades Union Providence] League,
while Lady Dilke exploits the movement in the political
interest of her husband.'[1] Louise, for her part, wrote on 'the
Power of Women' and other similar subjects.

Kautsky, however, was much annoyed now that Louise
began to play a public role under her married name which
naturally caused many 'painful misunderstandings'. He
asked Engels to advise his secretary to adopt her maiden
name and to call herself 'Strasser-Kautsky', but his master
challenged his right thus to ask. Moreover, wrote Engels,
Louise 'has become so dear to me that she is for me the same
as Pumps, Tussy, Laura, the same as if she were my own
child'. Kautsky had to accept all the results of his action,
he added, and Eleanor and Bebel, as he informed him, were
of the same opinion[2]—Eleanor because of her genuine sympathy with Louise, and Bebel obviously for tactical reasons.

The Marxian *Nachlass* had been slowly worked out by
Engels, who had edited the second volume of *Das Kapital* in
1885 and was then preparing the third volume for publication. With his constant eye trouble, however, he could not
hope for the completion by himself of 'the fourth volume',
which with Eleanor's approval he had decided to pass on
to Kautsky and Bernstein.[3] Yet Kautsky's divorce and all its
consequences led Engels to change his mind, and Kautsky
was secretly omitted from the list of the future administrators
of the literary remains.[4] Although Kautsky attributed his
exclusion solely to his personal relations with Engels, there
was another cause that could also account for this drastic step.

[1] *Arbeiterinnenzeitung*, 4 March 1892.
[2] Kautsky to Engels, 13 May 1892, Engels to Kautsky, 17 May 1892,
Kautsky, *Briefwechsel*, 340–2.
[3] Engels to Kautsky, 28 Jan. 1889, ibid. 227–8.   [4] Ibid. 447.

The Avelings' article on the British General Election of 1892 published in the *Neue Zeit* had been censored by the editor. Kautsky actually cut out critical comments on the S.D.F. and especially on the Fabian Society, which, in Engels's view, had become 'a real hindrance, the tail of the great Liberal Party'. Kautsky defended his action and the attitude of the Fabians, but he could not reasonably expect any good to come from such an affront, both personal and ideological.[1]

Louise had by now gained the full confidence of Engels. She not only got some revenge upon her former husband, but also her political mission appeared on the verge of success. Eleanor, having no inkling as yet of her real intentions, wrote as late as November 1893:

The General . . . is wonderfully well . . . Louise has him splendidly in hand; & he is happy as a school boy. Pumpsia's nose is hopelessly (at present) out of joint . . . When I remember how she treated our poor Nimmy, I can't help feeling a certain malicious pleasure in her discomfiture.—It is good news—I'm glad I have some!—that the General is working at Vol. III. & that a very good portion of it will be sent off to Meissner [the German publisher] immediately after Christmas—it would not be safe to send during the holiday traffic. Christmas! Oh! Laura, those awful festivities—becoming more & more terrible as one has less & less heart for them.[2]

*   *   *

Eleanor had grown to sobriety and even to melancholy. Many a death had deprived her Christmas of its association with her sweet childhood. Death also took away some of her personal friends. When a certain Charlotte died, she wrote to Dollie Radford:

I am thinking of her life, and what a terribly sad one it was after all. So wasted & so useless, & so miserable . . . You say, dear, that you often think that by the time your life is finished you will

[1] Engels to Kautsky, 12 Aug., 4 Sept. 1892, Kautsky to Engels, 3 Aug. 1892, Kautsky, *Briefwechsel*, 359–63.
[2] Eleanor Marx Aveling to Laura Lafargue, 11 Nov. 1893, Bottigelli Collection.

have learned just enough to begin it well. No, Dollie, we must just live our lives, & what we have missed, who knows? We may help others to realize. . . . Though each one must work out his own salvation we can make the work perhaps a little less hard for those that shall come after.[1]

She genuinely wanted to help others, and in this sense all her political work, all her Marxism, had a deep moral feeling at its root. 'The "movement" has a rapacious maw', she wrote to Ernest, Dollie's husband,

& swallows more work & time than most people would believe. The 'show' work of lectures & meetings is the least part of it. And then you know we are poor as the proverbial church mice, & find earning a living no such easy matter.—Ah well, I suppose the work will result in something some day.[2]

In the spring of 1893 the Avelings moved from Chancery Lane to 7 Gray's Inn Square, less than half a mile away. They were pressed for money at the time. The offer of $5 per article was the chief attraction of work for the *New Yorker Volkszeitung*, to which Aveling frequently contributed in those days. He often asked Hermann Schlüter, formerly manager of the Zurich *Sozialdemokrat* and now of the *Volkszeitung*, to send him an advance for the articles yet to be written. 'I am still doing no work & very needy. The $5 will help me to get to Zurich if 'tis sent at once,' he wrote shortly before the third congress of the International.[3]

It seems that coaching, his earliest occupation, was also the only constant source of income for him. He had written various textbooks designed to assist students for the matriculation examinations of London University. Among these his *Natural Philosophy* of 1886 and *Mechanics and Experimental Science* of 1888–9 were the most successful. For the series of 'Introductory Science Textbooks' he wrote two books, one

[1] Eleanor Marx Aveling to Dollie Radford, 14 April 1891, Radford Papers.

[2] Eleanor Marx Aveling to Ernest Radford, 15 July 1893, Radford Papers.

[3] Edward Aveling to Hermann Schlüter, 5 July 1893, IISH.

on botany in 1891 and the other on geology in 1893, and he spent a considerable time at the British Museum in preparing these textbooks. Yet coaching itself had become a fashionable occupation, and there were many competitors in the field. H. G. Wells, himself a product of South Kensington, obtained a London B.Sc. in 1890 and became a tutor of the University Correspondence College, 'one of the queerest outgrowths of the disorderly educational fermentations of that time' as he called it.[1] His classes, especially in biology, appeared quite successful. 'We got a number of ambitious teachers, engineering and technical students who wanted the B.Sc. degree. . . . We passed them neatly and surely. . . . One of those for whom we made life harder was Dr. Aveling, the son-in-law of old Karl Marx.'[2] It appears that even coaching ceased to be as lucrative an occupation as it had once been for Aveling.

Many years of experience as a coach in natural science had its effect upon his habit of thought. He attempted an analysis of the first volume of *Das Kapital* in his *Student's Marx* published in 1891, a book full of definitions, tables, and mathematical formulas. He believed that Marx had elevated the science of economics into a stable condition in which truths could and should be expressed in mathematical terms.[3] When an Italian translation of his book was suggested, Filippo Turati, the Milanese Socialist, thought that 'Aveling has rendered Marx still more arid and dry and that his manual, in Italy at least, could be good only for the students of mathematics'.[4] Another example of the barren treatment of his subject was his *Student's Darwin*, which is said to have been 'a great deal more difficult to read than the works of the distinguished scientist himself, and not by any means so interesting'.[5]

[1] H. G. Wells, *Experiment in Autobiography*, i (1934), 335.   [2] Ibid. 346–7.
[3] Edward Aveling, *The Student's Marx* (9th impression 1931), vii.
[4] Filippo Turati to Engels, 17 July 1893, *Annali* i (1958), 249.
[5] William Diack, op. cit. 105.

Aveling's failure as a dramatist, as we have seen, was by now complete. But he kept up his interest in literature and wrote reviews, mainly for *Neue Zeit*, protesting against the 'alarmingly low level' to which 'bourgeois' literary criticism had been reduced in England. Two successful recent novels attracted his attention—*Tess of the D'Urbervilles* by Thomas Hardy and *Esther Waters* by George Moore—chiefly because of their alleged immorality. He praised Hardy for his realistic treatment of agricultural workers, of many aspects of 'the capitalist society in its declining period', and lastly of Tess, whose whole life constituted a single struggle, 'a struggle between her conscience and her heart'. On the other hand, he thought that Moore had only superficially touched on the wounds of modern society and had 'not quite understood the natural history of the betting animals', the main theme of his novel. The working-class movement, he added, was 'very seriously hindered by the curse of betting. A working man, once he falls into the whirlpool of betting, is lost.'[1] His reviews were on the whole well written and well argued, at least from the Socialist point of view, but obviously there were few English journals that would publish his criticisms.

Aveling had been suffering from kidney disease and had been away occasionally for convalescence. On his doctor's recommendation he spent seven weeks in the Scilly Isles in the autumn of 1894. 'I am eagerly looking forward to his home-coming', wrote Eleanor at the time, 'for I am rather lonely—in spite of my many four-footed friends.'[2] Yet her husband thoroughly enjoyed his holiday—at least so it appears from his articles for the *Clarion*, written again under the pseudonym of Alec Nelson. He wrote on hotels, beaches, cliff walks, and 'a fair-haired, blue-eyed girl' whom he had met on the boat from Penzance: 'I had seen her the

[1] Edward Aveling, 'Ein englischer Roman', *Neue Zeit*, xi–ii, Nr. 51, 'Esther Waters', *Neue Zeit*, viii–i, Nr. 13.
[2] Eleanor Marx Aveling to Kautsky, 10 Nov, 1894, IISH.

day before in the Penzance Post-office, and invented a
telegram that I might stick on a stamp her hands had
touched. She was as easy and frank as she was beautiful.'[1]
Aveling also worked hard as a hack writer. His condition
grew worse, and when he returned he had an enormous
abscess in his side—'twice the size of my fist!', wrote
Eleanor to Laura. An operation was performed—'it has been
a bad & anxious week, I can tell you, and Edward is still
very ill & weak, but I hope on the mend now'.[2] Eleanor's
devotion to her pleasure-loving husband is already an old
story, but it has to be told again and again, indeed till her
very end.

*   *   *

An important part of the Marxian legacy, as far as
Eleanor was concerned, was her Jewishness. Max Beer, the
Socialist historian and himself a Jew, explained her devotion
to Edward by this trait of her personality and by the Jewish
conception of wedded life, sacred and indestructible.[3] Marx
himself, however, had regarded emancipation from Judaism
and from its secular God, Money, as equivalent to emancipation from bourgeois society, and had made no contact
with London Jewry. The Second International, for its part,
took no interest even in anti-Semitism, which originated, as
was emphasized at the Brussels congress, 'from the hatred
of the Christian capitalist against the Jewish capitalist,
cleverer than him'.[4] Indeed, Eleanor was the only member
of her family who felt drawn to Jewish people. 'My happiest
moments', she told Beer, 'are when I am in the East End
amidst Jewish workpeople.'[5]

[1] *Clarion*, 3, 10 Nov. 1894. An account of the Scilly Isles by Aveling
also appeared in *Neue Zeit*, xiii–ii (1894–5), Nr. 46, 631–6, under the
title of 'Eine eigenartiges Inselvolk'.

[2] Eleanor Marx Aveling to Laura Lafargue, 22 Nov. 1894, Bottigelli
Collection.

[3] Max Beer, *Fifty Years of International Socialism* (1935), 74.

[4] International Socialist Workers' Congress, 1891, *Rapport*, 43.

[5] Beer, op. cit. 72.

Amy Levy, the Jewish authoress, had been one of Eleanor's intimate friends. In 1888 she published a novel entitled *Reuben Sachs*, a brilliant description of the Jewish community in the West End, but nervous exhaustion led her to commit suicide in the following year. Beatrice Potter recorded in her diary on Amy's tragic death: 'in these terrible days of mental pressure it is courage to *live* that we most lack, not courage to die. It is the supreme courage of fighting a battle for an unknown leader, for an unknown cause, that fails us now and again.'[1] Eleanor was less critical than Beatrice in analysing Amy's death. Her whole sympathy was with Amy's 'hopeless melancholy', and she regarded her novel as her swan song. She translated it into German, and it was published in *Neue Zeit*.[2]

A 'great physician' in this novel was made to say that more than a half of his nervous patients were recruited from the ranks of the Jews and that this was the penalty that they had to pay for 'too high a civilisation'. The young educated Jews were struggling, each in his or her own fashion, to emerge 'from the tribal duck-pond into the wider and deeper waters of society'. Reuben Sachs became a Tory M.P., while his cousin Leopold Leuniger was a Socialist student at Cambridge. Leopold wanted to be free from 'our religion of materialism', 'our hereditary stain' as he called it. Reuben, on the other hand, greatly valued 'our virtues'—'our self-restraint, our self-respect, our industry, our power of endurance, our love of race, home and kindred', 'those unspeakable mysteries, affinity and—love', which would survive the emancipation not only of the Jews but also of the whole world. Judith Quixano, however, with whom Reuben was in love, married an Englishman mainly for the sake of expediency, and her marriage was closely followed by Reuben's premature death. Judith was frightened by the mysteries of life, and the bitter lesson of existence she drew

---

[1] Beatrice Webb, *My Apprenticeship*, 341.
[2] Beer, op. cit. 73; *Neue Zeit*, x–i, Nr. 1–12.

was that 'the sacred serves only to teach the full meaning of sacrilege; the beautiful of the hideous; modesty of outrage; joy of sorrow; life of death'.[1] What lessons Eleanor drew from the life of Reuben Sachs is not known, but she apparently sympathized with all the characters in the novel and even with its background characters, whether they were highly cultured Sephardim or nondescript tradesmen from Dalton or Hackney. 'What a mixture of races we Jews are!' she suggestively told Beer.

Beer, who had suffered imprisonment for his Socialist journalism in Germany, came to London in the summer of 1894. On his arrival he paid a visit to the headquarters of the German Workers' Educational Club at 49 Tottenham Street, where the executive of the Bloomsbury Socialist Society was also holding its meeting. He was introduced to the Avelings. He stood in awe before Eleanor but felt, as he said in his memoirs, that

she ought to have married some very great man, and not Aveling, who, my intuition told me, was a low comedian, and looked it, so I blurted out to her in German: 'Is *that* your husband?' But he, after all, had English manners, and said quite cheerfully: 'Comrade, let us go with Eleanor to the Horse Shoe and have a glass of English ale'.[2]

There he had a talk with Eleanor on Amy Levy and her novel, which he greatly admired; and he felt strongly that her Jewishness stood out conspicuously in her conversation.

*   *   *

Early in 1893 a young physician came from Vienna to attend the ageing Engels. Dr. Ludwig Freyberger, as his patient wrote in a letter, had been 'highly recommended to me by a prominent member of the Austrian Parliament'.[3] The man who recommended him was a certain Engelbert

[1] Amy Levy, *Reuben Sachs, a Sketch* (1888), *passim*.
[2] Beer, op. cit. 71.
[3] Engels to Thomas Cook & Son, 6 March 1893, photocopy, IML (Berlin).

Pernerstorfer, a German nationalist in Austria and a friend of Victor Adler's, Adler himself being a Doctor of Medicine.[1] Freyberger soon gained his patient's confidence and signed his name as witness—along with Lessner, the veteran of the 1848 revolution—when Engels made his last will on 29 July 1893. According to this testament, Samuel Moore, his old friend from his Manchester days, Edward Bernstein, and Louise Kautsky were to be appointed as the executors and were to be given £250 each for their trouble. £1,000 was left for the election funds of the German Social Democratic Party and £3,000 for his 'Pumps'—two bequests reflecting the two main interests of his life. The German party was also to receive, through its representatives Bebel and Paul Singer, all the books 'in [his] possession or control'—obviously including those once owned by Marx—and all his copyrights. All his manuscripts and letters were to be given to Bebel and Bernstein. All the manuscripts in Marx's handwriting and all family letters written by or addressed to him were to be returned by his executors to Eleanor. It was, however, Louise who was to receive the largest benefit by his will. His house, all the furniture, and other effects in and around the house, except what he otherwise assigned in the will, were to be hers. Moreover, she was to be given a quarter of the residue of his estate, mostly money and securities. Another quarter of the residue was to go to Eleanor, the third to Laura, and the fourth to Longuet's children, though the will, for technical reasons, did not mention the fourth, which was to be transferred through Eleanor and Laura.[2]

This remarkable document was rendered all the more striking by the fact that Eleanor was not included among the executors of an arrangement which would certainly affect her father's literary remains. In fact she had never been

[1] Kautsky, *Briefwechsel*, 356.
[2] Engels, Will, Somerset House; Engels to Laura Lafargue and Eleanor Marx Aveling, 14 Nov. 1894, *Correspondance*, iii. 370.

consulted by Engels in its preparation, and her exclusion was probably a result of the pressure exerted upon him by Bebel and Adler, who had even wanted to secure the whole of the Marxian *Nachlass* for the German party. It was presumably Engels's regard for his deceased friend as well as English law that prevented Eleanor from being deprived of her rightful possession of her father's papers.

She was, indeed, left in the dark about the fate of the Karl Marx manuscripts, and naturally began to suspect that some sinister scheme was being concocted around Engels. It was probably about this time that Louise asked Eleanor 'to sign a paper making *her* [Louise] the responsible owner of the papers for fear Pumps should get hold of them', and this gave her, as she recalled later, the first hint of something odd going on. Bebel, for his part, gave her a 'cool assurance' that she and Laura 'need not trouble about Mohr's papers as *he* knew it was all right'.[1] She began to wonder and made attempts to find out more about the possible fate of her father's papers. The matter suddenly came into the open in the autumn of 1893 when Louise, in a letter to Eleanor, declared that she would regard her friendship with Eleanor as broken because of the accusation of a 'breach of faith' which the latter had made—so she alleged—against her. On the back of the letter she received, Aveling wrote a reply in a cryptogram which Eleanor sent back to Louise with her decipherment. In this devious way the Avelings insisted that they were not responsible for the disclosure of 'your relations to Bebel'.[2] Eleanor's open conflict with Louise now began, and Aveling's hand in it did not promise any rational solution, for his selfish interests also played a part in the struggle.

Eleanor soon developed a hatred for Dr. Freyberger,

---

[1] Eleanor Marx Aveling to Laura Lafargue, 25 Dec. 1894, 2 Jan. 1895, Bottigelli Collection.
[2] Louise Kautsky to Eleanor Marx Aveling, 15 Sept. [1893]; Edward and Eleanor Marx Aveling to Louise Kautsky, n.d., Bottigelli Collection.

who had gained not merely Engels's full confidence but also Louise's affection. He married Louise early in the following year, and the newly wedded couple, upon Engels's suggestion, spent a fortnight at Eastbourne, the old man's favourite resort. 'I *can't* see how anyone can stand Freyberger', Eleanor wrote to her sister, '. . . I never could pretend to admire the profound sagacity & brilliant wit of the new bridegroom. Well, on the whole I'm glad Louise is married. She was too young for the rather dreary life at the General's.' Yet she thought it 'queer' for them to 'take the General a-honeymooning with them'. 'You ask me how he takes it', she wrote in the same letter:

I don't know, any more than I know what arrangements they are making. I've not seen or spoken to the General alone for many months, & whatever he may think he could hardly express his opinion before those most concerned. But you know the General is always under the thumb of the 'lady of the house'. When Pumps was with him, lo, she was good in his sight; now Pumps is dethroned & Louise is the queen who can do no wrong. But I *am* anxious to know what the household arrangements are to be, for frankly it will be intolerable if Freyberger permanently installs himself at Regents Park Road. It was unpleasant enough to constantly meet him there, but to know him always there![1]

Moreover, Louise remained as rude and insolent as ever. Eleanor had written to her about her marriage and got an irritating reply: 'You wrote "marriage is a lottery in whatever society". May I add out of experience that *no* society would tolerate a friendship between man and woman, without sneers and comments.'[2] Louise also told her that she and her husband were to remain with Engels. Eleanor was furious, and at once transmitted to her sister 'the latest news from the menage of Regents Park Road (oh! for a Balzac to paint it!)':

[1] Eleanor Marx Aveling to Laura Lafargue, 22 Feb. 1894, Bottigelli Collection.
[2] Louise Freyberger to Eleanor Marx Aveling, 22 Feb. [1894], Bottigelli Collection.

That Freyberger should hold 'at homes' at the General's is certainly coming it strong . . . The General, after all, *is* getting old . . . I question much if the Freyberger influence is likely to be a good one for the party. Anyone who has the slightest knowledge of human nature must know that this gentleman is playing his own game alone.

Eleanor apparently had got no exact knowledge as yet of the Freybergers' mission in London. Moreover, she still felt a certain pity for Louise. 'And poor Louise!' she added in her despatch to Laura, 'She *has* dropped from the frying pan into the fire. But then with us women it is generally a question of the frying pan or the fire & it is hard to say which is the worse. At the best our state is parlous.'[1]

Eleanor was now seriously worried about all the papers and letters which were at the General's. The Bernsteins also appear to have shared her anxiety. 'Should anything happen to the General, they said', she again wrote to Laura:

F[reyberger] is quite capable of getting hold of anything he can & selling it! For you must remember F[reyberger] is simply an anti-Semite (tho' I would wager my Jewish head that he's a Jew) & has nothing to do with the movement. It is no joking matter I assure you, for you know very well that anyone living with the General can manipulate him to any extent. Sam Moore (who is over again) also seemed doubtful . . . He was (& I believe is) a trustee under the General's will . . He told me he would try & get an opportunity of speaking to the General (who is sure to consult him as the other trustee under the will, Gumpert, is since dead) & of making sure about all papers . . . Mohr's MSS etc are things we can't be too careful about.[2]

Eleanor obviously did not know of the existence of Engels's last will, though she had been informed of a previous one.

There was a period of truce in her struggle, and in the summer Engels took the Avelings as well as Louise to a Handel Festival at the Crystal Palace. Eleanor also went to

[1] Eleanor Marx Aveling to Laura Lafargue, 2 March 1894, Bottigelli Collection.
[2] Ibid., 22 March 1894, Bottigelli Collection.

stay with the Lafargues in Paris at this time. Yet hostilities were resumed in the autumn in a more intense form. Eleanor sent an urgent message to Laura, begging her to come to London and to bring pressure to bear upon Engels:

When I tell you that Freyberger thro' Bax and others is spreading all through the S.D.F. all over London (so far as our acquaintance or political relations extend) that 'the Avelings have been turned out by the General, & that *now* that the things are in the hands of the Freybergers all will be different'; that Louise is spreading the same reports all over Germany (with personal calumnies about myself that I am ashamed to write) you will see to what a pass things have come.[1]

She went on to say that the Bernsteins and the Mendelsons (the Polish Socialist Stanislaw Mendelson and his wife Maria, who had come to London some time before) '*are* practically turned out' because they were friendly to Eleanor, and 'the poor old General . . . has come to the condition where he is a mere child in the hands of this monstrous pair'. Indeed, 'the wire-pulling of the F[rey- berger]s' had its effect upon Engels. 'For a long time things have been going from bad to worse', she continued: '& it is a positive pain to go to the General's. When he sees me alone—which is only for a moment, he seems glad enough— & then when the two others appear, he becomes like them, & in all but words I am told de trop.' When Engels con- fided the serious state of his health to Eleanor and Louise as a strict secret, the latter nevertheless revealed it to Adler. (His trouble was soon to be diagnosed as cancer in the throat, though the fact seems to have been concealed from him till the end.) Eleanor must have felt that the Germans and Austrians were speculating on his health for some shadowy purpose. 'Pumps *is* got rid of', she went on in this long and frantic message to Laura:

& even tho' the General will not treat me quite like Pumps, the

[1] Eleanor Marx Aveling to Laura Lafargue, 5 Nov. 1894, Bottigelli Collection.

result may come to the same. For despite all one owes the General, we cannot submit to everything. *You* are the one person Louise dreads, & you alone could help now . . . If you don't want to see the F[reyberger]s *sole literary* executors you must act, & that promptly. You will remember that Bebel wrote the papers would be in the right hands. If outsiders know, we should, for when all is said & done this is *our* business & no one else's. The papers—especially all the private papers—are *our* concern; they belong to us—not even to Engels.[1]

At last, on 14 November 1894, Engels disclosed part of his will to Eleanor and Laura. He told them that he had taken the liberty of disposing of all his books, including 'those received from you after Mohr's death', in favour of the German party, as these books together constituted a unique library for the study of Socialism, and as their transfer to Germany was 'a wish expressed to me long ago by Bebel' and other German leaders, 'the best people' in his opinion to use these books. While asking their consent to this arrangement, he informed Marx's daughters that he had made provision for them and for Longuet's children.[2] This letter from Engels about the books, as well as an announcement made at the time in *Vorwärts*, the organ of the German party, that the fourth volume of *Das Kapital* would not be issued, increased Eleanor's suspicions. For fear that the Freybergers might appropriate the manuscripts, she even volunteered to copy her father's rough draft for the fourth volume by herself or possibly with Laura's co-operation.

In December, shortly before Christmas, when Eleanor was away lecturing in the north, Aveling paid a visit to Engels at his new house at 41 Regents Park Road whence he had moved from 122 in the same street. There was a 'storm', he wrote in one of the 'war bulletins' the Avelings were sending to Laura at the time:

[1] Eleanor Marx Aveling to Laura Lafargue, 5 Nov. 1894, Bottigelli Collection.
[2] Engels to Laura Lafargue and Eleanor Marx Aveling, 14 Nov. 1894, *Correspondance*, iii. 370–1.

SEM

There was a conspiracy [said Engels] . . .—he knew all about it . . . you & Eleanor mistrusted him . . . All this in the spe [*sic*] spluttering vein & under the workings of a yeasty conscience, and with much marching up & down and more or less effective dodging of furniture. I said it was no good bullying me. I was only a messenger and he must have it out with you two women.[1]

Eleanor, upon her return from the north, immediately wrote to Engels, 'taking the tone of the offended party':

As to the general MSS. of Mohr, you surely must know that Laura & I are sure *you* would deal with them as Mohr himself would have done. But you can equally understand that we should not like the letters & papers (many of a purely personal nature) to fall into other hands than *yours* or ours. . . . Edward says you seemed to believe in some deep-laid scheme. I can quite believe you do, for I should be blind indeed if I had not seen the efforts to set you against us, & I can hardly wonder if you think what could never have occurred to you had our Nymmy been with you. . . . If you had not been very much poisoned against us you could never have thought so meanly of Mohr's children as to think they could mistrust *you*.[2]

On Christmas Day Engels had a private talk with Eleanor in his own room, 'as an appetiser for the festive meal', wrote Eleanor. He now made her a promise that Marx's papers were to be returned to her and Laura, and she replied that she was quite satisfied with his assurance. A few days later, when Engels came to lunch at the Avelings', she told him that Louise had been spreading all sorts of rumours and that 'we should ourselves have the greatest contempt for August [Bebel]' if he relied on Louise for information.[3] Eleanor thought that his tone had altered considerably after her mentioning Bebel, while Engels was convinced that these talks with Eleanor had 'settled everything' connected with Marx's papers and had 'left us as good friends as before'.[4]

[1] Edward Aveling to Laura Lafargue, 25 Dec. 1894, Bottigelli Collection.
[2] Quoted in Eleanor Marx Aveling to Laura Lafargue, 25 Dec. 1894, Bottigelli Collection.
[3] Eleanor Marx Aveling to Laura Lafargue, 2 Jan. 1895, Bottigelli Collection.
[4] Engels to Laura Lafargue, 19 Jan. 1895, *Correspondance*, iii. 391.

So open war came to an end as far as the manuscripts were concerned, but peace was only on the surface, for Louise's insolence and Eleanor's hatred for her grew as time went on.

*   *   *

One of the 'rumours' which Louise spread and of which Eleanor was 'ashamed' of speaking was about Freddy Demuth. The son of 'our Nymmy' had apparently become an object of curiosity and gossip, as he was allowed to appear at Engels's festivities.[1] Louise had heard from Engels that Freddy was Marx's son. Eleanor, who believed Engels to be his father, contradicted her so vigorously that Louise put the question to the old man. It is not unlikely that Eleanor suggested that Engels should make provision for Freddy in his will. 'The General was much astonished that Tussy stuck so stubbornly to her belief', wrote Louise, 'and he already gave me at the time the right to contradict, if need be, the gossip that he had disowned his son.'[2]

Eleanor still distrusted Louise's allegation, which she regarded as a part of her defamatory tactics against her. Meanwhile Samuel Moore, who usually spent much of his time on legal business in Africa, came to London and assisted Engels in making a codicil, which was completed on 26 July. One of the two important alterations made there was the reduction to £2,230 of the legacy to be given to Pumps. The other was that all the letters exchanged between Marx and Engels were to be regarded as Engels's and consequently to be handed over not to Eleanor but to the Germans. Obviously Eleanor did not gain from her struggle with Louise. Moreover, Engels, who was already seriously ill, confirmed to Moore that Freddy was Marx's son. Thereupon Moore went to Orpington, Kent, where the Avelings had moved shortly before, to bring the news to Eleanor. She,

[1] Engels to Natalie Liebknecht, 1 July 1894, photocopy, IML (Berlin).
[2] Louise Freyberger to Bebel, 2 Sept. 1898, quoted in Werner Blumenberg, *Karl Marx in Selbstzeugnissen und Bilddokumenten* (Hamburg, 1962), 115.

however, insisted that the old man had lied, and Engels told Moore on his return that 'Tussy wants to make an idol of her father'. On 4 August when Eleanor visited Regents Park Road, Engels, who was already too weak to speak, wrote the painful truth about Freddy down on a slate. According to Louise, 'Tussy, as she came out, was shaken so violently that she forgot all her hatred against me and wept bitterly on my neck'. Louise added, writing to Bebel, that Freddy looked very much like Marx, having a distinct Jewish countenance.[1] The revelation was at first a terrible blow to Eleanor, but she gradually reconciled herself to it. 'After all Marx the "Politiker" & "Denker" can take his chance', she later wrote to Laura, 'while Marx the Man . . . is less likely to fare as well.'[2] She also began to develop a special feeling of affinity for her half-brother.

On 5 August 1895, the day after she had had the fatal interview, the ailing General passed away, and she was informed of his death by a simple note sent by Louise, who had nursed him almost till his last minutes.[3] The funeral took place on 10 August, when his former friends and political disciples gathered together at the Necropolis Station at Waterloo to send off the body to Woking for cremation. On 27 August one of his last wishes was executed: a two-oared boat was hired at Eastbourne, and about six miles out to sea, almost straight out from Beachy Head, the urn containing his ashes was sunk. Only Eleanor, Aveling, Bernstein, and Lessner were present.[4] For an obituary Eleanor sent her memoir of Engels, which she had written for his seventieth birthday, to the new French journal *Devenir*

[1] Louise Freyberger to Bebel, 2 Sept. 1898, Blumenberg, op. cit. 116.
[2] Eleanor Marx Aveling to Laura Lafargue, 24 Dec. 1896, photocopy, IISH.
[3] Louise Freyberger to Eleanor Marx Aveling, 5 August 1895, Bottigelli Collection.
[4] Eleanor Marx Aveling to Kautsky, 29 Sept. 1895, IISH; Lessner, 'A Worker's Reminiscences of Friedrich Engels', in Marx-Engels, *Reminiscences*, 181.

Social, while Aveling wrote his own memoir for the *Labour Prophet,* the organ of the Labour Church movement, begging the readers to accept the 'historic truth' that Engels was an atheist.[1]

*   *   *

Meanwhile Louise kept herself busy with arrangements for settling Engels's estate. On 28 August probate of his will and codicil was granted to her and Bernstein, two of the executors. His effects were estimated at £25,155 3s. 11d. (re-sworn early in the following year at £25,265 0s. 11d.), of which, it appears, several thousand pounds came to Eleanor. But her immediate concern was her father's papers. In order to obtain these and other items due to her, she had to go through a number of irritating formalities which Louise imposed upon her. Louise went so far as to remind her of the receipts she had given Engels in return for borrowed money, although Engels had declared in his codicil that all money payments of this nature were to be regarded as free gifts.[2] Bebel, for his part, was complaining that the sum allotted for the German party was not large enough. 'A reduction in the amount of money which goes to private hands', he wrote to Adler, 'would have done no wrong. With the exception of what Louise receives, the money in the other hands will be squandered quite soon, and with this money will be created as little benefit for mankind as with the many thousand pounds that have already flowed into the same hands.' He accepted the circumstances in which Louise had 'let the Marx daughters gain everything to which they have a just claim', but he thought that the Engels papers which fell into the hands of the Germans would be of little value for publication without Marx's *Nachlass,* from which, he believed, Eleanor and Laura

[1] Eleanor Marx Aveling, 'Frédéric Engels', *Devenir Social,* August 1895, originally published in the Austrian *Sozialdemokratische Monatschrift,* Nov. 1890; *Labour Prophet,* Sept., Oct. 1895.

[2] Louise Freyberger to Eleanor Marx Aveling, 13 Sept. 1895, Bottigelli Collection.

expected material gains.[1] When twenty-seven cases of books arrived in Germany, Bebel and Singer made a 'very cool and unfair announcement'—complained Eleanor—and did not so much as mention Marx, though 'a good half' of the cases contained Marx's library 'presented to the German Party . . . by Marx's children. . . . It will be said that Louise graciously *gave* all the books to the Party, though she refused to give even the bookcases!' Eleanor was indignant when she heard that the Freybergers had been freely spending. 'The Duke and Duchess are "launching out" in grand style', she wrote to Laura: 'They have—or *say* they have, spent £3000 on new furniture, and speak only with contempt of what they made the poor old General buy.'[2]

Bebel, the splendid tactician, had skilfully intervened in the struggle over Engels's legacy, but Louise, his tool in the game, was more successful. She obtained the largest share of Engels's pecuniary wealth and quickly withdrew from political activities. Their manœuvring, though successful in securing Marx's library for the Germans, led to the division of the sacred scriptures of Marxism. Bebel, moreover, was no theoretician and made little contribution later on to the publication of these papers. Had not the party interests interfered in the name of 'mankind', the unity of these precious documents would have been maintained. Not only would Eleanor have been saved from unnecessary worry but she might even have established herself, possibly with the co-operation of Kautsky and Bernstein, as the successor of Engels in the field of Marxian scholarship. After all, she inherited the scholarly qualities of her father: it was not for material gain that she had fought a dreary struggle to secure his literary remains.

*　　　　*　　　　*

[1] Bebel to Adler, 18 Sept. 1895, Adler, *Briefwechsel*, 186–8.
[2] Eleanor Marx Aveling to Laura Lafargue, 24 Oct. 1895, Bottigelli Collection. See also Eleanor Marx Aveling to Liebknecht, 11 Nov. 1895, Liebknecht, *Briefwechsel*, 444.

In 1893 an English translation by Eleanor of Bernstein's introduction to Lassalle's *Reden und Schriften* appeared under the title *Ferdinand Lassalle as a Social Reformer*. It was a timely publication, for the book emphasized the need for the independent political activity of the working class, and very few—certainly not Eleanor—noticed the rudiments of the Revisionist heresy contained in it.[1] Bernstein was then working under Engels's close supervision. Moreover, his concern at the time was not so much with party politics as with Marxian scholarship, and he obtained Eleanor's eager cooperation in this field.[2]

Eleanor had wanted to write Mohr's biography and made a brief attempt in an article entitled 'Karl Marx, Stray Notes' written for the *Austrian Workers' Calendar* of 1895.[3] After the death of Engels she appealed to various persons who might have letters from her father to send them to her or to Laura, but there was little response. She began sorting Marx's papers at a depository at Chancery Lane. 'The most important letters *by far* are those to Engels', she wrote to Laura, 'and in preparing the necessary documents for a Biography we must have access to these letters.' Yet Engels's papers were then in the keeping of Julius Motteler, 'the business man of the German Social Democratic Party'—as he was often called—who lived in London at the time. 'There is a double lock to the box at Motteler's', wrote Eleanor: 'One key Ede Bernstein has—the other the female Freebooter [Louise] as Bebel's representative. Ede won't ask Louise to go to the Motteler's with him to get the letters

---

[1] 'A few years hence it [the movement] may, perhaps, be fighting in yet other ways, and still it will be the same movement', wrote Bernstein in his *Ferdinand Lassalle as a Social Reformer*, 192.

[2] He was able to use Marx's letters to Lassalle discovered among the Marx Papers, and Eleanor typed them for future publication. Engels to Bebel, 18 Oct. 1893, Bebel, *Briefwechsel*, 721; Engels to Laura Lafargue, 17 Dec. 1894, *Correspondance*, iii. 376.

[3] Eleanor Marx Aveling, 'Karl Marx, Lose Blätter', *Österreichische Arbeiter-Kalender* (Brünn, 1895), 51–54. The English original was printed in Marx-Engels, *Reminiscences*, 250–3.

268 THE MARXIAN LEGACY

& hence he is postponing the Engels' Life which he intended to write.'[1] Apart from those letters which were beyond her reach, there was yet another difficulty in writing her father's life, for Eleanor was strongly conscious of the fact that Marx had been 'intellectually many-sided'. 'Not only Science appealed to him—but Art & Literature', she wrote in a letter to Kautsky: 'Mohr's sympathy with *every* form of work was so perfect that it will take many men to deal with him from their own point of view. I only despair when I think of the task of gathering together all these loose threads & weaving them into a whole. Yet, it must be done . . .'[2]

Meanwhile, Eleanor sent Kautsky a letter from Heine to her father concerning his poetry, *Deutschland: ein Winter-märchen*, for publication in *Neue Zeit*. She declined to write an introduction, for she felt it 'too impudent', but she sent a few notes on the intimate friendship between the two great men which Kautsky made use of in his notes on the letter.[3] About this time she received from Caroline Smith, her cousin in Holland, a long letter Mohr had written to his father about his studies and his love for Jenny when he was a student at Berlin. She gave Kautsky permission to publish the letter, though she felt herself 'half a traitor in giving it to the world'.[4] She wrote an introductory note—'writing it was worse than having a tooth out!'—and told the readers that she had regarded this 'extraordinary human document' as material for the biography of Marx, which, she hoped, 'will be completed in the foreseeable future'.[5] Eleanor never

[1] Eleanor Marx Aveling to Laura Lafargue, 2 Jan. 1897, Bottigelli Collection.

[2] Eleanor Marx Aveling to Kautsky, 28 Dec. 1896, IISH.

[3] Ibid., 7 Sept. 1895, IISH; 'Heine an Marx', *Neue Zeit*, xiv–i (1895–6), Nr. 1, 14–19.

[4] Ibid., 19 July 1897, IISH.

[5] Ibid., 21 Sept. 1897, IISH; 'Ein Brief des jungen Marx', *Neue Zeit*, xvi–i (1897–8), Nr. 1, 4–12; an English translation of Eleanor's introduction in Marx-Engels, *Reminiscences*, 257. Her article on her father written for *Progress* in 1883 was reprinted in the *Social-Democrat*, June 1897.

completed a full life of her father, but the letter was used by Franz Mehring in his classical work on Marx. He detected in this letter 'the man striving after truth even to the point of moral and physical exhaustion, his insatiable thirst for knowledge, his inexhaustible capacity for work, his merciless self-criticism',[1] traits which one could also find in Eleanor herself.

*   *   *

In the course of her struggle with Louise, Kautsky recalled, 'Tussy changed herself finally from a fervent admirer to an inveterate foe of my first wife'.[2] This transformation drew her close once more to Kautsky. She asked him to resume the work on the fourth volume of *Das Kapital* and was surprised to know that Engels had 'stopped' him: 'he never said a word about it to me!'[3] She defied the ban and at once began negotiations for the publication of the fourth volume by appointing Kautsky as its editor. As there was difficulty about the terms of publication with Meissner, the publisher of the first three volumes of *Das Kapital*, she decided that the new volume was '*not* in the ordinary sense the 4th vol., being only certain notes which the editor has to work from' and that she would therefore not be bound by his copyright and would apply to Dietz, the publisher of *Neue Zeit* who had been recommended by Kautsky.[4] Meissner at last agreed to her conditions, and she wrote to Kautsky: 'I can't forget that Meissner was the only publisher in Germany who would even look at—let alone publish—Mohr's work.'[5] The publication of the fourth volume, however, was delayed, and when it came out, many years after Eleanor's death, it was published by Dietz under the title of *Theorien über Mehrwert*.

In the meantime Eleanor herself undertook to edit some of her father's English articles. In 1896 she compiled a book

[1] Mehring, *Karl Marx*, 10.   [2] Kautsky, *Briefwechsel*, 214.
[3] Eleanor Marx Aveling to Kautsky, 22 Aug., 27 Dec. 1895, IISH.
[4] Eleanor Marx Aveling to Kautsky, 30 April 1896, IISH.
[5] Ibid., 20 May 1896, IISH.

from a series of twenty articles bearing his signature in the *New York Tribune*, 'a wonderfully interesting history of /48', under the title of *Revolution and Counter-Revolution*.[1] The real author of these articles, however, turned out to have been Engels, but the blame for this unfortunate error should not be placed upon Eleanor, who had been deprived of access to the Marx-Engels correspondence, where this fact could be verified. She had also started editing the *Tribune* articles by her father on Palmerston and the Crimean war and those dealing with the diplomatic history of the eighteenth century published in David Urquhart's *Free Press*. The work of preparing these for the press took much of Aveling's time as well as hers. Here again there was trouble with the publisher. 'I tried—for Sonnenschein is *such* a thief—to get another publisher', she wrote to Laura: 'I have tried Methuen, Macmillan, Unwin (the only *likely* ones) & failed. I will make a last effort with Longman. If he fails too, we must go to Sonnenschein.'[2] As for the question of writing a preface, she thought it unfair to saddle her father's work with any 'views': 'his work must stand as it is, & we must all try & learn from it. And we can all "walk under his huge legs"— & find ourselves not *dis*honourable, but honourable graves.'[3] *The Eastern Question*, a collection of Marx's *Tribune* articles on the subject, edited by Eleanor and her husband, was published in 1897 by Sonnenschein. Here again the same unfortunate error that was to stain the reputation of the previous volume crept in, for several articles which Eleanor attributed to her father had been actually written by Engels. She wrote an introduction in which she merely reiterated her father's view: 'To-day the Russian Government . . . is, as it was in the "fifties", the greatest enemy of all advance, the greatest stronghold of reaction.' Eleanor, however, did

[1] Eleanor Marx Aveling to Laura Lafargue, 19 Oct. 1895, Bottigelli Collection.

[2] Ibid., 2 Jan. 1897, Bottigelli Collection.

[3] Eleanor Marx Aveling to Kautsky, 3 June 1897, IISH.

not live long enough to see the publication of the two other works she had prepared, *The Story of the Life of Palmerston* and *Secret Diplomatic History of the Eighteenth Century*, which came out in 1899. There was yet another volume by Mohr which she was preparing for publication. She had discovered among Marx's papers 'a simply *magnificent* paper . . . read by him (Oh! the work that man did!) to the Council of the I.W.M.A.' in 1865, 'an admirable economic exposition'.[1] Marx's *Value, Price, and Profit* edited by her appeared in 1898 with a preface by Aveling, for Eleanor was dead by that time.

* * *

Engels had once declared in a letter to Kautsky that Eleanor was the only person who could write a satisfactory history of the Socialist movement in England.[2] She soon gained a reputation, at least among the Continental Socialists, as an authority on English Socialism. In 1895 her 'Letters from England', written in collaboration with her husband, appeared in the *Russkoye Bogatstvo* (*'Russian Wealth'*), a monthly magazine published at St. Petersburg, in which she dealt with various topics of politics and literature with critical comments. She highly recommended to the Russian readers a new novel by her friend Clementina Black, *An Agitator*. She called it 'a really supreme and remarkably realistic account of certain stages of this complicated movement', i.e. the English working-class movement, for the hero in the novel, Christopher Brand, as she felt, combined the career of a John Burns and the character of a Champion.[3] In the same year her article on 'The Working-Class Movement in England' was published in Emanuel Wurm's *Volks-Lexikon* and was also issued as a separate pamphlet with a preface by Wilhelm Liebknecht. Her old 'Library' asserted

[1] Eleanor Marx Aveling to Kautsky, 27 April 1897, IISH.
[2] Engels to Kautsky, 29 Sept. 1892, Kautsky, *Briefwechsel*, 370.
[3] *Russkoye Bogatstvo*, Jan., Feb., April, May 1895.

that the author knew the subject 'almost by heredity' and 'from the heart', but she wrote to her sister: 'It is worth nothing because I had to cram the immense amount of material into a very small space.'[1] In fact it was an attempt to trace in a pamphlet of twenty-four pages the whole history of Socialism in England from the Peasant Rising of 1381 to the S.D.F. and I.L.P. of her own day when 'the spirit of Continental Socialism is permeating ever-widening circles of workers in the United Kingdom'.[2] It was by no means a scholarly work. Yet she was already steeped in the Marxian historiography which had begun at the time with Kautsky and Bernstein among its forerunners.

She had made researches in sixteenth-century English history and wrote an article on the 'Evil May Day' of 1517 when the London artisans attacked the foreigners in the city who, they thought, were threatening their own living. This article was intended to serve a practical purpose, as she emphasized the traditional prejudices of Englishmen against foreigners as a reminder for the May Day celebrations of the 1890's.[3] In the course of her studies, however, she became well versed in the documents on the social and economic conditions of England in those and earlier days and was able to challenge Lujo Brentano, the old critic of her father, on controversial quotations he had made in his study of the English guilds.[4] She also offered help in research to Kautsky, who was then working on such topics as the Lollards and the Anabaptists. When she received his work on *Wiedertäufer*

---

[1] Eleanor Marx Aveling to Laura Lafargue, 24 Oct. 1895, Bottigelli Collection.

[2] *Volks-Lexikon* ii (Nürnberg, 1895), 1236–59; Eleanor Marx Aveling, *Die Arbeiterclassen-Bewegung in England*, tr. by Gertrud Liebknecht (Nürnberg, 1895); an English edition was published by the Twentieth Century Press in 1896 under the title of *The Working Class Movement in England*.

[3] *Weekly Times & Echo*, 6 May 1894; a German translation, 'Der böse Maitag', *Neue Zeit*, xii–ii (1893–4), Nr. 30, 122–8.

[4] Eleanor Marx Aveling, 'Wie Lujo Brentano zitirt', *Neue Zeit*, xiii–i (1894–5), Nr. 9, 260–6.

early in 1895, she praised it in glowing terms—a book 'full of verve, of living, palpitating interest'. 'To me your researches are of very special interest', she added, 'because, as you know, I have dabbled somewhat in this sort of thing myself.'[1] When an English translation of his book was contemplated, she again wrote to Kautsky: 'I only regret (especially for England) that you could not deal more fully with the Anabaptists here. . . . My own work in the Record Office & Museum (I mean among the MSS & archives) has *convinced* me that the movement had a far greater hold here than is usually supposed. . . . There was a very *panic* in England about the Anabaptists.'[2] In spite of the time and labour she had put into her own researches, however, she could not establish herself as a Socialist historian. She seems to have been mentally too unstable to develop the necessary faculty of organizing and elaborating the results of her investigation into a unified whole.

*   *   *

Just as Engels's settlement in London had finally freed her father from perennial worries about money, so Eleanor at last found financial security in the ample provision made by her departed guardian. She at once started house-hunting. 'All the *nice* houses are too dear', she wrote to Laura, '& all the cheap ones are shoddy in shoddy neighbourhoods.'[3] In December 1895 she bought a house in Jews Walk, Sydenham, which she named 'The Den'. She was excited and at once reported to her sister, who was also house-hunting:

I am Jewishly proud of my house in Jew's Walk. Voilà. Ground floor—large room (Edward's study & general room combined);

[1] Eleanor Marx Aveling to Kautsky, 20 Feb. 1895, IISH. Kautsky's work was *Die Vorläufer des neuen Sozialismus*, erster Teil, 'Von Plato bis zu den Wiedertäufer' (Stuttgart, 1895).

[2] Ibid., 28 Dec. 1896, IISH.

[3] Eleanor Marx Aveling to Laura Lafargue, 19 Oct. 1895, Bottigelli Collection.

dining room (opens in back garden), kitchen, scullery, pantry, coal & wine cellars, cupboards, large entrance hall.—One flight of upstairs (easy)—bedroom—spare bedroom (*yours*), servants' room, bath room (large enough to be another spare room on special occasion), my *study*!!!—Everywhere we have electric light . . . tho' gas is laid on too, & I have a gas cooking stove & gas fires in most of the upper rooms.

As to furnishing, Edward, she said, paid for all the furniture with the money he had obtained by mortgaging his share in a property in Austinfriars, Central London. 'I want you to know this', she told Laura, 'as it would not be fair to think I was paying for it all.'[1]

The effect of this security on the Avelings' morale, however, was not entirely favourable: Edward revived his predilection for the theatre and found it within his or his wife's means to squander money as much on other women as on himself. Eleanor, for her part, plunged into hard work. We have already seen her achievements in Marxian scholarship and her frustration as a Socialist historian. Her greatest concern, however, was once more in the field of Socialist politics and the trade union movement. The employers' offensive against the unions still continued, and there were already signs of disintegration even within the Socialist movement of her father's school.

[1] Eleanor Marx Aveling to Laura Lafargue, 10 Dec. 1895, Bottigelli Collection.

XI ∽ SOCIAL DEMOCRACY IN DILEMMA

T HE death of Engels marked a new departure in the political life of the Avelings as well as in the history of Marxism. In their Socialist agitation they now definitely identified themselves with the S.D.F., even though that body was still dominated by Hyndman, whom the deceased General had anathematized. The S.D.F. now aspired to play its role in the international field as the only Marxist party in England, and through it the Avelings made an important contribution to the struggle against Anarchism. Indeed, they were at last accepted by the rest of the English Marxists not only as their colleagues but also as the custodians of the orthodoxy of their creed.

The removal of the personal pressure exerted by Engels, however, had its effect upon the orthodoxy itself, especially among the German party. Reassessments of doctrine, called forth by the emergence of new situations, now suddenly became a source of conflict, as the captains of the Marxist host began quarrelling over its sacred ordinances. In fact, Marxian Socialism after Engels, deprived of a powerful yet critical *eminence grise*, was left in a state of indecision, and under the cover of strict orthodoxy it proved easy for opportunistic tendencies to flourish. This was a line of development for the International that Eleanor Marx would certainly have deplored, had she lived on to see its culmination—the triumph of Revisionism under the name of orthodoxy.

*   *   *

The death of a man whom Hyndman had once regarded as his rival in the patronage of Marx removed a major obstacle to the *rapprochement* of the Avelings with the S.D.F. This had already begun, as we have seen, with Aveling's criticisms of Keir Hardie.[1] Reconciliation went on apace: in the summer, he was commissioned by *Justice* as well as by several Continental papers to attend the T.U.C. at Cardiff; and Eleanor was asked to give a series of lectures at Burnley, the stronghold of the S.D.F.[2] In the autumn the Avelings started on one week's tour for the S.D.F. and I.L.P. in Scotland and another week for the Lancashire District S.D.F.

Eleanor appeared at the Albion Hall, Glasgow, on 13 October and spoke about Engels. 'It was a labour of love on her part', reported the *Labour Leader*, 'the only blemish being her severe condemnation of hero worship in the movement, while at the same time almost deifying Engels.' Aveling had lectured in the same hall a few days before on a favourite subject, 'Socialism and Radicalism', and his speech was enthusiastically received as 'the cleverest and most cogent exposition' of Socialism.[3] Indeed, his reputation as the leading theoretician of Marxism in England rose high among the Glasgow Socialists, who even invited him to stand at the General Election of that year. The Avelings's Lancashire tour, which followed, covered ten towns in the weaving district, and on its last day, 1 December, they organized an entertainment—recitals, songs, character sketches, etc.—in St. James' Hall, Burnley.[4] This was a clear sign that their popularity was growing rapidly among the provincial

[1] Aveling was also entrusted with editing the May Day issue (1895) of *Clarion*, certainly no friend of Hardie, and it came out with international greetings and a piece of poetry by Laura Lafargue on the 'Eight Hour Day'. *Clarion*, 27 April 1895; Edward Aveling to Kautsky, 26 Feb. 1895, IISH.

[2] Eleanor Marx Aveling to Kautsky, 28 Aug. 1895, IISH; Eleanor Marx Aveling to Laura Lafargue, 4 Sept. 1895, Bottigelli Collection.

[3] *Labour Leader*, 19 Oct. 1895. The Twentieth Century Press of the S.D.F. published his pamphlet *Socialism and Radicalism* (n.d.).

[4] Ibid., 7 Dec. 1895.

Socialists. The executive of the S.D.F. could no longer ignore their work, though *Justice* only a year before had asserted that 'nothing . . . [could] make Dr. Aveling other than—Dr. Aveling'.[1]

The S.D.F., as we have seen, had made attempts to come to terms with the German Social Democrats, and Hyndman held out the olive-branch yet more earnestly to them after the death of Engels.[2] After all, the two Marxist parties, though unequal in size and strength, had adopted the same creed and the same tactics, and the S.D.F. always sought close relations with the more successful German party. It was under these circumstances that Bernstein suggested that the Avelings should rejoin the S.D.F.[3] The party leadership, however, was still unwilling to accept Aveling's formal affiliation. Indeed, the executive sought to put an end to all further communication with him by cautioning the branches, and went so far as to issue a statement to the effect that 'upon reliable information' Aveling had been using his influence to prevent the establishment of cordial relations between the S.D.F. and the German party. Thereupon Aveling sent a circular to the prominent Marxists on the Continent, denying the accusation and inviting them to write letters of recommendation on his behalf to the S.D.F. He asked Kautsky to lay stress in his letter upon 'my attempts with the General of late to make him less bitter against them [the S.D.F.]'.[4] The opposition to him came mainly from Hyndman, and probably also from Bax, who kept in touch with the Freybergers. But Hyndman was forced to alter his attitude when the S.D.F. began to receive letters

[1] *Justice*, 7 July 1894.
[2] Even when 'our courageous and thoroughgoing comrade' Bebel declined the S.D.F.'s invitation to come to England, *Justice* expressed hopes that 'our relations will become more and more cordial with our German fellow Social-Democrats'. *Justice*, 11 Jan. 1896.
[3] Eleanor Marx Aveling to Kautsky, 15 March 1898, IISH.
[4] Edward Aveling to Kautsky, also to F. Van der Goes, 8 Feb. 1896, IISH.

TEM

in his support from the Continental leaders.[1] 'In answer to the letter sent round', Eleanor wrote to her sister:

generally we had such replies that Hyndman *could* not hold out. As a matter of fact he was really taken in (this time) by the Freebooters [i.e. Freybergers], who made him believe the poor old General was *longing* to meet him, Hyndman—& that we prevented it. In the face of the execllent letters from *all* Continental people—including (& their letters were the strongest, because written before consultation with the Freebooters) Bebel & Adler, & of course Liebknecht, the Executive of the S.D.F on Tuesday *unanimously* withdrew their statement; everyone shook hands, & the Freebooters have thus *unwillingly* helped to bring about a very useful 'reconciliation' between us & the S.D.F. For years we have (to the General's distress) been on good terms with the S.D.F. *members*. Now we are *officially* to work together. You know what such 'official' friendship means—Edward & Hyndman no more love one another than do Paul & Brousse—but it is useful for the movement, & especially for the forthcoming Congress.[2]

*   *   *

The preparations for the London congress of the International had provided both sides with a special incentive for reconciliation. We have already seen how the Zurich Committee had become an organizational link between Aveling and the S.D.F. The co-operation that the Zurich Committee had gained from the T.U.C. had resulted in the setting up of a joint committee between these two bodies. Aveling, though nominally a translator for the new committee jointly with A. S. Headingley, was the leading spirit of the Zurich Committee, on which he had the close collaboration of Quelch for the S.D.F. and E. R. Pease for the Fabian Society. One of the main tasks set for the joint committee was to raise funds for the forthcoming congress, and the Zurich Committee, which represented the Socialist societies and trades councils, had to make greater efforts in this

[1] Hyndman, *Further Reminiscences*, 143.
[2] Eleanor Marx Aveling to Laura Lafargue, 5 March 1896, Bottigelli Collection.

line than the parliamentary committee of the T.U.C.

It was for this purpose that an entertainments committee was set up and placed under Aveling's care. In due course he managed to organize a musical and dramatic entertainment, which was held at the S.D.F. Hall in the Strand on 15 June 1895. For this he had secured the free services of several professional actors and actresses. There was a certain Miss Lilian Richardson who made a particularly favourable impression. She played the part of a charming widow in Alec Nelson's one-act drama, *In the Train*—a character with whom, according to the report in *Justice*, 'any travelling companion might certainly be pardoned for falling in love'.[1] The travelling companion, the Deputy Governor of Portsmouth Prison, was played by Aveling himself, while 'our indefatigable secretary, H. W. Lee, was a not too obtrusive guard'. Miss Richardson must have been the woman with whom, as Will Thorne, chairman of this entertainment, later recalled, 'Dr. Aveling became very familiar':[2] we shall hear more of her later. The Zurich Committee was nominally responsible for two more entertainments—one held at the Athenaeum Hall in December, and another at St. George's Hall in March in the following year. These gave Aveling an opportunity to revive his ambitions as a playwright by presenting some of his unsuccessful plays such as *Judith Shakespeare* and *Hundred Years Ago* to an uncritical audience.[3]

How far Eleanor co-operated in these dramatic efforts is not known, though her name was on one occasion advertised in *Justice* along with other artists.[4] She apparently preferred to continue and intensify her propaganda tour for the S.D.F. 'The last few weeks I've had very little time for anything', she wrote to Kautsky in April 1896, 'as I had long-standing lecturing engagements that I had to fulfil—

[1] *Justice*, 22 June 1895.
[2] Thorne, op. cit. 148. According to Thorne, the play in which this woman and Lee took part was called *The Railway Guard*, but this may be a slip of his memory.
[3] *Justice*, 18 Jan., 8 Feb. 1896.   [4] Ibid., 15 June 1895.

Edinburgh, Bristol, Aberdeen, in each case being away from early on Saturday till late on Tuesday. Then the accumulated correspondence & housework take another day! *And* the Congress! That takes no end of time one way or another, too.'[1] In Edinburgh Eleanor gave an 'encouraging' description of the German Social Democratic movement at an S.D.F. meeting. While she was away in Scotland, Aveling, surprisingly energetic for a sick man, was lecturing to a Burnley audience on 'How Fortunes are Made', condemning money-making as 'immoral'.[2] In spite of the unfavourable reputation which he still had in some quarters, Aveling was widely accepted as a talented speaker, entertainer, and even poet. A poem he wrote for recitation, entitled 'The Tramp of the Workers', was well received and was published by the Twentieth Century Press, the S.D.F.'s publisher.

Tramp, tramp, tramp—how they tramp along,
Thousands marching, an army strong,
Led by Generals Dire Distress,
Cold and Hunger and Nakedness.
    . . .
Sound the loudest, as is most meet,
Is the sound of the workers' feet
Keeping step as they march along,
Till their march is a psalm and song.
    . . .
Workers all! To the fight, the fight!
Length and breadth of the world unite!
What to lose but a galling chain?
What to win? Why a world to gain![3]

*   *   *

The joint committee of the London congress issued a circular declaring its adherence to the decision of the Zurich

[1] Eleanor Marx Aveling to Kautsky, 19 April 1896, IISH. Eleanor acted as secretary of the Hotel and Reception Committee for the congress.

[2] *Labour Leader*, 4 April 1896; *Justice*, 4 April 1896. The Aberdeen S.D.F. too was favoured with a visit by Edward as well as by Eleanor. *Justice*, 28 March, 9 May 1896.

[3] *Justice*, 4 April 1896.

congress on the terms of admission. All trade unions were to be admitted; so were all Socialist bodies which recognized 'the necessity of the organisation of the workers and of political action'.[1] The Avelings had apparently succeeded in inducing the committee to exclude Anarchists from the congress. This had in fact been one of their principal objects after the Zurich congress.

Anarchist outrages were again attracting attention, especially in France. Eleanor translated from the French original an article by Georgi Plekhanov on 'Anarchism and Socialism' in which the author traced the historical development of the Anarchist doctrine and sought to explain why it had lately become attractive:

In this society, satisfied and rotten to the marrow of its bones, where all faiths are long since dead, where all sincere opinions appear ridiculous, in this *monde où l'on s'ennui* . . . there are people who lend a willing ear to the song of the Anarchist siren. . . . By taking possession of the Anarchist doctrine, the decadent, *fin de siècle* writers restore to it its true character of bourgeois individualism.[2]

No doubt Eleanor fully shared these views. She firmly believed that Anarchism was merely a symptom of this sick society and that Marxism was the only effective cure. She declared in the preface to her translation, which was published by the Twentieth Century Press, that 'the Anarchists . . . must be taught once and for all, that they cannot be allowed to make the Congresses of the Revolutionary Socialists of the whole world a playground for reaction and international spydom'.[3]

[1] *Clarion*, 14 Dec. 1895; *Justice*, 11 Jan. 1896; *Labour Leader*, 11 Jan. 1896.

[2] Her translation was originally published in *Weekly Times and Echo*, 6 Jan.–24 Feb. 1895.

[3] Plekhanov, *Anarchism and Socialism* (1895), 6. Edward also contributed to the anti-Anarchist campaign by interviewing Vera Zassoulitch, then an exile in London, who, as she told him, had emancipated herself from terrorism and had since devoted herself to the work of 'teaching the Russian people the doctrines of scientific Socialism'. *Clarion*, 23 Feb. 1895.

The London congress was preceded by a propaganda tour by Liebknecht, whose mission it was to impress the British hosts with the strength of the German party and the efficacy of its political action. With the death of Engels, Eleanor had revived her old affection for her 'Library'. 'How *dare* you say you are glad we are not estranged from you?' she complained to Liebknecht.[1] 'Library', for his part, was 'very sore', as Eleanor wrote in a letter to Laura, 'at the General ignoring him so absolutely in his will. He says (openly) it is because he has not like Adler & Bebel "mitgeliebt" [loved together].'[2] Engels's will, as we have seen, did not satisfy Eleanor herself, and the fact that she and Liebknecht shared this grievance drew them closer together. It was probably on her initiative that the Zurich Committee invited Liebknecht to come to England.

A pamphlet entitled *Wilhelm Liebknecht and the German Social-Democratic Movement* was prepared by Aveling for the committee. He sent an urgent message to Liebknecht on counter-moves by the Anarchists and their sympathizers in England:

Domela Nieuwenhuis has been over here making much mischief, which you only can undo . . . .The danger is the I.L.P. and especially Hardie and Mann. They are both sentimentalists. . . . You have in this country at your back the Trade Unions with one or two exceptions, S.D.F. ditto (see *Justice*), Fabians, I think, foreign organisations generally, and the Organisation Committee to a man, except [Tom] Mann.[3]

Liebknecht began his campaign on 19 May at the Queen's Hall, Langham Place, London, with Aveling in the chair. The veteran Socialist with 'the appearance of an old English gentleman farmer', reported *Justice*, emphasized in his

[1] Eleanor Marx Aveling to Liebknecht, 15 Aug. 1895, Liebknecht, *Briefwechsel*, 440.

[2] Eleanor Marx Aveling to Laura Lafargue, 5 March 1896, Bottigelli Collection.

[3] Edward Aveling to Liebknecht, 8 May 1896, Liebknecht, *Briefwechsel*, 447n.

speech that 'the days of romantic fighting had gone by'.[1] 'It was disgusting', commented the Anarchist *Freedom*, 'to see Aveling inviting people who knew nothing of Liebknecht to break out into deafening applause at the mention of his name (just as other political tricksters use the name of G.O.M.).'[2] Liebknecht and Aveling visited Southampton and Bristol, and then proceeded to Oxford, where Eleanor joined them. After a series of lectures delivered successively at Glasgow, Edinburgh, and Bradford, they arrived in Manchester on 30 May. At a reception held at the Mosley Hotel, Dr. Pankhurst of the I.L.P. presented the German visitor with an address. His daughter Sylvia, later famous as a suffragette, has given her impression of Eleanor on this occasion: 'an attractive personality, with dark brows and strong, vivid colouring'. 'Beside her', she added, 'was the repellent figure of Edward Aveling.'[3] 'Dr. Aveling looked tragically about him', read an unfriendly *Labour Leader*, 'to see where that confounded draught was coming from; Mrs. Aveling, black-haired, buxom, and smiling, turned up the collar of his coat. Presently her husband rose and read the address, sitting down with an aspect of profound world-despair.'[4] After successful meetings at Manchester and Liverpool, Liebknecht's tour ended characteristically in the East End of London. On 6 June the Great Assembly Hall at Mile End was crammed with 'a mass of proletariat' who listened attentively to his speech, delivered partly in English and partly in German. Eleanor also spoke, in English, and there were speakers in Yiddish and in Polish.[5]

Before he returned to Germany, Liebknecht found time to visit the houses where Marx had lived in London and other places associated with the past. The past, indeed, overshadowed the present of the Socialist International. Just

[1] *Justice*, 23 May 1896.   [2] *Freedom*, June 1896.

[3] Sylvia Pankhurst, *The Suffragette Movement* (1931), 128.

[4] *Labour Leader*, 6 June 1896.

[5] *Justice*, 13 June 1896; a handbill on the Mile End meeting issued by the Twentieth Century Press, IISH.

as the English section of the First International had parted company with the authoritarian General Council, so now the British I.L.P. took a stand against the intolerance of the leaders of the Second International. The trade union allies of the Zurich Committee, too, remained suspicious of the Socialist intentions.[1] Shortly before the congress, Eleanor wrote to Liebknecht, saying that Hardie was 'as false as Galgenholz [gallows timber]' and was 'the devoted champion of Dutch, French and other Nieuwenhuises'.[2] She once made a harsh remark on the ex-parson Nieuwenhuis: 'if only the enemy had crucified him as they did Christ at the age of 30 how much better it would have been—for him'.[3] Now the Anarchists were to be crucified.

*   *   *

The fourth congress of the Second International, officially known as the International Socialist Workers and Trade Union Congress, began its proceedings on 27 July at the Queen's Hall, Langham Place. A Hyde Park demonstration held the previous day had been spoiled by the torrents of rain, and confusion prevailed in the congress hall as several hundred delegates, grouped by nationality, began discussing their attitude towards the Zurich resolution to exclude the Anarchists. The British section under the S.D.F. leadership had managed to overcome the opposition of the I.L.P., but the French split into two sections over the question. The Germans, the foremost advocates of exclusion, presented to their opponents an 'aggressively bourgeois appearance, sleek, well tailored, decked with all the appurtenances of the comfortable middle-class'.[4] Aveling acted as secretary,

[1] James Maudsley, general secretary of the Cotton Spinners and a member of the joint committee, demanded that the Zurich Committee should dissolve itself, and advocated tightening of the trade union grip over the whole congress. *Reynolds's Newspaper*, 31 May 1896.

[2] Eleanor Marx Aveling to Liebknecht, 11 July 1896, Liebknecht, *Briefwechsel*, 450.

[3] Eleanor Marx Aveling to [F. Van der Goes], 29 Dec. 1893, IISH.

[4] *Freedom*, Aug.–Sept. 1896.

and Eleanor as one of the translators. She had to complain, however, of the great noise, which continued even after the Zurich resolution had been adopted: almost the only distinguishable words on some occasions were 'Sit down', 'Turn him out', 'Vive l'Anarchie', and similar cries. The *Labour Leader* reported that 'Mrs. Aveling made so free with her translations, and showed such a tendency to give un-called-for directions, that the Englishmen were perplexed and distrustful'. It asserted that Aveling had been to the nearest police station, to ask them to prepare for an emergency in the hall.[1] A body of 'stalwart doorkeepers under the leadership of the sturdy Secretary of the Congress (Will Thorne)' was placed at the entrance.[2] The atmosphere was tense and turbulent.

It has been said that Anarchism dominated the London congress despite the exclusion of the Anarchists.[3] With the resignation of Nieuwenhuis from the Dutch delegation on the third day, however, the congress at last settled down to other business. Bebel boasted of the achievements of the German party with regard to political action, and Sidney Webb reported on the question of the 'educational and physical development' of the working class. The congress engaged in sober debate, but it allowed the trade union delegates little opportunity for the expression of their views.

Indeed, the British section was said to have 'all along swamped the trade unionists in it', and the Trade Union Congress, which was held within a month of the congress, openly declared its dissatisfaction with the proceedings.[4] Only the S.D.F. could derive any satisfaction from the congress, for Liebknecht now declared that the party had become 'the nucleus' of the English working class, worthy of its predecessors, the Chartists.[5] This flattering recognition

[1] *Labour Leader*, 1 Aug. 1896.   [2] *Justice*, 29, 30 July 1896.

[3] George Woodcock, *Anarchism* (Pelican Books, 1963), 247.

[4] London Congress, *Report of the Proceedings*, compiled by Edward Aveling (1896), 53; *Justice*, 19 Sept. 1896.

[5] *Justice*, 15 Aug. 1896.

of the S.D.F. by the Continental Marxists was largely due to the influence of the Avelings, and they were now allowed to carry on their propaganda work in the forefront of the S.D.F. leadership. Indeed, the reconciliation had gone so far as to induce an inside observer to declare: 'the friendship of H. M. Hyndman and Edward Aveling is touching to behold'.[1]

*   *   *

Eleanor, though constitutionally strong and healthy, often overworked herself and easily became 'a victim of the Influenza Demon'. When melancholy was added to forced inaction, she would write: 'I . . . now understand why so many people have committed suicide when in the Demon's clutches.'[2] In the autumn of 1896 she was again 'in the grip of the demon influenza' and 'quite hors de combat'. She consumed—so she claimed—only two spoonfuls of beef tea in ten days, but all the same she defied her doctor and started with her husband for a week's propaganda tour in the north—'where there's a will there's a way, & I think I shall risk it!'[3] The focus of this northern campaign was again Burnley, where on 13 December they spoke, Aveling on Evolution and Eleanor on Anarchism. Again an entertainment followed, and their recitations—'The Tramp of the Workers' by Aveling and 'The Pied Piper of Hamelin' by Eleanor—were well received. 'The gem of the evening', it was reported, was 'a reading by Dr. and Mrs. Aveling, entitled "By the Sea"'.[4] It may well have been a happy moment in Eleanor's life to join with her husband in rendering the old, familiar love story to an enthusiastic Socialist audience. Indeed, she declared that the tour was her 'cure' for the demon: 'a week of hard work in Lancashire . . . has done wonders', she wrote to Kautsky, 'and I am so well as

[1] *Labour Leader*, 29 Aug. 1896.
[2] Eleanor Marx Aveling to Laura Lafargue, 14 Jan. 1896, IISH.
[3] Eleanor Marx Aveling to Kautsky, 16 Nov., 3 Dec. 1896, IISH.
[4] *Justice*, 26 Dec. 1896.

ever. If I had followed the doctor's advice I should be quite
a confirmed invalid by now!'[1]

She was in great spirits, and this buoyancy in her mood
was reflected in her political speeches. Revolution had
already come, she declared at the New Year's meeting of
the S.D.F., and 'capitalist society was digging its grave so
rapidly that she was afraid it would tumble into it before
the Social-Democrats were ready'.[2] She believed that the
attitude of the Lancashire workers to child labour proved
her point. She and Aveling, in the 'suggestions for propaganda work' which they wrote after the tour, pointed to
'the horrible fact . . . that the great mass of the workers in
the north are devouring their children'. They had been
shocked by the sight of parents loudly protesting against a
proposal to raise the age of child labour. 'Not only the great
mass of the workers', they added, 'but a majority of the
Socialists, are as bad as can be on this question.' The S.D.F.,
they suggested, should at once organize and start an effective
campaign in the north to save the unfortunate children.[3]
Their proposals, however, were not immediately acted upon,
for the S.D.F. decided to wait for a convenient moment
when they could make political capital out of the issue.

At the same time the S.D.F. was attracting some publicity
by agitating against imperialism in South Africa and famine
in India. Eleanor got to know a certain Miss Colenso, the
daughter of the late Bishop of Natal, who was then touring
the country speaking about the 'horrors perpetrated in South
Africa by the British forces and Mr. Rhodes'. Eleanor compared her to Hyndman, whose vigorous campaign against
'British capitalist misrule in India' she thoroughly approved.
She herself chose 'Our glorious Empire' as a topic for her
lectures to S.D.F. branches.[4] She was in great demand as a
lecturer, and in June 1897, after having delivered forty-one

[1] Eleanor Marx Aveling to Kautsky, 28 Dec. 1896, IISH.
[2] *Justice*, 9 Jan. 1897.   [3] Ibid., 23 Jan. 1897.
[4] Ibid., 6 Feb., 8 May 1897.

lectures and spoken or taken the chair at ten meetings in the preceding eight months, she felt obliged to decline all open-air work, as 'my throat unfortunately will not stand the strain'.[1]

At the same time the Avelings were helping in the production of the S.D.F.'s new monthly journal, the *Social-Democrat*, the first issue of which came out in January 1897. It contained an article by Aveling on Julian Harney, which even Hyndman approved of. 'Poor old Harney will be 80 in a few weeks!' wrote Eleanor at the time: 'It is infamous that he should be in want. We are hoping the testimonial that is to be presented to him may not be too small!'[2] Indeed, Harney provided a living example of a forgotten champion of the workers' cause. She had to see to it that her own father was not similarly neglected by future generations. She translated part of Liebknecht's memoir of Marx for the S.D.F. journal and also reprinted in its pages her own article on the subject which had been published years before in *Progress*.[3] By now she had settled down to work for the S.D.F. and found it a reasonably congenial haven. Even Hyndman behaved in benign and friendly fashion, although he continued to be forthright at times. He later recalled her anger with him when he had declined to review her father's *Eastern Question*. 'The book was not, in my opinion, worthy of its author', he declared, and went on: 'She was very

---

[1] *Justice*, 26 July 1897.

[2] Eleanor Marx Aveling to Liebknecht, 12 Jan. 1897, Liebkneckt, *Briefwechsel*, 452–3. The testimonial fund amounted to £200, and its subscribers ranged from an S.D.F. branch to Joseph Chamberlain. A. R. Schoyen, *The Chartist Challenge* (1958), 284. Aveling's article was 'George Julian Harney: A Straggler of 1848', *Social-Democrat*, Jan. 1897.

[3] Liebknecht, 'A Bad Quarter of an Hour', translated by Eleanor Marx Aveling, *Social-Democrat*, Feb. 1897; Eleanor Marx, 'Karl Marx', ibid., June 1897. Edward also wrote a review of Olive Schreiner's new novel, *Peter Halket, Trooper*, in his 'Fillibuster Cecil Rhodes and his Chartered Company', *Social-Democrat*, Sept. 1897, and Eleanor's translation of *Siesta*, a short story by Alexander Kielland, appeared in the same journal, Jan. 1898.

angry . . . and declared my refusal was due partly to laziness and partly to incapacity to appreciate the book. I admired her filial devotion so much that I allowed her to have the last word, which, in any case, feminine fashion, she would have taken without my consent.'[1]

*   *   *

Eleanor's greatest contribution to the S.D.F., however, was the 'International Notes' which she wrote every week for *Justice*. With the enthusiasm of a fighter she reported the activities of the Russian League of Struggle for the Emancipation of the Working Class, a Marxist body which exerted considerable influence on the sensational strikes at St. Petersburg in 1896-7.[2] When she wrote on the German party, however, she could not conceal her misgivings as to its future development, though she refused to interfere in the growing differences among the German Social Democrats. In 1895, when Ignaz Auer, the Bavarian Socialist of the reformist wing, was attacked within the party for having compromised in his criticism of the Kaiser's aggressive intentions, she wrote to Liebknecht: 'At present the English press and people see only a big fight of the Socialists against the Mad Emperor. Surely it would be folly on our part to call attention to any fighting *inside* the ranks. It is not for us to point out the spots in the Socialist sun.'[3] In her account of the Gotha congress of the German party held in October 1896, she still found an excuse for the troubles caused by the reformist delegates. 'The German Social-Democrats cannot be broken either from without or within', she declared in *Justice*: '. . . In a great party it would be a serious symptom,

[1] Hyndman, *Further Reminiscences*, 139–40.

[2] *Justice*, 5 Sept. 1896, 30 Jan. 1897. Eleanor actively participated in the work of the Zurich Committee when it organized financial assistance for the St. Petersburg strikers. *Justice*, 4 July 1896.

[3] Eleanor Marx Aveling to Liebknecht, 25 Sept. 1895, Liebknecht, *Briefwechsel*, 443.

indeed a sure sign of decay, if no one member differed from his fellow upon any subject.'[1]

It soon became clear that the champion of the German reformism was Bernstein himself, who was still residing in England. In a controversy with Bax, he began formulating his famous theory of Revisionism which criticized the revolutionary aspects of Marxism. 'Just as the negro who takes the British whisky is ruined', retorted Bax, 'so is your Continental Socialist who takes to the English way of looking at things.'[2] Eleanor kept silence on the controversy even when Bernstein spoke of 'different kinds' of class struggle in a lecture delivered for the Fabian Society on 'What Marx Really Taught'.[3] But she wrote in *Justice* that the English people 'know—more or less vaguely—that there is a powerful Socialist Party in Germany. . . . If they [the Germans] had the advantage enjoyed by free born Britons they would only be—"Fabians"'', and she withheld her comment on this popular view.[4] She was apparently worried by the development of the Revisionist controversy. 'Yesterday we saw Hyndman (at a meeting of the 20th Century Press "shareholders!")' she wrote in a letter to Liebknecht: 'He is in a great state of mind about Bernstein's latest article. Of course, Hyndman forgets the way in which he attacked all of *us*—the General, you, and all. But it is an unfortunate business, and each side is becoming more and more embittered.'[5]

Several months later, almost at the end of her life, she revealed her real feeling on this matter in a letter to Kautsky in which she begged him to bring pressure to bear upon Bernstein—'you alone can make Ede our own *old* Ede again'. Bernstein's attitude had for some time been 'a matter of great pain to us', she said, because his position was exploited by the Fabians against the Marxists. '"Marx *must*

[1] *Justice*, 31 Oct. 1896.   [2] Ibid., 7 Nov. 1896.
[3] Ibid., 6 Feb. 1897.   [4] Ibid., 26 June 1897.
[5] Eleanor Marx Aveling to Liebknecht, 2 June 1897, Liebknecht, *Briefwechsel*, 453–4.

be played out" said one (this I heard at Portsmouth!) "when Bernstein has come over to us".—And you can imagine how this again is used by Bax & Co.' Yet it was impossible for her to speak to Bernstein, she added, because he was '*terribly* irritable' and regarded her not attacking the S.D.F. as a sign of her enmity against him. When Liebknecht paid a visit to the Den—in the summer of 1897—and made a casual reference to Hyndman as an authority on India, with which Eleanor agreed, Bernstein worked himself into 'the state of almost frantic rage'. How could she reason with such a man, she asked. The Mendelsons, who, as we have seen, had been 'turned out' by Engels, were mainly responsible in her view for his 'unhappy pessimism', and she asked Kautsky to remove him from their 'deadly influence'.[1] Bernstein stayed on in England till 1901, and in the meantime established himself as the founder and prophet of Revisionism. Kautsky significantly advised him to 'take the consequences and become an Englishman'.[2]

Eleanor found more pleasant developments to comment on in French Socialism. She enjoyed reporting on the achievements of the 'Socialist Communes', for instance the Lille Town Council's provision of free meals (*cantines scolaires*) and scholarships for school children and a grant of a subsidy to a theatre.[3] But she was outspoken in criticism of the support given by the French Socialists to Greece when that country invaded Crete, then under Turkish sovereignty, in 1897. 'Just now', she wrote in *Justice*,

all France, even Socialist France, seems quite—I mean Crete—mad. As the French Socialists . . . consider the Polish movement as 'Chauvinist', it is a little difficult to understand their present enthusiasm for the Greeks. And, personally, I must say I should be far more impressed by their diatribes against that much-damned

[1] Eleanor Marx Aveling to Kautsky, 15 March 1898, IISH.
[2] Kautsky to Bernstein, end of October 1898, quoted in Peter Gay, *The Dilemma of Democratic Socialism* (Collier Books, 1962), 80.
[3] *Justice*, 2, 9, 16 Jan. 1897.

Sultan if the French had even mildly damned the hideous Franco-Russian alliance.[1]

Indeed, the Cretan affair divided the European Socialists between those who, true to the Russophobe tradition of Marx, saw in the invasion a Russian plot—Eleanor, Hyndman, and Liebknecht among others—and those who regarded it as a spread of civilization—Bernstein, Kautsky, and the French. Her disapproval of the French attitude involved her in an indirect censure of the German reformism as well.

Meanwhile, the Dreyfus affair had involved the French Socialists in problems of political tactics. Eleanor at first regarded the affair as due to 'a Christian jealousy of superior Jewish money-making',[2] but she soon convinced herself that what was at stake was a matter of elementary justice. Zola's famous indictment of the irregular trial of which Dreyfus had been the victim appeared on 13 January 1898, and the following day she wrote to Mrs. Liebknecht:

It is not a pleasant fact that the one clear, honest note has been struck not by one of our party, but by Zola! . . . It is a disgrace that not one of our French 'Socialists' has dared to do what Library, Edward and I did in America—i.e. demand bare justice, even though we demanded it for opponents. What *does* it matter if Dreyfus is 'sympathique' or not? The only question is: was he even according to accepted standards *fairly tried*.[3]

Large sections of the French public now divided themselves between the Dreyfusards, many of them Radicals, who demanded a retrial of the case, and the Anti-Dreyfusards, who included most of the clericals and nationalists. But the Socialist group in the Chamber of Deputies issued a manifesto calling upon the workers to abstain from taking sides in the affair, which they regarded as a conflict between rival sections of the bourgeois society. The Socialist attitude was a

---

[1] *Justice*, 13 March 1897.   [2] Ibid., 27 Nov. 1897.
[3] Eleanor Marx Aveling to Natalie Liebknecht, 14 Jan. 1898, Liebknecht, *Briefwechsel*, 460.

great disappointment and really painful to Eleanor. She
declared in *Justice*: 'honour to whom honour is due—even
if we do not find these persons "sympathetic". And so all
honour to Clemenceau, and above all to Zola.'[1]

Eleanor had a sentimental attachment to Holland: 'it is
strange', she wrote in a letter to Henri Polak, the young
Dutch Socialist, 'that my father's semi-Dutch parentage
should be so little known.'[2] In March 1897 she visited the
land of dykes and dams for a week's lecturing at university
towns and assisted the Dutch Social Democrats in their
struggle against an Anarchist group.[3] Ireland was another
country to which Eleanor's memories of her childhood often
returned: even there a Socialist party had now come into
existence. When the youthful James Connolly founded the
Irish Socialist Republican Party in 1896, she sent him a
letter of congratulation, and Aveling was the first person to
avail himself of the associate membership of the party
designed mainly for the Irish in America.[4] The new ties that
she made with Polak and Connolly, however, were small
consolation in the face of the apostasy of Bernstein and the
confusion among the French Socialists.

In fact, Social Democracy found itself in a dilemma, and
the German party could no longer be regarded as a model
to be followed by the rest of the Marxist parties. She could
never come round to the view that her father's analysis of
capitalist society was no longer valid. It was all due to
Bernstein's 'pessimism'—so she persuaded herself. Her
trouble, however, was not limited to the political field.
Although her husband had at last secured a solid standing

[1] *Justice*, 22 Jan. 1898.
[2] Eleanor Marx Aveling to Henri Polak, 31 Oct. 1893, IISH.
'Though my father was half Dutch, I only read Dutch a very little—but
enough, I believe, to manage a newspaper!' Eleanor Marx Aveling to
Polak, 19 Oct. 1893, IISH, partly quoted in *International Review of Social
History* (1956), i. 56.
[3] *Justice*, 13 March, 3 April 1897.
[4] C. Desmond Greaves, *The Life & Times of James Connolly* (1961), 68.
81.

among the English Marxists, his ambitions lay also in the sphere of the drama, and here he was very unsuccessful. The result was a further deterioration of his character: and as a result of his behaviour, Eleanor began to grow increasingly disillusioned. The disappointment of her hopes, at once political and personal, began to overwhelm her altogether.

XII ⋄ CATASTROPHE

For a while after Engels's death, an ideal life had seemed to open up for Eleanor. Her letters struck a note of joy as she invited her friends to Sydenham. She asked Kautsky, for instance, to 'come to the Jews and the Den', telling him that her husband, himself 'neither a Jew nor the Den, but an unfortunate "Nonconformist"' as he protested, was also anxiously awaiting him.[1] And 'her face would beam with pleasure', recalled Bernstein, 'as she welcomed her friends to the "Den"'. In spite of all her friendliness and affection, however, an acute observer could perceive that her happiness was only momentary, for she could not hide her anxiety about the instability of her surroundings.[2] She would make excuses, as she had done for many years previously, for her husband, who was apparently the dark spot in her otherwise bright home. She hoped and told others that he would mend his ways, believing that he could not humanly be blind to her love and devotion. She was also convinced that hard work, especially in the cause of Socialism, would be an effective antidote against the moral sickness from which her husband seemed to suffer. She clung to this hope and conviction to a pathetic degree, and with it opened the final stage in her long struggle against fate.

*　　　*　　　*

[1] Eleanor Marx Aveling to Kautsky, 8 Feb. 1896, IISH.
[2] *Justice*, 30 July 1898.

The Avelings's work for Socialism had been largely educational, and education or instruction peculiarly suited their inclinations, as they were both experienced teachers in their own ways. Shortly after the London congress of the International, Eleanor offered to start language and debating classes, as she felt that the majority of the British delegates had been wanting in knowledge of foreign languages and also of the rules of debate observed on the Continent. Aveling seized the opportunity and proposed to offer science classes to prepare students for the Art and Science Examination at South Kensington. Coaching again! The S.D.F. executive adopted their suggestion, and classes were held at the hall of the S.D.F. under its auspices.[1] The advanced language classes under Eleanor's tutorship were soon reading and discussing the *Communist Manifesto* in German and the programme of the Parti Ouvrier in French.[2] The science classes were conducted in much the same way as their many predecessors with periodic examinations and an entertainment.

The 'Dramatic Entertainment' in aid of the funds of the science classes, which was held on 8 January 1897 at Social Hall, Wandsworth—a small hall owned by Mrs. Charlotte Despard, the Socialist sympathizer and suffragette—was in fact the last of its kind presented under the direction of Alec Nelson. It opened with an overture played by the S.D.F. String Band conducted by H. W. Lee, which was followed by Nelson's comedietta *The Landlady*. The chief characters in it were the author himself and Eva Frye, who sang 'Love's Old Sweet Song' in fine style to the delight of the audience and certainly of her co-actor.[3] Miss Frye, then 22 years old, the daughter of a music teacher, must have been the same person who under the name of Miss Richardson had played the part of a charming widow in one of the entertainments organized by the Zurich Committee, and apparently Alec Nelson was in love with her.

[1] *Justice*, 5 Sept., 3 Oct. 1896.   [2] Ibid., 2 Jan. 1897.
[3] Ibid., 30 Jan. 1897.

Aveling's classes were held every Wednesday evening, Eleanor's every Friday, and the S.D.F. Hall was conveniently situated in the Strand surrounded by the West End theatres, so that it was an easy matter for Aveling to continue his association with the young actress without being detected by his wife. Certainly such a liaison was by no means a novelty for him, and Eleanor would presumably not take the affair too seriously if she were aware of it. Moreover, she was fully occupied with her own work—lectures for the S.D.F., research at the British Museum, and translation for another international congress, that of the Miners, held in London in the second week of June 1897. There was in any case another source of concern—the behaviour of the children of her late sister Jenny. Jean Longuet, the eldest son, who often stayed with Eleanor at her house, began to worry her. 'Johnny is still here. . . . He is 21 and seems no more minded to work seriously than if he were 10', she wrote to Liebknecht in June: '. . . It is heartbreaking for me to see Jenny's children going wrong and to stand by helpless.'[1]

Furthermore, Aveling was a sick man, with an abscess still open in his side, and this gave her cause for serious anxiety. On his doctor's advice he left for St. Margaret's Bay on 19 June. While he was away, she invited Edith Lanchester, a 'new woman' and an executive member of the S.D.F., to stay with her. Miss Lanchester had gained a reputation in Socialist circles for her experiences as 'a lunatic' in a private asylum where she had been sent by her family after scandalizing them with a 'free-love' escapade. She became Eleanor's protégée, and, when out of work, was employed by her to copy Marx's articles at the Museum. As she was very ill after confinement, Eleanor asked her to come to the Den for a few weeks' nursing.[2] The cause of free love had to be defended

[1] Eleanor Marx Aveling to Liebknecht, 2 June 1897, Liebknecht, *Briefwechsel*, 453.

[2] Eleanor Marx Aveling to Kautsky, 19 June 1897, IISH. Eleanor Marx Aveling to Laura Lafargue, 12 Nov. 1896, photocopy, IISH; *Justice*, 2 Nov. 1895.

against the prejudice of society and those wounded in the struggle had to be upheld, but Eleanor had by now apparently begun to see herself as a victim of her own cause.

She longed to see her old friends, Kautsky and above all Liebknecht—'Dear, dear old Library, do you think there are so many of the *old* friends left that I can *afford* to not want *you*?'[1] Liebknecht came to the Den on 11 July for a holiday and rest. Aveling, who had returned from his seaside recuperation, was 'very vexed', wrote Eleanor, 'because he can't be with me' on the 11th when he had a lecture engagement to fulfil at Wigan.[2] Hyndman, who, as he described himself, had been 'churned up in the maelstrom of capitalism', proposed to visit Liebknecht at the Den.[3] It was probably on this occasion that Bernstein's bitter denunciation of him, to which we have already referred, took place. Aveling, for his part, behaved well to Liebknecht and found time to go out for a walk with him.[4] When, one day, Eleanor returned to the Den in good spirits after a round of her usual duties in London, Aveling said to his guest: 'She is as strong as a horse.'[5] Was he envious or contemptuous? Perhaps both. Liebknecht at any rate thoroughly enjoyed his stay in London. 'Just as the actor on an "off" night goes to some theatre, and a "cabby" drives alongside some pal', wrote Eleanor, 'so Liebknecht was attracted to the House of Commons', and from there he returned as 'a wiser but a sadder man' after having heard a debate on South Africa.[6] It was a happy reunion for Eleanor, but the day of catastrophe was fast approaching.

*　　　　*　　　　*

Isabel Campbell Aveling, Edward's legally married wife,

[1] Eleanor Marx Aveling to Liebknecht, 2 June 1897, Liebknecht, *Briefwechsel*, 454.

[2] Ibid., 7 July 1897, ibid. 455.

[3] Hyndman to Liebknecht, 15 July 1897, IML (Berlin).

[4] Eleanor Marx Aveling to Kautsky, 19 July 1897, IISH.

[5] *Vorwärts*, 5 April 1898.　　　　[6] *Justice*, 7 Aug. 1897.

had been dead nearly five years. She left no will, and administration of her personal property, estimated at £126, was granted to her lawful husband. This was not a large sum for a man who was extravagant in spending. He was apparently in debt to many persons, including William Morris, to whom he wrote in August 1895: 'Let us agree that it is £50. I enclose £5 on account & will go on enclosing as often as I can.'[1] In writing these words he was probably thinking of the money Eleanor had just inherited from Engels. Indeed, his 'sinister hand', as has been suggested,[2] was probably at work when Eleanor drew up her will on 16 October 1895, only two months after the death of Engels. In this she left all her interest in royalties from the works by her father to Jenny's children and the residue of her estate and effects to her 'husband', the sole executor of the will. Her insatiable husband, however, was not satisfied even with this generous arrangement. As a result she was obliged to make a codicil one year later, by which her interest in the royalties was also to be given to Aveling in his lifetime.[3] He continued to demand money from her, but Eleanor must have failed to see the full extent of his libertinism, the overt sign of which was his constantly penurious condition.

On 8 June 1897, at a time when Eleanor was attending the International Congress of the Miners held at St. Martin's Hall, Alec Nelson, widower, and the actress Eva Frye were married, and their marriage was solemnized at the Registry Office in Chelsea where Miss Frye then resided. The occasion was a masterpiece of sordid deceit by Aveling: even the name of his father was changed in registration to 'Thomas William Nelson'. His covert union with Miss Frye was nothing less than legalized adultery: for if he had decided to abandon the cause of free love, he could have persuaded

[1] Edward Aveling to William Morris, 27 Aug. 1895, B.M.Add.MSS. 45345.
[2] Felix Barker in *New Yorker*, 27 Nov. 1954.
[3] Eleanor Marx Aveling, Will, 16 Oct. 1895, Codicil, 28 Nov. 1896, Somerset House.

Eleanor to legalize their union long before. But in fact no matter of principle was involved in his behaviour. If he no longer loved Eleanor, he could have dissolved their union, and no doubt Miss Frye urged him to do so. But he could not take this step, as he was largely dependent upon Eleanor for his living as well as for the support of his new liaison. Thus the fictitious Alec Nelson began to play a sorry role in his actual life to cover up his weaknesses. But why had Miss Frye consented to this marriage, which was even more unorthodox than a free-love union? She must have known full well that Eleanor had been and would still remain devoted to Aveling. It is not altogether impossible that the disappointed play-wright and the amateur actress had agreed to put up a drama of deceit in which Aveling was to play a masterly villain. If they played well, they could even make a fortune at the expense of Eleanor, who was to play, though unwittingly, the part of a faithful woman awaiting a tragic end. Aveling was so successful in this real-life drama that Eleanor was left unaware of his lawful marriage. Knowledge of it was limited to a small coterie of his theatrical friends, and no Socialists, it seems, were allowed to penetrate into this culmination of his life of falsehood.

It is indeed difficult to believe him when, as we have seen, he assured Eleanor that he had spent almost a fortnight at St. Margaret's Bay for his health—this shortly after his marriage with Miss Frye. Yet he lied so well on every possible occasion for lying that Liebknecht, too, had no presentiment of this unfortunate affair during his visit to the Den in July. To the average Socialist, as to Liebknecht himself, he was still the son-in-law of Karl Marx. At the annual conference of the S.D.F. held in Northampton at the beginning of August, he was elected to its executive at the head of the poll. Further, he made a notable contribution to the proceedings of the conference by sponsoring a resolution in favour of close co-operation between trade unionists and members of the S.D.F., the latter joining their respective

trade unions.[1] With this position of esteem among his fellow
Socialists, he could not neglect his work for the S.D.F., at
least for the moment. In the middle of August he appeared
in South Wales and gave lectures for S.D.F. branches at
Barry and Aberdare. On 22 August he spoke at a mass
meeting in Trafalgar Square under the auspices of a Spanish
Atrocities Committee.[2] Mrs. Nelson became impatient.

*   *   *

It was probably after this Trafalgar Square demonstration
that he suddenly broke away from Eleanor. He took with
him everything he could find in the Den that could easily
be turned into money, and left Eleanor in the utmost
embarrassment. He told her that she should never know his
address, though she might write to him through an actor,
'M'. In a state of desperation she turned to Freddy Demuth
for help. 'I wrote once more to Edward this morning', she
told Freddy on 30 August:

No doubt it is weak, but one *can't* wipe out 14 years of one's life
as if they had not been. I think anyone with the least sense of
honour, not to mention any feeling of kindness and gratitude,
would answer that letter. Will he? I almost fear that he will
not. . . . To-morrow evening is the Executive of the S.[D.F.] I
can't go—because if he is not there I *can't* explain. I hate to give
you all this trouble, but could you go? . . . You could ask, if he
had been . . .[3]

---

[1] *Justice*, 7 Aug. 1897.   [2] Ibid., 21, 28 Aug. 1897.

[3] Eleanor Marx Aveling to Freddy Demuth, 30 Aug. 1897, *Labour
Leader*, 30 July 1898. This and the following letters from Eleanor to
Freddy were published in German translation in an article by Bernstein,
'Was Eleanor Marx in den Tod trieb', *Neue Zeit*, xvi–ii (1897–8), Nr. 42.
An English translation of his article containing these letters appeared
in *Justice* (30 July 1898). The *Labour Leader* (30 July 1898) also published
the same letters but in a slightly different version. One of these letters
had been quoted by Robert Banner, who seems to have known Freddy
personally, in the *Labour Leader* in its issue of 30 April 1898, more than
two months before its German translation, and the *Labour Leader* got all
the dates correct, while the German version made one obvious mistake in
this respect, which was copied by *Justice*. We give the *Labour Leader*
version in this and the following quotations from the Eleanor Marx-
Demuth correspondence.

She had also written to Arthur Wilson Crosse, her legal adviser, telling him that she would like to arrange a joint meeting between him, herself, and Aveling, if ever the latter would come.[1] From this it appears that Aveling had made fresh demands with regard to her will. It was stated in her testament that all the benefits provided for Aveling would, in case of his death during her lifetime, go to Jenny's children and that Bernstein would become the executor of her will. Aveling as a sick man probably felt that he could not live long, and Mrs. Nelson probably feared that Eleanor might very well outlive Aveling. Moreover, his debts appear to have increased as a result of the expensive life he lived with Mrs. Nelson in Chelsea. He even borrowed from Freddy! It is quite likely that he asked Eleanor to make immediate provision for himself. It was probably at this stage that he asked her to sell some of her father's literary remains, a monstrous demand which, when it was made, she naturally resisted.[2] By this time, it was alleged, 'fully one-half' of the fortune left by Engels for Eleanor had been dissipated, and upon her refusal to meet his fresh demands, Aveling had to disappear in order to 'escape imprisonment'.[3]

On the morning of 1 September Eleanor received a note from Aveling telling her that he was coming back. On his return to the Den in the afternoon, 'Edward seemed surprised and quite "offended" I did not rush into his arms', quoted Eleanor to Freddy:

He has so far made no apology and offered no explanation. I have—after waiting for him to begin—therefore said one *must* consider the business position—and that I should never forget the treatment I had been subjected to. He has said nothing. Meantime I said you *might* be down. . . . It is right he should have to face you in my presence, and me in yours.[4]

[1] Eleanor Marx Aveling to Freddy Demuth, 30 Aug. 1897.
[2] Bernstein in *Justice*, 30 July 1898.
[3] *Labour Leader*, 30 July 1898.
[4] Eleanor Marx Aveling to Freddy Demuth, 1 Sept. 1897, *Labour Leader*, 30 July 1898.

In the evening of the same day, just after Eleanor had sent the above letter, Aveling, it appears, threatened her with a cruel form of blackmail. He probably told her that he had been living with a woman from whom he could not separate without providing ample financial compensation. He did not tell Eleanor that he was already legally married, for this would certainly have led to her cutting him out of her will. But he could threaten her that he would have to marry his mistress legally if Eleanor refused to be generous to her. Next morning Eleanor sent an urgent message to Freddy:

Come, if you possibly can, this evening. It is a shame to trouble you; but I am so alone, and I am face to face with a most horrible position: *utter* ruin—everything, *to the last penny*, or utter, open disgrace. It is awful; worse than even I fancied it was.[1]

Freddy hurried to the Den, but his visit was almost useless. Eleanor had lost courage to tell him anything, Bernstein, another witness of the tragedy, recalled, and on the question of money 'Aveling had the advantage that neither Eleanor nor Demuth understood all. His declaration that the last penny of Eleanor's fortune was not claimed disarmed them.'[2] Apparently Aveling had a trump card in his hand—the secret about Freddy's birth—which, we may assume, he used skilfully in his negotiation with Eleanor. Obviously Aveling obtained a considerable sum of money and in return promised to leave his mistress and reform himself. Eleanor believed him, and the first serious crisis died down, to the chagrin of her friends, Freddy and possibly Bernstein, who had advised her to leave Aveling.

*   *   *

Aveling could play the part of a repentant husband quite well. In the middle of September he and Eleanor left for Paris and stayed with the Lafargues at Dravéil for about two weeks. The forest of Dénard and the banks of the Seine

[1] Eleanor Marx Aveling to Freddy Demuth, 2 Sept. 1897, ibid.
[2] *Justice*, 30 July 1898.

delighted Eleanor, and she began to recover from her days of terror.

Yet soon Eleanor became even more critical of her hosts than of her husband, who at least appeared willing to continue his work for Socialism. She found the Lafargues' new home to be much too lavish. Apparently they had invested in its purchase most of the fortune Laura had inherited from Engels. The house had about thirty rooms, apart from outhouses which contained a large billiard room and a studio. There was a large house for their gardener and greenhouses which seemed almost innumerable. There was a profusion of game in the grounds, and a huge 'orangerie' which, Eleanor thought, might be turned into a lecture and meeting hall. The garden was more like a park, with flowers and almost every vegetable and fruit one could think of. 'I don't think I would exchange my little Den with this palace', wrote Eleanor to Kautsky from Dravéil. It made her feel uneasy about the future of Marxism in France. 'The movement is all at sixes & sevens (this, of course, entre nous)', she added in her letter, '& the bosom friends of the London Congress are today mortal enemies & vice versa. Still, Paul declares, "que cela marche admirablement!"!!'[1]

*   *   *

In spite of or perhaps because of her unhappiness, both personal and political, she worked even harder for the cause of Socialism, and the last few months of her life were devoted to the great struggle of capital and labour that was fought in the engineering trade in England. The Amalgamated Society of Engineers, one of the oldest and wealthiest unions, under its new secretary, George Barnes, had determined to win an eight-hour day from employers in the London area. The Employers' Federation of Engineering Associations, which had been set up in 1896 with Colonel Dyer, the managing director of Armstrong Whitworths, as its president, inter-

[1] Eleanor Marx Aveling to Kautsky, 28 Sept. 1897, IISH.

vened in the dispute by setting up a London committee
headed by Alexander Siemens of the famous German firm.
This committee co-ordinated the action of the employers,
and a national lock-out of union members was decided on.
This began in July 1897.

A notable feature of this dispute was the considerable
financial help that came from workers on the Continent. The
union acknowledged Eleanor's help in securing this. 'In
translation of letters and in the giving of her time in writing
to the Press and friends abroad', the union journal stated,
she 'has been an invaluable connecting link between us and
Continental labour organisations'.[1] Siemens admitted that
the object of the lock-out was to 'smash' trade unions altogether, and a London correspondent of Liebknecht's
Vorwärts—probably Eleanor—wrote: 'It is no mere strike,
no mere lock-out—it is civil war.' With the 'foolish' utterance
by 'your Siemens'—'made in Germany!'—the struggle had
become one for the entire trade union movement not only
of England but of all countries: 'German workers, do your
duty!'[2] The German subscriptions amounted to more than
£14,000, about a half of the entire overseas contribution
to the lock-out funds.

But the lock-out became protracted and the suffering and
privation grew worse. Eleanor, in a signed article in *Vorwärts*,
stated that for the first time in history the employers had
resorted to a sympathetic strike—'they fight for their class,
not for their individual interests'. The class war had become
a fact, although some of the 'more intelligent' employers,
like 'the Quaker Cadbury', had actually contributed to the
lock-out funds of the workers, regarding it as a folly 'to
threaten with musket-ball when one could achieve the same
result with chocolate cream'. The workers, for their part,
were beginning to ask whether there was a shorter way to
their goal and were learning how to combine trade union

---

[1] *Amalgamated Engineers' Journal*, Feb. 1898.
[2] *Vorwärts*, 6 Nov. 1897.

methods with political action. The bravest elements in this struggle, she went on, were the unskilled workers: over 1,000 members of her union, the Gasworkers, of which she was a trustee, were involved in the lock-out. Many of the unskilled men, though they were capable of replacing their skilled brothers, refused to act as blacklegs.[1]

In fact, the employers were attempting to use blackleg labour, and had the services of the Free Labour Association, which existed to supply non-union workmen. But this manœuvre was not a success.[2] Eleanor knew the Association's founder, William Collison, a policeman's son, who had once taken an active part in the legal eight-hour movement. It was probably during the Engineers' struggle that Collison met her again. 'I said little', he wrote later, 'as we stood in the windy twilight at the corner of Chancery Lane, while I noted the faded beauty of her face and hopeless eyes and the grief inscribed in deep-drawn lines about the mouth.' Eleanor had certainly changed, but the cause of the workers she held dear had not. She looked at him seriously and told him: 'They will never forgive you; they would forgive others —but not you.'[3]

'I am translating all the many foreign letters Barnes gets, & I am writing or answering letters right & left on the great fight', she wrote to Kautsky on New Year's Day of 1898. She acknowledged with regret that 'the out & out S.D.F. people' were contemptuously treating it as 'mere' trade unionism. 'If only we could now spread our Socialist nets properly', she said, 'we should get a splendid haul—but I fear our fishers are not capable of using their opportunity.'[4] Even in the international field there was misinterpretation: Revisionist criticism of the Engineers' class struggle appeared in *Vorwärts* while Liebknecht, its editor, was in prison. 'The

[1] *Vorwärts*, 6 Nov. 1897.
[2] James B. Jefferys, *The Story of the Engineers* (1945), 146.
[3] William Collison, *The Apostle of Free Labour* (1913), 84–85.
[4] Eleanor Marx Aveling to Kautsky, 1 Jan. 1898, IISH.

"Vorwärts" is falling more & more under Bernstein's influence', she wrote in a letter to Laura:

> & his wet-blanket articles . . . are not exactly useful at the present moment. Assuredly the critical attitude is necessary & useful. But there are times when a little enthusiasm—even if 'uncritical'—is of greater value. Bernstein's position is a most unfortunate one for the movement, & one that makes *our* position very difficult. It is impossible to defend his attitude, & I am in daily fear that someone will tell Barnes & that Barnes will insist upon answering Bernstein—Barnes would be sure to get me to help him—& then I should be most awkwardly placed.—Unhappily there is no one, now we have not the General, to influence Bernstein, & pull him together.[1]

Meanwhile, the strain of the struggle became more severe as it dragged on through the winter days. The Engineers' executive finally withdrew its claim for an eight-hour day and accepted the employers' terms of settlement in the middle of January. 'This fight has been a heroic one and will be counted among the great battles of the world', wrote Eleanor on the 17th in her dispatch to the *Hamburger Echo*, the Socialist paper in the Hamburg district:

> . . . This fight was only a phase in the great, general class movement of the workers. We cannot be beaten. But we have our wounded to take care of. The lazarettos and hospitals of labour will be filled for a long time from now. May I ask help for these brave fighters who were wounded for our cause?[2]

Was not Eleanor herself wounded, almost mortally wounded in her struggles for her cause? She had just discovered—so she believed—that Bernstein was now using for his book her father's correspondence with Engels, access to which, as we have seen, had been denied to her.[3] Liebknecht, probably the only friend whom she could trust

[1] Eleanor Marx Aveling to Laura Lafargue, 8 Jan. 1898, Bottigelli Collection.
[2] *Hamburger Echo*, 20 Jan. 1898.
[3] Eleanor Marx Aveling to Laura Lafargue, 8 Jan. 1898, Bottigelli Collection.

politically, was in prison. Her husband was hopelessly sick, both morally and physically. At moments of despair she could now only turn to her half-brother Freddy. On 13 January, a few days before she wrote the sad message to the Hamburg workers, she sent him an even more sorrowful letter about the fate that awaited the children of Karl Marx:

I sometimes feel like you, Freddy, that *nothing* ever goes well with us. I mean you and me. Of course, poor Jenny had her full share of sorrow and of trouble, and Laura lost her children. But Jenny was fortunate enough to die, and sad as that was for her children, there are times when I think it fortunate. I would not have wished Jenny to have lived through what I have done. I don't think you and I have been very wicked people—and yet, dear Freddy, it does seem as if we got all the punishment.[1]

*　　　*　　　*

Aveling, on his return from Dravéil early in October, reopened his science classes with a soirée held at Holborn Town Hall. He also started an S.D.F. drama and elocution class, and this met sometimes at the S.D.F. Hall but more often at a coffee tavern near by.[2] It is a matter of conjecture whether and how far Eleanor tolerated his activities in the old, familiar line, which no doubt provided opportunities for him to visit Mrs. Nelson. Apparently her own language classes were not revived. Aveling still needed money for his adventures, and Eleanor, as we have seen, could not always meet his demands. He even turned to Ellen Terry, the Shakespearean actress, who in turn asked Bernard Shaw about him. 'His exploits as a borrower have grown into a Homeric legend', replied Shaw:

. . . For some years past he has been behaving well, because Marx's friend Engels left Eleanor £9,000. But the other day he tried the old familiar post-dated cheque on Sidney Webb—in

[1] Eleanor Marx Aveling to Freddy Demuth, 13 Jan. 1898, *Labour Leader*, 30 July 1898.
[2] *Justice*, 2 Oct., 6 Nov., 4 Dec. 1897.

vain. And then, I suppose, he tried you. Must I really not tell
anyone? If you only knew how utterly your delicacy is wasted![1]

By now there were very few people left from whom Aveling
could borrow money. So he returned to Eleanor and to the
Den.

In so far as he resumed his life with Eleanor, Aveling
could hardly neglect his work for the S.D.F. In November
both he and Eleanor spoke at various meetings in support
of S.D.F. candidates for the London School Board, and early
in December they left for Lancashire to assist Dan Irving,
Secretary of the Burnley S.D.F., who was a candidate for the
Burnley School Board.[2] The Executive of the S.D.F. had
just issued a leaflet entitled *The Campaign against Child Labour*,
written apparently by the Avelings for use in Irving's support.[3] Eleanor not only spoke for him but even sat for some
hours as his 'agent' in a polling booth. 'We fought the
campaign on the question of Child Labour', she wrote to
Liebknecht, 'and the "Free Maintenance [of school child-
ren]" question! And this in Burnley! And we made no concessions as to the horror of child labour! And yet we came
in victorious!'[4]

During the whole week of their Burnley campaign, the
weather had been bad—real Lancashire weather: 'certainly
if Dante could have dreamed of a Lancashire factory town
in bad weather', she wrote in a letter to Kautsky, 'he would

[1] George Bernard Shaw to Ellen Terry, 5 Jan. 1898, Christopher
St. John (ed.), *Ellen Terry and Bernard Shaw, A Correspondence* (1949),
262–3. £9,000 is an exaggeration, even allowing for the share for
Longuet's children included in it. Hardie's estimate of £4,000 seems
nearer the truth. *Labour Leader*, 30 July 1898.

[2] *Justice*, 20 Nov., 4 Dec. 1897.

[3] It condemned 'the comparatively well-paid spinners and weavers'
who were 'so chloroformed' by the capitalist system as to cling to 'the
commercial value of a child'. The S.D.F. now advocated the raising of
the age of child labour from eleven, the lowest among the major industrial nations, to sixteen, as a 'palliative' measure. S.D.F., *Campaign against
Child Labour* (n.d.), *passim*; *Justice*, 13 Nov. 1897.

[4] Eleanor Marx Aveling to Liebknecht, 24 Dec. 1897, Liebknecht,
Briefwechsel, 456. See also *Justice*, 18 Dec. 1897.

WEM

have added half a dozen circles to his hell, & to his "lowest depth, a lower deep".[1] As a result, Aveling, who had been ill, got worse, and by the time they returned to the Den influenza had developed into congestion of the lungs and pneumonia. Illness meant considerable expense in many ways, and she had to sacrifice still more to a man whose infidelity and ingratitude she knew well enough. 'I often feel this is not only "a mad world" but a very sad one too', she wrote in the same letter to Kautsky. But she took good care of him, and he gradually recovered. 'He is working again—though I wish he wouldn't', she wrote one week later to Laura:

. . . The doctor told me Edward might at any moment (his temperature was up to 103 at times) 'take a turn for the worse', & that I 'ought' at once to communicate with his relations. Of course I did not, because (except perhaps his sister, now living in Devonshire) there is not a relation he would want to see at any time. . . . Edward is better, but he is still terribly weak & terribly emaciated. He is a very skeleton—mere skin & bones. And so he is not yet out of the wood, & I am still very anxious. The slightest chill would, the doctors say, be absolutely fatal—& Edward is a most unmanageable person.—I write freely because he is in bed asleep (thank goodness he *does* sleep well!) . . . If I can I shall get him off to Hastings away from the awful fogs we are having here.[2]

On 13 January Aveling left for Hastings. Eleanor was anxious about his going alone. 'But I really *could* not go with him: these four weeks have cost too much to make this possible', she wrote to Mrs. Liebknecht.[3] In fact financial worries were looming large again, in spite of the fortune she had inherited from Engels. Towards the end of January *Justice* published a brief note from the Avelings: Edward

[1] Eleanor Marx Aveling to Kautsky, 1 Jan. 1898, IISH.

[2] Eleanor Marx Aveling to Laura Lafargue, 8 Jan. 1898. Bottigelli Collection. This letter among others would support our assumption that Eleanor was still unaware of Alex Nelson's lawful marriage.

[3] Eleanor Marx Aveling to Natalie Liebknecht, 14 Jan. 1898, Liebknecht, *Briefwechsel*, 458.

wrote from Hastings to say that his doctors 'do not prophesy very good things', while Eleanor asked for the cancellation of her own lecture engagements. And this was the end of their political work.[1]

*   *   *

In the warmer climate at Hastings Aveling's lung trouble disappeared, but the abscess on his side got worse and worried Eleanor. He returned to the Den shortly afterwards in order to have an operation, but at once began visiting his legal wife at her Chelsea home whenever he went to London, ostensibly to see his doctor. Eleanor's suspicions grew, and what she discovered, in combination with her financial worries, brought her to the verge of despair. 'I have to face such great trouble', she again wrote to Freddy:

And *quite* without help (for Edward does not help *even now*), and I hardly know what to do. I am daily getting demands for money, and how to meet them, and the operation, and all else, I don't know. . . . Edward has gone to London to-day. He is to see doctors, and so on. He *would not let me go with him*! That is mere *cruelty, and* there are things he does not want to tell me. Dear Freddy, you have your boy—I have nothing; and I see nothing worth living for.[2]

But when Aveling returned and, in the tone of a helpless husband, told her about the seriousness of his illness, she at once pulled herself together and, like an indulgent mother, treated him with tenderness and compassion. She persuaded herself that his moral degeneration was only another form of his disease and should be treated as such. 'I do see more and more that wrongdoing is just a moral disease', she now wrote to Freddy:

and the morally healthy (like yourself) are not fit judges of the condition of the morally diseased; just as the physically healthy

[1] *Justice*, 29 Jan. 1898.
[2] Eleanor Marx Aveling to Freddy Demuth, 3 Feb. 1898, *Labour Leader*, 30 July 1898.

person can hardly realise the condition of the physically diseased.
And I begin to understand that one has no more right to blame
the one disease than the other. We must try and cure, and, if no
cure is possible, do our best. I have learnt this through long
suffering in ways I would not tell even you.[1]

'There is a French saying that to *understand* is to *forgive*', she
wrote again. 'Much suffering has taught me to understand—
and so I have no need to forgive. I can only love.'[2]

Aveling's operation was finally arranged. Eleanor was
extremely agitated and sent a dispatch to Kautsky, giving
him the news and saying only 'I *can't* write'.[3] On 8 February
Aveling entered University College Hospital and Eleanor
took a room near by, in Gower Street. As he was a Fellow
of the college, he was placed under the special care of the
great surgeon Christopher Heath and every possible attention was given to his comfort. The operation, which took
place on the following day, was successful. 'What a day! To
sit waiting for such an operation!' Eleanor wrote to Liebknecht: 'It is horrible for the patient—but I would have
gladly changed places with Edward and have counted myself
happy. To sit there able to do nothing!' After the terrible
ordeal she spent all day with him, leaving him only at night.
'Well, so far things are going fairly', she added, '—and
where there is life there is hope.'[4] There were several visitors
while he stayed in hospital. Was Mrs. Nelson among them?
At any rate, Mrs. Hyndman, who, at Eleanor's request,
came to see her husband, had a long talk with Eleanor,
walking up and down the corridor of the hospital. 'The story
Mrs. Aveling told was most depressing', recorded Hyndman:

. . . She evidently had to open her heart to somebody, and the
tale she told of the misery and humiliation she had to undergo

---

[1] Eleanor Marx Aveling to Freddy Demuth, 5 Feb. 1898, *Labour Leader*,
30 July 1898.

[2] Ibid., 7 Feb. 1898, ibid.

[3] Eleanor Marx Aveling to Kautsky, 7 Feb. 1898, IISH.

[4] Eleanor Marx Aveling to Liebknecht, 9 Feb. 1898, Liebknecht,
Briefwechsel, 461.

indulged my wife to implore her to leave the man directly he was out of danger, and to come for a time to stay with us. She said she would gladly do so.[1]

The Hyndmans optimistically believed that Eleanor's 'martyrdom' was going to come to an end.

On the 17th Eleanor brought her husband to the Den— in a carriage direct from the hospital, for she would not risk the changing about of cab and train. His doctors had wanted him to go to Margate to convalesce; so she went there next day and booked rooms at a place recommended by Hyndman.[2] Another holiday for recuperation—this time, for them both—meant further expense, but 'it is all so surely going to the one thing that I am giving up all the little I have left', she wrote to Freddy. 'I can get on anyway', she added.[3]

So she took the invalid off to the seaside resort. 'For a week I looked after him alone', she wrote to Liebknecht on 1 March. But then she had a doctor friend, an old fellow student of Edward's brother, to help her. She often took the patient out in a bath-chair, but he could eat very little and could hardly walk a few yards. She spent the evening dressing his open wound. 'You can think what pain this is to Edward, and how awful it is to have to do this.' What troubled her, however, was not merely the serious state of his health. 'The actual material difficulties' were now felt even more acutely. 'Our joint income is (for London) very small and my present expenses are enormous.—Doctors, chemists' bills, "chairs" for going out, and so forth, added to the home that must be kept up—all this means a great deal.'[4] She was more frank when she addressed herself to Freddy. 'It is a bad time for me', she wrote to him on the same day: 'I fear there is

---

[1] Hyndman, *Further Reminiscences*, 144.

[2] Eleanor Marx Aveling to Kautsky, 20 Feb. 1898, IISH.

[3] Eleanor Marx Aveling to Freddy Demuth, 20 Feb. 1898, *Labour Leader*, 30 July 1898.

[4] Eleanor Marx Aveling to Liebknecht, 1 March 1898, Liebknecht, *Briefwechsel*, 463–4.

HUNT LIBRARY
CARNEGIE-MELLON UNIVERSITY

little hope, and there is much pain and suffering. Why we go on is the mystery to me. I am ready to go, and would gladly. But while he *wants* help I am bound to stay.'[1] If only Aveling recovered health, she would leave him gladly: till then, however, she would remain as a tender nurse—and devoted wife. 'I fear there is *very* little hope of ultimate recovery', she wrote to Kautsky on the 15th: 'Today he did —leaning on my arm & a stick—walk a little.'[2]

Eleanor had once been at Margate many years before with her father after his serious illness. On that occasion she had been engaged in a struggle between her own desire for freedom and her feelings of filial devotion. Now a similar conflict—one between her own emancipation and wifely duty—tormented her. She had come to an understanding with her father, but there was no such prospect with Aveling, who had been indulging himself both at her expense and at the expense of his own health. Yet Aveling was a sick man and appeared almost helpless. She looked after him with more attention than she had given to her father in his last days. She apparently felt that her devotion might cure his moral disease as well. In every aspect of her life, it seemed, the odds were piling up against her. She might even have to give up her home, the Den of which she was 'Jewishly proud'. It was no exaggeration when she said that she was envious of her dead sister Jenny. The final act of her life had now begun.

[1] Eleanor Marx Aveling to Freddy Demuth, 1 March 1898, *Labour Leader*, 30 July 1898.

[2] Eleanor Marx Aveling to Kautsky, 15 March 1898, IISH.

XIII ～ DEATH AND AFTERMATH

In spite of her innumerable difficulties Eleanor still hoped for the day when Aveling would recover sufficiently for her to devote herself solely to her own work. Even at Margate she found time to read the Danish critic Georg Brandes's study of Shakespeare, which she had been asked to review for the *Neue Zeit*: 'a re-hash—& not a good one—of all others have done' was her judgement.[1] Hyndman received several letters from her at the time and the last from Margate in the middle of March, all telling him encouragingly that her sphere of usefulness to the S.D.F was increasing.[2] She had promised Liebknecht an article on the conclusion of the Engineers' lock-out, in which, she believed, she had discovered 'treachery' of some kind, and this, she said, she would send by the time Liebknecht came out of prison, on 18 March.[3] On the 16th, 'Tussy and Edward' sent him a line from Margate, wishing that 'we could be with you in the flesh as well as the spirit' on the day of his release.[4] The burden and worry of nursing her husband, however,

[1] Eleanor Marx Aveling to Kautsky, 15 March 1898, IISH. Brandes's *Shakespeare* was later translated into English by William Archer and soon came to be recognized as an authoritative work on the subject.

[2] *Justice*, 9 April 1898.

[3] Eleanor Marx Aveling to Liebknecht, 9 Feb. 1898 (?), Liebknecht, *Briefwechsel*, 462.

[4] Eleanor Marx and Edward Aveling to Liebknecht, 16 March 1898, ibid. 465.

prevented Eleanor from carrying out her promises. Liebknecht became disturbed as he did not hear any more from her. 'I cannot wait any longer', he wrote her on the 23rd: 'How are you? How is Edward?'[1] He did not even know whether she was still at Margate or had returned to Sydenham.

The Avelings returned to the Den on Sunday the 27th.[2] Edward's condition had slightly improved and Eleanor hoped to apply herself to her own work in London. On her return she made arrangements with Sonnenschein for the publication of *Value, Price, and Profit*, her father's address to the General Council of the First International, to which we have already referred. She was preparing a preface and advertised through the press for a file of the *Eastern Post* which contained reports of the sittings of the General Council.[3] Apparently she had no thought of death at the time. Moreover, the Avelings, on their return, accepted an invitation to attend a dinner to be held in honour of Hyndman in May.[4] In fact, there was nothing to indicate the nearing of the final catastrophe of her life.

*   *   *

On the morning of Thursday 31 March, Eleanor received a letter which a subsequent reader described as throwing 'a very discreditable light on a certain person'.[5] This letter, whose author is not known, must have told her, as Bernstein assumed, that Aveling had legally married Miss Frye and that he no longer needed her.[6] The source of the terrible revelation may have been a friend of Eleanor's who resented Edward's cruelty to her, or possibly Mrs. Nelson herself, who apparently was losing her patience with Mrs. Aveling.

---

[1] Liebknecht to Eleanor Marx Aveling, 23 March 1898, Bottigelli Collection.

[2] *Vorwärts*, 5 April 1898.

[3] *Reynolds's Newspaper*, 3 April 1898; *Labour Leader*, 9 April 1898.

[4] *Reynolds's Newspaper*, 10 April 1898.

[5] *Labour Leader*, 30 April 1898.

[6] Bernstein, *My Years of Exile*, 165.

Indeed Mr. Nelson, Eva's legal husband, had on account of his health been chained to 'his mistress' at the Den! That this was the actual state of their entangled relations Eleanor was now for the first time forced to realize.

Eleanor had believed and told her friends that her union with Aveling was a true marriage 'just as much as if a dozen registrars had officiated'. She had stood firmly to her belief, and now at the end of all her endurance and self-sacrifice she found herself no more than a married man's mistress. The ideal of free love was degraded and reduced to the sin of adultery. It was said that 'a stormy interview' probably followed the painful discovery.[1] It is, however, more likely that the 'interview' was serious but restrained. It seems that she at once determined to end her life and in a grave tone asked her husband to do the same. Aveling perhaps did not take the threat seriously, for it was not the first time that she had declared her intention to destroy herself. But soon he realized that this time her threat was not idle. He told her—so we must assume—that he would share her fate. Eleanor's maid, Gertrude Gentry, whom she had called 'my very excellent but rather stupid Gerty',[2] was sent to a nearby chemist, bearing a visiting card of 'Dr. Aveling' and a note which said: 'Please give bearer chloroform and small quantity prussic acid for dog, E.A.'.[3] The maid testified at the inquest that she had been sent by Mrs. Aveling, but apparently her husband had been with her at the time. Certainly Eleanor had never signed her name as 'E.A.', which were Aveling's initials. Moreover, Aveling had acquired, as Hyndman later asserted, 'the power of writing . . . exactly like his wife'.[4] Or perhaps it may be truer to say that Eleanor's

[1] *Labour Leader*, 30 July 1898.

[2] Eleanor Marx Aveling to Laura Lafargue, 23 Dec. 1896, photocopy, IISH.

[3] *Forest Hill & Sydenham Examiner and Crystal Palace District Intelligencer*, 8 April 1898. The following references to the inquest regarding the cause of Eleanor's death are taken from a report published in this paper.

[4] Hyndman, *Further Reminiscences*, 145–6.

handwriting had come to resemble her husband's very closely—so that nobody could say for certain who actually wrote the order for the poison. If Eleanor had actually written the message, she must have done so in her husband's presence and with his tacit consent in order to reassure the chemist, who was under the impression that 'Dr. Aveling' was a qualified practitioner.

Gerty left the house just before ten o'clock and in a few minutes returned with a small white parcel which contained two ounces of chloroform and one drachm of prussic acid. This was the quantity normally used for poisoning a dog, but it was enough to kill several humans. She also brought back a book in which purchasers of poison were required to sign their names. Eleanor took the book into the front room where Aveling was at the time,[1] and, as the maid believed, she signed it. The signature was 'E. M. Aveling'. Apparently Aveling had become alarmed at the seriousness of the matter. He told Eleanor at this point, as he stated in his testimony at the inquest, that 'he was going up to town. She however did not wish him to do so on account of his health being so bad lately.' As Bernstein later pointed out, Aveling had been very weak even on the day before and had to be wheeled around in a bath-chair.[2] Still he insisted on going: anxious to avoid witnessing the crime he had engineered, he left the Den about ten minutes past ten.

After he had gone, Eleanor went upstairs and wrote a letter to her solicitor, A. R. Crosse, 'containing the names of several persons' as it was later stated. With it she enclosed the letter she had received that morning, and she addressed the envelope to Crosse.[3] It is quite likely that she gave him directions

[1] Robert Banner in *Labour Leader*, 30 April 1898.
[2] *Justice*, 30 July 1898.
[3] Robert Banner in *Labour Leader*, 30 April 1898. According to Banner, Eleanor wrote this letter immediately before taking the poison, but Keir Hardie in his article in the same paper (dated 30 July 1898) asserts that the letter was written soon after she had received 'some new revelation of disgrace'. If the letter contained, as it appears reasonable to assume

to alter her will and codicil so that the bulk of her property would go to Jenny's children or possibly to Freddy as well. Yet she also wrote a note to Aveling indicating her own loyalty to him even at the very last: 'Dear, it will soon be all over now. My last word to you is the same that I have said during all these long, sad years—love.'[1] She had a bath, dressed in white, and retired to bed.[2] Shortly afterwards, about a quarter to eleven, Gerty entered Eleanor's bedroom and found her unconscious but just breathing. She called in a neighbour and went for a doctor, but by the time the doctor arrived it was all over.

*　　　*　　　*

Meanwhile Aveling, on his arrival in London, went straight to the office of the S.D.F., where he met H. W. Lee and called his attention to the exact time of his visit.[3] He probably called on Mrs. Nelson to tell her what had happened, and then returned to Sydenham about five o'clock in the afternoon. When he saw the letters left behind by Eleanor he tried to destroy them, but was prevented from doing so by a police officer who had arrived on the scene.[4] He must have been afraid that Eleanor might have written something disclosing his complicity in her death, and perhaps he suspected that the letter to Crosse would deprive him of the benefit of her will. It was said that he did not even go to view the body and next day attended a cricket match![5]

An inquest to ascertain the circumstances of Eleanor's

it did, directions to alter her will, it must have been written at a time when Eleanor became convinced that Aveling would still be alive after her death, i.e. after his departure from the Den. According to her will and codicil all the benefits assigned for him would come to him only in case of his outliving Eleanor and otherwise would go to Jenny's children, and therefore Eleanor would have no incentive to alter the will as long as she felt or even wished that Aveling was going to die with her.

[1] *Reynolds's Newspaper*, 10 April 1898.
[2] *Justice*, 9 April 1898; Thorne, op. cit. 148.
[3] Hyndman, *Further Reminiscences*, 146.
[4] *Labour Leader*, 30 July 1898.
[5] Ibid. A football match seems more likely.

death was held on 2 August at the Park Hall, Sydenham. The first witness called was Dr. Aveling, who described himself as an author residing at the Den.

The Coroner: Was the deceased your wife?
Witness: Legally or not do you mean?
Coroner: You are a most difficult man to deal with. Were you married to the deceased?
Witness: Not legally.
Coroner: She lived with you as your wife do you mean?
Witness: Yes.
Coroner: What was her age?
Witness: I believe about 40, but I am not quite sure.
Coroner: Was her health usually good?
Witness: Very.

. . . .

Coroner: Had you any idea that she would destroy herself?
Witness: She has threatened to do it several times.
Coroner: Did you consider that the threats used were intentional?
Witness: I regarded them as idle, because they were so frequently repeated.
Coroner: Had you any quarrel before you left in the morning?
Witness: None whatever.
[Witness, questioned] by the Foreman [of the Jury]: They had had slight differences, but had never had any serious quarrel. The deceased was of a morbid disposition and several times suggested that they commit suicide together. When they had difficulties it was not infrequent for her to say 'Let us end all these difficulties together'.
Coroner: Do you mean pecuniary difficulties?
Witness: Yes, pecuniary, not, however, so much recently as in the past.

The coroner gave a warning not to Aveling but to the unfortunate chemist—against his 'perfunctory manner' of dealing with poison. And the jury returned the verdict of 'Suicide whilst in a state of temporary insanity'. After the verdict Aveling told the coroner and jury that he was not married to the deceased because he had been married before.[1] Nobody, however, brought out the fact of his second

[1] *Forest Hill & Sydenham Examiner and Crystal Palace District Intelligencer*, 8 April 1898.

marriage, which was the immediate cause of Eleanor's tragic death.

Eleanor's funeral took place on Tuesday 5 April at the Necropolis Station, Waterloo. A large number of mourners gathered around the coffin, on which were placed handsome wreaths from various Socialist organizations both in England and on the Continent and also from certain individuals such as the Hyndmans and Paul Lafargue. Mme Lafargue had been too much affected by grief to be able to leave Dravéil. Short addresses were delivered by several persons, including Aveling himself, who 'alone was dry-eyed and theatrical in speech and manner'.[1] Those who heard that he had sought relaxation at a football match on the previous day were shocked by his callousness.[2] 'If there were no party interest to take into consideration', later wrote Bernstein, who also spoke for the German party, 'the people would have torn Aveling to pieces.'[3] Will Thorne, on the other hand, was so overcome by strong emotion that 'he cried like a child' and his voice became almost inaudible as he tried to speak of the close friendship he had enjoyed with the deceased and the devoted work she had done on behalf of his union. Many of the friends present journeyed to Woking, where the body was cremated.[4]

Very few of her friends were satisfied with the result of the inquest, which established nothing beyond the fact of her suicide. Bernstein, who spent sleepless nights blaming himself for not having done his best to 'make the scoundrel impossible before', was determined to take legal action against Aveling.[5] Kautsky wrote from Berlin that he was 'in favour of proceeding relentlessly against the scoundrel'.[6] Robert Banner, who claimed to have known her 'perhaps longer than any living

---

[1] *Labour Leader*, 30 July 1898.   [2] *Justice*, 30 July 1898.
[3] Bernstein to Adler, 5 April 1898, Adler, *Briefwechsel*, 244.
[4] *Justice*, 9 April 1898.
[5] Bernstein to Adler, 5 April 1898, Kautsky to Adler, 9 April 1898, Adler, op. cit. 243–5.
[6] Kautsky to Adler, 9 April 1898, ibid.

British Socialist', called attention to certain facts which had been overlooked at the inquest, such as Aveling's presence at the time of the arrival of the poison, and also the failure to deliver the letter left for her solicitor.[1] An attempt was made to draw the attention of the Public Prosecutor to these facts,[2] but no fresh inquiry was held. Indeed, Eleanor's letter to Crosse and its enclosure, probably the most important documents in the whole affair, had been returned to Aveling without having received due consideration at the inquest. 'According to his statement to several persons', said Bernstein, Aveling 'destroyed' them.[3] Why had not Crosse claimed the letter? It looks as if Aveling had come to an understanding with him with regard to the letter and Eleanor's property, which was now his, and to this possibility we shall shortly return.

*   *   *

Meanwhile, some of Eleanor's closest friends found it difficult to speak ill of Aveling as they knew only too well of her devotion to him. An obituary by Liebknecht, in which he expressed surprise at the apparent restoration of Aveling's health, was still so restrained in its critical examination of the cause of the tragedy that Kautsky regarded it as a piece of 'propaganda for Aveling'.[4] Olive Schreiner, to whom Aveling had been simply abhorrent, hesitated to attack him in public. 'I have been desiring terribly further details with regard to Eleanor', she wrote from South Africa to Dollie Radford:

. . . I have little doubt in my mind she discovered a fresh infidelity of Aveling and that that ended all. I had thought of writing a short notice of her in one of the monthly reviews. Then I felt [that] as I could not speak the truth about him I could not write of her. It would have hurt her to have him blamed. . . . I am

---

[1] *Labour Leader*, 30 April 1898.   [2] Ibid. , 23 April 1898.
[3] *Justice*, 30 July 1898.
[4] *Vorwärts*, 5 April 1898; Kautsky to Adler, 9 April 1898, Adler, op. cit. 245.

so glad Eleanor is dead. It is such a mercy she has escaped from him.[1]

Moreover, Paul Lafargue and Charles Longuet, who had hurried to Sydenham upon receiving the sad news, did not see fit to investigate the tragic circumstances beyond what had been established at the official inquiry. They even went off, immediately after the inquest, to drink with Aveling at a near by public house. Aveling's insensitiveness distressed Bernstein, while theirs disappointed Hyndman, who almost believed that it was Aveling who had proposed the suicide pact.[2] Indeed, Eleanor's brothers-in-law had asked Aveling to go and see Crosse with them to settle certain matters, but he refused to do so 'as long as the two gentlemen stay in London'.[3] By the end of April there was no more talk, if there had been any, of a legal action against him by Eleanor's relations.[4]

A wider circle of her friends and acquaintances, however, were still interested in the possibility of incriminating Aveling. A. K. Donald, himself an intellectual of some sort, who had co-operated with the Avelings many years before in the Socialist League, took up the matter, but he soon found it difficult to proceed. 'It was rather funny', he wrote to J. L. Mahon, '—her friends came to me for advice as to whether Aveling could not be prosecuted for complicity in the suicide. I went into the matter and took additional evidence from what was given at the inquest but I strongly advised them not to proceed owing to want of evidence.'[5] By this time Aveling had managed to 'destroy' the oft-mentioned letter to Crosse. By getting rid of this document he doubly triumphed: not only had he escaped incrimination but he had also succeeded in preserving Eleanor's will from

[1] Olive Schreiner to Dollie Radford, June 1898, Radford Papers.
[2] *Justice*, 30 July 1898; Hyndman, *Further Reminiscences*, 145–7.
[3] Kautsky to Adler, 9 April 1898, Adler, op. cit. 245.
[4] Ibid., 29 April 1898, ibid. 247.
[5] A. K. Donald to J. L. Mahon, 4 June 1898, extracts published in E. P. Thomson, *William Morris*, 874.

any further alterations. This clearly shows, as Bernstein asserted, that 'after her death one thing of hers only was of value to him: her property, her money'.[1]

*   *   *

On 16 April probate of Eleanor's will and codicil was granted to Aveling. Her gross estate was sworn at £1,909. 3s. 10d., and the net property was £1,467. 7s. 8d.[2] Aveling had apparently consulted Crosse, and it is not impossible that he paid him hush-money.[3] Crosse was certainly given prominence in Aveling's own will, which he drew up three months later on 21 July. He was appointed as the sole executor of the will and was promised a legacy of £50. Moreover, he was entitled to 'charge . . . for all business whether strictly professional or not done by him as a Solicitor'. We may assume that the doctor and the lawyer had conspired against the helpless woman—helpless indeed in the matter of money—and had succeeded. Of course, Aveling was to bequeath to 'Eva Nelson' the bulk of the property he had just inherited from Eleanor. Shortly after her death he moved to No. 2 Stafford Mansions, Albert Bridge Road, Eva's residence, which he adorned with books, plate, china, glasses, pictures, and prints. All these and other household goods and articles were to be given to her, and the residue of his property was to be sold by Crosse for her benefit.[4] He had no power to bequeath his interest in the Marx literary remains, but he did manage to make some money out of it: he published Marx's *Value, Price, and Profit*, which had been

---

[1] *Justice*, 30 July 1898.

[2] Eleanor Marx Aveling, Will at Somerset House; *Reynolds's Newspaper*, 24 April 1898.

[3] Crosse told Bernstein that hardly one-fourth of the money left by Engels had remained at the time of her death. 'I do not know', wrote Bernstein, 'how much of it was spent as hush-money to cloak his infamies with women or children, but it must have been very much.' Bernstein to Adler, 5 April 1898, Adler, op. cit. 243–4.

[4] Edward Aveling, Will at Somerset House.

edited by Eleanor, with a preface of his own in which he
was shrewd enough to advertise his own *Student's Marx*.

Now Aveling was once again completely boycotted by the
Socialist and labour organizations, a lot to which he had
long been accustomed. Towards the end of April he resigned
his seat on the executive council of the S.D.F. and early in
June the auditorship of the Gasworkers' Union, which he
had held for some years.[1] It was rumoured that he was
intending to spend six months in New Zealand for his
health.[2] He was, however, only able to make a tour in
Ireland, and when he returned the six-month-old wound
caused by the operation reopened, and grave complications
ensued. He realized that he could not live long, and he
wanted to die in his study amid his books, facing Battersea
Park. On 2 August—only four months after the death of
Eleanor—in his room at Stafford Mansions, he 'closed his
eyes, having laid down a book he was perusing, and passed
away'.[3]

It was a surprisingly peaceful death for a man who had
involved others, and especially Eleanor, in such turmoil. The
mode of his death, however, has little to do with the pattern
of his life. There were not a few who felt that it would have
been better if he had died a few months earlier. 'What a
pity he didn't die a little before!' exclaimed Hyndman.[4] The
sentiment was widely echoed. 'Eleanor Marx, long known
by another name—which we shall try to forget—. . . [will
be] known by her own', now declared Liebknecht.[5]

Aveling's remains were cremated at Woking on 6 August.
Only his immediate relatives—about six of them—were
present, and there was no representative of the Socialist
movement. The most affected was 'a young lady attired in
deep mourning'—Mrs. Nelson—and on her arrival in chapel

---

[1] *Reynolds's Newspaper*, 1 May, 5 June 1898.
[2] *Labour Leader*, 14 May 1898.   [3] *Clarion*, 13 August 1898.
[4] Hyndman to Liebknecht, 10 Aug. 1898, IML (Berlin).
[5] *Social-Democrat*, Sept. 1898.

XEM

she sank into a chair in a state of collapse, unable to give a final farewell to Alec Nelson's body.[1] Shortly afterwards Crosse obtained probate of Aveling's will, his effects being estimated at £852, the greater part of which apparently went to Mrs. Nelson eventually. If only Engels could have known that the small remainder of his fortune was to pass into the hands of an obscure actress who had been the cause of Eleanor's sad end!

* * *

To anyone who knew Eleanor, her suicide was a shocking tragedy. A certain Lily Bell, who had met Eleanor once before, wrote a poem entitled 'Eleanor Marx Aveling':

> I never pray, for god is dead!
> I never weep, for tears are shed!
> I never hope, for hopes have fled!
> I only love such souls as thee,
> Oh, Sharer of Adversity!

She, however, blamed Eleanor's materialism—for 'materialism is the gospel of death'—and maintained that 'our sister comrade was in the innermost heart of her worthy of a nobler creed' and that 'her woman's soul craved for something more gratifying than the husks upon which it had fed'.[2] A similar argument has been presented by a recent writer, who asserted that 'the Marxian upbringing' had been responsible for the 'hopelessly unMarxian' outcome of the tragedy; in other words, 'the Marxian ethic', whatever it may be, 'negated itself' and produced the 'apotheosis of self-immolation', i.e. Eleanor's martyrdom.[3]

Eleanor Marx, however, was not a materialist in Lily Bell's sense nor even a Marxist in the sense used by this writer. Robert Banner is probably right when he contended

---

[1] *Reynolds's Newspaper*, 7 Aug. 1898.
[2] *Labour Leader*, 16 April 1898.
[3] Lewis S. Feuer, 'Marxian Tragedians: A Death in the Family', *Encounter*, Nov. 1962.

that Eleanor, in spite of her 'theoretical' materialism, had been an idealist in her practical life and that her misfortune was that she had invested love and hope and received nothing in return.[1] Indeed, as Collison, her political opponent, pointed out, Eleanor 'had all the Christian virtues, if she lacked faith'.[2] She would help anyone or anything in need of help. She spent hours teaching Will Thorne to read and write. She was devoted to children, fond of animals. The strong moral sense of compassion and fellow-feeling, the urge to do something to help others, underlay all her activities, her Socialism, her Internationalism, and her 'Marxism'. The result of her 'Marxian upbringing' was her especial loyalty to the cause of the workers, who, she felt, needed help more than anybody else. Eleanor once declared that Socialism would mean 'the real new birth of light' and ensure the attainment of man's salvation. She could be as fierce and uncompromising as a religious crusader in condemning the sins and wickedness of bourgeois society. Like her father, she was a warm friend and a fierce enemy, but, as Hyndman recalled, 'when she made up her mind that reconciliation was right as well as politic, she could be as generous and forgiving as she had before been bitter and unrelenting'.[3] Eleanor knew how to forgive, and after many years of suffering she only loved.

Yet Eleanor's whole life can also be represented as a conflict between love and duty. She probably agreed with Bernard Shaw when the latter asserted his Ibsenite conviction that 'progress must involve the repudiation of an established duty at every step'.[4] Yet she failed to be a Nora, however much she had wanted to be one, for duty, filial and then wifely duty, triumphed in her own struggle. Her Jewishness and her reverence for family ties may have been factors more potent in this than her desire for freedom, but

[1] *Labour Leader*, 23 April 1898.   [2] Collison, op. cit. 81.
[3] *Justice*, 9 April 1898.
[4] G. Bernard Shaw, *The Quintessence of Ibsenism* (1891), 7.

the fourteen years of her life with her demoralized husband could only be explained by her optimistic belief in the possibility of changing a bad character, her faith in herself as one who could cure evils by the strength of her devotion.

Eleanor once claimed that she had 'the power very strongly developed of seeing things from the "other side"'. By this dialectical power, it seems, she was led to perceive, among other things, the contradiction between the good Aveling, an innocent artist, and the wicked Aveling, the embodiment of greed and callousness. Indeed, her husband's private life provided an almost pathological case of man's alienation. She somehow believed that participation in a movement designed to overthrow the wicked capitalist society, as well as her own devotion to the good Aveling, would cure him of his moral disease. Yet dialectics failed her, for Aveling could argue that his alienation would go on till the advent of Socialism when a poor man like himself would for the first time be relieved of the need to borrow or extort. Further, he could contend that the need to seduce would also disappear only when property marriage was abolished. He seems to have come to believe that under the existing conditions his own association with Eleanor had to be based on property relations and was no longer 'free'. His alienation continued, and it was no use trying to argue him out of his 'degeneration'. When Eleanor realized how powerless her love and sacrifice had been and how irretrievably her self-respect had been damaged by Aveling's shameless behaviour, she chose to die. Had not her father made a memorable remark on the demise of the old International: 'the end must be voluntary and decent'?

*   *   *

When Dr. Aveling disowned 'Mrs. Aveling' at the inquest, his 'ingratitude, injustice, and hardness' at once became the object of universal hatred.[1] 'A long course of his low intrigues'

[1] *Labour Leader*, 7 May 1898.

was much talked about. 'Strange to say', read an obituary when he died,

in spite of an exterior that almost recalled Quasimodo, he always exercised a remarkable fascination for women, and the effect of his lecturing tours in the provinces was frequently discounted by tales of victims that he left behind him. That these offences were only known to a few persons, who were unable to speak in fear of injuring the innocent, is the explanation of the position he occupied in the political world. In order to shield the unfortunate lady who had united her fortunes with his own, silence was necessary.[1]

He was not only unorthodox in matters of sexual morality but also notorious for his irregularities in borrowing and spending. It was in this latter sense that one of his visits to Aberdeen became legendary. He took several of the local men, so the story runs, to the hotel where he was staying. He ordered a bottle of an expensive, special vintage sherry for himself, while his working-class friends contented themselves with lemonade. When the drinks were served, he paused a while in his streaming conversation, pointed to a stone-mason, and solemnly declared: 'And you'll pay'.[2] There must have been many other stories like this about the unpleasant features of his personality.

He is said to have been 'a moral wastrel'[3] and a 'real criminal type'[4] and his career 'best buried in oblivion'.[5] Bernard Shaw, however, eternalized him as Dubedat in his tragedy *The Doctor's Dilemma*. Dubedat, a young painter, committed bigamy and borrowed on all sides, but all his perversities were for the sake of his genius and his art, for he was 'a disciple of Bernard Shaw'. Moreover, Shaw made him die like a saint, and allowed Mrs. Dubedat to remarry happily. Certainly, Aveling was not a disciple of Shaw, and, unlike Dubedat, he was not an artistic genius either. 'At the

[1] *Reynolds's Newspaper*, 7 Aug. 1898.
[2] John Paton, *Proletarian Pilgrimage* (1935), 118. Paton, who was born in 1886, was too young to be an eye-witness of the occasion.
[3] Collison, op. cit. 52.   [4] *The Letters of Olive Schreiner*, 185.
[5] W. Stephen Sanders, *Early Socialist Days*, 82.

most', said Havelock Ellis, 'there were but traces' of artistic quality in him, and his 'air of virile and intellectual energy' was quite misleading.[1] But we can find other contemporaries who had a certain respect for him, such as Henry Salt, who found in him 'an odd mixture of fine qualities and bad' and a man whose 'duplicities were the result less of a calculated dishonesty than of a nature in which there was an excess of the emotional element'. Salt had been fascinated by his reading of Shelley's *Prometheus Unbound*, which he concluded with 'a storm of sobs and tears'.[2] Apparently he failed to see that Aveling was more of a sentimentalist than an inspired artist. It is probably not unjust to describe him, as Collison did, as 'a man of parts without stamina'.[3]

Shortly after the death of Eleanor, Dollie Radford set to writing an idyll based on her tragic life, which she published under the title *One Way of Love*. Sacha, obviously Eleanor herself,[4] was approached by a man whose 'self-preserving qualities' were astonishing. This man

relied invariably upon his head to bring him safely out of the dangerous places which his heart prompted him to penetrate. In all matters he relied, ultimately, upon his inherited and carefully developed gift of common-sense, and upon the faculty he had also inherited and prudently cultivated, of doing always the best for himself.

Yet Sacha fell in love with him, charmed with the magic of his caressing words. 'In the joy of that new speech, in the sweetness of his embrace, Sacha noticed not that he spoke no word again of his own love for her.' The end came swiftly: 'Long and patiently she had waited for her birthright, for the time in which to sing her song of triumph, and to-day she longed for it with a passionate longing'; Sacha drowned

---

[1] *Adelphi*, Sept., Oct. 1935.

[2] Henry Salt, *Seventy Years among Savages*, 80–81.

[3] Collison, op. cit. 82.

[4] Aveling had once called Eleanor 'Sacharissa'. See his *American Journey*, 73.

herself.[1] Unlike Salt, Dollie, one of Eleanor's closest friends, saw in Aveling a man of common selfishness and deceit. She firmly believed that he had not really loved Eleanor throughout their married life.

Even Engels, who had patronised Aveling not only as a Socialist but also as an aspiring dramatist, had to admit at one time: 'he had a capacity of neglecting facts, when they are contrary to his wishes, that is worthy of a more juvenile age'.[2] He could be as dishonest as he liked and was still able to pretend innocence. Apparently he did not believe in morality and did not understand demoralization. Thomas Okey, who had associated with him in the Secularist movement, emphasized 'the devastating effect of alcohol' on his moral character.[3] Yet an excess in drinking was rather a sympton of moral degeneration than its cause. There has been an attempt to place all the responsibilities upon his Marxism. 'The mandate to combat exploitation in its economic form', said a critic, 'could become a licence to exploit people in others.'[4] But again, Marxism had little to do with his deterioration, though he may have found an excuse in what appeared to him to be the general corruption of bourgeois society. Indeed, no such 'licence' was ever recognized among the Marxists of the nineteenth century. In fact Aveling had already been morally suspect before he became a Marxist; and his moral perversion had more to do with the militant atheism and the theatrical interests which he had cultivated earlier in his life.

We have seen that his atheism was mainly the result of his study of natural history. At one stage of his career he sought to integrate science and art in a crude materialism and aesthetic hedonism. He called this synthesis 'the gospel of Evolution' in which even human love was reduced to matter

---

[1] Dollie Radford, *One Way of Love* (1898), *passim*.
[2] Engels to Laura Lafargue, 23 July 1888, *Correspondance*, ii. 155.
[3] Thomas Okey, *A Basketful of Memoirs*, 62–63.
[4] Lewis Feuer, loc. cit.

and motion. He glorified the pleasure of living and asserted the right of all, but above all his own right, to every pleasure in this world. As a missionary dedicated to this gospel, he became an entertainer and dramatist as well as a science teacher. In such a life, however, the boundary between reality and fiction often became blurred, and he began to play various parts in his real life: the injured innocent, the honest poor man, the loving husband, the repentant husband, the seducer, and even the criminal. Disregard for truth became habitual and his depravity aggravated.

He attracted Eleanor into this drama of his own life when he became a Marxist. Their common interest was in the stage as much as in Socialism. Their favourite theme was adultery, for it could throw some light upon social evils and bourgeois conventions. Eleanor, however, upon the failure of her stage career, more or less abandoned the decadent world of smart intellectuals and devoted herself to the cause of the workers. Aveling went on seeking the best of every-thing in the name, strangely enough, of morality. Money-making was immoral—so he borrowed. Marriage without love was immoral—so he seduced. He lived in the same world of decadence and bohemian revolt where the *fin-de-siècle* writers in France showed their contempt for existing society by adhering to Anarchism and violence. In spite of the active part he played in the anti-Anarchist campaign he was in his private life perhaps more of an Anarchist than a Marxist, for on the whole the Marxists were disciplinarians rather than libertarians. The destruction of the daughter of Karl Marx was almost inevitable.

*   *   *

It has been asserted by a Communist critic that the truth about the final catastrophe in Eleanor's life 'is not really known' and 'never will be'. 'The issue has all along been bedevilled', added the same writer, 'by the desire of right-wing Social Democrats to exploit Aveling, blown up into an unrecognisable stage villain, against the Marxists,

especially against Engels.'[1] It is true that Hyndman deplored
the 'weakness of one of the great founders of modern
Socialism . . . in striving, in season and out of season, to force
upon the Party a particular person about whose character
opinion is now unanimous'.[2] And Bax wrote in similar terms
in his memoirs.[3] Yet both Hyndman and Bax more or less
knew 'the truth'; moreover, to deplore Engels's 'weakness' or
even his 'serious defect', as Bax put it, is not to diminish the
great contribution he had made to the wealth of Socialist
thought and tactics. Indeed, as we have seen, Marxism had
little to do with the tragedy itself. If there was anything
to be blamed in Marxism, it was not the creed as such but
individuals holding it or rather the peculiarities of certain
such individuals: Bebel and Adler's Machiavellism, Bernstein's sudden apostasy, and Lafargue's complacency.
Eleanor knew the personal foibles of her guardian 'General'
perhaps too well. The discovery that she had a half-brother
of her own must have been a shattering blow to her. At the
same time, the signs of disintegration in the Marxist movement after the death of Engels worried Eleanor. No doubt
she was politically disillusioned with many Marxists. Perhaps one could argue that even when all other hopes had
vanished, she would have retained a hope to live and work
if Marxism had remained as united a force as it had been
under her father's and guardian's tutorship. Yet our examination of the circumstances of her death shows that she was
still willing to live and work until a few hours before her end;
and this would seem to imply that the final tragedy was
caused solely by the criminal infidelity of her husband. Her
political disillusionment, however great and heart-breaking
it may have been, was only one, though an important one,
of the circumstances which led to the deepening of her
melancholy, and its absence would not have prevented her
from taking the fatal step.

[1] Allen Hutt, 'Eleanor Marx', *World News*, no. 22.
[2] *Justice*, 23 July 1898.   [3] Bax, *Reminiscences and Reflections*, 55–56.

Her contribution to the Socialist movement in England would have been greater if she had not been encumbered by her husband, for his presence inevitably brought the question of personality into the young movement, which was more puritanical than Bohemian. It is true that Aveling sincerely believed in Marxism, but his Marxism was grafted on to his curious gospel of evolution, and his treatment of it was mechanical.

While Engels was alive the Avelings always consulted him in their attempts to influence the movement. They sought to implant Marxian principles and Internationalism in the various organizations with which they came into contact. They were normally at first welcomed or tolerated but soon asked to withdraw. Engels's final judgement on the bodies which failed to accommodate Aveling—the S.D.F., Socialist League, and I.L.P.—was that each of these was a mere sect. He was at least partly right, for when the Avelings went directly to the workers their success was more remarkable. Their contribution, especially Eleanor's, to the growth of New Unionism has been fully acknowledged by Will Thorne. To Eleanor, the Gasworkers' Union was 'my union' in every sense of the word. Aveling's legal eight-hour movement with its annual May Day demonstrations appeared to grow into a power to be reckoned with. Yet as soon as he tried to make political capital out of it, failure awaited him. In a sense, their real work for the English movement began when they achieved reconciliation with the S.D.F. after the death of Engels. If they had been able to continue their work to convert trade unionists to Socialism, the history of the S.D.F., and possibly of the Labour Party, which was founded less than two years after Eleanor's death, would have been different. James Mawdsley, the 'old' unionist and by no means a Socialist, who had come to know Eleanor at the time of the London congress of the International, was much impressed by her undiluted devotion to the cause of the workers. 'I can scarcely call myself an intimate acquaintance', he wrote, 'but from what I have seen of her I am convinced that her heart was in her work, and that no one more honestly worked for the well-being of the Labour movement than she did.'[1]

*   *   *

When Eleanor died, Adler wrote to Kautsky: 'Poor Tussy! . . . No doubt the scamp has driven her to death. But the main thing—what will happen to the Nachlass? She had, I believe, many of Marx's letters in her hands.'[2] It is probably not surprising that Adler was more concerned about the fate of Marx's letters than about the tragic death of his daughter. The division of the Marx-Engels literary remains was regretted not only by Kautsky but also by Adler and Bebel. They soon discovered to their alarm that Eleanor had left all her interest in her father's works to Aveling, though only during his lifetime. Was he to come into possession of the *Nachlass* itself, which had come to Eleanor, in Engels's words, as 'the legal personal representative' of Karl Marx? He could not possibly claim any legal connexion with Marx. In fact no suggestion has ever been made that he sold the papers, and we can assume that the *Nachlass* passed more or less safely into Laura's hands. Kautsky, who had been appointed by Eleanor as the editor of Marx's manuscripts, went on co-operating with Laura. But a second tragedy befell the Marx family: in 1911 Laura committed suicide with her husband, having spent most of the fortune left by Engels. As they had no surviving child, there must have been a dispersion of Marx's papers at their death. Many of them, however, were collected by Jenny's children, especially her daughter Jenny, who espoused 'the cult of her grand-father's memory'.[3] Those documents that had been under Kautsky's control were later delivered to the party

---

[1] *Reynolds's Newspaper*, 10 April 1898.

[2] Adler to Kautsky, 4 April 1898, Adler, *Briefwechsel*, 242.

[3] Emile Bottigelli, introduction to 'Lettres et documents de Karl Marx', *Annali* (1958), 149.

archives of the German Social Democrats, where they joined Engels's *Nachlass*, which had been entrusted to Bernstein.[1] This did not bring about the consolidation of all the sacred documents, for Ryazanov was energetically collecting as many as he could for the Marx-Engels Institute in Moscow. Indeed, the story of the Marxian *Nachlass* ran parallel to the wider history of Marxism. Even after the close of the period of extermination and liquidation of political opponents, during which these documents also suffered, the division has continued between the Institute in Moscow and the International Institute of Social History in Amsterdam, the latter having obtained the German archives when the German Social Democratic Party was driven into exile in the 1930's. In spite of the great progress that has been made in publishing the *Nachlass*, the same party interest which deprived Eleanor of free access to her father's papers has not entirely disappeared.

Apart from the four children of Charles and Jenny Longuet, there was another line of descent from Karl Marx, by Freddy Demuth. But we know very little about his own later career. In 1910 he was living with a fellow workman at Upper Clapton, East London. He had a son who by then had married and obtained employment in a French taxicab company in London. Freddy was much troubled by his son's difficulties, as the young man's family was rapidly growing. 'I suppose it will go on', he wrote in a letter to Laura, 'till the time comes when the birth of children will be hailed with joy instead of sadness, as it is in many homes all the world over today.'[2] Shortly afterwards his son left for Australia, hoping to find employment on a farm. He seems to have had a rough time there, and his wife and four children, left behind in England, were looked after by Freddy for some time.[3] Whether his family joined him in Australia

---

[1] Kautsky, *Briefwechsel*, 448.
[2] Freddy Demuth to Laura Lafargue, 7 Oct. 1910, IISH.
[3] Freddy Demuth to Bernstein, 29 Aug. 1912, IISH.

or he returned to England later on is not known. Freddy and his descendants disappeared, at least for half a century, from the annals of the Socialist movement.

As for Eleanor's remains, for long they found no permanent resting place. Her ashes were not claimed by her husband, but were kept in an urn in the office of the S.D.F. They were transferred to the headquarters of the Communist Party of Great Britain in 1920 when the British Socialist Party, the successor of the S.D.F., merged in that new organization. In May 1921, when the police raided the premises of the party and seized documents under the Emergency Powers Act then in force, for no apparent reason they took away the urn. Later the urn was returned, and it was kept at the Karl Marx Memorial Library in Clerkenwell Green. About ten years ago, when the new family grave was erected at Highgate Cemetery, the ashes found a more permanent and, one may hope, a final resting place, beside those of her 'Mohr', 'Möhme', and 'Lenchen'.

SELECT BIBLIOGRAPHY

I. UNPUBLISHED SOURCES

1. Eleanor Marx Correspondence

Bottigelli Collection. By courtesy of M. Emile Bottigelli.
Ernest and Dollie Radford Papers. By courtesy of Dr. Muriel Radford.
Marx-Engels *Nachlass* (photocopy), IML (Berlin).
Marx-Engels *Nachlass*, IISH.
Karl Kautsky Archives, IISH.
Socialist League Archives, IISH.
Dutch Socialist Archives, IISH.
Bernard Shaw Papers, B.M.
John Burns Papers, B.M.Add.MSS. 46288, 46289.
Eleanor Marx-Karl Hirsch Correspondence, Ohara Institute for Social Research, Hosei University, Tokyo.

2. Other Manuscripts

Wilhelm Liebknecht Archives, IML (Berlin).
Wilhelm Liebknecht Archives, IISH.
Andreas Scheu Archives, IISH.
Hermann Schlüter Archives, IISH.
Eduard Bernstein Archives, IISH.
William Morris Papers, B.M.Add.MSS. 45345.
Bernard Shaw Diary and Notes, BLPES.

3. Thesis

Blumberg, Dorothy Rose. 'Florence Kelley: the Early Years', M.A. thesis, Columbia University.

II. WORKS BY ELEANOR MARX AND EDWARD AVELING

1. Published Letters of Eleanor Marx

Blumemberg, Werner (ed.), 'Ein unbekanntes Kapitel aus Marx' Leben: Briefe an die Hollandischen Verwandten', *International Review of Social History* (1956), i.

Eckert, Georg (ed.), *Wilhelm Liebknecht Briefwechsel mit Karl Marx und Friedrich Engels* (The Hague, 1963), vii. Briefe von Eleanor Marx-Aveling.

Ellis, Havelock (ed.), 'Eleanor Marx', *Adelphi*, vol. 10, no. 6 (Sept. 1935), vol. 11, no. 1 (Oct. 1935).

Gemkow, Heinrich (ed.), 'Zwei Briefe Eleanor Marx-Avelings an Friedrich Engels über den Parteitag der deutschen Sozialdemokratie zu Halle 1890', *Zeitschrift für Geschichtswissenschaft*, xiii Jahrgang (1965), Heft 7.

Thompson, E. P., *William Morris: Romantic to Revolutionary* (London, 1955). Appendix II. Correspondence between J. L. Mahon and Frederick Engels, Eleanor Marx Aveling and Others, 1884–98.

Tsuzuki, Chushichi (ed.), 'Japanese Archives Relating to British Labour History (2)—Eleanor Marx', *Bulletin of the Society for the Study of Labour History*, no. 8 (Spring 1964).

2. Books and Pamphlets

Marx Aveling, Eleanor. *Working Class Movement in England* (London, 1896). German translation: *Die Arbeiterclassen-Bewegung in England* übersetzt v. Gertrud Liebknecht, mit Vorwort v. W. Liebknecht, Nürnberg, 1895.

Aveling, Edward and Eleanor Marx. *The Factory Hell* (London, 1885).

— *The Woman Question* (London, 1886).

— *The Chicago Anarchists: a Statement of Facts* (London, 1887).

— *The Working-Class Movement in America* (London, 1888).

— *Shelley's Socialism: Two Lectures* (London, 1888).

(Aveling, Edward and Eleanor Marx). *Report from Great Britain and Ireland to the Delegates of the Brussels International Congress, 1891*, presented by the Gasworkers and General Labourers' Union, the Legal Eight Hours and International Labour League, the Bloomsbury Socialist Society, and the Battersea Labour League (London, 1891).

— Social-Democratic Federation, *Campaign against Child Labour* (London, 1897).

Marx Aveling, Eleanor and Israel Zangwill. '*A Doll's House*' *Repaired* (London, n.d.).

Aveling, Edward. *Botanical Tables, for the use of Students* (London, c. 1877).

— *Physiological Tables, for the use of Students* (London, 1877).

Aveling, Edward. *The Bookworm, and other Sketches* (London, c. 1878).
— *The Value of this Earthly Life: a Reply to 'Is Life worth living?'*
  by W. H. Mallock (London, 1879).
— *The Student's Darwin* (London, 1881).
— *Biological Discoveries and Problems* (London, 1881).
— *A Godless Life the Happiest and Most Useful* (London, c. 1881).
— *Works of Shakespeare* (London, 1882).
— *Science and Secularism* (London, 1882).
— *Science and Religion* (London, 1882).
— *The Sermon on the Mount* (London, n.d.).
— *On Superstition* (London, n.d.).
— *The Creed of an Atheist* (London, n.d.).
— *The Wickedness of God* (London, n.d.).
— *Irreligion of Science* (London, n.d.).
— *Why I dare not be a Christian* (London, n.d.).
— *God dies: Nature remains* (London, n.d.).
— *Darwinism and Small Families* (London, n.d.).
— *General Biology, Theoretical and Practical* (London, 1882).
— *The Borderland between Living and Non-Living Things* (London, 1883).
— *The Religious Views of Charles Darwin* (London, 1884).
— *The Gospel of Evolution* (London, 1884).
— *The Darwinian Theory: Its Meaning, Difficulties, Evidence, History* (London, 1884).
— *The Curse of Capital* (London, 1884).
— *Christianity and Capitalism* (London, 1884).
— *Comparative Physiology for London University Matriculation and Science and Art Examinations* (London, 1884).
— *Monkeys, Apes and Men* (London, 1885).
— *Natural Philosophy, for London University Matriculation* (revised ed., London, 1886).
— *An American Journey* (New York, n.d.).
— *Circular to the Sections of the American Socialistic Labor Party* (26 Feb. 1887).
— *Darwin Made Easy* (London, 1887).
— *Mechanics and Experimental Science as required for the Matriculation of the University of London* (London, 1888–9).
— *The Student's Marx* (London, 1891).
— *An Introduction to the Study of Botany* (London, 1891).
— *An Introduction to the Study of Geology* (London, 1893).
— *Charles Darwin and Karl Marx: A Comparison* (London, 1897).
— *Socialism and Radicalism* (London, n.d.).

3. Works edited and translated

Haeckel, Ernst. *The Pedigree of Man and other Essays*, translated by E. B. Aveling (London, 1883).

Lissagaray, Hippolyte Prosper Olivier. *History of the Commune of 1871*, translated by Eleanor Marx Aveling (London, 1886).

Marx, Karl. *Capital: A Critical Analysis of Capitalist Production*, translated by Samuel Moore and Edward Aveling and edited by Frederick Engels, 2 vols. (London, 1887).

Tikhomirov, Lev. *Russia, Political and Social*, translated by Edward Aveling, 2 vols. (London, 1888).

Ibsen, Henrik. *An Enemy of Society*, translated by Eleanor Marx Aveling (London, 1888). (Revised by William Archer as *An Enemy of the People* for the 1890 edition.)

— *The Lady from the Sea*, translated by Eleanor Marx Aveling (London, 1890).

Engels, Frederick. *Socialism Utopian and Scientific*, translated by Edward Aveling (London, 1892).

Bernstein, Edward. *Ferdinand Lassalle as a Social Reformer*, translated by Eleanor Marx Aveling (London, 1893).

Plekhanov, G. *Anarchism and Socialism*, translated by Eleanor Marx Aveling (London, 1895).

Marx, Karl. *Revolution and Counter-Revolution or Germany in 1848*, edited by Eleanor Marx Aveling (London, 1896). (Engels's work wrongly attributed to Marx.)

— *The Eastern Question: A Reprint of Letters written 1853–56 dealing with the events of the Crimean War*, edited by Eleanor Marx Aveling and Edward Aveling (London, 1897). (Containing letters by Engels.)

— *Value, Price, and Profit, addressed to Working Men*, edited by Eleanor Marx Aveling, with preface by Edward Aveling (London, 1898).

— *Secret Diplomatic History of the Eighteenth Century*, edited by Eleanor Marx Aveling (London, 1899).

— *The Story of the Life of Lord Palmerston*, edited by Eleanor Marx Aveling (London, 1899).

INDEX